# forall *x*: Calgary
## An Introduction to
## Formal Logic

By  **P. D. Magnus**
**Tim Button**
*with additions by*
**J. Robert Loftis**
**Robert Trueman**
*remixed and revised by*
**Aaron Thomas-Bolduc**
**Richard Zach**

**Fall 2021**

The LaTeX source for this book is available on GitHub and PDFs
at forallx.openlogicproject.org. This version is revision 52796bf
(2022-01-08).

The preparation of this textbook was made possible by a grant
from the Taylor Institute for Teaching and Learning.

**UNIVERSITY OF CALGARY**
Taylor Institute for Teaching and Learning

Cover design by Mark Lyall.

# Contents

# *Preface*

As the title indicates, this is a textbook on formal logic. Formal logic concerns the study of a certain kind of language which, like any language, can serve to express states of affairs. It is a formal language, i.e., its expressions (such as sentences) are defined formally. This makes it a very useful language for being very precise about the states of affairs its sentences describe. In particular, in formal logic it is impossible to be ambiguous. The study of these languages centres on the relationship of entailment between sentences, i.e., which sentences follow from which other sentences. Entailment is central because by understanding it better we can tell when some states of affairs must obtain provided some other states of affairs obtain. But entailment is not the only important notion. We will also consider the relationship of being satisfiable, i.e., of not being mutually contradictory. These notions can be defined semantically, using precise definitions of entailment based on interpretations of the language—or proof-theoretically, using formal systems of deduction.

Formal logic is of course a central sub-discipline of philosophy, where the logical relationship of assumptions to conclusions reached from them is important. Philosophers investigate the consequences of definitions and assumptions and evaluate these definitions and assumptions on the basis of their consequences. It is also important in mathematics and computer science. In mathematics, formal languages are used to describe not "everyday" states of affairs, but mathematical states of affairs. Mathematicians are also interested in the consequences of definitions and assumptions, and for them it is equally important to establish these consequences (which they call "theorems") using completely precise and rigorous methods. Formal logic provides such methods. In computer science, formal logic is applied to describe the state and behaviours of computational systems, e.g., circuits, programs, databases, etc. Methods of formal logic can likewise be used to establish consequences of such descriptions, such as whether a circuit is error-free, whether a program does what it's intended to do, whether a database is consistent or if something is true of the data in it.

The book is divided into nine parts. Part I introduces the topic and notions of logic in an informal way, without introducing a formal language yet. Parts II–IV concern truth-functional languages. In it, sentences are formed from basic sentences using a number of connectives ('or', 'and', 'not', 'if ... then') which just combine sentences into more complicated ones. We discuss logical notions such as entailment in two ways: semantically, using the method of truth tables (in Part III) and proof-theoretically, using a system of formal derivations (in Part IV). Parts V–VII deal with a more complicated language, that of first-order logic. It includes, in addition to the connectives of truth-functional logic, also names, predicates, identity, and the so-called quantifiers. These additional elements of the language make it much more expressive than the truth-functional language, and we'll spend a fair amount of time investigating just how much one can express in it. Again, logical notions for the language of first-order logic are defined semantically, using interpretations, and proof-theoretically, using a more complex version of the formal derivation system introduced in Part IV. Part VIII discusses the extension of TFL by non-truth-functional operators for possibility and necessity: modal logic. Part IX covers two advanced topics: that of conjunctive and disjunctive normal forms and the functional completeness of the truth-functional connectives, and the soundness of natural deduction for TFL.

In the appendices you'll find a discussion of alternative notations for the languages we discuss in this text, of alternative derivation systems, and a quick reference listing most of the important rules and definitions. The central terms are listed in a glossary at the very end.

**Credits**   This book is based on a text originally written by P. D. Magnus in the version revised and expanded by Tim Button. It also includes some material (mainly exercises) by J. Robert Loftis. The material in Part VIII is based on notes by Robert Trueman (but rewritten to use Fitch's original natural deduction rules for modal logic), and the material in chapters 43, 44, and 46 on two chapters from Tim Button's open text *Metatheory*. Aaron Thomas-Bolduc and Richard Zach have combined elements of these texts into the present version, changed some of the terminology and examples, rewritten some sections, and added material of their own. In particular, Richard Zach rewrote chapters 1 and 2, and added chapters 7, 17, 28, and 45. As of the Fall 2019 edition, the part on FOL uses the syntax more common in advanced texts (such as those based on the Open Logic Project) where arguments to predicate symbols are enclosed in parentheses (i.e., '$R(a,b)$' instead of '$Rab$'). The resulting text is licensed under a Creative Commons Attribution 4.0 license. There are several other "remixes" of *forall x*, including translations of this version.

**Notes for instructors**   The material in this book is suitable for a semester-long introduction to formal logic. I cover parts I–VII plus chapters 43, 44, and 45 in 12 weeks, although I leave out partial truth tables and derived inference rules.

The most recent version of this book is available in PDF at forallx.openlogicproject.org, but changes frequently. The CC BY license gives you the right to download and distribute the book yourself. In order to ensure that all your students have the same version of the book throughout the term you're using it, you should do so: upload the PDF you decide to use to your LMS rather than merely give your students the link. You are also free to have the PDFs printed by your bookstore, but some bookstores will be able to purchase and stock the softcover books available on Amazon.

Note that solutions to many exercises in the book are available at the above site as well (to everyone, including your students).

The syntax and proof systems (except those for modal logic) are supported by Graham Leach-Krouse's free, online logic teaching software application *Carnap* (carnap.io). This allows for submission and automated marking of exercises such as symbolization, truth tables, and natural deduction proofs. Instructors on carnap.io will be able to find samples of additional exercises they may wish to adapt or assign as-is.

# PART I

# *Key notions of logic*

# CHAPTER 1

# *Arguments*

Logic is the business of evaluating arguments; sorting the good from the bad.

In everyday language, we sometimes use the word 'argument' to talk about belligerent shouting matches. If you and a friend have an argument in this sense, things are not going well between the two of you. Logic is not concerned with such teeth-gnashing and hair-pulling. They are not arguments, in our sense; they are just disagreements.

An argument, as we will understand it, is something more like this:

> Either the butler or the gardener did it.
> The butler didn't do it.
> ∴ The gardener did it.

We here have a series of sentences. The three dots on the third line of the argument are read 'therefore.' They indicate that the final sentence expresses the *conclusion* of the argument. The two sentences before that are the *premises* of the argument. If you believe the premises, and you think the conclusion follows from the premises—that the argument, as we will say, is valid—then this (perhaps) provides you with a reason to believe the conclusion.

This is the sort of thing that logicians are interested in. We will say that an argument is any collection of premises, together with a conclusion.

This Part discusses some basic logical notions that apply to arguments in a natural language like English. It is important to begin with a clear understanding of what arguments are and of what it means for an argument to be valid. Later we will translate arguments from English into a formal language. We want formal validity, as defined in the formal language, to have at least some of the important features of natural-language validity.

In the example just given, we used individual sentences to express both of the argument's premises, and we used a third sentence to express the argument's conclusion. Many arguments are expressed in this way, but a single sentence can contain a complete argument. Consider:

> The butler has an alibi; so they cannot have done it.

This argument has one premise followed by a conclusion.

Many arguments start with premises, and end with a conclusion, but not all of them. The argument with which this section began might equally have been presented with the conclusion at the beginning, like so:

> The gardener did it. After all, it was either the butler or the gardener. And the butler didn't do it.

Equally, it might have been presented with the conclusion in the middle:

> The butler didn't do it. Accordingly, it was the gardener, given that it was either the gardener or the butler.

When approaching an argument, we want to know whether or not the conclusion follows from the premises. So the first thing to do is to separate out the conclusion from the premises. As a guide, these words are often used to indicate an argument's conclusion:

> so, therefore, hence, thus, accordingly, consequently

For this reason, they are sometimes called CONCLUSION INDICA-TOR WORDS.

By contrast, these expressions are PREMISE INDICATOR WORDS, as they often indicate that we are dealing with a premise, rather than a conclusion:

since, because, given that

But in analysing an argument, there is no substitute for a good nose.

## 1.1    Sentences

To be perfectly general, we can define an ARGUMENT as a series of sentences. The sentences at the beginning of the series are premises. The final sentence in the series is the conclusion. If the premises are true and the argument is a good one, then you have a reason to accept the conclusion.

In logic, we are only interested in sentences that can figure as a premise or conclusion of an argument, i.e., sentences that can be true or false. So we will restrict ourselves to sentences of this sort, and define a SENTENCE as a sentence that can be true or false.

You should not confuse the idea of a sentence that can be true or false with the difference between fact and opinion. Often, sentences in logic will express things that would count as facts—such as 'Kierkegaard was a hunchback' or 'Kierkegaard liked almonds.' They can also express things that you might think of as matters of opinion—such as, 'Almonds are tasty.' In other words, a sentence is not disqualified from being part of an argument because we don't know if it is true or false, or because its truth or falsity is a matter of opinion. If it is the kind of sentence that could be true or false it can play the role of premise or conclusion.

Also, there are things that would count as 'sentences' in a linguistics or grammar course that we will not count as sentences in logic.

**Questions**  In a grammar class, 'Are you sleepy yet?' would count as an interrogative sentence. Although you might be sleepy or you might be alert, the question itself is neither true nor false. For this reason, questions will not count as sentences in logic. Suppose you answer the question: 'I am not sleepy.' This is either true or false, and so it is a sentence in the logical sense. Generally, *questions* will not count as sentences, but *answers* will.

'What is this course about?' is not a sentence (in our sense). 'No one knows what this course is about' is a sentence.

**Imperatives**  Commands are often phrased as imperatives like 'Wake up!', 'Sit up straight', and so on. In a grammar class, these would count as imperative sentences. Although it might be good for you to sit up straight or it might not, the command is neither true nor false. Note, however, that commands are not always phrased as imperatives. 'You will respect my authority' *is* either true or false—either you will or you will not—and so it counts as a sentence in the logical sense.

**Exclamations**  'Ouch!' is sometimes called an exclamatory sentence, but it is neither true nor false. We will treat 'Ouch, I hurt my toe!' as meaning the same thing as 'I hurt my toe.' The 'ouch' does not add anything that could be true or false.

## Practice exercises

At the end of some chapters, there are exercises that review and explore the material covered in the chapter. There is no substitute for actually working through some problems, because learning logic is more about developing a way of thinking than it is about memorizing facts.

So here's the first exercise. Highlight the phrase which expresses the conclusion of each of these arguments:

1. It is sunny. So I should take my sunglasses.

2. It must have been sunny. I did wear my sunglasses, after all.

3. No one but you has had their hands in the cookie-jar. And the scene of the crime is littered with cookie-crumbs. You're the culprit!

4. Miss Scarlett and Professor Plum were in the study at the time of the murder. Reverend Green had the candlestick in the ballroom, and we know that there is no blood on his hands. Hence Colonel Mustard did it in the kitchen with the lead pipe. Recall, after all, that the gun had not been fired.

# CHAPTER 2

# *The scope of logic*

## 2.1 Consequence and validity

In §1, we talked about arguments, i.e., a collection of sentences (the premises), followed by a single sentence (the conclusion). We said that some words, such as "therefore," indicate which sentence is supposed to be the conclusion. "Therefore," of course, suggests that there is a connection between the premises and the conclusion, namely that the conclusion *follows from*, or *is a consequence of*, the premises.

This notion of consequence is one of the primary things logic is concerned with. One might even say that logic is the science of what follows from what. Logic develops theories and tools that tell us when a sentence follows from some others.

What about the main argument discussed in §1?

> Either the butler or the gardener did it.
> The butler didn't do it.
> ∴ The gardener did it.

We don't have any context for what the sentences in this argument refer to. Perhaps you suspect that "did it" here means "was

7

the perpetrator" of some unspecified crime. You might imagine
that the argument occurs in a mystery novel or TV show, perhaps spoken by a detective working through the evidence. But
even without having any of this information, you probably agree
that the argument is a good one in the sense that whatever the
premises refer to, if they are both true, the conclusion cannot but
be true as well. If the first premise is true, i.e., it's true that "the
butler did it or the gardener did it," then at least one of them
"did it," whatever that means. And if the second premise is true,
then the butler did not "do it." That leaves only one option: "the
gardener did it" must be true. Here, the conclusion follows from
the premises. We call arguments that have this property VALID.

By way of contrast, consider the following argument:

> If the driver did it, the maid didn't do it.
> The maid didn't do it.
> ∴ The driver did it.

We still have no idea what is being talked about here. But, again,
you probably agree that this argument is different from the previous one in an important respect. If the premises are true, it is
not guaranteed that the conclusion is also true. The premises of
this argument do not rule out, by themselves, that someone other
than the maid or the driver "did it." So there is a case where both
premises are true, and yet the driver didn't do it, i.e., the conclusion is not true. In this second argument, the conclusion does not
follow from the premises. If, like in this argument, the conclusion
does not follow from the premises, we say it is INVALID.

## 2.2   Cases and types of validity

How did we determine that the second argument is invalid? We
pointed to a case in which the premises are true and in which the
conclusion is not. This was the scenario where neither the driver
nor the maid did it, but some third person did. Let's call such a

case a COUNTEREXAMPLE to the argument. If there is a counterexample to an argument, the conclusion cannot be a consequence of the premises. For the conclusion to be a consequence of the premises, the truth of the premises must guarantee the truth of the conclusion. If there is a counterexample, the truth of the premises does not guarantee the truth of the conclusion.

As logicians, we want to be able to determine when the conclusion of an argument follows from the premises. And the conclusion is a consequence of the premises if there is no counterexample—no case where the premises are all true but the conclusion is not. This motivates a definition:

> A sentence $A$ is a CONSEQUENCE of sentences $B_1, \ldots, B_n$ if and only if there is no case where $B_1, \ldots, B_n$ are all true and $A$ is not true. (We then also say that $A$ FOLLOWS FROM $B_1, \ldots, B_n$ or that $B_1, \ldots, B_n$ ENTAIL $A$.)

This "definition" is incomplete: it does not tell us what a "case" is or what it means to be "true in a case." So far we've only seen an example: a hypothetical scenario involving three people. Of the three people in the scenario—a driver, a maid, and some third person—the driver and maid didn't do it, but the third person did. In this scenario, as described, the driver didn't do it, and so it is a case in which the sentence "the driver did it" is not true. The premises of our second argument are true, but the conclusion is not true: the scenario is a counterexample.

We said that arguments where the conclusion is a consequence of the premises are called valid, and those where the conclusion isn't a consequence of the premises are invalid. Since we now have at least a first stab at a definition of "consequence," we'll record this:

> An argument is VALID if and only if the conclusion is a consequence of the premises.

> An argument is INVALID if and only if it is not valid, i.e.,
> it has a counterexample.

Logicians are in the business of making the notion of "case" more precise, and investigating which arguments are valid when "case" is made precise in one way or another. If we take "case" to mean "hypothetical scenario" like the counterexample to the second argument, it's clear that the first argument counts as valid. If we imagine a scenario in which either the butler or the gardener did it, and also the butler didn't do it, we are automatically imagining a scenario in which the gardener did it. So any hypothetical scenario in which the premises of our first argument are true automatically makes the conclusion of our first argument true. This makes the first argument valid.

Making "case" more specific by interpreting it as "hypothetical scenario" is an advance. But it is not the end of the story. The first problem is that we don't know what to count as a hypothetical scenario. Are they limited by the laws of physics? By what is conceivable, in a very general sense? What answers we give to these questions determine which arguments we count as valid.

Suppose the answer to the first question is "yes." Consider the following argument:

> The spaceship *Rocinante* took six hours to reach Jupiter from Tycho space station.
> ∴ The distance between Tycho space station and Jupiter is less than 14 billion kilometers.

A counterexample to this argument would be a scenario in which the *Rocinante* makes a trip of over 14 billion kilometers in 6 hours, exceeding the speed of light. Since such a scenario is incompatible with the laws of physics, there is no such scenario if hypothetical scenarios have to conform to the laws of physics. If hypothetical scenarios are not limited by the laws of physics, however, there is a counterexample: a scenario where the *Rocinante* travels faster than the speed of light.

Suppose the answer to the second question is "yes," and consider another argument:

> Priya is an ophthalmologist.
> ∴ Priya is an eye doctor.

If we're allowing only conceivable scenarios, this is also a valid argument. If you imagine Priya being an ophthalmologist, you thereby imagine Priya being an eye doctor. That's just what "ophthalmologist" and "eye doctor" mean. A scenario where Priya is an ophthalmologist but not an eye doctor is ruled out by the conceptual connection between these words.

Depending on what kinds of cases we consider as potential counterexamples, then, we arrive at different notions of consequence and validity. We might call an argument NOMOLOGICALLY VALID if there are no counterexamples that don't violate the laws of nature, and an argument CONCEPTUALLY VALID if there are no counterexamples that don't violate conceptual connections between words. For both of these notions of validity, aspects of the world (e.g., what the laws of nature are) and aspects of the meaning of the sentences in the argument (e.g., that "ophthalmologist" just means a kind of eye doctor) figure into whether an argument is valid.

## 2.3 Formal validity

One distinguishing feature of *logical* consequence, however, is that it should not depend on the content of the premises and conclusion, but only on their logical form. In other words, as logicians we want to develop a theory that can make finer-grained distinctions still. For instance, both

> Either Priya is an ophthalmologist or a dentist.
> Priya isn't a dentist.

> ∴ Priya is an eye doctor.

and

> Either Priya is an ophthalmologist or a dentist.
> Priya isn't a dentist.
> ∴ Priya is an ophthalmologist.

are valid arguments. But while the validity of the first depends on the content (i.e., the meaning of "ophthalmologist" and "eye doctor"), the second does not. The second argument is FORMALLY VALID. We can describe the "form" of this argument as a pattern, something like this:

> Either $A$ is an $X$ or a $Y$.
> $A$ isn't a $Y$.
> ∴ $A$ is an $X$.

Here, $A$, $X$, and $Y$ are placeholders for appropriate expressions that, when substituted for $A$, $X$, and $Y$, turn the pattern into an argument consisting of sentences. For instance,

> Either Mei is a mathematician or a botanist.
> Mei isn't a botanist.
> ∴ Mei is a mathematician.

is an argument of the same form, but the first argument above is not: we would have to replace $Y$ by different expressions (once by "ophthalmologist" and once by "eye doctor") to obtain it from the pattern.

Moreover, the first argument is not formally valid. *Its* form is this:

> Either $A$ is an $X$ or a $Y$.
> $A$ isn't a $Y$.
> ∴ $A$ is a $Z$.

In this pattern we can replace $X$ by "ophthalmologist" and $Z$ by "eye doctor" to obtain the original argument. But here is another argument of the same form:

> Either Mei is a mathematician or a botanist.
> Mei isn't a botanist.
> ∴ Mei is an acrobat.

This argmuent is clearly not valid, since we can imagine a mathematician named Mei who is not an acrobat.

Our strategy as logicians will be to come up with a notion of "case" on which an argument turns out to be valid if it is formally valid. Clearly such a notion of "case" will have to violate not just some laws of nature but some laws of English. Since the first argument is invalid in this sense, we must allow as counterexample a case where Priya is an ophthalmologist but not an eye doctor. That case is not a conceivable situation: it is ruled out by the meanings of "ophthalmologist" and "eye doctor."

When we consider cases of various kinds in order to evaluate the validity of an argument, we will make a few assumptions. The first assumption is that every case makes every sentence true or not true—at least, every sentence in the argument under consideration. That means first of all that any imagined scenario which leaves it undetermined if a sentence in our argument is true will not be considered as a potential counterexample. For instance, a scenario where Priya is a dentist but not an ophthalmologist will count as a case to be considered in the first few arguments in this section, but not as a case to be considered in the last two: it doesn't tell us if Mei is a mathematician, a botanist, or an acrobat. If a case doesn't make a sentence true, we say it makes it FALSE. We'll thus assume that cases make sentences true or false but never both.[1]

---

[1] Even if these assumptions seem common-sensical to you, they are controversial among philosophers of logic. First of all, there are logicians who want to consider cases where sentences are neither true nor false, but have some kind of intermediate level of truth. More controversially, some philosophers think we should allow for the possibility of sentences to be both true and false at the same time. There are systems of logic in which sentences can be neither true nor false, or both, but we will not discuss them in this book.

## 2.4  Sound arguments

Before we go on and execute this strategy, a few clarifications. Arguments in our sense, as conclusions which (supposedly) follow from premises, are of course used all the time in everyday and scientific discourse. When they are, arguments are given to support or even prove their conclusions. Now, if an argument is valid, it will support its conclusion, but *only if* its premises are all true. Validity rules out the possibility that the premises are true and the conclusion is not true at the same time. It does not, by itself, rule out the possibility that the conclusion is not true, period. In other words, it is perfectly possibly for a valid argument to have a conclusion that isn't true!

Consider this example:

> Oranges are either fruit or musical instruments.
> Oranges are not fruit.
> ∴ Oranges are musical instruments.

The conclusion of this argument is ridiculous. Nevertheless, it follows from the premises. *If* both premises are true, *then* the conclusion just has to be true. So the argument is valid.

Conversely, having true premises and a true conclusion is not enough to make an argument valid. Consider this example:

> London is in England.
> Beijing is in China.
> ∴ Paris is in France.

The premises and conclusion of this argument are, as a matter of fact, all true, but the argument is invalid. If Paris were to declare independence from the rest of France, then the conclusion would no longer be true, even though both of the premises would remain true. Thus, there is a case where the premises of this argument are true without the conclusion being true. So the argument is invalid.

The important thing to remember is that validity is not about the actual truth or falsity of the sentences in the argument. It is about whether it is *possible* for all the premises to be true and the conclusion to be not true at the same time (in some hypothetical case). What is in fact the case has no special role to play; and what the facts are does not determine whether an argument is valid or not.[2] Nothing about the way things are can by itself determine if an argument is valid. It is often said that logic doesn't care about feelings. Actually, it doesn't care about facts, either.

When we use an argument to prove that its conclusion *is true*, then, we need two things. First, we need the argument to be valid, i.e., we need the conclusion to follow from the premises. But we also need the premises to be true. We will say that an argument is SOUND if and only if it is both valid and all of its premises are true.

The flip side of this is that when you want to rebut an argument, you have two options: you can show that (one or more of) the premises are not true, or you can show that the argument is not valid. Logic, however, will only help you with the latter!

## 2.5 Inductive arguments

Many good arguments are invalid. Consider this one:

> Every winter so far, it has snowed in Calgary.
> ∴ It will snow in Calgary this coming winter.

This argument generalises from observations about many (past) cases to a conclusion about all (future) cases. Such arguments are called INDUCTIVE arguments. Nevertheless, the argument is invalid. Even if it has snowed in Calgary every winter thus far, it remains *possible* that Calgary will stay dry all through the coming winter. In fact, even if it will henceforth snow every January in Calgary, we could still *imagine* a case in which this year is the first year it doesn't snow all winter. And that hypothetical scenario

---

[2]Well, there is one case where it does: if the premises are in fact true and the conclusion is in fact not true, then we live in a counterexample; so the argument is invalid.

is a case where the premises of the argument are true but the conclusion is not, making the argument invalid.

The point of all this is that inductive arguments—even good inductive arguments—are not (deductively) valid. They are not *watertight*. Unlikely though it might be, it is *possible* for their conclusion to be false, even when all of their premises are true. In this book, we will set aside (entirely) the question of what makes for a good inductive argument. Our interest is simply in sorting the (deductively) valid arguments from the invalid ones.

So: we are interested in whether or not a conclusion *follows from* some premises. Don't, though, say that the premises *infer* the conclusion. Entailment is a relation between premises and conclusions; inference is something we do. So if you want to mention inference when the conclusion follows from the premises, you could say that *one may infer* the conclusion from the premises.

## Practice exercises

**A**. Which of the following arguments are valid? Which are invalid?

1. Socrates is a man.
2. All men are carrots.
∴ Socrates is a carrot.

1. Abe Lincoln was either born in Illinois or he was once president.
2. Abe Lincoln was never president.
∴ Abe Lincoln was born in Illinois.

1. If I pull the trigger, Abe Lincoln will die.
2. I do not pull the trigger.
∴ Abe Lincoln will not die.

1. Abe Lincoln was either from France or from Luxemborg.
2. Abe Lincoln was not from Luxemborg.

∴ Abe Lincoln was from France.

1. If the world ends today, then I will not need to get up tomorrow morning.
2. I will need to get up tomorrow morning.
∴ The world will not end today.

1. Joe is now 19 years old.
2. Joe is now 87 years old.
∴ Bob is now 20 years old.

**B.** Could there be:

1. A valid argument that has one false premise and one true
   premise?
2. A valid argument that has only false premises?
3. A valid argument with only false premises and a false conclusion?
4. An invalid argument that can be made valid by the addition
   of a new premise?
5. A valid argument that can be made invalid by the addition
   of a new premise?

In each case: if so, give an example; if not, explain why not.

# CHAPTER 3
# *Other logical notions*

In §2, we introduced the ideas of consequence and of valid argument. This is one of the most important ideas in logic. In this section, we will introduce some similarly important ideas. They all rely, as did validity, on the idea that sentences are true (or not) in cases. For the rest of this section, we'll take cases in the sense of conceivable scenario, i.e., in the sense in which we used them to define conceptual validity. The points we made about different kinds of validity can be made about our new notions along similar lines: if we use a different idea of what counts as a "case" we will get different notions. And as logicians we will, eventually, consider a more permissive definition of case than we do here.

## 3.1   Joint possibility

Consider these two sentences:

B1. Jane's only brother is shorter than her.
B2. Jane's only brother is taller than her.

Logic alone cannot tell us which, if either, of these sentences is true. Yet we can say that *if* the first sentence (B1) is true, *then* the second sentence (B2) must be false. Similarly, if B2 is true, then B1 must be false. There is no possible scenario where both sentences are true together. These sentences are incompatible with each other, they cannot all be true at the same time. This motivates the following definition:

---

Sentences are JOINTLY POSSIBLE if and only if there is a case where they are all true together.

---

B1 and B2 are *jointly impossible*, while, say, the following two sentences are jointly possible:

B1. Jane's only brother is shorter than her.
B2. Jane's only brother is younger than her.

We can ask about the joint possibility of any number of sentences. For example, consider the following four sentences:

G1. There are at least four giraffes at the wild animal park.
G2. There are exactly seven gorillas at the wild animal park.
G3. There are not more than two martians at the wild animal park.
G4. Every giraffe at the wild animal park is a martian.

G1 and G4 together entail that there are at least four martian giraffes at the park. This conflicts with G3, which implies that there are no more than two martian giraffes there. So the sentences G1–G4 are jointly impossible. They cannot all be true together. (Note that the sentences G1, G3 and G4 are jointly impossible. But if sentences are already jointly impossible, adding an extra sentence to the mix cannot make them jointly possible!)

## 3.2  Necessary truths, necessary falsehoods, and contingency

In assessing arguments for validity, we care about what would be true *if* the premises were true, but some sentences just *must* be true. Consider these sentences:

1. It is raining.
2. Either it is raining here, or it is not.
3. It is both raining here and not raining here.

In order to know if sentence 1 is true, you would need to look outside or check the weather channel. It might be true; it might be false. A sentence which is capable of being true and capable of being false (in different circumstances, of course) is called CONTINGENT.

Sentence 2 is different. You do not need to look outside to know that it is true. Regardless of what the weather is like, it is either raining or it is not. That is a NECESSARY TRUTH.

Equally, you do not need to check the weather to determine whether or not sentence 3 is true. It must be false, simply as a matter of logic. It might be raining here and not raining across town; it might be raining now but stop raining even as you finish this sentence; but it is impossible for it to be both raining and not raining in the same place and at the same time. So, whatever the world is like, it is not both raining here and not raining here. It is a NECESSARY FALSEHOOD.

Something might *always* be true and still be contingent. For instance, if there never were a time when the universe contained fewer than seven things, then the sentence 'At least seven things exist' would always be true. Yet the sentence is contingent: the world could have been much, much smaller than it is, and then the sentence would have been false.

## 3.3   Necessary equivalence

We can also ask about the logical relations *between* two sentences. For example:

> John went to the store after he washed the dishes.
> John washed the dishes before he went to the store.

These two sentences are both contingent, since John might not have gone to the store or washed dishes at all. Yet they must have the same truth-value. If either of the sentences is true, then they both are; if either of the sentences is false, then they both are. When two sentences have the same truth value in every case, we say that they are NECESSARILY EQUIVALENT.

## Summary of logical notions

- ▷ An argument is VALID if there is no case where the premises are all true and the conclusion is not; it is INVALID otherwise.

- ▷ A NECESSARY TRUTH is a sentence that is true in every case.

- ▷ A NECESSARY FALSEHOOD is a sentence that is false in every case.

- ▷ A CONTINGENT SENTENCE is neither a necessary truth nor a necessary falsehood; a sentence that is true in some case and false in some other case.

- ▷ Two sentences are NECESSARILY EQUIVALENT if, in every case, they are both true or both false.

- ▷ A collection of sentences is JOINTLY POSSIBLE if there is a case where they are all true together; it is JOINTLY IMPOSSIBLE otherwise.

## Practice exercises

**A**. For each of the following: Is it a necessary truth, a necessary falsehood, or contingent?

  1. Caesar crossed the Rubicon.
  2. Someone once crossed the Rubicon.
  3. No one has ever crossed the Rubicon.
  4. If Caesar crossed the Rubicon, then someone has.
  5. Even though Caesar crossed the Rubicon, no one has ever crossed the Rubicon.
  6. If anyone has ever crossed the Rubicon, it was Caesar.

**B**. For each of the following: Is it a necessary truth, a necessary falsehood, or contingent?

  1. Elephants dissolve in water.
  2. Wood is a light, durable substance useful for building things.
  3. If wood were a good building material, it would be useful for building things.
  4. I live in a three story building that is two stories tall.
  5. If gerbils were mammals they would nurse their young.

**C**. Which of the following pairs of sentences are necessarily equivalent?

  1. Elephants dissolve in water.
     If you put an elephant in water, it will disintegrate.
  2. All mammals dissolve in water.
     If you put an elephant in water, it will disintegrate.
  3. George Bush was the 43rd president.
     Barack Obama is the 44th president.
  4. Barack Obama is the 44th president.
     Barack Obama was president immediately after the 43rd president.
  5. Elephants dissolve in water.
     All mammals dissolve in water.

**D.** Which of the following pairs of sentences are necessarily equivalent?

1. Thelonious Monk played piano.
   John Coltrane played tenor sax.
2. Thelonious Monk played gigs with John Coltrane.
   John Coltrane played gigs with Thelonious Monk.
3. All professional piano players have big hands.
   Piano player Bud Powell had big hands.
4. Bud Powell suffered from severe mental illness.
   All piano players suffer from severe mental illness.
5. John Coltrane was deeply religious.
   John Coltrane viewed music as an expression of spirituality.

**E.** Consider the following sentences:

G1 There are at least four giraffes at the wild animal park.

G2 There are exactly seven gorillas at the wild animal park.

G3 There are not more than two Martians at the wild animal park.

G4 Every giraffe at the wild animal park is a Martian.

Now consider each of the following collections of sentences. Which are jointly possible? Which are jointly impossible?

1. Sentences G2, G3, and G4
2. Sentences G1, G3, and G4
3. Sentences G1, G2, and G4
4. Sentences G1, G2, and G3

**F.** Consider the following sentences.

M1 All people are mortal.

M2 Socrates is a person.

M3 Socrates will never die.

M4 Socrates is mortal.

Which combinations of sentences are jointly possible? Mark each "possible" or "impossible."

1. Sentences M1, M2, and M3
2. Sentences M2, M3, and M4
3. Sentences M2 and M3
4. Sentences M1 and M4
5. Sentences M1, M2, M3, and M4

**G.** Which of the following is possible? If it is possible, give an example. If it is not possible, explain why.

1. A valid argument that has one false premise and one true premise
2. A valid argument that has a false conclusion
3. A valid argument, the conclusion of which is a necessary falsehood
4. An invalid argument, the conclusion of which is a necessary truth
5. A necessary truth that is contingent
6. Two necessarily equivalent sentences, both of which are necessary truths
7. Two necessarily equivalent sentences, one of which is a necessary truth and one of which is contingent
8. Two necessarily equivalent sentences that together are jointly impossible
9. A jointly possible collection of sentences that contains a necessary falsehood
10. A jointly impossible set of sentences that contains a necessary truth

**H.** Which of the following is possible? If it is possible, give an example. If it is not possible, explain why.

1. A valid argument, whose premises are all necessary truths, and whose conclusion is contingent

2. A valid argument with true premises and a false conclusion
3. A jointly possible collection of sentences that contains two sentences that are not necessarily equivalent
4. A jointly possible collection of sentences, all of which are contingent
5. A false necessary truth
6. A valid argument with false premises
7. A necessarily equivalent pair of sentences that are not jointly possible
8. A necessary truth that is also a necessary falsehood
9. A jointly possible collection of sentences that are all necessary falsehoods

# PART II

# *Truth-functional logic*

# CHAPTER 4

# *First steps to symbolization*

## 4.1 Validity in virtue of form

Consider this argument:

> It is raining outside.
> If it is raining outside, then Jenny is miserable.
> ∴ Jenny is miserable.

and another argument:

> Jenny is an anarcho-syndicalist.
> If Jenny is an anarcho-syndicalist, then Dipan is an avid
> reader of Tolstoy.
> ∴ Dipan is an avid reader of Tolstoy.

Both arguments are valid, and there is a straightforward sense in which we can say that they share a common structure. We might express the structure thus:

> $A$
> If $A$, then $C$
> ∴ $C$

This looks like an excellent argument *structure*. Indeed, surely any argument with this *structure* will be valid, and this is not the only good argument structure. Consider an argument like:

> Jenny is either happy or sad.
> Jenny is not happy.
> ∴ Jenny is sad.

Again, this is a valid argument. The structure here is something like:

> *A* or *B*
> not-*A*
> ∴ *B*

A superb structure! Here is another example:

> It's not the case that Jim both studied hard and acted in lots of plays.
> Jim studied hard
> ∴ Jim did not act in lots of plays.

This valid argument has a structure which we might represent thus:

> not-(*A* and *B*)
> *A*
> ∴ not-*B*

These examples illustrate an important idea, which we might describe as *validity in virtue of form*. The validity of the arguments just considered has nothing very much to do with the meanings of English expressions like 'Jenny is miserable', 'Dipan is an avid reader of Tolstoy', or 'Jim acted in lots of plays'. If it has to do with meanings at all, it is with the meanings of phrases like 'and', 'or', 'not,' and 'if..., then...'.

In Parts II–IV, we are going to develop a formal language which allows us to symbolize many arguments in such a way as to show that they are valid in virtue of their form. That language will be *truth-functional logic*, or TFL.

## 4.2 Validity for special reasons

There are plenty of arguments that are valid, but not for reasons relating to their form. Take an example:

Juanita is a vixen
∴ Juanita is a fox

It is impossible for the premise to be true and the conclusion false. So the argument is valid. However, the validity is not related to the form of the argument. Here is an invalid argument with the same form:

Juanita is a vixen
∴ Juanita is a cathedral

This might suggest that the validity of the first argument *is* keyed to the meaning of the words 'vixen' and 'fox'. But, whether or not that is right, it is not simply the *shape* of the argument that makes it valid. Equally, consider the argument:

The sculpture is green all over.
∴ The sculpture is not red all over.

Again, it seems impossible for the premise to be true and the conclusion false, for nothing can be both green all over and red all over. So the argument is valid, but here is an invalid argument with the same form:

The sculpture is green all over.
∴ The sculpture is not shiny all over.

The argument is invalid, since it is possible to be green all over and shiny all over. (One might paint their nails with an elegant shiny green varnish.) Plausibly, the validity of the first argument is keyed to the way that colours (or colour-words) interact, but, whether or not that is right, it is not simply the *shape* of the argument that makes it valid.

The important moral can be stated as follows. *At best, TFL will help us to understand arguments that are valid due to their form.*

## 4.3  Atomic sentences

We started isolating the form of an argument, in §4.1, by replacing *subsentences* of sentences with individual letters. Thus in the first example of this section, 'it is raining outside' is a subsentence of 'If it is raining outside, then Jenny is miserable', and we replaced this subsentence with '$A$'.

Our artificial language, TFL, pursues this idea absolutely ruthlessly. We start with some *sentence letters*. These will be the basic building blocks out of which more complex sentences are built. We will use single uppercase letters as sentence letters of TFL. There are only twenty-six letters of the alphabet, but there is no limit to the number of sentence letters that we might want to consider. By adding subscripts to letters, we obtain new sentence letters. So, here are five different sentence letters of TFL:

$$A, P, P_1, P_2, A_{234}$$

We will use sentence letters to represent, or *symbolize*, certain English sentences. To do this, we provide a SYMBOLIZATION KEY, such as the following:

> $A$: It is raining outside
> $C$: Jenny is miserable

In doing this, we are not fixing this symbolization *once and for all*. We are just saying that, for the time being, we will think of the sentence letter of TFL, '$A$', as symbolizing the English sentence 'It is raining outside', and the sentence letter of TFL, '$C$', as symbolizing the English sentence 'Jenny is miserable'. Later, when we are dealing with different sentences or different arguments, we can provide a new symbolization key; as it might be:

> $A$: Jenny is an anarcho-syndicalist
> $C$: Dipan is an avid reader of Tolstoy

It is important to understand that whatever structure an English sentence might have is lost when it is symbolized by a sentence letter of TFL. From the point of view of TFL, a sentence letter is just a letter. It can be used to build more complex sentences, but it cannot be taken apart.

# CHAPTER 5
# *Connectives*

In the previous chapter, we considered symbolizing fairly basic English sentences with sentence letters of TFL. This leaves us wanting to deal with the English expressions 'and', 'or', 'not', and so forth. These are *connectives*—they can be used to form new sentences out of old ones. In TFL, we will make use of logical connectives to build complex sentences from atomic components. There are five logical connectives in TFL. This table summarises them, and they are explained throughout this section.

| symbol | what it is called | rough meaning |
|--------|-------------------|---------------|
| ¬ | negation | 'It is not the case that...' |
| ∧ | conjunction | 'Both... and ...' |
| ∨ | disjunction | 'Either... or ...' |
| → | conditional | 'If ... then ...' |
| ↔ | biconditional | '... if and only if ...' |

These are not the only connectives of English of interest. Others are, e.g., 'unless', 'neither ... nor ...', and 'because'. We will see that the first two can be expressed by the connectives we will discuss, while the last cannot. 'Because', in contrast to the others, is not *truth functional*.

## 5.1  Negation

Consider how we might symbolize these sentences:

1. Mary is in Barcelona.
2. It is not the case that Mary is in Barcelona.
3. Mary is not in Barcelona.

In order to symbolize sentence 1, we will need a sentence letter. We might offer this symbolization key:

   $B$:  Mary is in Barcelona.

Since sentence 2 is obviously related to sentence 1, we will not want to symbolize it with a completely different sentence letter. Roughly, sentence 2 means something like 'It is not the case that $B$'. In order to symbolize this, we need a symbol for negation. We will use '¬'. Now we can symbolize sentence 2 with '¬$B$'.

Sentence 3 also contains the word 'not', and it is obviously equivalent to sentence 2. As such, we can also symbolize it with '¬$B$'.

> A sentence can be symbolized as ¬$\mathcal{A}$ if it can be paraphrased in English as 'It is not the case that…'.

It will help to offer a few more examples:

4. The widget can be replaced.
5. The widget is irreplaceable.
6. The widget is not irreplaceable.

Let us use the following representation key:

   $R$:  The widget is replaceable

Sentence 4 can now be symbolized by '$R$'. Moving on to sentence 5: saying the widget is irreplaceable means that it is not the case that the widget is replaceable. So even though sentence 5 does not contain the word 'not', we will symbolize it as follows: '$\neg R$'.

Sentence 6 can be paraphrased as 'It is not the case that the widget is irreplaceable.' Which can again be paraphrased as 'It is not the case that it is not the case that the widget is replaceable'. So we might symbolize this English sentence with the TFL sentence '$\neg\neg R$'.

But some care is needed when handling negations. Consider:

7. Jane is happy.
8. Jane is unhappy.

If we let the TFL-sentence '$H$' symbolize 'Jane is happy', then we can symbolize sentence 7 as '$H$'. However, it would be a mistake to symbolize sentence 8 with '$\neg H$'. If Jane is unhappy, then she is not happy; but sentence 8 does not mean the same thing as 'It is not the case that Jane is happy'. Jane might be neither happy nor unhappy; she might be in a state of blank indifference. In order to symbolize sentence 8, then, we would need a new sentence letter of TFL.

## 5.2   Conjunction

Consider these sentences:

9. Adam is athletic.
10. Barbara is athletic.
11. Adam is athletic, and also Barbara is athletic.

We will need separate sentence letters of TFL to symbolize sentences 9 and 10; perhaps

$A$: Adam is athletic.
$B$: Barbara is athletic.

Sentence 9 can now be symbolized as '$A$', and sentence 10 can be symbolized as '$B$'. Sentence 11 roughly says 'A and B'. We need another symbol, to deal with 'and'. We will use '∧'. Thus we will symbolize it as '$(A \land B)$'. This connective is called CON-JUNCTION. We also say that '$A$' and '$B$' are the two CONJUNCTS of the conjunction '$(A \land B)$'.

Notice that we make no attempt to symbolize the word 'also' in sentence 11. Words like 'both' and 'also' function to draw our attention to the fact that two things are being conjoined. Maybe they affect the emphasis of a sentence, but we will not (and cannot) symbolize such things in TFL.

Some more examples will bring out this point:

12. Barbara is athletic and energetic.
13. Barbara and Adam are both athletic.
14. Although Barbara is energetic, she is not athletic.
15. Adam is athletic, but Barbara is more athletic than him.

Sentence 12 is obviously a conjunction. The sentence says two things (about Barbara). In English, it is permissible to refer to Barbara only once. It *might* be tempting to think that we need to symbolize sentence 12 with something along the lines of '$B$ and energetic'. This would be a mistake. Once we symbolize part of a sentence as '$B$', any further structure is lost, as '$B$' is a sentence letter of TFL. Conversely, 'energetic' is not an English sentence at all. What we are aiming for is something like '$B$ and Barbara is energetic'. So we need to add another sentence letter to the symbolization key. Let '$E$' symbolize 'Barbara is energetic'. Now the entire sentence can be symbolized as '$(B \land E)$'.

Sentence 13 says one thing about two different subjects. It says of both Barbara and Adam that they are athletic, even though in English we use the word 'athletic' only once. The sentence can be paraphrased as 'Barbara is athletic, and Adam is athletic'. We can symbolize this in TFL as '$(B \land A)$', using the same symbolization key that we have been using.

Sentence 14 is slightly more complicated. The word 'although' sets up a contrast between the first part of the sentence and the second part. Nevertheless, the sentence tells us both that Barbara is energetic and that she is not athletic. In order to make each of the conjuncts a sentence letter, we need to replace 'she' with 'Barbara'. So we can paraphrase sentence 14 as, '*Both* Barbara is energetic, *and* Barbara is not athletic'. The second conjunct contains a negation, so we paraphrase further: '*Both* Barbara is energetic *and it is not the case that* Barbara is athletic'. Now we can symbolize this with the TFL sentence '$(E \land \neg B)$'. Note that we have lost all sorts of nuance in this symbolization. There is a distinct difference in tone between sentence 14 and 'Both Barbara is energetic and it is not the case that Barbara is athletic'. TFL does not (and cannot) preserve these nuances.

Sentence 15 raises similar issues. There is a contrastive structure, but this is not something that TFL can deal with. So we can paraphrase the sentence as '*Both* Adam is athletic, *and* Barbara is more athletic than Adam'. (Notice that we once again replace the pronoun 'him' with 'Adam'.) How should we deal with the second conjunct? We already have the sentence letter '$A$', which is being used to symbolize 'Adam is athletic', and the sentence '$B$' which is being used to symbolize 'Barbara is athletic'; but neither of these concerns their relative athleticity. So, to symbolize the entire sentence, we need a new sentence letter. Let the TFL sentence '$R$' symbolize the English sentence 'Barbara is more athletic than Adam'. Now we can symbolize sentence 15 by '$(A \land R)$'.

---

A sentence can be symbolized as $(\mathscr{A} \land \mathscr{B})$ if it can be paraphrased in English as 'Both..., and...', or as '..., but ...', or as 'although ..., ...'.

---

You might be wondering why we put brackets around the conjunctions. The reason can be brought out by thinking about how negation interacts with conjunction. Consider:

16. It's not the case that you will get both soup and salad.
17. You will not get soup but you will get salad.

Sentence 16 can be paraphrased as 'It is not the case that: both you will get soup and you will get salad'. Using this symbolization key:

> $S_1$: You will get soup.
> $S_2$: You will get salad.

we would symbolize 'both you will get soup and you will get salad' as '$(S_1 \wedge S_2)$'. To symbolize sentence 16, then, we simply negate the whole sentence, thus: '$\neg(S_1 \wedge S_2)$'.

Sentence 17 is a conjunction: you *will not* get soup, and you *will* get salad. 'You will not get soup' is symbolized by '$\neg S_1$'. So to symbolize sentence 17 itself, we offer '$(\neg S_1 \wedge S_2)$'.

These English sentences are very different, and their symbolizations differ accordingly. In one of them, the entire conjunction is negated. In the other, just one conjunct is negated. Brackets help us to keep track of things like the *scope* of the negation.

## 5.3 Disjunction

Consider these sentences:

18. Either Fatima will play videogames, or she will watch movies.
19. Either Fatima or Omar will play videogames.

For these sentences we can use this symbolization key:

> $F$: Fatima will play videogames.
> $O$: Omar will play videogames.
> $M$: Fatima will watch movies.

However, we will again need to introduce a new symbol. Sentence 18 is symbolized by '$(F \vee M)$'. The connective is called DISJUNCTION. We also say that '$F$' and '$M$' are the DISJUNCTS of the disjunction '$(F \vee M)$'.

Sentence 19 is only slightly more complicated. There are two subjects, but the English sentence only gives the verb once. However, we can paraphrase sentence 19 as 'Either Fatima will play videogames, or Omar will play videogames'. Now we can obviously symbolize it by '$(F \vee O)$' again.

> A sentence can be symbolized as $(\mathcal{A} \vee \mathcal{B})$ if it can be paraphrased in English as 'Either..., or....'

Sometimes in English, the word 'or' is used in a way that excludes the possibility that both disjuncts are true. This is called an EXCLUSIVE OR. An *exclusive or* is clearly intended when it says, on a restaurant menu, 'Entrees come with either soup or salad': you may have soup; you may have salad; but, if you want *both* soup *and* salad, then you have to pay extra.

At other times, the word 'or' allows for the possibility that both disjuncts might be true. This is probably the case with sentence 19, above. Fatima might play videogames alone, Omar might play videogames alone, or they might both play. Sentence 19 merely says that *at least* one of them plays videogames. This is an INCLUSIVE OR. The TFL symbol '$\vee$' always symbolizes an *inclusive or*.

It will also help to see how negation interacts with disjunction. Consider:

20. Either you will not have soup, or you will not have salad.
21. You will have neither soup nor salad.
22. You get either soup or salad, but not both.

Using the same symbolization key as before, sentence 20 can be paraphrased in this way: '*Either* it is not the case that you get soup, *or* it is not the case that you get salad'. To symbolize this in TFL, we need both disjunction and negation. 'It is not the case that you get soup' is symbolized by '$\neg S_1$'. 'It is not the case that you get salad' is symbolized by '$\neg S_2$'. So sentence 20 itself is symbolized by '$(\neg S_1 \vee \neg S_2)$'.

Sentence 21 also requires negation. It can be paraphrased as, '*It is not the case that:* either you get soup or you get salad'. Since this negates the entire disjunction, we symbolize sentence 21 with '$\neg(S_1 \vee S_2)$'.

Sentence 22 is an *exclusive or*. We can break the sentence into two parts. The first part says that you get one or the other. We symbolize this as '$(S_1 \vee S_2)$'. The second part says that you do not get both. We can paraphrase this as: 'It is not the case both that you get soup and that you get salad'. Using both negation and conjunction, we symbolize this with '$\neg(S_1 \wedge S_2)$'. Now we just need to put the two parts together. As we saw above, 'but' can usually be symbolized with '$\wedge$'. So sentence 22 can be symbolized as '$((S_1 \vee S_2) \wedge \neg(S_1 \wedge S_2))$'.

This last example shows something important. Although the TFL symbol '$\vee$' always symbolizes *inclusive or*, we can symbolize an *exclusive or* in TFL. We just have to use a few other symbols as well.

## 5.4   Conditional

Consider these sentences:

23. If Jean is in Paris, then Jean is in France.
24. Jean is in France only if Jean is in Paris.

Let's use the following symbolization key:

$P$: Jean is in Paris.
$F$: Jean is in France

Sentence 23 is roughly of this form: 'if $P$, then $F$'. We will use the symbol '$\rightarrow$' to symbolize this 'if..., then...' structure. So we symbolize sentence 23 by '$(P \rightarrow F)$'. The connective is called THE CONDITIONAL. Here, '$P$' is called the ANTECEDENT of the conditional '$(P \rightarrow F)$', and '$F$' is called the CONSEQUENT.

Sentence 24 is also a conditional. Since the word 'if' appears in the second half of the sentence, it might be tempting to symbolize this in the same way as sentence 23. That would be a mistake. Your knowledge of geography tells you that sentence 23 is unproblematically true: there is no way for Jean to be in Paris that doesn't involve Jean being in France. But sentence 24 is not so straightforward: were Jean in Dieppe, Lyons, or Toulouse, Jean would be in France without being in Paris, thereby rendering sentence 24 false. Since geography alone dictates the truth of sentence 23, whereas travel plans (say) are needed to know the truth of sentence 24, they must mean different things.

In fact, sentence 24 can be paraphrased as 'If Jean is in France, then Jean is in Paris'. So we can symbolize it by '$(F \to P)$'.

> A sentence can be symbolized as $\mathscr{A} \to \mathscr{B}$ if it can be paraphrased in English as 'If A, then B' or 'A only if B'.

In fact, the conditional can represent many English expressions. Consider:

25. For Jean to be in Paris, it is necessary that Jean be in France.
26. It is a necessary condition on Jean's being in Paris that she be in France.
27. For Jean to be in France, it is sufficient that Jean be in Paris.
28. It is a sufficient condition on Jean's being in France that she be in Paris.

If we think about it, all four of these sentences mean the same as 'If Jean is in Paris, then Jean is in France'. So they can all be symbolised by '$(P \to F)$'.

It is important to bear in mind that the connective '$\to$' tells us only that, if the antecedent is true, then the consequent is true. It says nothing about a *causal* connection between two events (for example). In fact, we lose a huge amount when we use '$\to$' to symbolize English conditionals. We will return to this in §§10.3 and 12.5.

## 5.5   Biconditional

Consider these sentences:

29. Laika is a dog only if she is a mammal
30. Laika is a dog if she is a mammal
31. Laika is a dog if and only if she is a mammal

We will use the following symbolization key:

> *D*: Laika is a dog
> *M*: Laika is a mammal

For reasons discussed above, sentence 29 can be symbolised by '$(D \rightarrow M)$'.

Sentence 30 is importantly different. It can be paraphrased as, 'If Laika is a mammal then Laika is a dog'. So it can be symbolized by '$M \rightarrow D$'.

Sentence 31 says something stronger than either 29 or 30. It can be paraphrased as 'Laika is a dog if Laika is a mammal, and Laika is a dog only if Laika is a mammal'. This is just the conjunction of sentences 29 and 30. So we can symbolize it as '$(D \rightarrow M) \wedge (M \rightarrow D)$'. We call this a BICONDITIONAL, because it amounts to stating both directions of the conditional.

We could treat every biconditional this way. So, just as we do not need a new TFL symbol to deal with *exclusive or*, we do not really need a new TFL symbol to deal with biconditionals. Because the biconditional occurs so often, however, we will use the symbol '$\leftrightarrow$' for it. We can then symbolize sentence 31 with the TFL sentence '$(D \leftrightarrow M)$'.

The expression 'if and only if' occurs a lot especially in philosophy, mathematics, and logic. For brevity, we can abbreviate it with the snappier word 'iff'. We will follow this practice. So 'if' with only *one* 'f' is the English conditional. But 'iff' with *two* 'f's is the English biconditional. Armed with this we can say:

A sentence can be symbolized as $\mathcal{A} \leftrightarrow \mathcal{B}$ if it can be paraphrased in English as 'A iff B'; that is, as 'A if and only if B'.

A word of caution. Ordinary speakers of English often use 'if ..., then...' when they really mean to use something more like '...if and only if ...'. Perhaps your parents told you, when you were a child: 'if you don't eat your greens, you won't get any dessert'. Suppose you ate your greens, but that your parents refused to give you any dessert, on the grounds that they were only committed to the *conditional* (roughly 'if you get dessert, then you will have eaten your greens'), rather than the biconditional (roughly, 'you get dessert iff you eat your greens'). Well, a tantrum would rightly ensue. So, be aware of this when interpreting people; but in your own writing, make sure you use the biconditional iff you mean to.

## 5.6 Unless

We have now introduced all of the connectives of TFL. We can use them together to symbolize many kinds of sentences. An especially difficult case is when we use the English-language connective 'unless':

32. Unless you wear a jacket, you will catch a cold.
33. You will catch a cold unless you wear a jacket.

These two sentences are clearly equivalent. To symbolize them, we will use the symbolization key:

J: You will wear a jacket.
D: You will catch a cold.

Both sentences mean that if you do not wear a jacket, then you will catch a cold. With this in mind, we might symbolize them as '$(\neg J \to D)$'.

Equally, both sentences mean that if you do not catch a cold, then you must have worn a jacket. With this in mind, we might symbolize them as '$(\neg D \to J)$'.

Equally, both sentences mean that either you will wear a jacket or you will catch a cold. With this in mind, we might symbolize them as '$(J \lor D)$'.

All three are correct symbolizations. Indeed, in chapter 12 we will see that all three symbolizations are equivalent in TFL.

> If a sentence can be paraphrased as 'Unless $A$, $B$,' then it can be symbolized as '$(\mathcal{A} \lor \mathcal{B})$'.

Again, though, there is a little complication. 'Unless' can be symbolized as a conditional; but as we said above, people often use the conditional (on its own) when they mean to use the biconditional. Equally, 'unless' can be symbolized as a disjunction; but there are two kinds of disjunction (exclusive and inclusive). So it will not surprise you to discover that ordinary speakers of English often use 'unless' to mean something more like the biconditional, or like exclusive disjunction. Suppose someone says: 'I will go running unless it rains'. They probably mean something like 'I will go running iff it does not rain' (i.e., the biconditional), or 'either I will go running or it will rain, but not both' (i.e., exclusive disjunction). Again: be aware of this when interpreting what other people have said, but be precise in your writing.

## Practice exercises

**A.** Using the symbolization key given, symbolize each English sentence in TFL.

$M$: Those creatures are men in suits.
$C$: Those creatures are chimpanzees.
$G$: Those creatures are gorillas.

1. Those creatures are not men in suits.

2. Those creatures are men in suits, or they are not.

3. Those creatures are either gorillas or chimpanzees.

4. Those creatures are neither gorillas nor chimpanzees.

5. If those creatures are chimpanzees, then they are neither gorillas nor men in suits.

6. Unless those creatures are men in suits, they are either chimpanzees or they are gorillas.

**B**. Using the symbolization key given, symbolize each English sentence in TFL.

 *A*: Mister Ace was murdered.
 *B*: The butler did it.
 *C*: The cook did it.
 *D*: The Duchess is lying.
 *E*: Mister Edge was murdered.
 *F*: The murder weapon was a frying pan.

1. Either Mister Ace or Mister Edge was murdered.

2. If Mister Ace was murdered, then the cook did it.

3. If Mister Edge was murdered, then the cook did not do it.

4. Either the butler did it, or the Duchess is lying.

5. The cook did it only if the Duchess is lying.

6. If the murder weapon was a frying pan, then the culprit must have been the cook.

7. If the murder weapon was not a frying pan, then the culprit was either the cook or the butler.

8. Mister Ace was murdered if and only if Mister Edge was not murdered.

9. The Duchess is lying, unless it was Mister Edge who was murdered.

10. If Mister Ace was murdered, he was done in with a frying pan.

11. Since the cook did it, the butler did not.

12. Of course the Duchess is lying!

**C.** Using the symbolization key given, symbolize each English sentence in TFL.

> $E_1$: Ava is an electrician.
> $E_2$: Harrison is an electrician.
> $F_1$: Ava is a firefighter.
> $F_2$: Harrison is a firefighter.
> $S_1$: Ava is satisfied with her career.
> $S_2$: Harrison is satisfied with his career.

1. Ava and Harrison are both electricians.
2. If Ava is a firefighter, then she is satisfied with her career.
3. Ava is a firefighter, unless she is an electrician.
4. Harrison is an unsatisfied electrician.
5. Neither Ava nor Harrison is an electrician.
6. Both Ava and Harrison are electricians, but neither of them find it satisfying.
7. Harrison is satisfied only if he is a firefighter.
8. If Ava is not an electrician, then neither is Harrison, but if she is, then he is too.
9. Ava is satisfied with her career if and only if Harrison is not satisfied with his.
10. If Harrison is both an electrician and a firefighter, then he must be satisfied with his work.
11. It cannot be that Harrison is both an electrician and a firefighter.
12. Harrison and Ava are both firefighters if and only if neither of them is an electrician.

**D.** Using the symbolization key given, symbolize each English-language sentence in TFL.

> $J_1$: John Coltrane played tenor sax.
> $J_2$: John Coltrane played soprano sax.
> $J_3$: John Coltrane played tuba
> $M_1$: Miles Davis played trumpet
> $M_2$: Miles Davis played tuba

1. John Coltrane played tenor and soprano sax.
2. Neither Miles Davis nor John Coltrane played tuba.
3. John Coltrane did not play both tenor sax and tuba.
4. John Coltrane did not play tenor sax unless he also played soprano sax.
5. John Coltrane did not play tuba, but Miles Davis did.
6. Miles Davis played trumpet only if he also played tuba.
7. If Miles Davis played trumpet, then John Coltrane played at least one of these three instruments: tenor sax, soprano sax, or tuba.
8. If John Coltrane played tuba then Miles Davis played neither trumpet nor tuba.
9. Miles Davis and John Coltrane both played tuba if and only if Coltrane did not play tenor sax and Miles Davis did not play trumpet.

**E.** Give a symbolization key and symbolize the following English sentences in TFL.

1. Alice and Bob are both spies.
2. If either Alice or Bob is a spy, then the code has been broken.
3. If neither Alice nor Bob is a spy, then the code remains unbroken.
4. The German embassy will be in an uproar, unless someone has broken the code.
5. Either the code has been broken or it has not, but the German embassy will be in an uproar regardless.
6. Either Alice or Bob is a spy, but not both.

**F.** Give a symbolization key and symbolize the following English sentences in TFL.

1. If there is food to be found in the pridelands, then Rafiki will talk about squashed bananas.
2. Rafiki will talk about squashed bananas unless Simba is alive.

3. Rafiki will either talk about squashed bananas or he won't, but there is food to be found in the pridelands regardless.
4. Scar will remain as king if and only if there is food to be found in the pridelands.
5. If Simba is alive, then Scar will not remain as king.

**G.** For each argument, write a symbolization key and symbolize all of the sentences of the argument in TFL.

1. If Dorothy plays the piano in the morning, then Roger wakes up cranky. Dorothy plays piano in the morning unless she is distracted. So if Roger does not wake up cranky, then Dorothy must be distracted.
2. It will either rain or snow on Tuesday. If it rains, Neville will be sad. If it snows, Neville will be cold. Therefore, Neville will either be sad or cold on Tuesday.
3. If Zoog remembered to do his chores, then things are clean but not neat. If he forgot, then things are neat but not clean. Therefore, things are either neat or clean; but not both.

**H.** For each argument, write a symbolization key and symbolize the argument as well as possible in TFL. The part of the passage in italics is there to provide context for the argument, and doesn't need to be symbolized.

1. It is going to rain soon. I know because my leg is hurting, and my leg hurts if it's going to rain.
2. *Spider-man tries to figure out the bad guy's plan.* If Doctor Octopus gets the uranium, he will blackmail the city. I am certain of this because if Doctor Octopus gets the uranium, he can make a dirty bomb, and if he can make a dirty bomb, he will blackmail the city.
3. *A westerner tries to predict the policies of the Chinese government.* If the Chinese government cannot solve the water shortages in Beijing, they will have to move the capital. They don't want to move the capital. Therefore they must solve the

water shortage. But the only way to solve the water shortage is to divert almost all the water from the Yangzi river
northward. Therefore the Chinese government will go with
the project to divert water from the south to the north.

**I.** We symbolized an *exclusive or* using '∨', '∧', and '¬'. How could
you symbolize an *exclusive or* using only two connectives? Is there
any way to symbolize an *exclusive or* using only one connective?

# CHAPTER 6

# *Sentences of TFL*

The sentence 'either apples are red, or berries are blue' is a sentence of English, and the sentence '$(A \lor B)$' is a sentence of TFL. Although we can identify sentences of English when we encounter them, we do not have a formal definition of 'sentence of English'. But in this chapter, we will *define* exactly what will count as a sentence of TFL. This is one respect in which a formal language like TFL is more precise than a natural language like English.

## 6.1 Expressions

We have seen that there are three kinds of symbols in TFL:

| | |
|---|---|
| Atomic sentences with subscripts, as needed | $A, B, C, \ldots, Z$<br>$A_1, B_1, Z_1, A_2, A_{25}, J_{375}, \ldots$ |
| Connectives | $\neg, \land, \lor, \rightarrow, \leftrightarrow$ |
| Brackets | ( , ) |

Define an EXPRESSION OF TFL as any string of symbols of TFL. So: write down any sequence of symbols of TFL, in any order,

49

and you have an expression of TFL.

## 6.2  Sentences

Given what we just said, '$(A \wedge B)$' is an expression of TFL, and so
is '$\neg)(\vee()\wedge(\neg\neg())((B$'. But the former is a *sentence*, and the latter
is *gibberish*. We want some rules to tell us which TFL expressions
are sentences.

Obviously, individual sentence letters like '$A$' and '$G_{13}$' should
count as sentences. (We'll also call them *atomic* sentences.) We
can form further sentences out of these by using the various connectives. Using negation, we can get '$\neg A$' and '$\neg G_{13}$'. Using
conjunction, we can get '$(A \wedge G_{13})$', '$(G_{13} \wedge A)$', '$(A \wedge A)$', and
'$(G_{13} \wedge G_{13})$'. We could also apply negation repeatedly to get
sentences like '$\neg\neg A$' or apply negation along with conjunction to
get sentences like '$\neg(A \wedge G_{13})$' and '$\neg(G_{13} \wedge \neg G_{13})$'. The possible
combinations are endless, even starting with just these two sen-
tence letters, and there are infinitely many sentence letters. So
there is no point in trying to list all the sentences one by one.

Instead, we will describe the process by which sentences can
be *constructed*. Consider negation: Given any sentence $\mathscr{A}$ of TFL,
$\neg\mathscr{A}$ is a sentence of TFL. (Why the funny fonts? We return to this
in §8.3.)

We can say similar things for each of the other connectives.
For instance, if $\mathscr{A}$ and $\mathscr{B}$ are sentences of TFL, then $(\mathscr{A} \wedge \mathscr{B})$
is a sentence of TFL. Providing clauses like this for all of the
connectives, we arrive at the following formal definition for a
SENTENCE OF TFL:

1. Every sentence letter is a sentence.

2. If $\mathcal{A}$ is a sentence, then $\neg\mathcal{A}$ is a sentence.

3. If $\mathcal{A}$ and $\mathcal{B}$ are sentences, then $(\mathcal{A} \wedge \mathcal{B})$ is a sentence.

4. If $\mathcal{A}$ and $\mathcal{B}$ are sentences, then $(\mathcal{A} \vee \mathcal{B})$ is a sentence.

5. If $\mathcal{A}$ and $\mathcal{B}$ are sentences, then $(\mathcal{A} \rightarrow \mathcal{B})$ is a sentence.

6. If $\mathcal{A}$ and $\mathcal{B}$ are sentences, then $(\mathcal{A} \leftrightarrow \mathcal{B})$ is a sentence.

7. Nothing else is a sentence.

Definitions like this are called *inductive*. inductive definitions begin with some specifiable base elements, and then present ways to generate indefinitely many more elements by compounding together previously established ones. To give you a better idea of what an inductive definition is, we can give an inductive definition of the idea of *an ancestor of mine*. We specify a base clause.

- My parents are ancestors of mine.

and then offer further clauses like:

- If $x$ is an ancestor of mine, then $x$'s parents are ancestors of mine.
- Nothing else is an ancestor of mine.

Using this definition, we can easily check to see whether someone is my ancestor: just check whether she is the parent of the parent of... one of my parents. And the same is true for our inductive definition of sentences of TFL. Just as the inductive definition allows complex sentences to be built up from simpler parts, the definition allows us to decompose sentences into their simpler parts. Once we get down to sentence letters, then we know we are ok.

Let's consider some examples.

Suppose we want to know whether or not '¬¬¬$D$' is a sentence of TFL. Looking at the second clause of the definition, we know that '¬¬¬$D$' is a sentence *if* '¬¬$D$' is a sentence. So now we need to ask whether or not '¬¬$D$' is a sentence. Again looking at the second clause of the definition, '¬¬$D$' is a sentence *if* '¬$D$' is. So, '¬$D$' is a sentence *if* '$D$' is a sentence. Now '$D$' is a sentence letter of TFL, so we know that '$D$' is a sentence by the first clause of the definition. So for a compound sentence like '¬¬¬$D$', we must apply the definition repeatedly. Eventually we arrive at the sentence letters from which the sentence is built up.

Next, consider the example '¬($P \land \neg(\neg Q \lor R)$)'. Looking at the second clause of the definition, this is a sentence if '($P \land \neg(\neg Q \lor R)$)' is, and this is a sentence if *both* '$P$' *and* '¬($\neg Q \lor R$)' are sentences. The former is a sentence letter, and the latter is a sentence if '($\neg Q \lor R$)' is a sentence. It is. Looking at the fourth clause of the definition, this is a sentence if both '¬$Q$' and '$R$' are sentences, and both are!

Ultimately, every sentence is constructed nicely out of sentence letters. When we are dealing with a *sentence* other than a sentence letter, we can see that there must be some sentential connective that was introduced *last*, when constructing the sentence. We call that connective the MAIN LOGICAL OPERATOR of the sentence. In the case of '¬¬¬$D$', the main logical operator is the very first '¬' sign. In the case of '($P \land \neg(\neg Q \lor R)$)', the main logical operator is '$\land$'. In the case of '(($\neg E \lor F$) $\to$ ¬¬$G$)', the main logical operator is '$\to$'.

As a general rule, you can find the main logical operator for a sentence by using the following method:

- If the first symbol in the sentence is '¬', then that is the main logical operator
- Otherwise, start counting the brackets. For each open-bracket, i.e., '(', add 1; for each closing-bracket, i.e., ')', subtract 1. When your count is at exactly 1, the first operator you hit (*apart* from a '¬') is the main logical operator.

(Note: if you do use this method, then make sure to include *all* the brackets in the sentence, rather than omitting some as per the conventions of §6.3!)

The inductive structure of sentences in TFL will be important when we consider the circumstances under which a particular sentence would be true or false. The sentence '¬¬¬D' is true if and only if the sentence '¬¬D' is false, and so on through the structure of the sentence, until we arrive at the atomic components. We will return to this point in Part III.

The inductive structure of sentences in TFL also allows us to give a formal definition of the *scope* of a negation (mentioned in §5.2). The scope of a '¬' is the subsentence for which '¬' is the main logical operator. Consider a sentence like:

$$(P \wedge (\neg(R \wedge B) \leftrightarrow Q))$$

which was constructed by conjoining '*P*' with '(¬(*R* ∧ *B*) ↔ *Q*)'. This last sentence was constructed by placing a biconditional between '¬(*R* ∧ *B*)' and '*Q*'. The former of these sentences—a subsentence of our original sentence—is a sentence for which '¬' is the main logical operator. So the scope of the negation is just '¬(*R* ∧ *B*)'. More generally:

> The SCOPE of a connective (in a sentence) is the subsentence for which that connective is the main logical operator.

## 6.3 Bracketing conventions

Strictly speaking, the brackets in '(*Q* ∧ *R*)' are an indispensable part of the sentence. Part of this is because we might use '(*Q* ∧ *R*)' as a subsentence in a more complicated sentence. For example, we might want to negate '(*Q* ∧ *R*)', obtaining '¬(*Q* ∧ *R*)'. If we just had '*Q* ∧ *R*' without the brackets and put a negation in front of it, we would have '¬*Q* ∧ *R*'. It is most natural to read this as meaning the same thing as '$(\neg Q \wedge R)$', but as we saw in §5.2, this is very different from '$\neg(Q \wedge R)$'.

Strictly speaking, then, '$Q \wedge R$' is *not* a sentence. It is a mere *expression*.

When working with TFL, however, it will make our lives easier if we are sometimes a little less than strict. So, here are some convenient conventions.

First, we allow ourselves to omit the *outermost* brackets of a sentence. Thus we allow ourselves to write '$Q \wedge R$' instead of the sentence '$(Q \wedge R)$'. However, we must remember to put the brackets back in, when we want to embed the sentence into a more complicated sentence!

Second, it can be a bit painful to stare at long sentences with many nested pairs of brackets. To make things a bit easier on the eyes, we will allow ourselves to use square brackets, '[' and ']', instead of rounded ones. So there is no logical difference between '$(P \vee Q)$' and '$[P \vee Q]$', for example.

Combining these two conventions, we can rewrite the unwieldy sentence

$$(((H \rightarrow I) \vee (I \rightarrow H)) \wedge (J \vee K))$$

rather more clearly as follows:

$$\big[(H \rightarrow I) \vee (I \rightarrow H)\big] \wedge (J \vee K)$$

The scope of each connective is now much easier to pick out.

## Practice exercises

**A.** For each of the following: (a) Is it a sentence of TFL, strictly speaking? (b) Is it a sentence of TFL, allowing for our relaxed bracketing conventions?

   1. $(A)$
   2. $J_{374} \vee \neg J_{374}$
   3. $\neg\neg\neg\neg F$

4. $\neg \wedge S$
5. $(G \wedge \neg G)$
6. $(A \rightarrow (A \wedge \neg F)) \vee (D \leftrightarrow E)$
7. $[(Z \leftrightarrow S) \rightarrow W] \wedge [J \vee X]$
8. $(F \leftrightarrow \neg D \rightarrow J) \vee (C \wedge D)$

**B.** Are there any sentences of TFL that contain no sentence letters? Explain your answer.

**C.** What is the scope of each connective in the sentence

$$\big[(H \rightarrow I) \vee (I \rightarrow H)\big] \wedge (J \vee K)$$

# CHAPTER 7
# *Ambiguity*

In English, sentences can be AMBIGUOUS, i.e., they can have more than one meaning. There are many sources of ambiguity. One is *lexical ambiguity:* a sentence can contain words which have more than one meaning. For instance, 'bank' can mean the bank of a river, or a financial institution. So I might say that 'I went to the bank' when I took a stroll along the river, or when I went to deposit a check. Depending on the situation, a different meaning of 'bank' is intended, and so the sentence, when uttered in these different contexts, expresses different meanings.

A different kind of ambiguity is *structural ambiguity*. This arises when a sentence can be interpreted in different ways, and depending on the interpretation, a different meaning is selected. A famous example due to Noam Chomsky is the following:

> Flying planes can be dangerous.

There is one reading in which 'flying' is used as an adjective which modifies 'planes'. In this sense, what's claimed to be dangerous are airplanes which are in the process of flying. In another reading, 'flying' is a gerund: what's claimed to be dangerous is the act of flying a plane. In the first case, you might use the sentence to warn someone who's about to launch a hot air baloon. In the second case, you might use it to counsel someone against becoming a pilot.

When the sentence is uttered, usually only one meaning is intended. Which of the possible meanings an utterance of a sentence intends is determined by context, or sometimes by how it is uttered (which parts of the sentence are stressed, for instance). Often one interpretation is much more likely to be intended, and in that case it will even be difficult to "see" the unintended reading. This is often the reason why a joke works, as in this example from Groucho Marx:

> One morning I shot an elephant in my pajamas.
> How he got in my pajamas, I don't know.

Ambiguity is related to, but not the same as, vagueness. An adjective, for instance 'rich' or 'tall,' is VAGUE when it is not always possible to determine if it applies or not. For instance, a person who's 6 ft 4 in (1.9 m) tall is pretty clearly tall, but a building that size is tiny. Here, context has a role to play in determining what the clear cases and clear non-cases are ('tall for a person,' 'tall for a basketball player,' 'tall for a building'). Even when the context is clear, however, there will still be cases that fall in a middle range.

In TFL, we generally aim to avoid ambiguity. We will try to give our symbolization keys in such a way that they do not use ambiguous words or disambiguate them if a word has different meanings. So, e.g., your symbolization key will need two different sentence letters for 'Rebecca went to the (money) bank' and 'Rebecca went to the (river) bank.' Vagueness is harder to avoid. Since we have stipulated that every case (and later, every valuation) must make every basic sentence (or sentence letter) either true or false and nothing in between, we cannot accommodate borderline cases in TFL.

It is an important feature of sentences of TFL that they *cannot* be structurally ambiguous. Every sentence of TFL can be read in one, and only one, way. This feature of TFL is also a strength. If an English sentence is ambiguous, TFL can help us make clear what the different meanings are. Although we are pretty good at dealing with ambiguity in everyday conversation, avoiding it can sometimes be terribly important. Logic can then be usefully applied: it helps philosophers express their thoughts clearly, mathematicians to state their theorems rigorously, and software engineers to specify loop conditions, database queries, or verification criteria unambiguously.

Stating things without ambiguity is of crucial importance in the law as well. Here, ambiguity can, without exaggeration, be a matter of life and death. Here is a famous example of where a death sentence hinged on the interpretation of an ambiguity in the law. Roger Casement (1864–1916) was a British diplomat who was famous in his time for publicizing human-rights violations in the Congo and Peru (for which he was knighted in 1911). He was also an Irish nationalist. In 1914–16, Casement secretly travelled to Germany, with which Britain was at war at the time, and tried to recruit Irish prisoners of war to fight against Britain and for Irish independence. Upon his return to Ireland, he was captured by the British and tried for high treason.

The law under which Casement was tried is the *Treason Act of 1351*. That act specifies what counts as treason, and so the prosecution had to establish at trial that Casement's actions met the criteria set forth in the Treason Act. The relevant passage stipulated that someone is guilty of treason

> if a man is adherent to the King's enemies in his realm, giving to them aid and comfort in the realm, or elsewhere.

Casement's defense hinged on the last comma in this sentence, which is not present in the original French text of the law from 1351. It was not under dispute that Casement had been 'adherent to the King's enemies', but the question was whether being adherent to the King's enemies constituted treason only when it was done in the realm, or also when it was done abroad. The defense argued that the law was ambiguous. The claimed ambiguity hinged on whether 'or elsewhere' attaches only to 'giving aid and comfort to the King's enemies' (the natural reading without the comma), or to both 'being adherent to the King's enemies' and 'giving aid and comfort to the King's enemies' (the natural reading with the comma). Although the former interpretation might seem far fetched, the argument in its favor was actually not unpersuasive. Nevertheless, the court decided that the passage should be read with the comma, so Casement's antics in Germany were treasonous, and he was sentenced to death. Casement himself wrote that he was 'hanged by a comma'.

We can use TFL to symbolize both readings of the passage, and thus to provide a disambiguiation. First, we need a symbolization key:

> $A$: Casement was adherent to the King's enemies in the realm.
> $G$: Casement gave aid and comfort to the King's enemies in the realm.
> $B$: Casement was adherent to the King's enemies abroad.
> $H$: Casement gave aid and comfort to the King's enemies abroad.

The interpretation according to which Casement's behavior was not treasonous is this:

> $A \lor (G \lor H)$

The interpretation which got him executed, on the other hand, can be symbolized by:

> $(A \lor B) \lor (G \lor H)$

Remember that in the case we're dealing with Casement, was adherent to the King's enemies abroad ($B$ is true), but not in the realm, and he did not give the King's enemies aid or comfort in or outside the realm ($A$, $G$, and $H$ are false).

One common source of structural ambiguity in English arises from its lack of parentheses. For instance, if I say 'I like movies that are not long and boring', you will most likely think that what

I dislike are movies that are long and boring. A less likely, but possible, interpretation is that I like movies that are both (a) not long and (b) boring. The first reading is more likely because who likes boring movies? But what about 'I like dishes that are not sweet and flavorful'? Here, the more likely interpretation is that I like savory, flavorful dishes. (Of course, I could have said that better, e.g., 'I like dishes that are not sweet, yet flavorful'.) Similar ambiguities result from the interaction of 'and' with 'or'. For instance, suppose I ask you to send me a picture of a small and dangerous or stealthy animal. Would a leopard count? It's stealthy, but not small. So it depends whether I'm looking for small animals that are dangerous or stealthy (leopard doesn't count), or whether I'm after either a small, dangerous animal or a stealthy animal (of any size).

These kinds of ambiguities are called *scope ambiguities*, since they depend on whether or not a connective is in the scope of another. For instance, the sentence, '*Avengers: Endgame* is not long and boring' is ambiguous between:

1. *Avengers: Endgame* is not: both long and boring.
2. *Avengers: Endgame* is both: not long and boring.

Sentence 2 is certainly false, since *Avengers: Endgame* is over three hours long. Whether you think 1 is true depends on if you think it is boring or not. We can use the symbolization key:

B: *Avengers: Endgame* is boring.
L: *Avengers: Endgame* is long.

Sentence 1 can now be symbolized as '$\neg(L \wedge B)$', whereas sentence 2 would be '$\neg L \wedge B$'. In the first case, the '$\wedge$' is in the scope of '$\neg$', in the second case '$\neg$' is in the scope of '$\wedge$'.

The sentence 'Tai Lung is small and dangerous or stealthy' is ambiguous between:

3. Tai Lung is either both small and dangerous or stealthy.
4. Tai Lung is both small and either dangerous or stealthy.

We can use the following symbolization key:

> $D$: Tai Lung is dangerous.
> $S$: Tai Lung is small.
> $T$: Tai Lung is stealthy.

The symbolization of sentence 3 is '$(S \wedge D) \vee T$' and that of sentence 4 is '$S \wedge (D \vee T)$'. In the first, $\wedge$ is in the scope of $\vee$, and in the second $\vee$ is in the scope of $\wedge$.

## Practice exercises

**A.** The following sentences are ambiguous. Give symbolization keys for each and symbolize the different readings.

1. Haskell is a birder and enjoys watching cranes.
2. The zoo has lions or tigers and bears.
3. The flower is not red or fragrant.

**CHAPTER 8**

# *Use and mention*

In this Part, we have talked a lot *about* sentences. So we should pause to explain an important, and very general, point.

## 8.1 Quotation conventions

Consider these two sentences:

- Justin Trudeau is the Prime Minister.
- The expression 'Justin Trudeau' is composed of two uppercase letters and eleven lowercase letters

When we want to talk about the Prime Minister, we *use* his name. When we want to talk about the Prime Minister's name, we *mention* that name, which we do by putting it in quotation marks.

There is a general point here. When we want to talk about things in the world, we just *use* words. When we want to talk about words, we typically have to *mention* those words. We need to indicate that we are mentioning them, rather than using them. To do this, some convention is needed. We can put them in quotation marks, or display them centrally in the page (say). So this sentence:

- 'Justin Trudeau' is the Prime Minister.

says that some *expression* is the Prime Minister. That's false. The *man* is the Prime Minister; his *name* isn't. Conversely, this sentence:

- Justin Trudeau is composed of two uppercase letters and eleven lowercase letters.

also says something false: Justin Trudeau is a man, made of flesh rather than letters. One final example:

- " 'Justin Trudeau' " is the name of 'Justin Trudeau'.

On the left-hand-side, here, we have the name of a name. On the right hand side, we have a name. Perhaps this kind of sentence only occurs in logic textbooks, but it is true nonetheless.

Those are just general rules for quotation, and you should observe them carefully in all your work! To be clear, the quotation-marks here do not indicate reported speech. They indicate that you are moving from talking about an object, to talking about a name of that object.

## 8.2  Object language and metalanguage

These general quotation conventions are very important for us. After all, we are describing a formal language here, TFL, and so we must often *mention* expressions from TFL.

When we talk about a language, the language that we are talking about is called the OBJECT LANGUAGE. The language that we use to talk about the object language is called the METALAN-GUAGE.

For the most part, the object language in this chapter has been the formal language that we have been developing: TFL. The metalanguage is English. Not conversational English exactly, but English supplemented with some additional vocabulary to help us get along.

Now, we have used uppercase letters as sentence letters of TFL:

$$A, B, C, Z, A_1, B_4, A_{25}, J_{375}, \ldots$$

These are sentences of the object language (TFL). They are not sentences of English. So we must not say, for example:

- $D$ is a sentence letter of TFL.

Obviously, we are trying to come out with an English sentence that says something about the object language (TFL), but '$D$' is a sentence of TFL, and not part of English. So the preceding is gibberish, just like:

- Schnee ist weiß is a German sentence.

What we surely meant to say, in this case, is:

- 'Schnee ist weiß' is a German sentence.

Equally, what we meant to say above is just:

- '$D$' is a sentence letter of TFL.

The general point is that, whenever we want to talk in English about some specific expression of TFL, we need to indicate that we are *mentioning* the expression, rather than *using* it. We can either deploy quotation marks, or we can adopt some similar convention, such as placing it centrally in the page.

## 8.3   Metavariables

However, we do not just want to talk about *specific* expressions of TFL. We also want to be able to talk about *any arbitrary* sentence of TFL. Indeed, we had to do this in §6.2, when we presented the inductive definition of a sentence of TFL. We used uppercase script letters to do this, namely:

$$\mathcal{A}, \mathcal{B}, \mathcal{C}, \mathcal{D}, \ldots$$

These symbols do not belong to TFL. Rather, they are part of our (augmented) metalanguage that we use to talk about *any* expression of TFL. To explain why we need them, recall the second clause of the recursive definition of a sentence of TFL:

2. If $\mathcal{A}$ is a sentence, then $\neg\mathcal{A}$ is a sentence.

This talks about *arbitrary* sentences. If we had instead offered:

- If '$A$' is a sentence, then '$\neg A$' is a sentence.

this would not have allowed us to determine whether '$\neg B$' is a sentence. To emphasize:

> '$\mathcal{A}$' is a symbol (called a METAVARIABLE) in augmented English, which we use to talk about expressions of TFL. '$A$' is a particular sentence letter of TFL.

But this last example raises a further complication, concerning quotation conventions. We did not include any quotation marks in the second clause of our inductive definition. Should we have done so?

The problem is that the expression on the right-hand-side of this rule, i.e., '$\neg\mathcal{A}$', is not a sentence of English, since it contains '$\neg$'. So we might try to write:

2′. If $\mathcal{A}$ is a sentence, then '$\neg\mathcal{A}$' is a sentence.

But this is no good: '$\neg\mathcal{A}$' is not a TFL sentence, since '$\mathcal{A}$' is a symbol of (augmented) English rather than a symbol of TFL.

What we really want to say is something like this:

2″. If $\mathcal{A}$ is a sentence, then the result of concatenating the symbol '$\neg$' with the sentence $\mathcal{A}$ is a sentence.

This is impeccable, but rather long-winded. But we can avoid long-windedness by creating our own conventions. We can perfectly well stipulate that an expression like '$\neg\mathcal{A}$' should simply be read *directly* in terms of rules for concatenation. So, *officially*, the metalanguage expression '$\neg\mathcal{A}$' simply abbreviates:

the result of concatenating the symbol '$\neg$' with the sentence $\mathcal{A}$

and similarly, for expressions like '$(\mathcal{A} \land \mathcal{B})$', '$(\mathcal{A} \lor \mathcal{B})$', etc.

## 8.4   Quotation conventions for arguments

One of our main purposes for using TFL is to study arguments, and that will be our concern in chapter III. In English, the premises of an argument are often expressed by individual sentences, and the conclusion by a further sentence. Since we can symbolize English sentences, we can symbolise English arguments using TFL.

Or rather, we can use TFL to symbolize each of the *sentences* used in an English argument. However, TFL itself has no way to flag some of them as the *premises* and another as the *conclusion* of an argument. (Contrast this with natural English, which uses words like 'so', 'therefore', etc., to mark that a sentence is the *conclusion* of an argument.)

So, we need another bit of notation. Suppose we want to symbolize the premises of an argument with $\mathcal{A}_1, \ldots, \mathcal{A}_n$ and the conclusion with $\mathcal{C}$. Then we will write:

$$\mathcal{A}_1, \ldots, \mathcal{A}_n \therefore \mathcal{C}$$

The role of the symbol '$\therefore$' is simply to indicate which sentences are the premises and which is the conclusion.

Strictly, the symbol '$\therefore$' will not be a part of the object language, but of the *metalanguage*. As such, one might think that we would need to put quote-marks around the TFL-sentences which flank it. That is a sensible thought, but adding these quote-marks would make things harder to read. Moreover—and as above—recall that *we* are stipulating some new conventions. So, we can simply stipulate that these quote-marks are unnecessary. That is, we can simply write:

$$A, A \rightarrow B \therefore B$$

*without any quotation marks*, to indicate an argument whose premises are (symbolized by) '$A$' and '$A \rightarrow B$' and whose conclusion is (symbolized by) '$B$'.

# PART III

# *Truth tables*

## CHAPTER 9

# *Characteristic truth tables*

Any sentence of TFL is composed of sentence letters, possibly combined using sentential connectives. The truth value of the compound sentence depends only on the truth value of the sentence letters that comprise it. In order to know the truth value of '$(D \wedge E)$', for instance, you only need to know the truth value of '$D$' and the truth value of '$E$'.

We introduced five connectives in chapter 5. So we just need to explain how they map between truth values. For convenience, we abbreviate 'True' with 'T' and 'False' with 'F'. (But, to be clear, the two truth values are True and False; the truth values are not *letters*!)

**Negation.** For any sentence $\mathcal{A}$: If $\mathcal{A}$ is true, then $\neg \mathcal{A}$ is false; and if $\neg \mathcal{A}$ is true, then $\mathcal{A}$ is false. We can summarize this in the *characteristic truth table* for negation:

| $\mathcal{A}$ | $\neg \mathcal{A}$ |
|---|---|
| T | F |
| F | T |

69

**Conjunction.**  For any sentences $\mathcal{A}$ and $\mathcal{B}$, $\mathcal{A} \wedge \mathcal{B}$ is true if and only if both $\mathcal{A}$ and $\mathcal{B}$ are true. We can summarize this in the characteristic truth table for conjunction:

| $\mathcal{A}$ | $\mathcal{B}$ | $\mathcal{A} \wedge \mathcal{B}$ |
|:---:|:---:|:---:|
| T | T | T |
| T | F | F |
| F | T | F |
| F | F | F |

Note that conjunction is *symmetrical*. The truth value for $\mathcal{A} \wedge \mathcal{B}$ is always the same as the truth value for $\mathcal{B} \wedge \mathcal{A}$.

**Disjunction.**  Recall that '$\vee$' always represents inclusive or. So, for any sentences $\mathcal{A}$ and $\mathcal{B}$, $\mathcal{A} \vee \mathcal{B}$ is true if and only if either $\mathcal{A}$ or $\mathcal{B}$ is true. We can summarize this in the characteristic truth table for disjunction:

| $\mathcal{A}$ | $\mathcal{B}$ | $\mathcal{A} \vee \mathcal{B}$ |
|:---:|:---:|:---:|
| T | T | T |
| T | F | T |
| F | T | T |
| F | F | F |

Like conjunction, disjunction is symmetrical.

**Conditional.**  We're just going to come clean and admit it: Conditionals are a mess in TFL. Exactly how much of a mess they are is *philosophically* contentious. We'll discuss a few of the subtleties in §§10.3 and 12.5. For now, we are going to stipulate the following: $\mathcal{A} \rightarrow \mathcal{B}$ is false if and only if $\mathcal{A}$ is true and $\mathcal{B}$ is false. We can summarize this with a characteristic truth table for the conditional.

| $\mathscr{A}$ | $\mathscr{B}$ | $\mathscr{A} \rightarrow \mathscr{B}$ |
|:---:|:---:|:---:|
| T | T | T |
| T | F | F |
| F | T | T |
| F | F | T |

The conditional is *asymmetric*. You cannot swap the antecedent and consequent without changing the meaning of the sentence; $\mathscr{A} \rightarrow \mathscr{B}$ and $\mathscr{B} \rightarrow \mathscr{A}$ have different truth tables.

**Biconditional.**   Since a biconditional is to be the same as the conjunction of the conditionals running in both directions, we will want the truth table for the biconditional to be:

| $\mathscr{A}$ | $\mathscr{B}$ | $\mathscr{A} \leftrightarrow \mathscr{B}$ |
|:---:|:---:|:---:|
| T | T | T |
| T | F | F |
| F | T | F |
| F | F | T |

Unsurprisingly, the biconditional is symmetrical.

# CHAPTER 10

# *Truth-functional connectives*

## 10.1   The idea of truth-functionality

Let's introduce an important idea.

> A connective is TRUTH-FUNCTIONAL iff the truth value of
> a sentence with that connective as its main logical oper-
> ator is uniquely determined by the truth value(s) of the
> constituent sentence(s).

Every connective in TFL is truth-functional. The truth value
of a negation is uniquely determined by the truth value of the
unnegated sentence. The truth value of a conjunction is uniquely
determined by the truth value of both conjuncts. The truth value
of a disjunction is uniquely determined by the truth value of both
disjuncts, and so on. To determine the truth value of some TFL
sentence, we only need to know the truth value of its components.

This is what gives TFL its name: it is *truth-functional logic*.

Many languages use connectives that are not truth-functional. In English, for example, we can form a new sentence from any simpler sentence by prefixing it with 'It is necessarily the case that...'. The truth value of this new sentence is not fixed solely by the truth value of the original sentence. For consider two true sentences:

1. $2 + 2 = 4$
2. Shostakovich wrote fifteen string quartets

Whereas it is necessarily the case that $2 + 2 = 4$, it is not *necessarily* the case that Shostakovich wrote fifteen string quartets. If Shostakovich had died earlier, he would have failed to finish Quartet no. 15; if he had lived longer, he might have written a few more. So 'It is necessarily the case that...' is not *truth-functional*.

## 10.2  Symbolizing versus translating

All of the connectives of TFL are truth-functional, but more than that: they really do nothing *but* map us between truth values.

When we symbolize a sentence or an argument in TFL, we ignore everything *besides* the contribution that the truth values of a component might make to the truth value of the whole. There are subtleties to our ordinary claims that far outstrip their mere truth values. Sarcasm; poetry; snide implicature; emphasis; these are important parts of everyday discourse, but none of this is retained in TFL. As remarked in §5, TFL cannot capture the subtle differences between the following English sentences:

1. Dana is a logician and Dana is a nice person
2. Although Dana is a logician, Dana is a nice person
3. Dana is a logician despite being a nice person
4. Dana is a nice person, but also a logician
5. Dana's being a logician notwithstanding, he is a nice person

All of the above sentences will be symbolized with the same TFL sentence, perhaps '$L \wedge N$'.

Now, we keep saying that we use TFL sentences to *symbolize* English sentences. Many other textbooks talk about *translating* English sentences into TFL. However, a good translation should preserve certain facets of meaning, and—as we just saw—TFL just cannot do that. This is why we will speak of *symbolizing* English sentences, rather than of *translating* them.

This affects how we should understand our symbolization keys. Consider a key like:

$L$: Dana is a logician.
$N$: Dana is a nice person.

Other textbooks will understand this as a stipulation that the TFL sentence '$L$' should *mean* that Dana is a logician, and that the TFL sentence '$N$' should *mean* that Dana is a nice person. But TFL just is totally unequipped to deal with *meaning*. The preceding symbolization key is doing no more and no less than stipulating that the TFL sentence '$L$' should take the same truth value as the English sentence 'Dana is a logician' (whatever that might be), and that the TFL sentence '$N$' should take the same truth value as the English sentence 'Dana is a nice person' (whatever that might be).

> When we treat a TFL sentence as *symbolizing* an English sentence, we are stipulating that the TFL sentence is to take the same truth value as that English sentence.

## 10.3   Indicative versus subjunctive conditionals

We want to bring home the point that TFL can *only* deal with truth functions by considering the case of the conditional. When we introduced the characteristic truth table for the material conditional in §9, we did not say anything to justify it. Let's now offer a justification, which follows Dorothy Edgington.[1]

Suppose that Lara has drawn some shapes on a piece of paper, and coloured some of them in. We have not seen them, but nevertheless claim:

If any shape is grey, then that shape is also circular.

As it happens, Lara has drawn the following:

In this case, our claim is surely true. Shapes C and D are not grey, and so can hardly present *counterexamples* to our claim. Shape A *is* grey, but fortunately it is also circular. So our claim has no counterexamples. It must be true. That means that each of the following *instances* of our claim must be true too:

- If A is grey, then it is circular     (true antecedent, true consequent)
- If C is grey, then it is circular     (false antecedent, true consequent)
- If D is grey, then it is circular     (false antecedent, false consequent)

However, if Lara had drawn a fourth shape, thus:

then our claim would have been false. So this claim must also be false:

- If B is grey, then it is circular     (true antecedent, false consequent)

---

[1]Dorothy Edgington, 'Conditionals', 2014, in the *Stanford Encyclopedia of Philosophy* (http://plato.stanford.edu/entries/conditionals/).

Now, recall that every connective of TFL has to be truth-functional. This means that merely the truth values of the antecedent and consequent must uniquely determine the truth value of the conditional as a whole. Thus, from the truth values of our four claims—which provide us with all possible combinations of truth and falsity in antecedent and consequent—we can read off the truth table for the material conditional.

What this argument shows is that '→' is the *best* candidate for a truth-functional conditional. Otherwise put, *it is the best conditional that TFL can provide.* But is it any good, as a surrogate for the conditionals we use in everyday language? Consider two sentences:

1. If Hillary Clinton had won the 2016 election, then she would have been the first woman president of the USA.
2. If Hillary Clinton had won the 2016 election, then she would have turned into a helium-filled balloon and floated away into the night sky.

Sentence 1 is true; sentence 2 is false, but both have false antecedents and false consequents. (Hillary did not win; she did not become the first woman president of the US; and she did not fill with helium and float away.) So the truth value of the whole sentence is not uniquely determined by the truth value of the parts.

The crucial point is that sentences 1 and 2 employ *subjunctive* conditionals, rather than *indicative* conditionals. They ask us to imagine something contrary to fact—after all, Hillary Clinton lost the 2016 election—and then ask us to evaluate what *would* have happened in that case. Such considerations simply cannot be tackled using '→'.

We will say more about the difficulties with conditionals in §12.5. For now, we will content ourselves with the observation that '→' is the only candidate for a truth-functional conditional for TFL, but that many English conditionals cannot be represented adequately using '→'. TFL is an intrinsically limited language.

# CHAPTER 11

# *Complete truth tables*

So far, we have used symbolization keys to assign truth values to TFL sentences *indirectly*. For example, we might say that the TFL sentence '*B*' is to be true iff Big Ben is in London. Since Big Ben *is* in London, this symbolisation would make '*B*' true. But we can also assign truth values *directly*. We can simply stipulate that '*B*' is to be true, or stipulate that it is to be false. Such stipulations are called *valuations*:

A VALUATION is any assignment of truth values to particular sentence letters of TFL.

The power of truth tables lies in the following. Each row of a truth table represents a possible valuation. The complete truth table represents all possible valuations. And the truth table provides us with a means to calculate the truth value of complex sentences, on each possible valuation. But all of this is easiest to explain by example.

## 11.1   A worked example

Consider the sentence '$(H \land I) \to H$'. There are four possible ways to assign True and False to the sentence letter '$H$' and '$I$'—four valuations—which we can represent as follows:

| $H$ | $I$ | $(H \land I) \to H$ |
|---|---|---|
| T | T | |
| T | F | |
| F | T | |
| F | F | |

To calculate the truth value of the entire sentence '$(H \land I) \to H$', we first copy the truth values for the sentence letters and write them underneath the letters in the sentence:

| $H$ | $I$ | $(H \land I) \to H$ | | |
|---|---|---|---|---|
| T | T | T | T | T |
| T | F | T | F | T |
| F | T | F | T | F |
| F | F | F | F | F |

Now consider the subsentence '$(H \land I)$'. This is a conjunction, $(\mathscr{A} \land \mathscr{B})$, with '$H$' as $\mathscr{A}$ and with '$I$' as $\mathscr{B}$. The characteristic truth table for conjunction gives the truth conditions for *any* sentence of the form $(\mathscr{A} \land \mathscr{B})$, whatever $\mathscr{A}$ and $\mathscr{B}$ might be. It represents the point that a conjunction is true iff both conjuncts are true. In this case, our conjuncts are just '$H$' and '$I$'. They are both true on (and only on) the first line of the truth table. Accordingly, we can calculate the truth value of the conjunction on all four rows.

| | | $\mathscr{A} \land \mathscr{B}$ | | |
|---|---|---|---|---|
| $H$ | $I$ | $(H \land I) \to H$ | | |
| T | T | T T T | | T |
| T | F | T F F | | T |
| F | T | F F T | | F |
| F | F | F F F | | F |

Now, the entire sentence that we are dealing with is a conditional, $\mathscr{A} \to \mathscr{B}$, with '$(H \land I)$' as $\mathscr{A}$ and with '$H$' as $\mathscr{B}$. On the second row, for example, '$(H \land I)$' is false and '$H$' is true. Since a conditional is true when the antecedent is false, we write a 'T' in the second row underneath the conditional symbol. We continue for the other three rows and get this:

|     |     | $\mathscr{A}$ | $\to$ | $\mathscr{B}$ |
| --- | --- | :---: | :---: | :---: |
| $H$ | $I$ | $(H \land I)$ | $\to$ | $H$ |
| T | T | T | T T |
| T | F | F | T T |
| F | T | F | T F |
| F | F | F | T F |

The conditional is the main logical operator of the sentence, so the column of 'T's underneath the conditional tells us that the sentence '$(H \land I) \to H$' is true regardless of the truth values of '$H$' and '$I$'. They can be true or false in any combination, and the compound sentence still comes out true. Since we have considered all four possible assignments of truth and falsity to '$H$' and '$I$'—since, that is, we have considered all the different *valuations*—we can say that '$(H \land I) \to H$' is true on every valuation.

   In this example, we have not repeated all of the entries in every column in every successive table. When actually writing truth tables on paper, however, it is impractical to erase whole columns or rewrite the whole table for every step. Although it is more crowded, the truth table can be written in this way:

| $H$ | $I$ | $(H \land I) \to H$ |
| --- | --- | :---: |
| T | T | T T T **T** T |
| T | F | T F F **T** T |
| F | T | F F T **T** F |
| F | F | F F F **T** F |

Most of the columns underneath the sentence are only there for bookkeeping purposes. The column that matters most is the column underneath the *main logical operator* for the sentence, since this tells you the truth value of the entire sentence. We have emphasized this, by putting this column in bold. When you work through truth tables yourself, you should similarly emphasize it (perhaps by highlighting).

## 11.2   Building complete truth tables

A COMPLETE TRUTH TABLE has a line for every possible assignment of True and False to the relevant sentence letters. Each line represents a *valuation*, and a complete truth table has a line for all the different valuations.

The size of the complete truth table depends on the number of different sentence letters in the table. A sentence that contains only one sentence letter requires only two rows, as in the characteristic truth table for negation. This is true even if the same letter is repeated many times, as in the sentence '$[(C \leftrightarrow C) \rightarrow C] \wedge \neg(C \rightarrow C)$'. The complete truth table requires only two lines because there are only two possibilities: '$C$' can be true or it can be false. The truth table for this sentence looks like this:

| $C$ | $[(C \leftrightarrow C) \rightarrow C] \wedge \neg(C \rightarrow C)$ |
|---|---|
| T | T T T  T T  **F F**  T T T |
| F | F T F  F F  **F F**  F T F |

Looking at the column underneath the main logical operator, we see that the sentence is false on both rows of the table; i.e., the sentence is false regardless of whether '$C$' is true or false. It is false on every valuation.

There will be four lines in the complete truth table for a sentence containing two sentence letters, as in the characteristic truth tables, or the truth table for '$(H \wedge I) \rightarrow H$'.

There will be eight lines in the complete truth table for a sentence containing three sentence letters, e.g.:

| $M$ | $N$ | $P$ | $M \wedge (N \vee P)$ |
|---|---|---|---|
| T | T | T | T **T** T T T |
| T | T | F | T **T** T T F |
| T | F | T | T **T** F T T |
| T | F | F | T **F** F F F |
| F | T | T | F **F** T T T |
| F | T | F | F **F** T T F |
| F | F | T | F **F** F T T |
| F | F | F | F **F** F F F |

From this table, we know that the sentence '$M \wedge (N \vee P)$' can be true or false, depending on the truth values of '$M$', '$N$', and '$P$'.

A complete truth table for a sentence that contains four different sentence letters requires 16 lines. Five letters, 32 lines. Six letters, 64 lines. And so on. To be perfectly general: If a complete truth table has $n$ different sentence letters, then it must have $2^n$ lines.

In order to fill in the columns of a complete truth table, begin with the right-most sentence letter and alternate between 'T' and 'F'. In the next column to the left, write two 'T's, write two 'F's, and repeat. For the third sentence letter, write four 'T's followed by four 'F's. This yields an eight line truth table like the one above. For a 16 line truth table, the next column of sentence letters should have eight 'T's followed by eight 'F's. For a 32 line table, the next column would have 16 'T's followed by 16 'F's, and so on.

## 11.3  More about brackets

Consider these two sentences:

$$((A \wedge B) \wedge C)$$
$$(A \wedge (B \wedge C))$$

These are truth functionally equivalent. Consequently, it will never make any difference from the perspective of truth value—

which is all that TFL cares about (see §10)—which of the two sentences we assert (or deny). Even though the order of the brackets does not matter as to their truth, we should not just drop them. The expression

$$A \wedge B \wedge C$$

is ambiguous between the two sentences above. The same observation holds for disjunctions. The following sentences are logically equivalent:

$$((A \vee B) \vee C)$$
$$(A \vee (B \vee C))$$

But we should not simply write:

$$A \vee B \vee C$$

In fact, it is a specific fact about the characteristic truth table of $\vee$ and $\wedge$ that guarantees that any two conjunctions (or disjunctions) of the same sentences are truth functionally equivalent, however you place the brackets. *This is only true of conjunctions and disjunctions*, however. The following two sentences have *different* truth tables:

$$((A \rightarrow B) \rightarrow C)$$
$$(A \rightarrow (B \rightarrow C))$$

So if we were to write:

$$A \rightarrow B \rightarrow C$$

it would be dangerously ambiguous. Leaving out brackets in this case would be disastrous. Equally, these sentences have different truth tables:

$$((A \vee B) \wedge C)$$
$$(A \vee (B \wedge C))$$

So if we were to write:

$$A \vee B \wedge C$$

it would be dangerously ambiguous. *Never write this.* The moral is: never drop brackets (except the outermost ones).

## Practice exercises

**A.** Offer complete truth tables for each of the following:

1. $A \to A$
2. $C \to \neg C$
3. $(A \leftrightarrow B) \leftrightarrow \neg(A \leftrightarrow \neg B)$
4. $(A \to B) \vee (B \to A)$
5. $(A \wedge B) \to (B \vee A)$
6. $\neg(A \vee B) \leftrightarrow (\neg A \wedge \neg B)$
7. $\big[(A \wedge B) \wedge \neg(A \wedge B)\big] \wedge C$
8. $[(A \wedge B) \wedge C] \to B$
9. $\neg\big[(C \vee A) \vee B\big]$

**B.** Check all the claims made in introducing the new notational conventions in §11.3, i.e. show that:

1. '$((A \wedge B) \wedge C)$' and '$(A \wedge (B \wedge C))$' have the same truth table
2. '$((A \vee B) \vee C)$' and '$(A \vee (B \vee C))$' have the same truth table
3. '$((A \vee B) \wedge C)$' and '$(A \vee (B \wedge C))$' do not have the same truth table
4. '$((A \to B) \to C)$' and '$(A \to (B \to C))$' do not have the same truth table

Also, check whether:

5. '$((A \leftrightarrow B) \leftrightarrow C)$' and '$(A \leftrightarrow (B \leftrightarrow C))$' have the same truth table

**C.** Write complete truth tables for the following sentences and mark the column that represents the possible truth values for the whole sentence.

1. $\neg(S \leftrightarrow (P \rightarrow S))$
2. $\neg[(X \wedge Y) \vee (X \vee Y)]$
3. $(A \rightarrow B) \leftrightarrow (\neg B \leftrightarrow \neg A)$
4. $[C \leftrightarrow (D \vee E)] \wedge \neg C$
5. $\neg(G \wedge (B \wedge H)) \leftrightarrow (G \vee (B \vee H))$

**D**. Write complete truth tables for the following sentences and mark the column that represents the possible truth values for the whole sentence.

1. $(D \wedge \neg D) \rightarrow G$
2. $(\neg P \vee \neg M) \leftrightarrow M$
3. $\neg\neg(\neg A \wedge \neg B)$
4. $[(D \wedge R) \rightarrow I] \rightarrow \neg(D \vee R)$
5. $\neg[(D \leftrightarrow O) \leftrightarrow A] \rightarrow (\neg D \wedge O)$

If you want additional practice, you can construct truth tables for any of the sentences and arguments in the exercises for the previous chapter.

# CHAPTER 12

# *Semantic concepts*

In the previous section, we introduced the idea of a valuation and showed how to determine the truth value of any TFL sentence, on any valuation, using a truth table. In this section, we will introduce some related ideas, and show how to use truth tables to test whether or not they apply.

## 12.1 Tautologies and contradictions

In §3, we explained *necessary truth* and *necessary falsity*. Both notions have surrogates in TFL. We will start with a surrogate for necessary truth.

> $\mathcal{A}$ is a TAUTOLOGY iff it is true on every valuation.

We can use truth tables to decide whether a sentence is a tautology. If the sentence is true on every line of its complete truth table, then it is true on every valuation, so it is a tautology. In the example of §11, '$(H \land I) \to H$' is a tautology.

This is only, though, a *surrogate* for necessary truth. There are some necessary truths that we cannot adequately symbolize in TFL. One example is '2+2 = 4'. This *must* be true, but if we try to symbolize it in TFL, the best we can offer is an sentence letter, and no sentence letter is a tautology. Still, if we can adequately symbolize some English sentence using a TFL sentence which is a tautology, then that English sentence expresses a necessary truth.

We have a similar surrogate for necessary falsity:

> $\mathscr{A}$ is a CONTRADICTION (in TFL) iff it is false on every valuation.

We can use truth tables to decide whether a sentence is a contradiction. If the sentence is false on every line of its complete truth table, then it is false on every valuation, so it is a contradiction. In the example of §11, '$[(C \leftrightarrow C) \to C] \land \neg(C \to C)$' is a contradiction.

## 12.2 Equivalence

Here is a similar useful notion:

> $\mathscr{A}$ and $\mathscr{B}$ are EQUIVALENT (in TFL) iff, for every valuation, their truth values agree, i.e., if there is no valuation in which they have opposite truth values.

We have already made use of this notion, in effect, in §11.3; the point was that '$(A \land B) \land C$' and '$A \land (B \land C)$' are equivalent. Again, it is easy to test for equivalence using truth tables. Consider the sentences '$\neg(P \lor Q)$' and '$\neg P \land \neg Q$'. Are they equivalent? To find out, we construct a truth table.

| $P$ | $Q$ | $\neg(P \lor Q)$ | $\neg P \land \neg Q$ |
|---|---|---|---|
| T | T | **F** T T T | F T **F** F T |
| T | F | **F** T T F | F T **F** T F |
| F | T | **F** F T T | T F **F** F T |
| F | F | **T** F F F | T F **T** T F |

Look at the columns for the main logical operators; negation for the first sentence, conjunction for the second. On the first three rows, both are false. On the final row, both are true. Since they match on every row, the two sentences are equivalent.

## 12.3 Satisfiability

In §3, we said that sentences are jointly possible iff it is possible for all of them to be true at once. We can offer a surrogate for this notion too:

$\mathcal{A}_1, \mathcal{A}_2, \ldots, \mathcal{A}_n$ are JOINTLY SATISFIABLE (in TFL) iff there is some valuation which makes them all true.

Derivatively, sentences are JOINTLY UNSATISFIABLE iff no valuation makes them all true. Again, it is easy to test for joint satisfiability using truth tables.

## 12.4 Entailment and validity

The following idea is closely related to that of joint satisfiability:

The sentences $\mathcal{A}_1, \mathcal{A}_2, \ldots, \mathcal{A}_n$ ENTAIL (in TFL) the sentence $\mathcal{C}$ iff no valuation of the relevant sentence letters makes all of $\mathcal{A}_1, \mathcal{A}_2, \ldots, \mathcal{A}_n$ true and $\mathcal{C}$ false.

Again, it is easy to test this with a truth table. To check whether '$\neg L \rightarrow (J \vee L)$' and '$\neg L$' entail '$J$', we simply need to check whether there is any valuation which makes both '$\neg L \rightarrow (J \vee L)$' and '$\neg L$' true whilst making '$J$' false. So we use a truth table:

| $J$ | $L$ | $\neg L \to (J \vee L)$ | $\neg L$ | $J$ |
|-----|-----|-------------------------|----------|-----|
| T | T | F T **T** T T T | **F** T | **T** |
| T | F | T F **T** T T F | **T** F | **T** |
| F | T | F T **T** F T T | **F** T | **F** |
| F | F | T F **F** F F F | **T** F | **F** |

The only row on which both '$\neg L \to (J \vee L)$' and '$\neg L$' are true is the second row, and that is a row on which '$J$' is also true. So '$\neg L \to (J \vee L)$' and '$\neg L$' entail '$J$'.

We now make an important observation:

> If $\mathcal{A}_1, \mathcal{A}_2, \ldots, \mathcal{A}_n$ entail $\mathcal{C}$, in TFL then $\mathcal{A}_1, \mathcal{A}_2, \ldots, \mathcal{A}_n \therefore \mathcal{C}$ is valid.

Here's why. If $\mathcal{A}_1, \mathcal{A}_2, \ldots, \mathcal{A}_n$ entail $\mathcal{C}$, then there is no valuation which makes all of $\mathcal{A}_1, \mathcal{A}_2, \ldots, \mathcal{A}_n$ true and also makes $\mathcal{C}$ false. Any case in which all of $\mathcal{A}_1, \mathcal{A}_2, \ldots, \mathcal{A}_n$ are true and $\mathcal{C}$ is false would generate a valuation with this property: take the truth value of any sentence letter to be just the truth value the corresponding sentence in that case. Since there is no such valuation, there is no case in which all of $\mathcal{A}_1, \mathcal{A}_2, \ldots, \mathcal{A}_n$ are true and $\mathcal{C}$ is false. But this is just what it takes for an argument, with premises $\mathcal{A}_1, \mathcal{A}_2, \ldots, \mathcal{A}_n$ and conclusion $\mathcal{C}$, to be valid!

In short, we have a way to test for the validity of English arguments. First, we symbolize them in TFL; then we test for entailment in TFL using truth tables.

## 12.5  The limits of these tests

This is an important milestone: a test for the validity of arguments! However, we should not get carried away just yet. It is important to understand the *limits* of our achievement. We will illustrate these limits with three examples.

First, consider the argument:

1. Daisy has four legs. So Daisy has more than two legs.

To symbolize this argument in TFL, we would have to use two different sentence letters—perhaps '$F$' and '$T$'—for the premise and the conclusion respectively. Now, it is obvious that '$F$' does not entail '$T$'. But the English argument is surely valid!

Second, consider the sentence:

2. Jan is neither bald nor not-bald.

To symbolize this sentence in TFL, we would offer something like '$\neg J \wedge \neg\neg J$'. This a contradiction (check this with a truth-table), but sentence 2 does not itself seem like a contradiction; for we might have happily added 'Jan is on the borderline of baldness'!

Third, consider the following sentence:

3. It's not the case that, if God exists, She answers malevolent prayers.

Symbolizing this in TFL, we would offer something like '$\neg(G \to M)$'. Now, '$\neg(G \to M)$' entails '$G$' (again, check this with a truth table). So if we symbolize sentence 3 in TFL, it seems to entail that God exists. But that's strange: surely even an atheist can accept sentence 3, without contradicting herself!

One lesson of this is that the symbolization of 3 as '$\neg(G \to M)$' shows that 3 does not express what we intend. Perhaps we should rephrase it as

3. If God exists, She does not answer malevolent prayers.

and symbolize 3 as '$G \to \neg M$'. Now, if atheists are right, and there is no God, then '$G$' is false and so '$G \to \neg M$' is true, and the puzzle disappears. However, if '$G$' is false, '$G \to M$', i.e. 'If God exists, She answers malevolent prayers', is *also* true!

In different ways, these four examples highlight some of the limits of working with a language (like TFL) that can *only* handle truth-functional connectives. Moreover, these limits give rise to some interesting questions in philosophical logic. The case of Jan's baldness (or otherwise) raises the general question of what logic we should use when dealing with *vague* discourse. The case of the atheist raises the question of how to deal with the (so-called) *paradoxes of the material conditional*. Part of the purpose of this course is to equip you with the tools to explore these questions of *philosophical logic*. But we have to walk before we can run; we have to become proficient in using TFL, before we can adequately discuss its limits, and consider alternatives.

## 12.6   The double turnstile

In what follow, we will use the notion of entailment rather a lot in this book. It will help us, then, to introduce a symbol that abbreviates it. Rather than saying that the TFL sentences $\mathscr{A}_1$, $\mathscr{A}_2, \ldots$ and $\mathscr{A}_n$ together entail $\mathscr{C}$, we will abbreviate this by:

$$\mathscr{A}_1, \mathscr{A}_2, \ldots, \mathscr{A}_n \vDash \mathscr{C}$$

The symbol '$\vDash$' is known as *the double turnstile*, since it looks like a turnstile with two horizontal beams.

Let's be clear. '$\vDash$' is not a symbol of TFL. Rather, it is a symbol of our metalanguage, augmented English (recall the difference between object language and metalanguage from §8). So the metalanguage sentence:

- $P, P \rightarrow Q \vDash Q$

is *just* an abbreviation for this metalanguage sentence:

- The TFL sentences '$P$' and '$P \rightarrow Q$' entail '$Q$'

Note that there is no limit on the number of TFL sentences that can be mentioned before the symbol '$\vDash$'. Indeed, we can even consider the limiting case:

$$\vDash \mathscr{C}$$

This says that there is no valuation which makes all the sentences mentioned on the left side of '$\vDash$' true whilst making $\mathscr{C}$ false. Since *no* sentences are mentioned on the left side of '$\vDash$' in this case, this just means that there is no valuation which makes $\mathscr{C}$ false. Otherwise put, it says that every valuation makes $\mathscr{C}$ true. Otherwise put, it says that $\mathscr{C}$ is a tautology. Equally, to say that $\mathscr{A}$ is a contradiction, we can write:

$$\mathscr{A} \models$$

For this says that no valuation makes $\mathscr{A}$ true.

Sometimes, we will want to deny that there is a tautological entailment, and say something of this shape:

> it is *not* the case that $\mathscr{A}_1, \ldots, \mathscr{A}_n \models \mathscr{C}$

In that case, we can just slash the turnstile through, and write:

$$\mathscr{A}_1, \mathscr{A}_2, \ldots, \mathscr{A}_n \nvDash \mathscr{C}$$

This means that *some* valuation makes all of $\mathscr{A}_1, \ldots, \mathscr{A}_n$ true whilst making $\mathscr{C}$ false. (But note that it does *not* immediately follow that $\mathscr{A}_1, \ldots, \mathscr{A}_n \models \neg\mathscr{C}$, for that would mean that *every* valuation makes all of $\mathscr{A}_1, \ldots, \mathscr{A}_n$ true whilst making $\mathscr{C}$ false.)

## 12.7  '⊨' versus '→'

We now want to compare and contrast '⊨' and '→'.

Observe: $\mathscr{A} \models \mathscr{C}$ iff no valuation of the sentence letters makes $\mathscr{A}$ true and $\mathscr{C}$ false.

Observe: $\mathscr{A} \to \mathscr{C}$ is a tautology iff no valuation of the sentence letters makes $\mathscr{A} \to \mathscr{C}$ false. Since a conditional is true except when its antecedent is true and its consequent false, $\mathscr{A} \to \mathscr{C}$ is a tautology iff no valuation makes $\mathscr{A}$ true and $\mathscr{C}$ false.

Combining these two observations, we see that $\mathscr{A} \to \mathscr{C}$ is a tautology iff $\mathscr{A} \models \mathscr{C}$. But there is a really, really important difference between '⊨' and '→':

> '→' is a sentential connective of TFL.
> '⊨' is a symbol of augmented English.

Indeed, when '→' is flanked with two TFL sentences, the result is a longer TFL sentence. By contrast, when we use '⊨', we form a metalinguistic sentence that *mentions* the surrounding TFL sentences.

## Practice exercises

**A.** Revisit your answers to §11A. Determine which sentences were tautologies, which were contradictions, and which were neither tautologies nor contradictions.

**B.** Use truth tables to determine whether these sentences are jointly satisfiable, or jointly unsatisfiable:

1. $A → A, ¬A → ¬A, A ∧ A, A ∨ A$
2. $A ∨ B, A → C, B → C$
3. $B ∧ (C ∨ A), A → B, ¬(B ∨ C)$
4. $A ↔ (B ∨ C), C → ¬A, A → ¬B$

**C.** Use truth tables to determine whether each argument is valid or invalid.

1. $A → A ∴ A$
2. $A → (A ∧ ¬A) ∴ ¬A$
3. $A ∨ (B → A) ∴ ¬A → ¬B$
4. $A ∨ B, B ∨ C, ¬A ∴ B ∧ C$
5. $(B ∧ A) → C, (C ∧ A) → B ∴ (C ∧ B) → A$

**D.** Determine whether each sentence is a tautology, a contradiction, or a contingent sentence, using a complete truth table.

1. $¬B ∧ B$
2. $¬D ∨ D$
3. $(A ∧ B) ∨ (B ∧ A)$
4. $¬[A → (B → A)]$
5. $A ↔ [A → (B ∧ ¬B)]$

6. $[(A \land B) \leftrightarrow B] \rightarrow (A \rightarrow B)$

**E.** Determine whether each the following sentences are logically equivalent using complete truth tables. If the two sentences really are logically equivalent, write "equivalent." Otherwise write, "Not equivalent."

1. $A$ and $\neg A$
2. $A \land \neg A$ and $\neg B \leftrightarrow B$
3. $[(A \lor B) \lor C]$ and $[A \lor (B \lor C)]$
4. $A \lor (B \land C)$ and $(A \lor B) \land (A \lor C)$
5. $[A \land (A \lor B)] \rightarrow B$ and $A \rightarrow B$

**F.** Determine whether each the following sentences are logically equivalent using complete truth tables. If the two sentences really are equivalent, write "equivalent." Otherwise write, "not equivalent."

1. $A \rightarrow A$ and $A \leftrightarrow A$
2. $\neg(A \rightarrow B)$ and $\neg A \rightarrow \neg B$
3. $A \lor B$ and $\neg A \rightarrow B$
4. $(A \rightarrow B) \rightarrow C$ and $A \rightarrow (B \rightarrow C)$
5. $A \leftrightarrow (B \leftrightarrow C)$ and $A \land (B \land C)$

**G.** Determine whether each collection of sentences is jointly satisfiable or jointly unsatisfiable using a complete truth table.

1. $A \land \neg B$, $\neg(A \rightarrow B)$, $B \rightarrow A$
2. $A \lor B$, $A \rightarrow \neg A$, $B \rightarrow \neg B$
3. $\neg(\neg A \lor B)$, $A \rightarrow \neg C$, $A \rightarrow (B \rightarrow C)$
4. $A \rightarrow B$, $A \land \neg B$
5. $A \rightarrow (B \rightarrow C)$, $(A \rightarrow B) \rightarrow C$, $A \rightarrow C$

**H.** Determine whether each collection of sentences is jointly satisfiable or jointly unsatisfiable, using a complete truth table.

1. $\neg B$, $A \rightarrow B$, $A$

2. $\neg(A \vee B), A \leftrightarrow B, B \to A$

3. $A \vee B, \neg B, \neg B \to \neg A$

4. $A \leftrightarrow B, \neg B \vee \neg A, A \to B$

5. $(A \vee B) \vee C, \neg A \vee \neg B, \neg C \vee \neg B$

**I.** Determine whether each argument is valid or invalid, using a complete truth table.

1. $A \to B, B \therefore A$
2. $A \leftrightarrow B, B \leftrightarrow C \therefore A \leftrightarrow C$
3. $A \to B, A \to C \therefore B \to C$
4. $A \to B, B \to A \therefore A \leftrightarrow B$

**J.** Determine whether each argument is valid or invalid, using a complete truth table.

1. $A \vee \left[ A \to (A \leftrightarrow A) \right] \therefore A$
2. $A \vee B, B \vee C, \neg B \therefore A \wedge C$
3. $A \to B, \neg A \therefore \neg B$
4. $A, B \therefore \neg(A \to \neg B)$
5. $\neg(A \wedge B), A \vee B, A \leftrightarrow B \therefore C$

**K.** Answer each of the questions below and justify your answer.

1. Suppose that $\mathcal{A}$ and $\mathcal{B}$ are logically equivalent. What can you say about $\mathcal{A} \leftrightarrow \mathcal{B}$?
2. Suppose that $(\mathcal{A} \wedge \mathcal{B}) \to \mathcal{C}$ is neither a tautology nor a contradiction. What can you say about whether $\mathcal{A}, \mathcal{B} \therefore \mathcal{C}$ is valid?
3. Suppose that $\mathcal{A}$, $\mathcal{B}$ and $\mathcal{C}$ are jointly unsatisfiable. What can you say about $(\mathcal{A} \wedge \mathcal{B} \wedge \mathcal{C})$?
4. Suppose that $\mathcal{A}$ is a contradiction. What can you say about whether $\mathcal{A}, \mathcal{B} \vDash \mathcal{C}$?
5. Suppose that $\mathcal{C}$ is a tautology. What can you say about whether $\mathcal{A}, \mathcal{B} \vDash \mathcal{C}$?
6. Suppose that $\mathcal{A}$ and $\mathcal{B}$ are logically equivalent. What can you say about $(\mathcal{A} \vee \mathcal{B})$?

7. Suppose that $\mathscr{A}$ and $\mathscr{B}$ are *not* logically equivalent. What can you say about $(\mathscr{A} \vee \mathscr{B})$?

**L.** Consider the following principle:

- Suppose $\mathscr{A}$ and $\mathscr{B}$ are logically equivalent. Suppose an argument contains $\mathscr{A}$ (either as a premise, or as the conclusion). The validity of the argument would be unaffected, if we replaced $\mathscr{A}$ with $\mathscr{B}$.

Is this principle correct? Explain your answer.

## CHAPTER 13

# *Truth table shortcuts*

With practice, you will quickly become adept at filling out truth tables. In this section, we consider (and justify) some shortcuts which will help you along the way.

## 13.1 Working through truth tables

You will quickly find that you do not need to copy the truth value of each sentence letter, but can simply refer back to them. So you can speed things up by writing:

| $P$ | $Q$ | $(P \lor Q) \leftrightarrow \neg P$ | | |
|---|---|---|---|---|
| T | T | T | **F** | F |
| T | F | T | **F** | F |
| F | T | T | **T** | T |
| F | F | F | **F** | T |

You also know for sure that a disjunction is true whenever one of the disjuncts is true. So if you find a true disjunct, there is no need to work out the truth values of the other disjuncts. Thus you might offer:

96

| P | Q | $(\neg P \vee \neg Q) \vee \neg P$ |
|---|---|---|
| T | T | F   F F   **F** F |
| T | F | F   T T   **T** F |
| F | T |              **T** T |
| F | F |              **T** T |

Equally, you know for sure that a conjunction is false whenever one of the conjuncts is false. So if you find a false conjunct, there is no need to work out the truth value of the other conjunct. Thus you might offer:

| P | Q | $\neg (P \wedge \neg Q) \wedge \neg P$ |
|---|---|---|
| T | T |              **F** F |
| T | F |              **F** F |
| F | T | T   F   **T** T |
| F | F | T   F   **T** T |

A similar short cut is available for conditionals. You immediately know that a conditional is true if either its consequent is true, or its antecedent is false. Thus you might present:

| P | Q | $((P \rightarrow Q) \rightarrow P) \rightarrow P$ |
|---|---|---|
| T | T |              **T** |
| T | F |              **T** |
| F | T |    T   F   **T** |
| F | F |    T   F   **T** |

So '$((P \rightarrow Q) \rightarrow P) \rightarrow P$' is a tautology. In fact, it is an instance of *Peirce's Law*, named after Charles Sanders Peirce.

## 13.2   Testing for validity and entailment

In §12, we saw how to use truth tables to test for validity. In that test, we look for *bad* lines: lines where the premises are all true and the conclusion is false. Now:

- If the conclusion is true on a line, then that line is not bad. (And we don't need to evaluate anything *else* on that line to confirm this.)

- If any premise is false on a line, then that line is not bad. (And we don't need to evaluate anything *else* on that line to confirm this.)

With this in mind, we can speed up our tests for validity quite considerably.

Let's consider how we might test the following:

$$\neg L \to (J \lor L), \neg L \therefore J$$

The *first* thing we should do is evaluate the conclusion. If we find that the conclusion is *true* on some line, then that is not a bad line. So we can simply ignore the rest of the line. So, after our first stage, we are left with something like this:

| $J$ | $L$ | $\neg L \to (J \lor L)$ | $\neg L$ | $J$ |
|---|---|---|---|---|
| T | T |   |   | T |
| T | F |   |   | T |
| F | T | ? | ? | F |
| F | F | ? | ? | F |

where the blanks indicate that we won't bother with any more investigation (since the line is not bad), and the question marks indicate that we need to keep digging.

The easiest premise to evaluate is the second, so we do that next, and get:

| $J$ | $L$ | $\neg L \to (J \lor L)$ | $\neg L$ | $J$ |
|---|---|---|---|---|
| T | T |   |   | T |
| T | F |   |   | T |
| F | T |   | F | F |
| F | F | ? | T | F |

Note that we no longer need to consider the third line on the table: it is certainly not bad, because some premise is false on that line. And finally, we complete the truth table:

| J | L | $\neg L \to (J \vee L)$ | $\neg L$ | J |
|---|---|---|---|---|
| T | T | | | T |
| T | F | | | T |
| F | T | | F | F |
| F | F | T **F** F | T | F |

The truth table has no bad lines, so the argument is valid. Any valuation which makes every premise true makes the conclusion true.

It's probably worth illustrating the tactic again. Consider this argument:

$$A \vee B, \neg(B \wedge C) \therefore (A \vee \neg C)$$

Again, we start by evaluating the conclusion. Since this is a disjunction, it is true whenever either disjunct is true, so we can speed things along a bit.

| A | B | C | $A \vee B$ | $\neg(B \wedge C)$ | $(A \vee \neg C)$ |
|---|---|---|---|---|---|
| T | T | T | | | **T** |
| T | T | F | | | **T** |
| T | F | T | | | **T** |
| T | F | F | | | **T** |
| F | T | T | ? | ? | **F** F |
| F | T | F | | | **T** T |
| F | F | T | ? | ? | **F** F |
| F | F | F | | | **T** T |

We can now ignore all but the two lines where the sentence after the turnstile is false. Evaluating the two sentences on the left of the turnstile, we get:

| A | B | C | $A \vee B$ | $\neg(B \wedge C)$ | $(A \vee \neg C)$ |
|---|---|---|---|---|---|
| T | T | T |   |   | **T** |
| T | T | F |   |   | **T** |
| T | F | T |   |   | **T** |
| T | F | F |   |   | **T** |
| F | T | T | **T** | **F**   T | **F** F |
| F | T | F |   |   | **T** T |
| F | F | T | **F** |   | **F** F |
| F | F | F |   |   | **T** T |

So the entailment holds! And our shortcuts saved us a *lot* of work.

We have been discussing shortcuts in testing for validity. But exactly the same shortcuts can be used in testing for entailment. By employing a similar notion of bad lines, you can save yourself a huge amount of work.

## Practice exercises

**A.** Using shortcuts, check whether each sentence is a tautology, a contradiction, or neither.

1. $\neg B \wedge B$
2. $\neg D \vee D$
3. $(A \wedge B) \vee (B \wedge A)$
4. $\neg[A \rightarrow (B \rightarrow A)]$
5. $A \leftrightarrow [A \rightarrow (B \wedge \neg B)]$
6. $\neg(A \wedge B) \leftrightarrow A$
7. $A \rightarrow (B \vee C)$
8. $(A \wedge \neg A) \rightarrow (B \vee C)$
9. $(B \wedge D) \leftrightarrow [A \leftrightarrow (A \vee C)]$

# CHAPTER 14

# *Partial truth tables*

Sometimes, we do not need to know what happens on every line of a truth table. Sometimes, just a line or two will do.

**Tautology.** In order to show that a sentence is a tautology, we need to show that it is true on every valuation. That is to say, we need to know that it comes out true on every line of the truth table. So we need a complete truth table.

To show that a sentence is *not* a tautology, however, we only need one line: a line on which the sentence is false. Therefore, in order to show that some sentence is not a tautology, it is enough to provide a single valuation—a single line of the truth table—which makes the sentence false.

Suppose that we want to show that the sentence '$(U \land T) \to (S \land W)$' is *not* a tautology. We set up a PARTIAL TRUTH TABLE:

| S | T | U | W | $(U \land T) \to (S \land W)$ |
|---|---|---|---|:---:|
|   |   |   |   | **F** |

We have only left space for one line, rather than 16, since we are only looking for one line, on which the sentence is false (hence, also, the 'F').

The main logical operator of the sentence is a conditional. In order for the conditional to be false, the antecedent must be true and the consequent must be false. So we fill these in on the table:

| $S$ | $T$ | $U$ | $W$ | $(U \wedge T) \rightarrow (S \wedge W)$ |
|---|---|---|---|---|
|  |  |  |  | T    **F**    F |

In order for the '$(U \wedge T)$' to be true, both '$U$' and '$T$' must be true.

| $S$ | $T$ | $U$ | $W$ | $(U \wedge T) \rightarrow (S \wedge W)$ |
|---|---|---|---|---|
|  | T | T |  | T T T **F**    F |

Now we just need to make '$(S \wedge W)$' false. To do this, we need to make at least one of '$S$' and '$W$' false. We can make both '$S$' and '$W$' false if we want. All that matters is that the whole sentence turns out false on this line. Making an arbitrary decision, we finish the table in this way:

| $S$ | $T$ | $U$ | $W$ | $(U \wedge T) \rightarrow (S \wedge W)$ |
|---|---|---|---|---|
| F | T | T | F | T T T **F** F F F |

We now have a partial truth table, which shows that '$(U \wedge T) \rightarrow (S \wedge W)$' is not a tautology. Put otherwise, we have shown that there is a valuation which makes '$(U \wedge T) \rightarrow (S \wedge W)$' false, namely, the valuation which makes '$S$' false, '$T$' true, '$U$' true and '$W$' false.

**Contradicitions**.   Showing that something is a contradiciction in TFL requires a complete truth table: we need to show that there is no valuation which makes the sentence true; that is, we need to show that the sentence is false on every line of the truth table.

However, to show that something is *not* a contradiction, all we need to do is find a valuation which makes the sentence true, and a single line of a truth table will suffice. We can illustrate this with the same example.

| S | T | U | W | $(U \wedge T) \rightarrow (S \wedge W)$ |
|---|---|---|---|---|
|   |   |   |   | **T** |

To make the sentence true, it will suffice to ensure that the antecedent is false. Since the antecedent is a conjunction, we can just make one of them false. Making an arbitrary choice, let's make '$U$' false; we can then assign any truth value we like to the other sentence letters.

| S | T | U | W | $(U \wedge T) \rightarrow (S \wedge W)$ |
|---|---|---|---|---|
| F | T | F | F | F F T **T** F F F |

**Equivalence.**   To show that two sentences are equivalent, we must show that the sentences have the same truth value on every valuation. So this requires a complete truth table.

To show that two sentences are *not* equivalent, we only need to show that there is a valuation on which they have different truth values. So this requires only a one-line partial truth table: make the table so that one sentence is true and the other false.

**Consistency.**   To show that some sentences are jointly satisfiable, we must show that there is a valuation which makes all of the sentences true ,so this requires only a partial truth table with a single line.

To show that some sentences are jointly unsatisfiable, we must show that there is no valuation which makes all of the sentence true. So this requires a complete truth table: You must show that on every row of the table at least one of the sentences is false.

**Validity and entailment.**   To show that an argument is valid, we must show that there is no valuation which makes all of the premises true and the conclusion false. So this requires a complete truth table. (Likewise for entailment.)

To show that argument is *invalid*, we must show that there is a valuation which makes all of the premises true and the conclusion false. So this requires only a one-line partial truth table on which all of the premises are true and the conclusion is false. (Likewise for a failure of entailment.)

This table summarises what is required:

|                | Yes              | No               |
|----------------|------------------|------------------|
| tautology?     | complete         | one-line partial |
| contradiction? | complete         | one-line partial |
| equivalent?    | complete         | one-line partial |
| satisfiable?   | one-line partial | complete         |
| valid?         | complete         | one-line partial |
| entailment?    | complete         | one-line partial |

## Practice exercises

**A**. Use complete or partial truth tables (as appropriate) to determine whether these pairs of sentences are logically equivalent:

1. $A$, $\neg A$
2. $A$, $A \lor A$
3. $A \to A$, $A \leftrightarrow A$
4. $A \lor \neg B$, $A \to B$
5. $A \land \neg A$, $\neg B \leftrightarrow B$
6. $\neg(A \land B)$, $\neg A \lor \neg B$
7. $\neg(A \to B)$, $\neg A \to \neg B$
8. $(A \to B)$, $(\neg B \to \neg A)$

**B**. Use complete or partial truth tables (as appropriate) to determine whether these sentences are jointly satisfiable, or jointly unsatisfiable:

1. $A \land B$, $C \to \neg B$, $C$
2. $A \to B$, $B \to C$, $A$, $\neg C$
3. $A \lor B$, $B \lor C$, $C \to \neg A$
4. $A$, $B$, $C$, $\neg D$, $\neg E$, $F$
5. $A \land (B \lor C)$, $\neg(A \land C)$, $\neg(B \land C)$
6. $A \to B$, $B \to C$, $\neg(A \to C)$

**C.** Use complete or partial truth tables (as appropriate) to determine whether each argument is valid or invalid:

1. $A \vee [A \to (A \leftrightarrow A)] \therefore A$
2. $A \leftrightarrow \neg(B \leftrightarrow A) \therefore A$
3. $A \to B, B \therefore A$
4. $A \vee B, B \vee C, \neg B \therefore A \wedge C$
5. $A \leftrightarrow B, B \leftrightarrow C \therefore A \leftrightarrow C$

**D.** Determine whether each sentence is a tautology, a contradiction, or a contingent sentence. Justify your answer with a complete or partial truth table where appropriate.

1. $A \to \neg A$
2. $A \to (A \wedge (A \vee B))$
3. $(A \to B) \leftrightarrow (B \to A)$
4. $A \to \neg(A \wedge (A \vee B))$
5. $\neg B \to [(\neg A \wedge A) \vee B]$
6. $\neg(A \vee B) \leftrightarrow (\neg A \wedge \neg B)$
7. $[(A \wedge B) \wedge C] \to B$
8. $\neg[(C \vee A) \vee B]$
9. $[(A \wedge B) \wedge \neg(A \wedge B)] \wedge C$
10. $(A \wedge B)] \to [(A \wedge C) \vee (B \wedge D)]$

**E.** Determine whether each sentence is a tautology, a contradiction, or a contingent sentence. Justify your answer with a complete or partial truth table where appropriate.

1. $\neg(A \vee A)$
2. $(A \to B) \vee (B \to A)$
3. $[(A \to B) \to A] \to A$
4. $\neg[(A \to B) \vee (B \to A)]$
5. $(A \wedge B) \vee (A \vee B)$
6. $\neg(A \wedge B) \leftrightarrow A$

   7. $A \rightarrow (B \vee C)$

   8. $(A \wedge \neg A) \rightarrow (B \vee C)$

   9. $(B \wedge D) \leftrightarrow [A \leftrightarrow (A \vee C)]$

 10. $\neg[(A \rightarrow B) \vee (C \rightarrow D)]$

**F.** Determine whether each the following pairs of sentences are logically equivalent using complete truth tables. If the two sentences really are logically equivalent, write "equivalent." Otherwise write, "not equivalent."

   1. $A$ and $A \vee A$

   2. $A$ and $A \wedge A$

   3. $A \vee \neg B$ and $A \rightarrow B$

   4. $(A \rightarrow B)$ and $(\neg B \rightarrow \neg A)$

   5. $\neg(A \wedge B)$ and $\neg A \vee \neg B$

   6. $((U \rightarrow (X \vee X)) \vee U)$ and $\neg(X \wedge (X \wedge U))$

   7. $((C \wedge (N \leftrightarrow C)) \leftrightarrow C)$ and $(\neg\neg\neg N \rightarrow C)$

   8. $[(A \vee B) \wedge C]$ and $[A \vee (B \wedge C)]$

   9. $((L \wedge C) \wedge I)$ and $L \vee C$

**G.** Determine whether each collection of sentences is jointly satisfiable or jointly unsatisfiable. Justify your answer with a complete or partial truth table where appropriate.

   1. $A \rightarrow A, \neg A \rightarrow \neg A, A \wedge A, A \vee A$

   2. $A \rightarrow \neg A, \neg A \rightarrow A$

   3. $A \vee B, A \rightarrow C, B \rightarrow C$

   4. $A \vee B, A \rightarrow C, B \rightarrow C, \neg C$

   5. $B \wedge (C \vee A), A \rightarrow B, \neg(B \vee C)$

   6. $(A \leftrightarrow B) \rightarrow B, B \rightarrow \neg(A \leftrightarrow B), A \vee B$

   7. $A \leftrightarrow (B \vee C), C \rightarrow \neg A, A \rightarrow \neg B$

   8. $A \leftrightarrow B, \neg B \vee \neg A, A \rightarrow B$

   9. $A \leftrightarrow B, A \rightarrow C, B \rightarrow D, \neg(C \vee D)$

 10. $\neg(A \wedge \neg B), B \rightarrow \neg A, \neg B$

**H.** Determine whether each argument is valid or invalid. Justify your answer with a complete or partial truth table where appropriate.

1. $A \rightarrow (A \wedge \neg A) \therefore \neg A$
2. $A \vee B, A \rightarrow B, B \rightarrow A \therefore A \leftrightarrow B$
3. $A \vee (B \rightarrow A) \therefore \neg A \rightarrow \neg B$
4. $A \vee B, A \rightarrow B, B \rightarrow A \therefore A \wedge B$
5. $(B \wedge A) \rightarrow C, (C \wedge A) \rightarrow B \therefore (C \wedge B) \rightarrow A$
6. $\neg(\neg A \vee \neg B), A \rightarrow \neg C \therefore A \rightarrow (B \rightarrow C)$
7. $A \wedge (B \rightarrow C), \neg C \wedge (\neg B \rightarrow \neg A) \therefore C \wedge \neg C$
8. $A \wedge B, \neg A \rightarrow \neg C, B \rightarrow \neg D \therefore A \vee B$
9. $A \rightarrow B \therefore (A \wedge B) \vee (\neg A \wedge \neg B)$
10. $\neg A \rightarrow B, \neg B \rightarrow C, \neg C \rightarrow A \therefore \neg A \rightarrow (\neg B \vee \neg C)$

**I.** Determine whether each argument is valid or invalid. Justify your answer with a complete or partial truth table where appropriate.

1. $A \leftrightarrow \neg(B \leftrightarrow A) \therefore A$
2. $A \vee B, B \vee C, \neg A \therefore B \wedge C$
3. $A \rightarrow C, E \rightarrow (D \vee B), B \rightarrow \neg D \therefore (A \vee C) \vee (B \rightarrow (E \wedge D))$
4. $A \vee B, C \rightarrow A, C \rightarrow B \therefore A \rightarrow (B \rightarrow C)$
5. $A \rightarrow B, \neg B \vee A \therefore A \leftrightarrow B$

# PART IV

# *Natural deduction for TFL*

## CHAPTER 15

# *The very idea of natural deduction*

Way back in §2, we said that an argument is valid iff there is no case in which all of the premises are true and the conclusion is false.

In the case of TFL, this led us to develop truth tables. Each line of a complete truth table corresponds to a valuation. So, when faced with a TFL argument, we have a very direct way to assess whether there is a valuation on which the premises are true and the conclusion is false: just thrash through the truth table.

However, truth tables may not give us much *insight*. Consider two arguments in TFL:

$$P \lor Q, \neg P \therefore Q$$
$$P \to Q, P \therefore Q$$

Clearly, these are valid arguments. You can confirm that they are valid by constructing four-line truth tables, but we might say that they make use of different *forms* of reasoning. It might be nice to keep track of these different forms of inference.

One aim of a *natural deduction system* is to show that particular arguments are valid, in a way that allows us to understand the reasoning that the arguments might involve. We begin with very basic rules of inference. These rules can be combined to offer more complicated arguments. Indeed, with just a small starter pack of rules of inference, we hope to capture all valid arguments.

*This is a very different way of thinking about arguments.*

With truth tables, we directly consider different ways to make sentences true or false. With natural deduction systems, we manipulate sentences in accordance with rules that we have set down as good rules. The latter promises to give us a better insight—or at least, a different insight—into how arguments work.

The move to natural deduction might be motivated by more than the search for insight. It might also be motivated by *necessity*. Consider:

$$A_1 \to C_1 \therefore (A_1 \land A_2 \land A_3 \land A_4 \land A_5) \to (C_1 \lor C_2 \lor C_3 \lor C_4 \lor C_5)$$

To test this argument for validity, you might use a 1024-line truth table. If you do it correctly, then you will see that there is no line on which all the premises are true and on which the conclusion is false. So you will know that the argument is valid. (But, as just mentioned, there is a sense in which you will not know *why* the argument is valid.) But now consider:

$$A_1 \to C_1 \therefore (A_1 \land A_2 \land A_3 \land A_4 \land A_5 \land A_6 \land A_7 \land A_8 \land A_9 \land A_{10}) \to$$
$$(C_1 \lor C_2 \lor C_3 \lor C_4 \lor C_5 \lor C_6 \lor C_7 \lor C_8 \lor C_9 \lor C_{10})$$

This argument is also valid—as you can probably tell—but to test it requires a truth table with $2^{20} = 1048576$ lines. In principle, we can set a machine to grind through truth tables and report back when it is finished. In practice, complicated arguments in TFL can become *intractable* if we use truth tables.

When we get to first-order logic (FOL) (beginning in chapter 22), though, the problem gets dramatically worse. There is nothing like the truth table test for FOL. To assess whether or not an argument is valid, we have to reason about *all* interpretations, but, as we will see, there are infinitely many possible interpretations. We cannot even in principle set a machine to grind through infinitely many possible interpretations and report back when it is finished: it will *never* finish. We either need to come up with some more efficient way of reasoning about all interpretations, or we need to look for something different.

There are, indeed, systems that codify ways to reason about all possible interpretations. They were developed in the 1950s by Evert Beth and Jaakko Hintikka, but we will not follow this path. We will, instead, look to natural deduction.

Rather than reasoning directly about all valuations (in the case of TFL), we will try to select a few basic rules of inference. Some of these will govern the behaviour of the sentential connectives. Others will govern the behaviour of the quantifiers and identity that are the hallmarks of FOL. The resulting system of rules will give us a new way to think about the validity of arguments. The modern development of natural deduction dates from simultaneous and unrelated papers by Gerhard Gentzen and Stanisław Jaśkowski (1934). However, the natural deduction system that we will consider is based largely around work by Frederic Fitch (first published in 1952).

**CHAPTER 16**

# *Basic rules for TFL*

We will develop a NATURAL DEDUCTION system. For each connective, there will be INTRODUCTION rules, that allow us to prove a sentence that has that connective as the main logical operator, and ELIMINATION rules, that allow us to prove something given a sentence that has that connective as the main logical operator.

## 16.1 The idea of a formal proof

A *formal proof* or *derivation* is a sequence of sentences, some of which are marked as being initial assumptions (or premises). The last line of the formal proof is the conclusion. (Henceforth, we will simply call these 'proofs' or 'derivations', but be aware that there are *informal proofs* too.)

As an illustration, consider:

$$\neg(A \lor B) \therefore \neg A \land \neg B$$

We will start a proof by writing the premise:

1 | $\neg(A \lor B)$

Note that we have numbered the premise, since we will want to refer back to it. Indeed, every line of the proof is numbered, so that we can refer back to it.

Note also that we have drawn a line underneath the premise. Everything written above the line is an *assumption*. Everything written below the line will either be something which follows from the assumptions, or it will be some new assumption. We are hoping to conclude '$\neg A \wedge \neg B$'; so we are hoping ultimately to conclude our proof with

$n \quad \Big| \quad \neg A \wedge \neg B$

for some number $n$. It doesn't matter what line number we end on, but we would obviously prefer a short proof to a long one.

Similarly, suppose we wanted to consider:

$$A \vee B, \neg(A \wedge C), \neg(B \wedge \neg D) \therefore \neg C \vee D$$

The argument has three premises, so we start by writing them all down, numbered, and drawing a line under them:

$1 \quad \Big| \quad A \vee B$

$2 \quad \Big| \quad \neg(A \wedge C)$

$3 \quad \Big| \quad \neg(B \wedge \neg D)$

and we are hoping to conclude with some line:

$n \quad \Big| \quad \neg C \vee D$

All that remains to do is to explain each of the rules that we can use along the way from premises to conclusion. The rules are broken down by our logical connectives.

## 16.2   Reiteration

The very first rule is so breathtakingly obvious that it is surprising we bother with it at all.

If you already have shown something in the course of a proof, the *reiteration rule* allows you to repeat it on a new line. For example:

$$
\begin{array}{r|l}
4 & A \wedge B \\
\vdots & \vdots \\
10 & A \wedge B \quad \text{R } 4
\end{array}
$$

This indicates that we have written '$A \wedge B$' on line 4. Now, at some later line—line 10, for example—we have decided that we want to repeat this. So we write it down again. We also add a citation which justifies what we have written. In this case, we write 'R', to indicate that we are using the reiteration rule, and we write '4', to indicate that we have applied it to line 4.

Here is a general expression of the rule:

$$
\begin{array}{r|l}
m & \mathcal{A} \\
 & \mathcal{A} \quad \text{R } m
\end{array}
$$

The point is that, if any sentence $\mathcal{A}$ occurs on some line, then we can repeat $\mathcal{A}$ on later lines. Each line of our proof must be justified by some rule, and here we have 'R $m$'. This means: Reiteration, applied to line $m$.

Two things need emphasizing. First '$\mathcal{A}$' is not a sentence of TFL. Rather, it a symbol in the metalanguage, which we use when we want to talk about any sentence of TFL (see §8). Second, and similarly, '$m$' is not a symbol that will appear on a proof. Rather, it is a symbol in the metalanguage, which we use when we want to talk about any line number of a proof. In an actual proof, the lines are numbered '1', '2', '3', and so forth. But when we define

the rule, we use variables like '$m$' to underscore the point that
the rule may be applied at any point.

## 16.3  Conjunction

Suppose we want to show that Ludwig is both reactionary and
libertarian. One obvious way to do this would be as follows: first
we show that Ludwig is reactionary; then we show that Ludwig
is libertarian; then we put these two demonstrations together, to
obtain the conjunction.

Our natural deduction system will capture this thought
straightforwardly. In the example given, we might adopt the following symbolization key:

$R$: Ludwig is reactionary
$L$: Ludwig is libertarian

Perhaps we are working through a proof, and we have obtained
'$R$' on line 8 and '$L$' on line 15. Then on any subsequent line we
can obtain '$R \wedge L$' thus:

8 | $R$
15 | $L$
| $R \wedge L$    $\wedge$I 8, 15

Note that every line of our proof must either be an assumption, or
must be justified by some rule. We cite '$\wedge$I 8, 15' here to indicate
that the line is obtained by the rule of conjunction introduction
($\wedge$I) applied to lines 8 and 15. We could equally well obtain:

8 | $R$
15 | $L$
| $L \wedge R$    $\wedge$I 15, 8

with the citation reversed, to reflect the order of the conjuncts. More generally, here is our conjunction introduction rule:

$$
\begin{array}{r|l}
m & \mathcal{A} \\[4pt]
n & \mathcal{B} \\[4pt]
  & \mathcal{A} \wedge \mathcal{B} \quad \wedge\mathrm{I}\ m,\, n
\end{array}
$$

To be clear, the statement of the rule is *schematic*. It is not itself a proof. '$\mathcal{A}$' and '$\mathcal{B}$' are not sentences of TFL. Rather, they are symbols in the metalanguage, which we use when we want to talk about any sentence of TFL (see §8). Similarly, '$m$' and '$n$' are not a numerals that will appear on any actual proof. Rather, they are symbols in the metalanguage, which we use when we want to talk about any line number of any proof. In an actual proof, the lines are numbered '1', '2', '3', and so forth, but when we define the rule, we use variables to emphasize that the rule may be applied at any point. The rule requires only that we have both conjuncts available to us somewhere in the proof. They can be separated from one another, and they can appear in any order.

The rule is called 'conjunction *introduction*' because it introduces the symbol '$\wedge$' into our proof where it may have been absent. Correspondingly, we have a rule that *eliminates* that symbol. Suppose you have shown that Ludwig is both reactionary and libertarian. You are entitled to conclude that Ludwig is reactionary. Equally, you are entitled to conclude that Ludwig is libertarian. Putting this together, we obtain our conjunction elimination rule(s):

$$
\begin{array}{r|l}
m & \mathcal{A} \wedge \mathcal{B} \\[4pt]
  & \mathcal{A} \quad\quad \wedge\mathrm{E}\ m
\end{array}
$$

and equally:

$$m \quad \mathcal{A} \wedge \mathcal{B}$$

$$\mathcal{B} \qquad \wedge E \; m$$

The point is simply that, when you have a conjunction on some line of a proof, you can obtain either of the conjuncts by $\wedge E$. One point is worth emphasising: you can only apply this rule when conjunction is the main logical operator. So you cannot infer '$D$' just from '$C \vee (D \wedge E)$'!

Even with just these two rules, we can start to see some of the power of our formal proof system. Consider:

$$[(A \vee B) \rightarrow (C \vee D)] \wedge [(E \vee F) \rightarrow (G \vee H)]$$
$$\therefore \; [(E \vee F) \rightarrow (G \vee H)] \wedge [(A \vee B) \rightarrow (C \vee D)]$$

The main logical operator in both the premise and conclusion of this argument is '$\wedge$'. In order to provide a proof, we begin by writing down the premise, which is our assumption. We draw a line below this: everything after this line must follow from our assumptions by (repeated applications of) our rules of inference. So the beginning of the proof looks like this:

1 | $[(A \vee B) \rightarrow (C \vee D)] \wedge [(E \vee F) \rightarrow (G \vee H)]$

From the premise, we can get each of the conjuncts by $\wedge E$. The proof now looks like this:

| 1 | $[(A \vee B) \rightarrow (C \vee D)] \wedge [(E \vee F) \rightarrow (G \vee H)]$ | |
|---|---|---|
| 2 | $[(A \vee B) \rightarrow (C \vee D)]$ | $\wedge E \; 1$ |
| 3 | $[(E \vee F) \rightarrow (G \vee H)]$ | $\wedge E \; 1$ |

So by applying the $\wedge I$ rule to lines 3 and 2 (in that order), we arrive at the desired conclusion. The finished proof looks like this:

| 1 | $[(A \lor B) \to (C \lor D)] \land [(E \lor F) \to (G \lor H)]$ | |
|---|---|---|
| 2 | $[(A \lor B) \to (C \lor D)]$ | $\land$E 1 |
| 3 | $[(E \lor F) \to (G \lor H)]$ | $\land$E 1 |
| 4 | $[(E \lor F) \to (G \lor H)] \land [(A \lor B) \to (C \lor D)]$ | $\land$I 3, 2 |

This is a very simple proof, but it shows how we can chain rules of proof together into longer proofs. In passing, note that investigating this argument with a truth table would have required 256 lines; our formal proof required only four lines.

It is worth giving another example. Back in §11.3, we noted that this argument is valid:

$$A \land (B \land C) \therefore (A \land B) \land C$$

To provide a proof corresponding to this argument, we start by writing:

| 1 | $A \land (B \land C)$ |
|---|---|

From the premise, we can get each of the conjuncts by applying $\land$E twice. We can then apply $\land$E twice more, so our proof looks like:

| 1 | $A \land (B \land C)$ | |
|---|---|---|
| 2 | $A$ | $\land$E 1 |
| 3 | $B \land C$ | $\land$E 1 |
| 4 | $B$ | $\land$E 3 |
| 5 | $C$ | $\land$E 3 |

But now we can merrily reintroduce conjunctions in the order we wanted them, so that our final proof is:

$$
\begin{array}{r|ll}
1 & A \land (B \land C) & \\
\hline
2 & A & \land\text{E } 1 \\
3 & B \land C & \land\text{E } 1 \\
4 & B & \land\text{E } 3 \\
5 & C & \land\text{E } 3 \\
6 & A \land B & \land\text{I } 2, 4 \\
7 & (A \land B) \land C & \land\text{I } 6, 5
\end{array}
$$

Recall that our official definition of sentences in TFL only allowed conjunctions with two conjuncts. The proof just given suggests that we could drop inner brackets in all of our proofs. However, this is not standard, and we will not do this. Instead, we will maintain our more austere bracketing conventions. (Though we will still allow ourselves to drop outermost brackets, for legibility.)

Let's give one final illustration. When using the $\land$I rule, there is no requirement to apply it to different sentences. So, if we want, we can formally prove '$A \land A$' from '$A$' thus:

$$
\begin{array}{r|ll}
1 & A & \\
\hline
2 & A \land A & \land\text{I } 1, 1
\end{array}
$$

Simple, but effective.

## 16.4 Conditional

Consider the following argument:

> If Jane is smart then she is fast.
> Jane is smart.
> ∴ Jane is fast.

This argument is certainly valid, and it suggests a straightforward conditional elimination rule (→E):

$$
\begin{array}{ll}
m & \mathcal{A} \rightarrow \mathcal{B} \\[6pt]
n & \mathcal{A} \\[6pt]
  & \mathcal{B} \qquad\qquad \rightarrow\text{E } m, n
\end{array}
$$

This rule is also sometimes called *modus ponens*. Again, this is an elimination rule, because it allows us to obtain a sentence that may not contain '→', having started with a sentence that did contain '→'. Note that the conditional $\mathcal{A} \rightarrow \mathcal{B}$ and the antecedent $\mathcal{A}$ can be separated from one another in the proof, and they can appear in any order. However, in the citation for →E, we always cite the conditional first, followed by the antecedent.

The rule for conditional introduction is also quite easy to motivate. The following argument should be valid:

> Ludwig is reactionary. Therefore if Ludwig is libertarian, then Ludwig is both reactionary *and* libertarian.

If someone doubted that this was valid, we might try to convince them otherwise by explaining ourselves as follows:

> Assume that Ludwig is reactionary. Now, *additionally* assume that Ludwig is libertarian. Then by conjunction introduction—which we just discussed—Ludwig is both reactionary and libertarian. Of course, that's conditional on the assumption that Ludwig is libertarian. But this just means that, if Ludwig is libertarian, then he is both reactionary and libertarian.

Transferred into natural deduction format, here is the pattern of reasoning that we just used. We started with one premise, 'Ludwig is reactionary', thus:

1 | $R$

The next thing we did is to make an *additional* assumption ('Ludwig is libertarian'), for the sake of argument. To indicate that we are no longer dealing *merely* with our original assumption ('$R$'), but with some additional assumption, we continue our proof as follows:

1 | $R$
2 | | $L$

Note that we are *not* claiming, on line 2, to have proved '$L$' from line 1, so we do not write in any justification for the additional assumption on line 2. We do, however, need to mark that it is an additional assumption. We do this by drawing a line under it (to indicate that it is an assumption) and by indenting it with a further vertical line (to indicate that it is additional).

With this extra assumption in place, we are in a position to use $\wedge$I. So we can continue our proof:

1 | $R$
2 | | $L$
3 | | $R \wedge L$    $\wedge$I 1, 2

So we have now shown that, on the additional assumption, '$L$', we can obtain '$R \wedge L$'. We can therefore conclude that, if '$L$' obtains, then so does '$R \wedge L$'. Or, to put it more briefly, we can conclude '$L \rightarrow (R \wedge L)$':

1 | $R$
2 | | $L$
3 | | $R \wedge L$       $\wedge$I 1, 2
4 | $L \rightarrow (R \wedge L)$     $\rightarrow$I 2–3

Observe that we have dropped back to using one vertical line on the left. We have *discharged* the additional assumption, 'L', since the conditional itself follows just from our original assumption, 'R'.

The general pattern at work here is the following. We first make an additional assumption, $\mathcal{A}$; and from that additional assumption, we prove $\mathcal{B}$. In that case, we know the following: If $\mathcal{A}$ is true, then $\mathcal{B}$ is true. This is wrapped up in the rule for conditional introduction:

$$
\begin{array}{ll}
i & \quad \mathcal{A} \\
j & \quad \mathcal{B} \\
& \mathcal{A} \to \mathcal{B} \quad \to\text{I } i\text{-}j
\end{array}
$$

There can be as many or as few lines as you like between lines $i$ and $j$.

It will help to offer a second illustration of $\to$I in action. Suppose we want to consider the following:

$$P \to Q, Q \to R \therefore P \to R$$

We start by listing *both* of our premises. Then, since we want to arrive at a conditional (namely, '$P \to R$'), we additionally assume the antecedent to that conditional. Thus our main proof starts:

$$
\begin{array}{ll}
1 & P \to Q \\
2 & Q \to R \\
3 & \quad P
\end{array}
$$

Note that we have made '$P$' available, by treating it as an additional assumption, but now, we can use $\to$E on the first premise. This will yield '$Q$'. We can then use $\to$E on the second premise.

So, by assuming '$P$' we were able to prove '$R$', so we apply the $\rightarrow$I rule—discharging '$P$'—and finish the proof. Putting all this together, we have:

$$
\begin{array}{ll}
1 \quad P \rightarrow Q & \\
2 \quad Q \rightarrow R & \\
3 \quad\quad P & \\
4 \quad\quad Q & \rightarrow\text{E } 1, 3 \\
5 \quad\quad R & \rightarrow\text{E } 2, 4 \\
6 \quad P \rightarrow R & \rightarrow\text{I } 3\text{–}5 \\
\end{array}
$$

## 16.5   Additional assumptions and subproofs

The rule $\rightarrow$I invoked the idea of making additional assumptions. These need to be handled with some care. Consider this proof:

$$
\begin{array}{ll}
1 \quad A & \\
2 \quad\quad B & \\
3 \quad\quad B & \text{R } 2 \\
4 \quad B \rightarrow B & \rightarrow\text{I } 2\text{–}3 \\
\end{array}
$$

This is perfectly in keeping with the rules we have laid down already, and it should not seem particularly strange. Since '$B \rightarrow B$' is a tautology, no particular premises should be required to prove it.

But suppose we now tried to continue the proof as follows:

```
1 │ A
2 │ │ B
3 │ │ B      R 2
4 │ B → B    →I 2–3
5 │ B        naughty attempt
             to invoke →E 4, 3
```

If we were allowed to do this, it would be a disaster. It would allow us to prove any sentence letter from any other sentence letter. However, if you tell me that Anne is fast (symbolized by '*A*'), we shouldn't be able to conclude that Queen Boudica stood twenty-feet tall (symbolized by '*B*')! We must be prohibited from doing this, but how are we to implement the prohibition?

We can describe the process of making an additional assumption as one of performing a *subproof*: a subsidiary proof within the main proof. When we start a subproof, we draw another vertical line to indicate that we are no longer in the main proof. Then we write in the assumption upon which the subproof will be based. A subproof can be thought of as essentially posing this question: *what could we show, if we also make this additional assumption?*

When we are working within the subproof, we can refer to the additional assumption that we made in introducing the subproof, and to anything that we obtained from our original assumptions. (After all, those original assumptions are still in effect.) At some point though, we will want to stop working with the additional assumption: we will want to return from the subproof to the main proof. To indicate that we have returned to the main proof, the vertical line for the subproof comes to an end. At this point, we say that the subproof is CLOSED. Having closed a subproof, we have set aside the additional assumption, so it will be illegitimate to draw upon anything that depends upon that additional assumption. Thus we stipulate:

> To cite an individual line when applying a rule:
>
> 1. the line must come before the line where the rule is applied, but
>
> 2. not occur within a subproof that has been closed before the line where the rule is applied.

This stipulation rules out the disastrous attempted proof above. The rule of →E requires that we cite two individual lines from earlier in the proof. In the purported proof, above, one of these lines (namely, line 4) occurs within a subproof that has (by line 5) been closed. This is illegitimate.

Closing a subproof is called DISCHARGING the assumptions of that subproof. So we can put the point this way: *you cannot refer back to anything that was obtained using discharged assumptions.*

Subproofs, then, allow us to think about what we could show, if we made additional assumptions. The point to take away from this is not surprising—in the course of a proof, we have to keep very careful track of what assumptions we are making, at any given moment. Our proof system does this very graphically. (Indeed, that's precisely why we have chosen to use *this* proof system.)

Once we have started thinking about what we can show by making additional assumptions, nothing stops us from posing the question of what we could show if we were to make *even more* assumptions? This might motivate us to introduce a subproof within a subproof. Here is an example using only the rules which we have considered so far:

| 1 | $A$ | |
|---|---|---|
| 2 | $\quad B$ | |
| 3 | $\qquad C$ | |
| 4 | $\qquad A \land B$ | $\land$I 1, 2 |
| 5 | $\quad C \rightarrow (A \land B)$ | $\rightarrow$I 3–4 |
| 6 | $B \rightarrow (C \rightarrow (A \land B))$ | $\rightarrow$I 2–5 |

Notice that the citation on line 4 refers back to the initial assumption (on line 1) and an assumption of a subproof (on line 2). This is perfectly in order, since neither assumption has been discharged at the time (i.e., by line 4).

Again, though, we need to keep careful track of what we are assuming at any given moment. Suppose we tried to continue the proof as follows:

| 1 | $A$ | |
|---|---|---|
| 2 | $\quad B$ | |
| 3 | $\qquad C$ | |
| 4 | $\qquad A \land B$ | $\land$I 1, 2 |
| 5 | $\quad C \rightarrow (A \land B)$ | $\rightarrow$I 3–4 |
| 6 | $B \rightarrow (C \rightarrow (A \land B))$ | $\rightarrow$I 2–5 |
| 7 | $C \rightarrow (A \land B)$ | naughty attempt |
| | | to invoke $\rightarrow$I 3–4 |

This would be awful. If we tell you that Anne is smart, you should not be able to infer that, if Cath is smart (symbolized by '$C$') then *both* Anne is smart and Queen Boudica stood 20-feet tall! But this is just what such a proof would suggest, if it were permissible.

The essential problem is that the subproof that began with the assumption '$C$' depended crucially on the fact that we had assumed '$B$' on line 2. By line 6, we have *discharged* the assumption '$B$': we have stopped asking ourselves what we could show, if we also assumed '$B$'. So it is simply cheating, to try to help ourselves (on line 7) to the subproof that began with the assumption '$C$'. Thus we stipulate, much as before, that a subproof can only be cited on a line if it does not occur within some other subproof which is already closed at that line. The attempted disastrous proof violates this stipulation. The subproof of lines 3–4 occurs within a subproof that ends on line 5. So it cannot be invoked on line 7.

Here is one further case we have to exclude:

| | | |
|---|---|---|
| 1 | $A$ | |
| 2 | $B$ | |
| 3 | $C$ | |
| 4 | $B \wedge C$ | $\wedge$I 2, 3 |
| 5 | $C$ | $\wedge$E 4 |
| 6 | $B \rightarrow C$ | naughty attempt |
| | | to invoke $\rightarrow$I 2–5 |

Here we are trying to cite a subproof that begins on line 2 and ends on line 5—but the sentence on line 5 depends not only on the assumption on line 2, but also on one another assumption (line 3) which we have not discharged at the end of the subproof. The subproof started on line 3 is still open at line 3. But $\rightarrow$I requires that the last line of the subproof *only* relies on the assumption of the subproof being cited, i.e., the subproof beginning on line 2 (and anything before it), and not on assumptions of any subproofs within it. In particular, the last line of the subproof cited must not itself lie within a nested subproof.

To cite a subproof when applying a rule:

1. the cited subproof must come entirely before the application of the rule where it is cited,

2. the cited subproof must not lie within some other closed subproof which is closed at the line it is cited, and

3. its last line of the cited subproof must not occur inside a nested subproof.

One last point to emphasize how rules can be applied: where a rule requires you to cite an individual line, you cannot cite a subproof instead; and where it requires you to cite a subproof, you cannot cite an individual line instead. So for instance, this is incorrect:

| | | | |
|---|---|---|---|
| 1 | $A$ | | |
| 2 | | $B$ | |
| 3 | | | $C$ |
| 4 | | | $B \wedge C$ | $\wedge$I 2, 3 |
| 5 | | | $C$ | $\wedge$E 4 |
| 6 | | $C$ | naughty attempt to invoke R 3–5 |
| 7 | $B \to C$ | $\to$I 2–6 |

Here, we have tried to justify $C$ on line 6 by the reiteration rule, but we have cited the subproof on lines 3–5 with it. That subproof is closed and can in principle be cited on line 6. (For instance, we could use it to justify $C \to C$ by $\to$I.) But the reiteration rule R requires you to cite an individual line, so citing the entire subproof is inadmissible (even if that subproof contains the sentence $C$ we want to reiterate).

It is always permissible to open a subproof with any assumption. However, there is some strategy involved in picking a useful assumption. Starting a subproof with an arbitrary, wacky assumption would just waste lines of the proof. In order to obtain a conditional by →I, for instance, you must assume the antecedent of the conditional in a subproof.

Equally, it is always permissible to close a subproof (and discharge its assumptions). However, it will not be helpful to do so until you have reached something useful. Once the subproof is closed, you can only cite the entire subproof in any justification. Those rules that call for a subproof or subproofs, in turn, require that the last line of the subproof is a sentence of some form or other. For instance, you are only allowed to cite a subproof for →I if the line you are justifying is of the form $\mathcal{A} \rightarrow \mathcal{B}$, $\mathcal{A}$ is the assumption of your subproof, and $\mathcal{B}$ is the last line of your subproof.

## 16.6 Biconditional

The rules for the biconditional will be like double-barrelled versions of the rules for the conditional.

In order to prove '$F \leftrightarrow G$', for instance, you must be able to prove '$G$' on the assumption '$F$' *and* prove '$F$' on the assumption '$G$'. The biconditional introduction rule (↔I) therefore requires two subproofs. Schematically, the rule works like this:

$$
\begin{array}{l|l}
i & \mathscr{A} \\
j & \mathscr{B} \\
k & \mathscr{B} \\
l & \mathscr{A} \\
\hline
& \mathscr{A} \leftrightarrow \mathscr{B} \quad \leftrightarrow\text{I } i\text{--}j,\, k\text{--}l
\end{array}
$$

There can be as many lines as you like between $i$ and $j$, and as many lines as you like between $k$ and $l$. Moreover, the subproofs can come in any order, and the second subproof does not need to come immediately after the first.

The biconditional elimination rule ($\leftrightarrow$E) lets you do a bit more than the conditional rule. If you have the left-hand subsentence of the biconditional, you can obtain the right-hand subsentence. If you have the right-hand subsentence, you can obtain the left-hand subsentence. So we allow:

$$
\begin{array}{l|l}
m & \mathscr{A} \leftrightarrow \mathscr{B} \\
n & \mathscr{A} \\
& \mathscr{B} \quad\quad \leftrightarrow\text{E } m,\, n
\end{array}
$$

and equally:

$$
\begin{array}{l|l}
m & \mathscr{A} \leftrightarrow \mathscr{B} \\
n & \mathscr{B} \\
& \mathscr{A} \quad\quad \leftrightarrow\text{E } m,\, n
\end{array}
$$

Note that the biconditional, and the right or left half, can be separated from one another, and they can appear in any order.

However, in the citation for ↔E, we always cite the biconditional first.

## 16.7 Disjunction

Suppose Ludwig is reactionary. Then Ludwig is either reactionary or libertarian. After all, to say that Ludwig is either reactionary or libertarian is to say something weaker than to say that Ludwig is reactionary.

Let's emphasize this point. Suppose Ludwig is reactionary. It follows that Ludwig is *either* reactionary *or* a kumquat. Equally, it follows that *either* Ludwig is reactionary *or* that kumquats are the only fruit. Equally, it follows that *either* Ludwig is reactionary *or* that God is dead. Many of these are strange inferences to draw, but there is nothing *logically* wrong with them (even if they maybe violate all sorts of implicit conversational norms).

Armed with all this, we present the disjunction introduction rule(s):

$$m \quad | \quad \mathcal{A}$$

$$\mathcal{A} \vee \mathcal{B} \quad \vee\text{I } m$$

and

$$m \quad | \quad \mathcal{A}$$

$$\mathcal{B} \vee \mathcal{A} \quad \vee\text{I } m$$

Notice that $\mathcal{B}$ can be *any* sentence whatsoever, so the following is a perfectly acceptable proof:

$$1 \quad | \quad M$$

$$2 \quad | \quad M \vee ([(A \leftrightarrow B) \to (C \wedge D)] \leftrightarrow [E \wedge F]) \quad \vee\text{I } 1$$

Using a truth table to show this would have taken 128 lines.

The disjunction elimination rule is, though, slightly trickier. Suppose that either Ludwig is reactionary or he is libertarian. What can you conclude? Not that Ludwig is reactionary; it might be that he is libertarian instead. Equally, not that Ludwig is libertarian; for he might merely be reactionary. Disjunctions, just by themselves, are hard to work with.

But suppose that we could somehow show both of the following: first, that Ludwig's being reactionary entails that he is an Austrian economist: second, that Ludwig's being libertarian entails that he is an Austrian economist. Then if we know that Ludwig is either reactionary or libertarian, then we know that, whichever he is, Ludwig is an Austrian economist. This insight can be expressed in the following rule, which is our disjunction elimination ($\lor$E) rule:

$$
\begin{array}{cl}
m & \mathcal{A} \lor \mathcal{B} \\[4pt]
i & \quad | \;\; \mathcal{A} \\
j & \quad | \;\; \mathcal{C} \\[4pt]
k & \quad | \;\; \mathcal{B} \\
l & \quad | \;\; \mathcal{C} \\[4pt]
& \mathcal{C} \qquad \lor\text{E } m,\, i\text{--}j,\, k\text{--}l
\end{array}
$$

This is obviously a bit clunkier to write down than our previous rules, but the point is fairly simple. Suppose we have some disjunction, $\mathcal{A} \lor \mathcal{B}$. Suppose we have two subproofs, showing us that $\mathcal{C}$ follows from the assumption that $\mathcal{A}$, and that $\mathcal{C}$ follows from the assumption that $\mathcal{B}$. Then we can infer $\mathcal{C}$ itself. As usual, there can be as many lines as you like between $i$ and $j$, and as many lines as you like between $k$ and $l$. Moreover, the subproofs and the disjunction can come in any order, and do not have to be adjacent.

Some examples might help illustrate this. Consider this argument:

$$(P \wedge Q) \vee (P \wedge R) \therefore P$$

An example proof might run thus:

| | | |
|---|---|---|
| 1 | $(P \wedge Q) \vee (P \wedge R)$ | |
| 2 | $P \wedge Q$ | |
| 3 | $P$ | $\wedge$E 2 |
| 4 | $P \wedge R$ | |
| 5 | $P$ | $\wedge$E 4 |
| 6 | $P$ | $\vee$E 1, 2–3, 4–5 |

Here is a slightly harder example. Consider:

$$A \wedge (B \vee C) \therefore (A \wedge B) \vee (A \wedge C)$$

Here is a proof corresponding to this argument:

| | | |
|---|---|---|
| 1 | $A \wedge (B \vee C)$ | |
| 2 | $A$ | $\wedge$E 1 |
| 3 | $B \vee C$ | $\wedge$E 1 |
| 4 | $B$ | |
| 5 | $A \wedge B$ | $\wedge$I 2, 4 |
| 6 | $(A \wedge B) \vee (A \wedge C)$ | $\vee$I 5 |
| 7 | $C$ | |
| 8 | $A \wedge C$ | $\wedge$I 2, 7 |
| 9 | $(A \wedge B) \vee (A \wedge C)$ | $\vee$I 8 |
| 10 | $(A \wedge B) \vee (A \wedge C)$ | $\vee$E 3, 4–6, 7–9 |

Don't be alarmed if you think that you wouldn't have been able to come up with this proof yourself. The ability to come up with novel proofs comes with practice, and we'll cover some strategies for finding proofs in §17. The key question at this stage is whether, looking at the proof, you can see that it conforms to the rules that we have laid down. That just involves checking every line, and making sure that it is justified in accordance with the rules we have laid down.

## 16.8   Contradiction and negation

We have only one connective left to deal with: negation. But to tackle it, we must connect negation with *contradiction*.

An effective form of argument is to argue your opponent into contradicting themselves. At that point, you have them on the ropes. They have to give up at least one of their assumptions. We are going to make use of this idea in our proof system, by adding a new symbol, '⊥', to our proofs. This should be read as something like 'contradiction!' or 'reductio!' or 'but that's absurd!' The rule for introducing this symbol is that we can use it whenever we explicitly contradict ourselves, i.e., whenever we find both a sentence and its negation appearing in our proof:

$$
\begin{array}{r|ll}
m & \neg \mathscr{A} & \\
& & \\
n & \mathscr{A} & \\
& & \\
& \bot & \neg\text{E } m, n \\
\end{array}
$$

It does not matter what order the sentence and its negation appear in, and they do not need to appear on adjacent lines. However, we always cite the line number of the negation first, followed by that of the sentence it is a negation of.

There is obviously a tight link between contradiction and negation. The rule ¬E lets us proceed from two contradictory sentences—$\mathscr{A}$ and its negation $\neg\mathscr{A}$—to an explicit contradition $\bot$. We choose the label for a reason: it is the the most basic rule that lets us proceed from a premise containing a negation, i.e., $\neg\mathscr{A}$, to a sentence not containing it, i.e., $\bot$. So it is a rule that *eliminates* $\neg$.

We have said that '$\bot$' should be read as something like 'contradiction!' but this does not tell us much about the symbol. There are, roughly, three ways to approach the symbol.

- We might regard '$\bot$' as a new atomic sentence of TFL, but one which can only ever have the truth value False.
- We might regard '$\bot$' as an abbreviation for some canonical contradiction, such as '$A \wedge \neg A$'. This will have the same effect as the above—obviously, '$A \wedge \neg A$' only ever has the truth value False—but it means that, officially, we do not need to add a new symbol to TFL.
- We might regard '$\bot$', not as a symbol of TFL, but as something more like a *punctuation mark* that appears in our proofs. (It is on a par with the line numbers and the vertical lines, say.)

There is something very philosophically attractive about the third option, but here we will *officially* adopt the first. '$\bot$' is to be read as a sentence letter that is always false. This means that we can manipulate it, in our proofs, just like any other sentence.

We still have to state a rule for negation introduction. The rule is very simple: if assuming something leads you to a contradiction, then the assumption must be wrong. This thought motivates the following rule:

$$
\begin{array}{ll}
i & \quad \mathscr{A} \\
j & \quad \bot \\
& \neg\mathscr{A} \qquad \neg\text{I } i\text{–}j
\end{array}
$$

There can be as many lines between *i* and *j* as you like. To see this in practice, and interacting with negation, consider this proof:

$$\begin{array}{ll} 1 & D \\ 2 & \quad \neg D \\ 3 & \quad \bot \qquad \neg E\ 2,\ 1 \\ 4 & \neg\neg D \qquad \neg I\ 2\text{--}3 \end{array}$$

If the assumption that $\mathcal{A}$ is true leads to a contradiction, $\mathcal{A}$ cannot be true, i.e., it must be false, i.e., $\neg\mathcal{A}$ must be true. Of course, if the assumption that $\mathcal{A}$ is false (i.e., the assumption that $\neg\mathcal{A}$ is true) leads to a contradiction, then $\mathcal{A}$ cannot be false, i.e., $\mathcal{A}$ must be true. So we can consider the following rule:

$$\begin{array}{ll} i & \quad \neg\mathcal{A} \\ j & \quad \bot \\ & \mathcal{A} \qquad \text{IP } i\text{--}j \end{array}$$

This rule is called *indirect proof*, since it allows us to prove $\mathcal{A}$ indirectly, by assuming its negation. Formally, the rule is very similar to ¬I, but $\mathcal{A}$ and $\neg\mathcal{A}$ have changed places. Since $\neg\mathcal{A}$ is not the conclusion of the rule, we are not introducing ¬, so IP is not a rule that introduces any connective. It also doesn't eliminate a connective, since it has no free-standing premises which contain ¬, only a subproof with an assumption of the form $\neg\mathcal{A}$. By contrast, ¬E does have a premise of the form $\neg\mathcal{A}$: that's why ¬E eliminates ¬, but IP does not.[1]

---

[1] There are logicians who have qualms about IP, but not about ¬E. They are called "intuitionists." Intuitionists don't buy our basic assumption that every sentence has one of two truth values, true or false. They also think that ¬ works differently—for them, a proof of $\bot$ from $\mathcal{A}$ guarantees $\neg\mathcal{A}$, but a proof

Using ¬I, we were able to give a proof of ¬¬𝒟 from 𝒟. Using IP, we can go the other direction (with essentially the same proof).

```
1 │ ¬¬D
2 │ │ ¬D
3 │ │ ⊥       ¬E 1, 2
4 │ D         IP 2–3
```

We need one last rule. It is a kind of elimination rule for '⊥', and known as *explosion*.[2] If we obtain a contradiction, symbolized by '⊥', then we can infer whatever we like. How can this be motivated, as a rule of argumentation? Well, consider the English rhetorical device '...and if *that's* true, I'll eat my hat'. Since contradictions simply cannot be true, if one *is* true then not only will I eat my hat, I'll have it too. Here is the formal rule:

```
m │ ⊥
  │ 𝒜     X m
```

Note that 𝒜 can be *any* sentence whatsoever.

The explosion rule is a bit odd. It looks like 𝒜 arrives in our proof like a bunny out of a hat. When trying to find proofs, it is very tempting to try to use it everywhere, since it seems so powerful. Resist this temptation: you can only apply it when you already have ⊥! And you get ⊥ only when your assumptions are contradictory.

Still, isn't it odd that from a contradiction anything whatsoever should follow? Not according to our notion of entailment

---

of ⊥ from ¬𝒜 does not guarantee that 𝒜, but only ¬¬𝒜. So, for them, 𝒜 and ¬¬𝒜 are not equivalent.

[2]The latin name for this principle is *ex contradictione quod libet*, "from contradiction, anything."

and validity. For $\mathcal{A}$ entails $\mathcal{B}$ iff there is no valuation of the sentence letters which makes $\mathcal{A}$ true and $\mathcal{B}$ false at the same time. Now $\bot$ is a contradiction—it is never true, whatever the valuation of the sentence letters. Since there is no valuation which makes $\bot$ true, there of course is also no valuation that makes $\bot$ true and $\mathcal{B}$ false! So according to our definition of entailment, $\bot \vDash \mathcal{B}$, whatever $\mathcal{B}$ is. A contradiction entails anything.[3]

*These are all of the basic rules for the proof system for TFL.*

## Practice exercises

**A.** The following two 'proofs' are *incorrect*. Explain the mistakes they make.

| | | |
|---|---|---|
| 1 | $(\neg L \wedge A) \vee L$ | |
| 2 | $\neg L \wedge A$ | |
| 3 | $\neg L$ | $\wedge$E 3 |
| 4 | $A$ | $\wedge$E 1 |
| 5 | $L$ | |
| 6 | $\bot$ | $\neg$E 3, 5 |
| 7 | $A$ | X 6 |
| 8 | $A$ | $\vee$E 1, 2–4, 5–7 |

---

[3]There are some logicians who don't buy this. They think that if $\mathcal{A}$ entails $\mathcal{B}$, there must be some *relevant connection* between $\mathcal{A}$ and $\mathcal{B}$—and there isn't one between $\bot$ and some arbitrary sentence $\mathcal{B}$. So these logicians develop other, "relevant" logics in which you aren't allowed the explosion rule.

1 | $A \wedge (B \wedge C)$
2 | $(B \vee C) \rightarrow D$
———
3 | $B$          $\wedge$E 1
4 | $B \vee C$      $\vee$I 3
5 | $D$          $\rightarrow$E 4, 2

**B.** The following three proofs are missing their citations (rule and line numbers). Add them, to turn them into *bona fide* proofs. Additionally, write down the argument that corresponds to each proof.

1 | $P \wedge S$
2 | $S \rightarrow R$
———
3 | $P$
4 | $S$
5 | $R$
6 | $R \vee E$

1 | $A \rightarrow D$
———
2 |    $A \wedge B$
———
3 |    $A$
4 |    $D$
5 |    $D \vee E$
6 | $(A \wedge B) \rightarrow (D \vee E)$

1 | $\neg L \rightarrow (J \vee L)$
2 | $\neg L$
———
3 | $J \vee L$
4 |    $J$
———
5 |    $J \wedge J$
6 |    $J$
7 |    $L$
———
8 |    $\bot$
9 |    $J$
10 | $J$

**C.** Give a proof for each of the following arguments:

1. $J \rightarrow \neg J \therefore \neg J$

2. $Q \to (Q \land \neg Q) \therefore \neg Q$
3. $A \to (B \to C) \therefore (A \land B) \to C$
4. $K \land L \therefore K \leftrightarrow L$
5. $(C \land D) \lor E \therefore E \lor D$
6. $A \leftrightarrow B, B \leftrightarrow C \therefore A \leftrightarrow C$
7. $\neg F \to G, F \to H \therefore G \lor H$
8. $(Z \land K) \lor (K \land M), K \to D \therefore D$
9. $P \land (Q \lor R), P \to \neg R \therefore Q \lor E$
10. $S \leftrightarrow T \therefore S \leftrightarrow (T \lor S)$
11. $\neg(P \to Q) \therefore \neg Q$
12. $\neg(P \to Q) \therefore P$

# CHAPTER 17

# *Constructing proofs*

There is no simple recipe for finding proofs, and there is no substitute for practice. Here, though, are some rules of thumb and strategies to keep in mind.

## 17.1   Working backward from what we want

So you're trying to find a proof of some conclusion $\mathscr{C}$, which will be the last line of your proof. The first thing you do is look at $\mathscr{C}$ and ask what the introduction rule is for its main logical operator. This gives you an idea of what should happen *before* the last line of the proof. The justifications for the introduction rule require one or two other sentences above the last line, or one or two subproofs. Moreover, you can tell from $\mathscr{C}$ what those sentences are, or what the assumptions and conclusions of the subproof(s) are. Then you can write down those sentence or outline the subproof(s) above the last line, and treat those as your new goals.

For example: If your conclusion is a conditional $\mathscr{A} \rightarrow \mathscr{B}$, plan to use the $\rightarrow$I rule. This requires starting a subproof in which you assume $\mathscr{A}$. The subproof ought to end with $\mathscr{B}$. Then, continue by thinking about what you should do to get $\mathcal{B}$ inside that subproof, and how you can use the assumption $\mathcal{A}$.

If your goal is a conjunction, conditional, or negated sentence, you should start by working backward in this way. We'll describe what you have to do in each of these cases in detail.

### Working backward from a conjunction

If we want to prove $\mathcal{A} \wedge \mathcal{B}$, working backward means we should write $\mathcal{A} \wedge \mathcal{B}$ at the bottom of our proof, and try to prove it using $\wedge$I. At the top, we'll write out the premises of the proof, if there are any. Then, at the bottom, we write the sentence we want to prove. If it is a conjunction, we'll prove it using $\wedge$I.

$$
\begin{array}{r|ll}
1 & \mathcal{P}_1 & \\
& \vdots & \\
k & \mathcal{P}_k & \\
\cline{2-2}
& \vdots & \\
n & \mathcal{A} & \\
& \vdots & \\
m & \mathcal{B} & \\
m+1 & \mathcal{A} \wedge \mathcal{B} & \wedge\text{I } n,\, m
\end{array}
$$

For $\wedge$I, we need to prove $\mathcal{A}$ first, then prove $\mathcal{B}$. For the last line, we have to cite the lines where we (will have) proved $\mathcal{A}$ and $\mathcal{B}$, and use $\wedge$I. The parts of the proof labelled $\vdots$ have to still be filled in. We'll mark the line numbers $m$, $n$ for now. When the proof is complete, these placeholders can be replaced by actual numbers.

### Working backward from a conditional

If our goal is to prove a conditional $\mathcal{A} \rightarrow \mathcal{B}$, we'll have to use $\rightarrow$I. This requires a subproof starting with $\mathcal{A}$ and ending with $\mathcal{B}$. We'll set up our proof as follows:

$$
\begin{array}{ll}
n & \quad \begin{array}{|l} \mathcal{A} \\ \vdots \end{array} \\
m & \quad \begin{array}{|l} \mathcal{B} \end{array} \\
m+1 & \mathcal{A} \rightarrow \mathcal{B} \quad \rightarrow\text{I } n\text{--}m
\end{array}
$$

Again we'll leave placeholders in the line number slots. We'll record the last inference as $\rightarrow$I, citing the subproof.

### Working backward from a negated sentence

If we want to prove $\neg\mathcal{A}$, we'll have to use $\neg$I.

$$
\begin{array}{ll}
n & \quad \begin{array}{|l} \mathcal{A} \\ \vdots \end{array} \\
m & \quad \begin{array}{|l} \bot \end{array} \\
m+1 & \neg\mathcal{A} \quad \neg\text{I } n\text{--}m
\end{array}
$$

For $\neg$I, we have to start a subproof with assumption $\mathcal{A}$; the last line of the subproof has to be $\bot$. We'll cite the subproof, and use $\neg$I as the rule.

When working backward, continue to do so as long as you can. So if you're working backward to prove $\mathcal{A} \rightarrow \mathcal{B}$ and have set up a subproof in which you want to prove $\mathcal{B}$. Now look at $\mathcal{B}$. If, say, it is a conjunction, work backward from it, and write down the two conjuncts inside your subproof. Etc.

### Working backward from a disjunction

Of course, you can also work backward from a disjunction $\mathcal{A} \vee \mathcal{B}$, if that is your goal. The $\vee$I rule requires that you have one of the disjuncts in order to infer $\mathcal{A} \vee \mathcal{B}$. So to work backward, you pick a disjunct, infer $\mathcal{A} \vee \mathcal{B}$ from it, and then continue to look for a proof of the disjunct you picked:

$$
\begin{array}{r|ll}
& \vdots & \\
n & \mathcal{A} & \\
n+1 & \mathcal{A} \vee \mathcal{B} & \vee\text{I } n
\end{array}
$$

However, you may not be able to prove the disjunct you picked.

In that case you have to backtrack. When you can't fill in the $\vdots$, delete everything, and try with the other disjunct:

$$
\begin{array}{r|ll}
& \vdots & \\
n & \mathcal{B} & \\
n+1 & \mathcal{A} \vee \mathcal{B} & \vee\text{I } n
\end{array}
$$

Obviously, deleting everything and starting over is frustrating, so you should avoid it. If your goal is a disjunction, therefore, you should *not start* by working backward: try working forward first, and apply the $\vee$I strategy only when working forward (and working backward using $\wedge$I, $\rightarrow$I, and $\neg$I) no longer work.

## 17.2   Work forward from what you have

Your proof may have premises. And if you've worked backward in order to prove a conditional or a negated sentence, you will have set up subproofs with an assumption, and be looking to prove a final sentence in the subproof. These premises and assumptions are sentences you can work forward from in order to fill in the missing steps in your proof. That means applying elimination rules for the main operators of these sentences. The form of the rules will tell you what you'll have to do.

### Working forward from a conjunction

To work forward from a sentence of the form $\mathscr{A} \wedge \mathscr{B}$, we use $\wedge$E. That rule allows us to do two things: infer $\mathscr{A}$, and infer $\mathscr{B}$. So in a proof where we have $\mathscr{A} \wedge \mathscr{B}$, we can work forward by writing $\mathscr{A}$ and/or $\mathscr{B}$ immediately below the conjunction:

$$
\begin{array}{r|ll}
n & \mathscr{A} \wedge \mathscr{B} & \\
n+1 & \mathscr{A} & \wedge\text{E } n \\
n+2 & \mathscr{B} & \wedge\text{E } n
\end{array}
$$

Usually it will be clear in the particular situation you're in which one of $\mathscr{A}$ or $\mathscr{B}$ you'll need. It doesn't hurt, however, to write them both down.

### Working forward from a disjunction

Working forward from a disjunction works a bit differently. To use a disjunction, we use the $\vee$E rule. In order to apply that rule, it is not enough to know what the disjuncts of the disjunction are that we want to use. We must also keep in mind what we want to prove. Suppose we want to prove $\mathscr{C}$, and we have $\mathscr{A} \vee B$ to work with. (That $\mathscr{A} \vee B$ may be a premise of the proof, an assumption of a subproof, or something already proved.) In order to be able to apply the $\vee$E rule, we'll have to set up two subproofs:

$$
\begin{array}{ll}
n & \mathcal{A} \vee \mathcal{B} \\[4pt]
n+1 & \quad \mathcal{A} \\[2pt]
& \quad \vdots \\[2pt]
m & \quad \mathcal{C} \\[4pt]
m+1 & \quad \mathcal{B} \\[2pt]
& \quad \vdots \\[2pt]
k & \quad \mathcal{C} \\[4pt]
k+1 & \mathcal{C} \qquad \vee\text{E } n,\, (n+1)\text{--}m,\, (m+1)\text{--}k
\end{array}
$$

The first subproof starts with the first disjunct, $\mathcal{A}$, and ends with the sentence we're looking for, $\mathcal{C}$. The second subproof starts with the other disjunct, $\mathcal{B}$, and also ends with the goal sentence $\mathcal{C}$. Each of these subproofs have to be filled in further. We can then justify the goal sentence $\mathcal{C}$ by using $\vee$E, citing the line with $\mathcal{A} \vee \mathcal{B}$ and the two subproofs.

## Working forward from a conditional

In order to use a conditional $\mathcal{A} \to \mathcal{B}$, you also need the antecedent $\mathcal{A}$ in order to apply $\to$E. So to work forward from a conditional, you will derive $\mathcal{B}$, justify it by $\to$E, and set up $\mathcal{A}$ as a new subgoal.

$$
\begin{array}{ll}
n & \mathcal{A} \to \mathcal{B} \\[2pt]
& \vdots \\[2pt]
m & \mathcal{A} \\[4pt]
m+1 & \mathcal{B} \qquad \to\text{E } n,\, m
\end{array}
$$

**Working forward from a negated sentence**

Finally, to use a negated sentence $\neg\mathcal{A}$, you would apply $\neg$E. It requires, in addition to $\neg\mathcal{A}$, also the corresponding sentence $\mathcal{A}$ without the negation. The sentence you'll get is always the same: $\bot$. So working forward from a negated sentence works especially well inside a subproof that you'll want to use for $\neg$I (or IP). You work forward from $\neg\mathcal{A}$ if you already have $\neg\mathcal{A}$ and you want to prove $\bot$. To do it, you set up $\mathcal{A}$ as a new subgoal.

$$
\begin{array}{r|ll}
n & \neg\mathcal{A} & \\
 & \vdots & \\
m & \mathcal{A} & \\
m+1 & \bot & \neg\text{E } n, m
\end{array}
$$

## 17.3  Strategies at work

Suppose we want to show that the argument $(A \wedge B) \vee (A \wedge C)$ $\therefore$ $A \wedge (B \vee C)$ is valid. We start the proof by writing the premise and conclusion down. (On a piece of paper, you would want as much space as possible between them, so write the premises at the top of the sheet and the conclusion at the bottom.)

$$
\begin{array}{r|l}
1 & (A \wedge B) \vee (A \wedge C) \\
 & \vdots \\
n & A \wedge (B \vee C)
\end{array}
$$

We now have two options: either work backward from the conclusion, or work forward from the premise. We'll pick the second strategy: we use the disjunction on line 1, and set up the subproofs we need for $\vee$E. The disjunction on line 1 has two disjuncts, $A \wedge B$ and $A \wedge C$. The goal sentence you want to prove is $A \wedge (B \vee C)$. So in this case you have to set up two subproofs, one with assumption $A \wedge B$ and last line $A \wedge (B \vee C)$, the other with assumption $A \wedge C$ and last line $A \wedge (B \vee C)$. The justification for the conclusion on line $n$ will be $\vee$E, citing the disjunction on line 1 and the two subproofs. So your proof now looks like this:

$$
\begin{array}{ll}
1 & (A \wedge B) \vee (A \wedge C) \\[4pt]
2 & \quad A \wedge B \\
  & \quad \vdots \\
n & \quad A \wedge (B \vee C) \\[4pt]
n+1 & \quad A \wedge C \\
  & \quad \vdots \\
m & \quad A \wedge (B \vee C) \\[4pt]
m+1 & A \wedge (B \vee C) \qquad \vee\text{E } 1, 2\text{–}n, n+1\text{–}m
\end{array}
$$

You now have two separate tasks, namely to fill in each of the two subproofs. In the first subproof, we now work backward from the conclusion $A \wedge (B \vee C)$. That is a conjunction, so inside the first subproof, you will have two separate subgoals: proving $A$, and proving $B \vee C$. These subgoals will let you justify line $n$ using $\wedge$I. Your proof now looks like this:

$$
\begin{array}{r|l}
1 & (A \wedge B) \vee (A \wedge C) \\
\cline{2-2}
2 & \quad A \wedge B \\
 & \qquad \vdots \\
i & \quad A \\
 & \qquad \vdots \\
n-1 & \quad B \vee C \\
n & \quad A \wedge (B \vee C) \qquad \wedge\text{I } i, n-1 \\
n+1 & \quad A \wedge C \\
 & \qquad \vdots \\
m & \quad A \wedge (B \vee C) \\
m+1 & A \wedge (B \vee C) \qquad \vee\text{E } 1, 2\text{--}n, (n+1)\text{--}m
\end{array}
$$

We immediately see that we can get line $i$ from line 2 by $\wedge$E. So line $i$ is actually line 3, and can be justified with $\wedge$E from line 2. The other subgoal $B \vee C$ is a disjunction. We'll apply the strategy for working backward from a disjunctions to line $n-1$. We have a choice of which disjunct to pick as a subgoal, $B$ or $C$. Picking $C$ wouldn't work and we'd end up having to backtrack. And you can already see that if you pick $B$ as a subgoal, you could get that by working forward again from the conjunction $A \wedge B$ on line 2. So we can complete the first subproof as follows:

| 1     | $(A \land B) \lor (A \land C)$ |                       |
|-------|--------------------------------|-----------------------|
| 2     | $A \land B$                    |                       |
| 3     | $A$                            | $\land$E 2            |
| 4     | $B$                            | $\land$E 2            |
| 5     | $B \lor C$                     | $\lor$I 4             |
| 6     | $A \land (B \lor C)$           | $\land$I 3, 5         |
| 7     | $A \land C$                    |                       |
|       | $\vdots$                       |                       |
| $m$   | $A \land (B \lor C)$           |                       |
| $m+1$ | $A \land (B \lor C)$           | $\lor$E 1, 2–6, 7–$m$ |

Like line 3, we get line 4 from 2 by $\land$E. Line 5 is justified by $\lor$I from line 4, since we were working backward from a disjunction there.

That's it for the first subproof. The second subproof is almost exactly the same. We'll leave it as an exercise.

Remember that when we started, we had the option of working forward from the premise, or working backward from the conclusion, and we picked the first option. The second option also leads to a proof, but it will look different. The first steps would be to work backward from the conclusion and set up two subgoals, $A$ and $B \lor C$, and then work forward from the premise to prove them, e.g.,:

| | | |
|---|---|---|
| 1 | $(A \wedge B) \vee (A \wedge C)$ | |
| 2 |    $A \wedge B$ | |
| |    $\vdots$ | |
| $k$ |    $A$ | |
| $k+1$ |    $A \wedge C$ | |
| |    $\vdots$ | |
| $n-1$ |    $A$ | |
| $n$ | $A$ | $\vee$E 1, 2–$k$, ($k+1$)–($n-1$) |
| $n+1$ |    $A \wedge B$ | |
| |    $\vdots$ | |
| $l$ |    $B \vee C$ | |
| $l+1$ |    $A \wedge C$ | |
| |    $\vdots$ | |
| $m-1$ |    $B \vee C$ | |
| $m$ | $B \vee C$ | $\vee$E 1, ($n+1$)–$l$, ($l+1$)–($m-1$) |
| $m+1$ | $A \wedge (B \vee C)$ | $\wedge$I $n, m$ |

We'll leave you to fill in the missing pieces indicated by $\vdots$.

Let's give another example to illustrate how to apply the strategies to deal with conditionals and negation. The sentence $(A \to B) \to (\neg B \to \neg A)$ is a tautology. Let's see if we can find a proof of it, from no premises, using the strategies. We first write the sentence at the bottom of a sheet of paper. Since working forward is not an option (there is nothing to work forward from), we work backward, and set up a subproof to establish the sentence we want $(A \to B) \to (\neg B \to \neg A)$ using $\to$I. Its assumption must be the antecedent of the conditional we want to prove, i.e., $A \rightarrow B$, and its last line the consequent $\neg B \rightarrow \neg A$.

$$
\begin{array}{ll}
1 & \quad \boxed{\begin{array}{l} A \rightarrow B \\[4pt] \vdots \\[4pt] \end{array}} \\[2pt]
n & \quad \neg B \rightarrow \neg A \\[4pt]
n+1 & (A \rightarrow B) \rightarrow (\neg B \rightarrow \neg A) \qquad \rightarrow\!\mathrm{I}\ 1\text{--}n
\end{array}
$$

The new goal, $\neg B \rightarrow \neg A$ is itself a conditional, so working backward we set up another subproof:

$$
\begin{array}{ll}
1 & \quad A \rightarrow B \\[4pt]
2 & \qquad \neg B \\[4pt]
  & \qquad \vdots \\[4pt]
n-1 & \qquad \neg A \\[4pt]
n & \quad \neg B \rightarrow \neg A \qquad\qquad\qquad \rightarrow\!\mathrm{I}\ 2\text{--}(n-1) \\[4pt]
n+1 & (A \rightarrow B) \rightarrow (\neg B \rightarrow \neg A) \qquad \rightarrow\!\mathrm{I}\ 1\text{--}n
\end{array}
$$

From $\neg A$ we again work backward. To do this, look at the $\neg\mathrm{I}$ rule. It requires a subproof with $A$ as assumption, and $\bot$ as its last line. So the proof is now:

$$
\begin{array}{lll}
1 & A \to B \\
2 & \quad \neg B \\
3 & \quad\quad A \\
 & \quad\quad \vdots \\
n-2 & \quad\quad \bot \\
n-1 & \quad\quad \neg A & \neg\text{I } 3\text{-}(n-2) \\
n & \quad \neg B \to \neg A & \to\text{I } 2\text{-}(n-1) \\
n+1 & (A \to B) \to (\neg B \to \neg A) & \to\text{I } 1\text{-}n
\end{array}
$$

Now our goal is to prove $\bot$. We said above, when discussing how to work forward from a negated sentence, that the $\neg$E rule allows you to prove $\bot$, which is our goal in the innermost subproof. So we look for a negated sentence which we can work forward from: that would be $\neg B$ on line 2. That means we have to derive $B$ inside the subproof, since $\neg$E requires not just $\neg B$ (which we have already), but also $B$. And $B$, in turn, we get by working forward from $A \to B$, since $\to$E will allow us to justify the consequent of that conditional $B$ by $\to$E. The rule $\to$E also requires the antecedent $A$ of the conditional, but that is also already available (on line 3). So we finish with:

| 1 | $A \rightarrow B$ | |
|---|---|---|
| 2 | $\neg B$ | |
| 3 | $A$ | |
| 4 | $B$ | $\rightarrow$E 1, 3 |
| 5 | $\bot$ | $\neg$E 2, 4 |
| 6 | $\neg A$ | $\neg$I 3–5 |
| 7 | $\neg B \rightarrow \neg A$ | $\rightarrow$I 2–6 |
| 8 | $(A \rightarrow B) \rightarrow (\neg B \rightarrow \neg A)$ | $\rightarrow$I 1–7 |

## 17.4   Working forward from $\bot$

When applying the strategies, you will sometimes find yourself in a situation where you can justify $\bot$. Using the explosion rule, this would allow you to justify *anything*. So $\bot$ works like a wild-card in proofs. For instance, suppose you want to give a proof of the argument $A \lor B, \neg A \therefore B$. You set up your proof, writing the premises $A \lor B$ and $\neg A$ at the top on lines 1 and 2, and the conclusion $B$ at the bottom of the page. $B$ has no main connective, so you can't work backward from it. Instead, you must work forward from $A \lor B$: That requires two subproofs, like so:

```
1      │ A ∨ B
2      │ ¬A
       ├──────
3      │ │ A
       │ │ ⋮
m      │ │ B
m + 1  │ │ B
       │ ├──────
       │ │ ⋮
k      │ │ B
k + 1  │ B        ∨E 1, 3–m, (m + 1)–k
```

Notice that you have $\neg A$ on line 2 and $A$ as the assumption of your first subproof. That gives you ⊥ using ¬E, and from ⊥ you get the conclusion $B$ of the first subroof using X. Recall that you can repeat a sentence you already have by using the reiteration rule R. So our proof would be:

```
1   │ A ∨ B
2   │ ¬A
    ├──────
3   │ │ A
4   │ │ ⊥      ¬E 2, 3
5   │ │ B      X 4
6   │ │ B
    │ ├──────
7   │ │ B      R 6
8   │ B        ∨E 1, 3–5, 6–7
```

## 17.5   Proceed indirectly

In very many cases, the strategies of working forward and backward will eventually pan out. But there are cases where they do not work. If you cannot find a way to show $\mathscr{A}$ directly using those, use IP instead. To do this, set up a subproof in which you assume $\neg\mathscr{A}$ and look for a proof of $\bot$ inside that subproof.

$$
\begin{array}{r|l|l}
n & \quad \neg A & \\
 & \quad \vdots & \\
m & \quad \bot & \\
m+1 & \mathscr{A} & \text{IP } n\text{--}m
\end{array}
$$

Here, we have to start a subproof with assumption $\neg\mathscr{A}$; the last line of the subproof has to be $\bot$. We'll cite the subproof, and use IP as the rule. In the subproof, we now have an additional assumption (on line $n$) to work with.

Suppose we used the indirect proof strategy, or we're in some other situation where we're looking for a proof of $\bot$. What's a good candidate? Of course the obvious candidate would be to use a negated sentence, since (as we saw above) $\neg$E always yields $\bot$. If you set up a proof as above, trying to prove $\mathscr{A}$ using IP, you will have $\neg\mathscr{A}$ as the assumption of your subproof—so working forward from it to justify $\bot$ inside your subproof, you would next set up $\mathscr{A}$ as a goal inside your subproof. If you are using this IP strategy, you will find yourself in the following situation:

$$
\begin{array}{r|l|l}
n & \quad \neg\mathscr{A} & \\
 & \quad \vdots & \\
m-1 & \quad \mathscr{A} & \\
m & \quad \bot & \neg\text{E } n, m-1 \\
m+1 & \mathscr{A} & \text{IP } n\text{--}m
\end{array}
$$

This looks weird: We wanted to prove $\mathscr{A}$ and the strategies failed us; so we used IP as a last resort. And now we find ourselves in the same situation: we are again looking for a proof of $\mathscr{A}$. But notice that we are now *inside* a subproof, and in that subproof we have an additional assumption ($\neg\mathscr{A}$) to work with which we didn't have before. Let's look at an example.

## 17.6  Indirect proof of excluded middle

The sentence $A \lor \neg A$ is a tautology, and so should have a proof even without any premises. But working backward fails us: to get $A \lor \neg A$ using $\lor$I we would have to prove either $A$ or $\neg A$—again, from no premises. Neither of these is a tautology, so we won't be able to prove either. Working forward doesn't work either, since there is nothing to work forward from. So, the only option is indirect proof.

| | | |
|---|---|---|
| 1 | $\neg(A \lor \neg A)$ | |
| | $\vdots$ | |
| $m$ | $\bot$ | |
| $m+1$ | $A \lor \neg A$ | IP 1–$m$ |

Now we do have something to work forward from: the assumption $\neg(A \lor \neg A)$. To use it, we justify $\bot$ by $\neg$E, citing the assumption on line 1, and also the corresponding unnegated sentence $A \lor \neg A$, yet to be proved.

| | | |
|---|---|---|
| 1 | $\neg(A \lor \neg A)$ | |
| | $\vdots$ | |
| $m-1$ | $A \lor \neg A$ | |
| $m$ | $\bot$ | $\neg$E 1, $m-1$ |
| $m+1$ | $A \lor \neg A$ | IP 1–$m$ |

At the outset, working backward to prove $A \vee \neg A$ by $\vee$I did not work. But we are now in a different situation: we want to prove $A \vee \neg A$ inside a subproof. In general, when dealing with new goals we should go back and start with the basic strategies. In this case, we should first try to work backward from the disjunction $A \vee \neg A$, i.e., we have to pick a disjunct and try to prove it. Let's pick $\neg A$. This would let us justify $A \vee \neg A$ on line $m - 1$ using $\vee$I. Then working backward from $\neg A$, we start another subproof in order to justify $\neg A$ using $\neg$I. That subproof must have $A$ as the assumption and $\perp$ as its last line.

| | | |
|---|---|---|
| 1 | $\neg(A \vee \neg A)$ | |
| 2 | $A$ | |
| | $\vdots$ | |
| $m - 3$ | $\perp$ | |
| $m - 2$ | $\neg A$ | $\neg$I 2–$(m - 3)$ |
| $m - 1$ | $A \vee \neg A$ | $\vee$I $m - 2$ |
| $m$ | $\perp$ | $\neg$E 1, $m - 1$ |
| $m + 1$ | $A \vee \neg A$ | IP 1–$m$ |

Inside this new subproof, we again need to justify $\perp$. The best way to do this is to work forward from a negated sentence; $\neg(A \vee \neg A)$ on line 1 is the only negated sentence we can use. The corresponding unnegated sentence, $A \vee \neg A$, however, directly follows from $A$ (which we have on line 2) by $\vee$I. Our complete proof is:

| | | |
|---|---|---|
| 1 | $\neg(A \vee \neg A)$ | |
| 2 | $A$ | |
| 3 | $A \vee \neg A$ | $\vee$I 2 |
| 4 | $\bot$ | $\neg$E 1, 3 |
| 5 | $\neg A$ | $\neg$I 2–4 |
| 6 | $A \vee \neg A$ | $\vee$I 5 |
| 7 | $\bot$ | $\neg$E 1, 6 |
| 8 | $A \vee \neg A$ | IP 1–7 |

## Practice exercises

**A.** Use the strategies to find proofs for each of the following arguments:

1. $A \rightarrow B, A \rightarrow C \therefore A \rightarrow (B \wedge C)$
2. $(A \wedge B) \rightarrow C \therefore A \rightarrow (B \rightarrow C)$
3. $A \rightarrow (B \rightarrow C) \therefore (A \rightarrow B) \rightarrow (A \rightarrow C)$
4. $A \vee (B \wedge C) \therefore (A \vee B) \wedge (A \vee C)$
5. $(A \wedge B) \vee (A \wedge C) \therefore A \wedge (B \vee C)$
6. $A \vee B, A \rightarrow C, B \rightarrow D \therefore C \vee D$
7. $\neg A \vee \neg B \therefore \neg(A \wedge B)$
8. $A \wedge \neg B \therefore \neg(A \rightarrow B)$

**B.** Formulate strategies for working backward and forward from $\mathcal{A} \leftrightarrow \mathcal{B}$.

**C.** Use the strategies to find proofs for each of the following sentences:

1. $\neg A \rightarrow (A \rightarrow \bot)$
2. $\neg(A \wedge \neg A)$
3. $[(A \rightarrow C) \wedge (B \rightarrow C)] \rightarrow [(A \vee B) \rightarrow C]$
4. $\neg(A \rightarrow B) \rightarrow (A \wedge \neg B)$

5. $(\neg A \lor B) \to (A \to B)$

Since these should be proofs of sentences from no premises, you will start with the respective sentence at the *bottom* of the proof, which will have no premises.

**D.** Use the strategies to find proofs for each one of the following arguments and sentences:

1. $\neg\neg A \to A$
2. $\neg A \to \neg B \therefore B \to A$
3. $A \to B \therefore \neg A \lor B$
4. $\neg(A \land B) \to (\neg A \lor \neg B)$
5. $A \to (B \lor C) \therefore (A \to B) \lor (A \to C)$
6. $(A \to B) \lor (B \to A)$
7. $((A \to B) \to A) \to A$

These all will require the IP strategy. The last three especially are quite hard!

## CHAPTER 18
# *Additional rules for TFL*

In §16, we introduced the basic rules of our proof system for TFL. In this section, we will add some additional rules to our system. Our extended proof system is a bit easier to work with. (However, in §20 we will see that they are not strictly speaking *necessary*.)

## 18.1 Disjunctive syllogism

Here is a very natural argument form.

> Elizabeth is either in Massachusetts or in DC. She is not in DC. So, she is in Massachusetts.

This is called *disjunctive syllogism*. We add it to our proof system as follows:

| | | |
|---|---|---|
| $m$ | $\mathcal{A} \lor \mathcal{B}$ | |
| $n$ | $\neg\mathcal{A}$ | |
| | $\mathcal{B}$ | DS $m$, $n$ |

and

$$
\begin{array}{r|l}
m & \mathcal{A} \lor \mathcal{B} \\[4pt]
n & \neg\mathcal{B} \\[4pt]
  & \mathcal{A} \qquad \text{DS } m,\, n
\end{array}
$$

As usual, the disjunction and the negation of one disjunct may occur in either order and need not be adjacent. However, we always cite the disjunction first.

## 18.2   Modus tollens

Another useful pattern of inference is embodied in the following argument:

> If Hilary has won the election, then he is in the White House. She is not in the White House. So she has not won the election.

This inference pattern is called *modus tollens*. The corresponding rule is:

$$
\begin{array}{r|l}
m & \mathcal{A} \to \mathcal{B} \\[4pt]
n & \neg\mathcal{B} \\[4pt]
  & \neg\mathcal{A} \qquad \text{MT } m,\, n
\end{array}
$$

As usual, the premises may occur in either order, but we always cite the conditional first.

## 18.3  Double-negation elimination

Another useful rule is *double-negation elimination*. It does exactly what it says on the tin:

$$
\begin{array}{ll}
m & \neg\neg\mathcal{A} \\[2mm]
   & \mathcal{A} \qquad \text{DNE } m
\end{array}
$$

The justification for this is that, in natural language, double-negations tend to cancel out.

That said, you should be aware that context and emphasis can prevent them from doing so. Consider: 'Jane is not *not* happy'. Arguably, one cannot infer 'Jane is happy', since the first sentence should be understood as meaning the same as 'Jane is not *un*happy'. This is compatible with 'Jane is in a state of profound indifference'. As usual, moving to TFL forces us to sacrifice certain nuances of English expressions.

## 18.4  Excluded middle

Suppose that we can show that if it's sunny outside, then Bill will have brought an umbrella (for fear of burning). Suppose we can also show that, if it's not sunny outside, then Bill will have brought an umbrella (for fear of rain). Well, there is no third way for the weather to be. So, *whatever the weather*, Bill will have brought an umbrella.

This line of thinking motivates the following rule:

$$
\begin{array}{ll}
i & \quad \mathcal{A} \\
j & \quad \mathcal{B} \\
k & \quad \neg\mathcal{A} \\
l & \quad \mathcal{B} \\
& \mathcal{B} \qquad \text{LEM } i\text{-}j,\, k\text{-}l
\end{array}
$$

The rule is sometimes called the law of *excluded middle*, since it encapsulates the idea that $\mathcal{A}$ may be true or $\neg\mathcal{A}$ may be true, but there is no middle way where neither is true.[1] There can be as many lines as you like between $i$ and $j$, and as many lines as you like between $k$ and $l$. Moreover, the subproofs can come in any order, and the second subproof does not need to come immediately after the first.

To see the rule in action, consider:

$$P \therefore (P \land D) \lor (P \land \neg D)$$

Here is a proof corresponding with the argument:

---

[1] You may sometimes find logicians or philosophers talking about "tertium non datur." That's the same principle as excluded middle; it means "no third way." Logicians who have qualms about indirect proof also have qualms about LEM.

```
1 │ P
  │
2 │   │ D
  │   ├─────
3 │   │ P ∧ D                    ∧I 1, 2
  │   │
4 │   │ (P ∧ D) ∨ (P ∧ ¬D)      ∨I 3
  │   │
5 │   │ ¬D
  │   ├─────
6 │   │ P ∧ ¬D                   ∧I 1, 5
  │   │
7 │   │ (P ∧ D) ∨ (P ∧ ¬D)      ∨I 6
  │
8 │ (P ∧ D) ∨ (P ∧ ¬D)          LEM 2–4, 5–7
```

Here is another example:

```
1 │ A → ¬A
  ├────────
2 │   │ A
  │   ├─────
3 │   │ ¬A        →E 1, 2
  │   │
4 │   │ ¬A
  │   ├─────
5 │   │ ¬A        R 4
  │
6 │ ¬A            LEM 2–3, 4–5
```

## 18.5  De Morgan Rules

Our final additional rules are called De Morgan's Laws (named after Augustus De Morgan). The shape of the rules should be familiar from truth tables.

The first De Morgan rule is:

$$m \quad | \quad \neg(\mathscr{A} \wedge \mathscr{B})$$

$$\quad | \quad \neg\mathscr{A} \vee \neg\mathscr{B} \quad \text{DeM } m$$

The second De Morgan is the reverse of the first:

$$m \quad | \quad \neg\mathscr{A} \vee \neg\mathscr{B}$$

$$\quad | \quad \neg(\mathscr{A} \wedge \mathscr{B}) \quad \text{DeM } m$$

The third De Morgan rule is the *dual* of the first:

$$m \quad | \quad \neg(\mathscr{A} \vee \mathscr{B})$$

$$\quad | \quad \neg\mathscr{A} \wedge \neg\mathscr{B} \quad \text{DeM } m$$

And the fourth is the reverse of the third:

$$m \quad | \quad \neg\mathscr{A} \wedge \neg\mathscr{B}$$

$$\quad | \quad \neg(\mathscr{A} \vee \mathscr{B}) \quad \text{DeM } m$$

*These are all of the additional rules of our proof system for TFL.*

## Practice exercises

**A.** The following proofs are missing their citations (rule and line numbers). Add them wherever they are required:

1.

| | 1 | $W \rightarrow \neg B$ |
|---|---|---|
| | 2 | $A \wedge W$ |
| | 3 | $B \vee (J \wedge K)$ |
| | 4 | $W$ |
| | 5 | $\neg B$ |
| | 6 | $J \wedge K$ |
| | 7 | $K$ |

2.

| | 1 | $L \leftrightarrow \neg O$ |
|---|---|---|
| | 2 | $L \vee \neg O$ |
| | 3 | $\neg L$ |
| | 4 | $\neg O$ |
| | 5 | $L$ |
| | 6 | $\bot$ |
| | 7 | $\neg\neg L$ |
| | 8 | $L$ |

3.

| | | |
|---|---|---|
| 1 | $Z \rightarrow (C \wedge \neg N)$ | |
| 2 | $\neg Z \rightarrow (N \wedge \neg C)$ | |
| 3 | $\neg(N \vee C)$ | |
| 4 | $\neg N \wedge \neg C$ | |
| 5 | $\neg N$ | |
| 6 | $\neg C$ | |
| 7 | $Z$ | |
| 8 | $C \wedge \neg N$ | |
| 9 | $C$ | |
| 10 | $\bot$ | |
| 11 | $\neg Z$ | |
| 12 | $N \wedge \neg C$ | |
| 13 | $N$ | |
| 14 | $\bot$ | |
| 15 | $\neg\neg(N \vee C)$ | |
| 16 | $N \vee C$ | |

**B.** Give a proof for each of these arguments:

1. $E \vee F$, $F \vee G$, $\neg F$ $\therefore E \wedge G$
2. $M \vee (N \rightarrow M)$ $\therefore \neg M \rightarrow \neg N$
3. $(M \vee N) \wedge (O \vee P)$, $N \rightarrow P$, $\neg P$ $\therefore M \wedge O$
4. $(X \wedge Y) \vee (X \wedge Z)$, $\neg(X \wedge D)$, $D \vee M$ $\therefore M$

# CHAPTER 19
# *Proof-theoretic concepts*

In this chapter we will introduce some new vocabulary. The following expression:

$$\mathcal{A}_1, \mathcal{A}_2, \ldots, \mathcal{A}_n \vdash \mathcal{C}$$

means that there is some proof which ends with $\mathcal{C}$ whose undischarged assumptions are among $\mathcal{A}_1, \mathcal{A}_2, \ldots, \mathcal{A}_n$. When we want to say that it is *not* the case that there is some proof which ends with $\mathcal{C}$ from $\mathcal{A}_1, \mathcal{A}_2, \ldots, \mathcal{A}_n$, we write:

$$\mathcal{A}_1, \mathcal{A}_2, \ldots, \mathcal{A}_n \nvdash \mathcal{C}$$

The symbol '$\vdash$' is called the *single turnstile*. We want to emphasize that this is not the double turnstile symbol ('$\vDash$') that we introduced in chapter 12 to symbolize entailment. The single turnstile, '$\vdash$', concerns the existence of proofs; the double turnstile, '$\vDash$', concerns the existence of valuations (or interpretations, when used for FOL). *They are very different notions.*

Armed with our '$\vdash$' symbol, we can introduce some more terminology. To say that there is a proof of $\mathcal{A}$ with no undischarged assumptions, we write: $\vdash \mathcal{A}$. In this case, we say that $\mathcal{A}$ is a THEOREM.

$\mathcal{A}$ is a THEOREM iff $\vdash \mathcal{A}$

To illustrate this, suppose we want to show that '$\neg(A \wedge \neg A)$' is a theorem. So we need a proof of '$\neg(A \wedge \neg A)$' which has *no* undischarged assumptions. However, since we want to prove a sentence whose main logical operator is a negation, we will want to start with a *subproof* within which we assume '$A \wedge \neg A$', and show that this assumption leads to contradiction. All told, then, the proof looks like this:

| | | |
|---|---|---|
| 1 | $A \wedge \neg A$ | |
| 2 | $A$ | $\wedge$E 1 |
| 3 | $\neg A$ | $\wedge$E 1 |
| 4 | $\bot$ | $\neg$E 3, 2 |
| 5 | $\neg(A \wedge \neg A)$ | $\neg$I 1–4 |

We have therefore proved '$\neg(A \wedge \neg A)$' on no (undischarged) assumptions. This particular theorem is an instance of what is sometimes called *the Law of Non-Contradiction*.

To show that something is a theorem, you just have to find a suitable proof. It is typically much harder to show that something is *not* a theorem. To do this, you would have to demonstrate, not just that certain proof strategies fail, but that *no* proof is possible. Even if you fail in trying to prove a sentence in a thousand different ways, perhaps the proof is just too long and complex for you to make out. Perhaps you just didn't try hard enough.

Here is another new bit of terminology:

Two sentences $\mathcal{A}$ and $\mathcal{B}$ are PROVABLY EQUIVALENT iff each can be proved from the other; i.e., both $\mathcal{A} \vdash \mathcal{B}$ and $\mathcal{B} \vdash \mathcal{A}$.

As in the case of showing that a sentence is a theorem, it is relatively easy to show that two sentences are provably equivalent:

it just requires a pair of proofs. Showing that sentences are *not* provably equivalent would be much harder: it is just as hard as showing that a sentence is not a theorem.

Here is a third, related, bit of terminology:

> The sentences $\mathcal{A}_1, \mathcal{A}_2, \ldots, \mathcal{A}_n$ are JOINTLY INCONSISTENT iff the contradiction $\bot$ can be proved from them, i.e., $\mathcal{A}_1, \mathcal{A}_2, \ldots, \mathcal{A}_n \vdash \bot$. If they are not INCONSISTENT, we call them JOINTLY CONSISTENT.

It is easy to show that some sentences are inconsistent: you just need to prove the contradiction $\bot$, assuming all the sentences as premises. Showing that some sentences are *not* inconsistent is much harder. It would require more than just providing a proof or two; it would require showing that no proof of a certain kind is *possible*.

This table summarises whether one or two proofs suffice, or whether we must reason about all possible proofs.

|  | **Yes** | **No** |
|---|---|---|
| theorem? | one proof | all possible proofs |
| inconsistent? | one proof | all possible proofs |
| equivalent? | two proofs | all possible proofs |
| consistent? | all possible proofs | one proof |

## Practice exercises

**A.** Show that each of the following sentences is a theorem:

1. $O \to O$
2. $N \vee \neg N$
3. $J \leftrightarrow [J \vee (L \wedge \neg L)]$
4. $((A \to B) \to A) \to A$

**B.** Provide proofs to show each of the following:

1. $C \to (E \wedge G), \neg C \to G \vdash G$
2. $M \wedge (\neg N \to \neg M) \vdash (N \wedge M) \vee \neg M$
3. $(Z \wedge K) \leftrightarrow (Y \wedge M), D \wedge (D \to M) \vdash Y \to Z$
4. $(W \vee X) \vee (Y \vee Z), X \to Y, \neg Z \vdash W \vee Y$

**C.** Show that each of the following pairs of sentences are provably equivalent:

1. $R \leftrightarrow E, E \leftrightarrow R$
2. $G, \neg\neg\neg\neg G$
3. $T \to S, \neg S \to \neg T$
4. $U \to I, \neg(U \wedge \neg I)$
5. $\neg(C \to D), C \wedge \neg D$
6. $\neg G \leftrightarrow H, \neg(G \leftrightarrow H)$

**D.** If you know that $\mathscr{A} \vdash \mathscr{B}$, what can you say about $(\mathscr{A} \wedge \mathscr{C}) \vdash \mathscr{B}$? What about $(\mathscr{A} \vee \mathscr{C}) \vdash \mathscr{B}$? Explain your answers.

**E.** In this chapter, we claimed that it is just as hard to show that two sentences are not provably equivalent, as it is to show that a sentence is not a theorem. Why did we claim this? (*Hint*: think of a sentence that would be a theorem iff $\mathscr{A}$ and $\mathscr{B}$ were provably equivalent.)

# CHAPTER 20

# *Derived rules*

In this section, we will see why we introduced the rules of our proof system in two separate batches. In particular, we want to show that the additional rules of §18 are not strictly speaking necessary, but can be derived from the basic rules of §16.

## 20.1  Derivation of Reiteration

To illustrate what it means to derive a *rule* from other rules, first consider reiteration. It is a basic rule of our system, but it is also not necessary. Suppose you have some sentence on some line of your deduction:

$$m \quad \big| \quad \mathcal{A}$$

You now want to repeat yourself, on some line $k$. You could just invoke the rule R. But equally well, you can do this with other basic rules of §16:

| | | |
|---|---|---|
| $m$ | $\mathcal{A}$ | |
| $k$ | $\mathcal{A} \wedge \mathcal{A}$ | $\wedge$I $m, m$ |
| $k+1$ | $\mathcal{A}$ | $\wedge$E $k$ |

173

To be clear: this is not a proof. Rather, it is a proof *scheme*. After all, it uses a variable, '$\mathcal{A}$', rather than a sentence of TFL, but the point is simple: Whatever sentences of TFL we plugged in for '$\mathcal{A}$', and whatever lines we were working on, we could produce a bona fide proof. So you can think of this as a recipe for producing proofs.

Indeed, it is a recipe which shows us the following: anything we can prove using the rule R, we can prove (with one more line) using just the basic rules of §16 without R. That is what it means to say that the rule R can be derived from the other basic rules: anything that can be justified using R can be justified using only the other basic rules.

## 20.2 Derivation of Disjunctive Syllogism

Suppose that you are in a proof, and you have something of this form:

$$m \quad | \quad \mathcal{A} \lor \mathcal{B}$$

$$n \quad | \quad \neg\mathcal{A}$$

You now want, on line $k$, to prove $\mathcal{B}$. You can do this with the rule of DS, introduced in §18, but equally well, you can do this with the *basic* rules of §16:

| | | | |
|---|---|---|---|
| $m$ | $\mathcal{A} \vee \mathcal{B}$ | | |
| $n$ | $\neg\mathcal{A}$ | | |
| $k$ | | $\mathcal{A}$ | |
| $k+1$ | | $\bot$ | $\neg$E $n, k$ |
| $k+2$ | | $\mathcal{B}$ | X $k+1$ |
| $k+3$ | | $\mathcal{B}$ | |
| $k+4$ | | $\mathcal{B}$ | R $k+3$ |
| $k+5$ | $\mathcal{B}$ | | $\vee$E $m, k$–$k+2, k+3$–$k+4$ |

So the DS rule, again, can be derived from our more basic rules. Adding it to our system did not make any new proofs possible. Anytime you use the DS rule, you could always take a few extra lines and prove the same thing using only our basic rules. It is a *derived* rule.

## 20.3 Derivation of Modus Tollens

Suppose you have the following in your proof:

| | |
|---|---|
| $m$ | $\mathcal{A} \to \mathcal{B}$ |
| $n$ | $\neg\mathcal{B}$ |

You now want, on line $k$, to prove $\neg\mathcal{A}$. You can do this with the rule of MT, introduced in §18. Equally well, you can do this with the *basic* rules of §16:

$$
\begin{array}{r|ll}
m & \mathscr{A} \to \mathscr{B} & \\
n & \neg\mathscr{B} & \\
k & \quad\mid \mathscr{A} & \\
k+1 & \quad\mid \mathscr{B} & \to\!\text{E } m,\, k \\
k+2 & \quad\mid \bot & \neg\text{E } n,\, k+1 \\
k+3 & \neg\mathscr{A} & \neg\text{I } k\text{--}k+2
\end{array}
$$

Again, the rule of MT can be derived from the *basic* rules of §16.

## 20.4  Derivation of Double-Negation Elimination

Consider the following deduction scheme:

$$
\begin{array}{r|ll}
m & \neg\neg\mathscr{A} & \\
k & \quad\mid \neg\mathscr{A} & \\
k+1 & \quad\mid \bot & \neg\text{E } m,\, k \\
k+2 & \mathscr{A} & \text{IP } k\text{--}k+1
\end{array}
$$

Again, we can derive the DNE rule from the *basic* rules of §16.

## 20.5  Derivation of Excluded Middle

Suppose you want to prove something using the LEM rule, i.e., you have in your proof

$$
\begin{array}{c|l}
m & \mathcal{A} \\
 & \overline{\phantom{xx}} \\
n & \mathcal{B} \\
k & \neg\mathcal{A} \\
 & \overline{\phantom{xx}} \\
l & \mathcal{B}
\end{array}
$$

You now want, on line $l+1$, to prove $\mathcal{B}$. The rule LEM from §18 would allow you to do it. But can do this with the *basic* rules of §16?

One option is to first prove $\mathcal{A} \vee \neg\mathcal{A}$, and then apply $\vee$E, i.e. proof by cases:

$$
\begin{array}{c|l}
m & \mathcal{A} \\
 & \overline{\phantom{xx}} \\
n & \mathcal{B} \\
k & \neg\mathcal{A} \\
 & \overline{\phantom{xx}} \\
l & \mathcal{B} \\
 & \vdots \\
i & \mathcal{A} \vee \neg\mathcal{A} \\
i+1 & \mathcal{B} \qquad \vee\text{E } i,\ m\text{--}n,\ k\text{--}l
\end{array}
$$

(We gave a proof of $\mathcal{A} \vee \neg\mathcal{A}$ using only our basic rules in §17.6.)

Here is another way that is a bit more complicated than the ones before. What you have to do is embed your two subproofs inside another subproof. The assumption of the subproof will be $\neg\mathcal{B}$, and the last line will be $\bot$. Thus, the complete subproof is the kind you need to conclude $\mathcal{B}$ using IP. Inside the proof, you'd have to do a bit more work to get $\bot$:

$$
\begin{array}{lll}
m & \neg\mathcal{B} & \\
m+1 & \quad \mathcal{A} & \\
& \quad \vdots & \\
n & \quad \mathcal{B} & \\
n+1 & \quad \bot & \neg\text{E } m,\, n \\
n+2 & \quad \neg\mathcal{A} & \\
& \quad \vdots & \\
l & \quad \mathcal{B} & \\
l+1 & \quad \bot & \neg\text{E } m,\, l \\
l+2 & \quad \neg\mathcal{A} & \neg\text{I } (m+1)\text{–}(n+1) \\
l+3 & \quad \neg\neg\mathcal{A} & \neg\text{I } (n+2)\text{–}(l+1) \\
l+4 & \quad \bot & \neg\text{E } l+3,\, l+2 \\
l+5 & \mathcal{B} & \text{IP } m\text{–}(l+4)
\end{array}
$$

Note that because we add an assumption at the top and additional conclusions inside the subproofs, the line numbers change. You may have to stare at this for a while before you understand what's going on.

## 20.6 Derivation of De Morgan rules

Here is a demonstration of how we could derive the first De Morgan rule:

| | | |
|---|---|---|
| $m$ | $\neg(\mathcal{A} \wedge \mathcal{B})$ | |
| $k$ | $\mathcal{A}$ | |
| $k+1$ | $\mathcal{B}$ | |
| $k+2$ | $\mathcal{A} \wedge \mathcal{B}$ | $\wedge$I $k, k+1$ |
| $k+3$ | $\bot$ | $\neg$E $m, k+2$ |
| $k+4$ | $\neg\mathcal{B}$ | $\neg$I $k+1$–$k+3$ |
| $k+5$ | $\neg\mathcal{A} \vee \neg\mathcal{B}$ | $\vee$I $k+4$ |
| $k+6$ | $\neg\mathcal{A}$ | |
| $k+7$ | $\neg\mathcal{A} \vee \neg\mathcal{B}$ | $\vee$I $k+6$ |
| $k+8$ | $\neg\mathcal{A} \vee \neg\mathcal{B}$ | LEM $k$–$k+5$, $k+6$–$k+7$ |

Here is a demonstration of how we could derive the second De Morgan rule:

| | | |
|---|---|---|
| $m$ | $\neg\mathcal{A} \vee \neg\mathcal{B}$ | |
| $k$ | $\mathcal{A} \wedge \mathcal{B}$ | |
| $k+1$ | $\mathcal{A}$ | $\wedge$E $k$ |
| $k+2$ | $\mathcal{B}$ | $\wedge$E $k$ |
| $k+3$ | $\neg\mathcal{A}$ | |
| $k+4$ | $\bot$ | $\neg$E $k+3, k+1$ |
| $k+5$ | $\neg\mathcal{B}$ | |
| $k+6$ | $\bot$ | $\neg$E $k+5, k+2$ |
| $k+7$ | $\bot$ | $\vee$E $m, k+3$–$k+4$, $k+5$–$k+6$ |
| $k+8$ | $\neg(\mathcal{A} \wedge \mathcal{B})$ | $\neg$I $k$–$k+7$ |

Similar demonstrations can be offered explaining how we could derive the third and fourth De Morgan rules. These are left as exercises.

## Practice exercises

**A**. Provide proof schemes that justify the addition of the third and fourth De Morgan rules as derived rules.

**B**. The proofs you offered in response to the practice exercises of §§18–19 used derived rules. Replace the use of derived rules, in such proofs, with only basic rules. You will find some 'repetition' in the resulting proofs; in such cases, offer a streamlined proof using only basic rules. (This will give you a sense, both of the power of derived rules, and of how all the rules interact.)

**C**. Give a proof of $\mathcal{A} \vee \neg \mathcal{A}$. Then give a proof that *uses only the basic rules.*

**D**. Show that if you had LEM as a basic rule, you could justify IP as a derived rule. That is, suppose you had the proof:

$$
\begin{array}{c|c|l}
m & & \neg\mathcal{A} \\
 & & \overline{\phantom{xxx}} \\
 & & \cdots \\
n & & \bot
\end{array}
$$

How could you use it to prove $\mathcal{A}$ without using IP but with using LEM as well as all the other basic rules?

**E**. Give a proof of the first De Morgan rule, but using only the basic rules, in particular, *without using LEM.* (Of course, you can combine the proof using LEM with the proof *of* LEM. Try to find a proof directly.)

# CHAPTER 21

# *Soundness and completeness*

In §19, we saw that we could use derivations to test for the same concepts we used truth tables to test for. Not only could we use derivations to prove that an argument is valid, we could also use them to test if a sentence is a tautology or a pair of sentences are equivalent. We also started using the single turnstile the same way we used the double turnstile. If we could prove that $\mathcal{A}$ was a tautology using a truth table, we wrote $\vDash \mathcal{A}$, and if we could prove it using a derivation, we wrote $\vdash \mathcal{A}$.

You may have wondered at that point if the two kinds of turnstiles always worked the same way. If you can show that $\mathcal{A}$ is a tautology using truth tables, can you also always show that it is a theorem using a derivation? Is the reverse true? Are these things also true for valid arguments and pairs of equivalent sentences? As it turns out, the answer to all these questions and many more like them is yes. We can show this by defining all these concepts separately and then proving them equivalent. That is, we imag-

181

ine that we actually have two notions of validity, valid$_\vDash$ and valid$_\vdash$ and then show that the two concepts always work the same way.

To begin with, we need to define all of our logical concepts separately for truth tables and derivations. A lot of this work has already been done. We handled all of the truth table definitions in §12. We have also already given proof-theoretic definitions for theorems and pairs of logically equivalent sentences. The other definitions follow naturally. For most logical properties we can devise a test using derivations, and those that we cannot test for directly can be defined in terms of the concepts that we can define.

For instance, we defined a theorem as a sentence that can be derived without any premises (p. 170). Since the negation of a contradiction is a tautology, we can define an INCONSISTENT SENTENCE IN TFL as a sentence whose negation can be derived without any premises.[1] The syntactic definition of a contingent sentence is a little different. We don't have any practical, finite method for proving that a sentence is contingent using derivations, the way we did using truth tables. So we have to content ourselves with defining "contingent sentence" negatively. A sentence is PROOF-THEORETICALLY CONTINGENT IN TFL if it is neither a theorem nor an inconsistent sentence.

A collection of sentences is INCONSISTENT IN TFL if and only if one can derive the contradiction $\bot$ from them. Consistency, on the other hand, is like contingency, in that we do not have a practical finite method to test for it directly. So again, we have to define a term negatively. A collection of sentences is CONSISTENT IN TFL if and only if they are not inconsistent.

Finally, an argument is PROVABLY VALID IN TFL if and only if there is a derivation of its conclusion from its premises. All of these definitions are given in Table 21.1.

All of our concepts have now been defined both semantically (using valuations and truth tables) and proof-theoretically (on the basis of natural deduction). How can we establish that these

---

[1] Note that $\neg\mathcal{A}$ is a theorem iff $\mathcal{A} \vdash \bot$.

| Concept | Truth table (semantic) definition | Proof-theoretic (syntactic) definition |
|---|---|---|
| Tautology/ theorem | A sentence whose truth table only has Ts under the main connective | A sentence that can be derived without any premises. |
| Contradiction/ inconsistent sentence | A sentence whose truth table only has Fs under the main connective | A sentence whose negation can be derived without any premises |
| Contingent sentence | A sentence whose truth table contains both Ts and Fs under the main connective | A sentence that is not a theorem or contradiction |
| Equivalent sentences | The columns under the main connectives are identical. | The sentences can be derived from each other |
| Unsatisfiable/ inconsistent sentences | Sentences which do not have a single line in their truth table where they are all true. | Sentences from which one can derive the contradiction $\bot$ |
| Satisfiable/ Consistent sentences | Sentences which have at least one line in their truth table where they are all true. | Sentences from which one cannot derive the contradiction $\bot$ |
| Valid argument | An argument whose truth table has no lines where there are all Ts under main connectives for the premises and an F under the main connective for the conclusion. | An argument where one can derive the conclusion from the premises |

*Table 21.1: Two ways to define logical concepts.*

definitions always work the same way? A full proof here goes well beyond the scope of this book. However, we can sketch what it would be like. We will focus on showing the two notions of validity to be equivalent. From that the other concepts will follow quickly. The proof will have to go in two directions. First we will have to show that things which are proof-theoretically valid will also be semantically valid. In other words, everything that we can prove using derivations could also be proven using truth tables. Put symbolically, we want to show that valid⊢ implies valid⊨. Afterwards, we will need to show things in the other directions, valid⊨ implies valid⊢.

This argument from ⊢ to ⊨ is the problem of SOUNDNESS. A proof system is SOUND if there are no derivations of arguments that can be shown invalid by truth tables. Demonstrating that the proof system is sound would require showing that *any* possible proof is the proof of a valid argument. It would not be enough simply to succeed when trying to prove many valid arguments and to fail when trying to prove invalid ones.

The proof that we will sketch depends on the fact that we initially defined a sentence of TFL using an inductive definition (see p. 51). We could have also used inductive definitions to define a proper proof in TFL and a proper truth table (although we didn't.) If we had these definitions, we could then use an *inductive proof* to show the soundness of TFL. An inductive proof works the same way as an inductive definition. With the inductive definition, we identified a group of base elements that were stipulated to be examples of the thing we were trying to define. In the case of a TFL sentence, the base class was the set of sentence letters $A, B, C, \ldots$. We just announced that these were sentences. The second step of an inductive definition is to say that anything that is built up from your base class using certain rules also counts as an example of the thing you are defining. In the case of a definition of a sentence, the rules corresponded to the five sentential connectives (see p. 51). Once you have established an inductive definition, you can use that definition to show that all the members of the class you have defined have a certain property. You simply prove that the property is true of the members of the base class, and then you prove that the rules for extending the base class don't change the property. This is what it means to give an inductive proof.

Even though we don't have an inductive definition of a proof in TFL, we can sketch how an inductive proof of the soundness of TFL would go. Imagine a base class of one-line proofs, one for each of our eleven rules of inference. The members of this class would look like this $\mathcal{A}, \mathcal{B} \vdash \mathcal{A} \wedge \mathcal{B}$; $\mathcal{A} \wedge \mathcal{B} \vdash \mathcal{A}$; $\mathcal{A} \vee \mathcal{B}, \neg \mathcal{A} \vdash \mathcal{B} \ldots$ etc. Since some rules have a couple different forms, we would have to have add some members to this base class, for instance $\mathcal{A} \wedge \mathcal{B} \vdash \mathcal{B}$ Notice that these are all statements in the metalanguage. The proof that TFL is sound is not a part of TFL, because TFL does not have the power to talk about itself.

You can use truth tables to prove to yourself that each of these one-line proofs in this base class is valid$_\vDash$. For instance the proof $\mathcal{A}, \mathcal{B} \vdash \mathcal{A} \wedge \mathcal{B}$ corresponds to a truth table that shows $\mathcal{A}, \mathcal{B} \vDash \mathcal{A} \wedge \mathcal{B}$ This establishes the first part of our inductive proof.

The next step is to show that adding lines to any proof will never change a valid$_\vDash$ proof into an invalid$_\vDash$ one. We would need to do this for each of our eleven basic rules of inference. So, for instance, for $\wedge$I we need to show that for any proof $\mathcal{A}_1, \ldots,$ $\mathcal{A}_n \vdash \mathcal{B}$ adding a line where we use $\wedge$I to infer $\mathcal{C} \wedge \mathcal{D}$, where $\mathcal{C} \wedge \mathcal{D}$ can be legitimately inferred from $\mathcal{A}_1, \ldots, \mathcal{A}_n, \mathcal{B}$, would not change a valid proof into an invalid proof. But wait, if we can legitimately derive $\mathcal{C} \wedge \mathcal{D}$ from these premises, then $\mathcal{C}$ and $\mathcal{D}$ must be already available in the proof. They are either already among $\mathcal{A}_1, \ldots, \mathcal{A}_n, \mathcal{B}$, or can be legitimately derived from them. As such, any truth table line in which the premises are true must be a truth table line in which $\mathcal{C}$ and $\mathcal{D}$ are true. According to the characteristic truth table for $\wedge$, this means that $\mathcal{C} \wedge \mathcal{D}$ is also true on that line. Therefore, $\mathcal{C} \wedge \mathcal{D}$ validly follows from the premises. This means that using the $\wedge$E rule to extend a valid proof produces another valid proof.

In order to show that the proof system is sound, we would need to show this for the other inference rules. Since the derived rules are consequences of the basic rules, it would suffice to provide similar arguments for the 11 other basic rules. You can find the details of this proof worked out in Chapter 46.

So we have shown that $\mathcal{A} \vdash \mathcal{B}$ implies $\mathcal{A} \vDash \mathcal{B}$. What about the other direction, that is, why think that *every* argument that can be shown valid using truth tables can also be proven using a derivation?

This is the problem of completeness. A proof system has the property of COMPLETENESS if and only if there is a derivation of every semantically valid argument. Proving that a system is complete is generally harder than proving that it is sound. Proving that a system is sound amounts to showing that all of the rules of your proof system work the way they are supposed to. Showing that a system is complete means showing that you have included *all* the rules you need, that you haven't left any out. Showing this is beyond the scope of this book. The important point is that, happily, the proof system for TFL is both sound and complete. This is not the case for all proof systems or all formal languages. Because it is true of TFL, we can choose to give proofs or give truth tables—whichever is easier for the task at hand.

Now that we know that the truth table method is interchangeable with the method of derivations, you can chose which method you want to use for any given problem. Students often prefer to use truth tables, because they can be produced purely mechanically, and that seems 'easier'. However, we have already seen that truth tables become impossibly large after just a few sentence letters. On the other hand, there are a couple situations where using proofs simply isn't possible. We syntactically defined a contingent sentence as a sentence that couldn't be proven to be a tautology or a contradiction. There is no practical way to prove this kind of negative statement. We will never know if there isn't some proof out there that a statement is a contradiction and we just haven't found it yet. We have nothing to do in this situation but resort to truth tables. Similarly, we can use derivations to prove two sentences equivalent, but what if we want to prove that they are *not* equivalent? We have no way of proving that we will never find

| Logical property | To prove it present | To prove it absent |
|---|---|---|
| Being a theorem | Derive the sentence | Find a false line in the truth table for the sentence |
| Being a contradiction | Derive the negation of the sentence | Find a true line in the truth table for the sentence |
| Contingency | Find a false line and a true line in the truth table for the sentence | Prove the sentence or its negation |
| Equivalence | Derive each sentence from the other | Find a line in the truth tables for the sentence where they have different values |
| Consistency | Find a line in truth table for the sentence where they all are true | Derive a contradiction from the sentences |
| Validity | Derive the conclusion from the premises | Find a line in the truth table where the premises are true and the conclusion false. |

*Table 21.2: When to provide a truth table and when to provide a proof.*

the relevant proof. So we have to fall back on truth tables again.

Table 21.2 summarizes when it is best to give proofs and when it is best to give truth tables.

## Practice exercises

**A.** Use either a derivation or a truth table for each of the following.

1. Show that $A \rightarrow [((B \wedge C) \vee D) \rightarrow A]$ is a theorem.

2. Show that $A \rightarrow (A \rightarrow B)$ is not a theorem.

3. Show that the sentence $A \rightarrow \neg A$ is not a contradiction.

4. Show that the sentence $A \leftrightarrow \neg A$ is a contradiction.

5. Show that the sentence $\neg(W \rightarrow (J \lor J))$ is contingent.

6. Show that the sentence $\neg(X \lor (Y \lor Z)) \lor (X \lor (Y \lor Z))$ is not contingent.

7. Show that the sentence $B \rightarrow \neg S$ is equivalent to the sentence $\neg\neg B \rightarrow \neg S$.

8. Show that the sentence $\neg(X \lor O)$ is not equivalent to the sentence $X \land O$.

9. Show that the sentences $\neg(A \lor B)$, $C$, $C \rightarrow A$ are jointly inconsistent.

10. Show that the sentences $\neg(A \lor B)$, $\neg B$, $B \rightarrow A$ are jointly consistent.

11. Show that $\neg(A \lor (B \lor C)) \therefore \neg C$ is valid.

12. Show that $\neg(A \land (B \lor C)) \therefore \neg C$ is invalid.

**B**. Use either a derivation or a truth table for each of the following.

1. Show that $A \rightarrow (B \rightarrow A)$ is a theoremy.

2. Show that $\neg(((N \leftrightarrow Q) \lor Q) \lor N)$ is not a theorem.

3. Show that $Z \lor (\neg Z \leftrightarrow Z)$ is contingent.

4. show that $(L \leftrightarrow ((N \rightarrow N) \rightarrow L)) \lor H$ is not contingent.

5. Show that $(A \leftrightarrow A) \land (B \land \neg B)$ is a contradiction.

6. Show that $(B \leftrightarrow (C \lor B))$ is not a contradiction.

7. Show that $((\neg X \leftrightarrow X) \vee X)$ is equivalent to $X$.

8. Show that $F \wedge (K \wedge R)$ is not equivalent to $(F \leftrightarrow (K \leftrightarrow R))$.

9. Show that the sentences $\neg(W \rightarrow W)$, $(W \leftrightarrow W) \wedge W$, $E \vee (W \rightarrow \neg(E \wedge W))$ are jointly inconsistent.

10. Show that the sentences $\neg R \vee C$, $(C \wedge R) \rightarrow \neg R$, $(\neg(R \vee R) \rightarrow R)$ are jointly consistent.

11. Show that $\neg\neg(C \leftrightarrow \neg C), ((G \vee C) \vee G) \therefore ((G \rightarrow C) \wedge G)$ is valid.

12. Show that $\neg\neg L, (C \rightarrow \neg L) \rightarrow C) \therefore \neg C$ is invalid.

# PART V

# *First-order logic*

# CHAPTER 22

# *Building blocks of FOL*

## 22.1   The need to decompose sentences

Consider the following argument, which is obviously valid in English:

> Willard is a logician.
> All logicians wear funny hats.
> ∴ Willard wears a funny hat.

To symbolize it in TFL, we might offer a symbolization key:

> $L$: Willard is a logician.
> $A$: All logicians wear funny hats.
> $F$: Willard wears a funny hat.

And the argument itself becomes:

$$L, A \therefore F$$

But the truth-table test will now indicate that this is *invalid*. What has gone wrong?

The problem is not that we have made a mistake while symbolizing the argument. This is the best symbolization we can give *in TFL*. The problem lies with TFL itself. 'All logicians wear funny hats' is about both logicians and hat-wearing. By not retaining this structure in our symbolization, we lose the connection between Willard's being a logician and Willard's wearing a hat.

The basic units of TFL are sentence letters, and TFL cannot decompose these. To symbolize arguments like the preceding one, we will have to develop a new logical language which will allow us to *split the atom*. We will call this language *first-order logic*, or *FOL*.

The details of FOL will be explained throughout this chapter, but here is the basic idea for splitting the atom.

First, we have *names*. In FOL, we indicate these with lowercase italic letters. For instance, we might let '$b$' stand for Bertie, or let '$i$' stand for Willard.

Second, we have predicates. English predicates are expressions like '_____ is a dog' or '_____ is a logician'. These are not complete sentences by themselves. In order to make a complete sentence, we need to fill in the gap. We need to say something like 'Bertie is a dog' or 'Willard is a logician'. In FOL, we indicate predicates with uppercase italic letters. For instance, we might let the FOL predicate '$D$' symbolize the English predicate '_____ is a dog'. Then the expression '$D(b)$' will be a sentence in FOL, which symbolizes the English sentence 'Bertie is a dog'. Equally, we might let the FOL predicate '$L$' symbolize the English predicate '_____ is a logician'. Then the expression '$L(i)$' will symbolize the English sentence 'Willard is a logician'.

Third, we have quantifiers. For instance, '$\exists$' will roughly convey 'There is at least one …'. So we might symbolize the English sentence 'there is a dog' with the FOL sentence '$\exists x\, D(x)$', which we might read aloud as 'there is at least one thing, $x$, such that $x$ is a dog'.

That is the general idea, but FOL is significantly more subtle than TFL, so we will come at it slowly.

## 22.2 Names

In English, a *singular term* is a word or phrase that refers to a *specific* person, place, or thing. The word 'dog' is not a singular term, because there are a great many dogs. The phrase 'Bertie' is a singular term, because it refers to a specific terrier. Likewise, the phrase 'Philip's dog Bertie' is a singular term, because it refers to a specific little terrier.

*Proper names* are a particularly important kind of singular term. These are expressions that pick out individuals without describing them. The name 'Emerson' is a proper name, and the name alone does not tell you anything about Emerson. Of course, some names are traditionally given to boys and other are traditionally given to girls. If 'Hilary' is used as a singular term, you might guess that it refers to a woman. You might, though, be guessing wrongly. Indeed, the name does not necessarily mean that the person referred to is even a person: Hilary might be a giraffe, for all you could tell just from the name.

In FOL, our NAMES are lower-case letters '$a$' through to '$r$'. We can add subscripts if we want to use some letter more than once. So here are some singular terms in FOL:

$$a, b, c, \ldots, r, a_1, f_{32}, j_{390}, m_{12}$$

These should be thought of along the lines of proper names in English, but with one difference. 'Tim Button' is a proper name, but there are several people with this name. (Equally, there are at least two people with the name 'P.D. Magnus'.) We live with this kind of ambiguity in English, allowing context to individuate the fact that 'Tim Button' refers to an author of this book, and not some other Tim. In FOL, we do not tolerate any such ambiguity. Each name must pick out *exactly* one thing. (However, two different names may pick out the same thing.)

As with TFL, we can provide symbolization keys. These indicate, temporarily, what a name will pick out. So we might offer:

$e$: Elsa

> *g*: Gregor
> *m*: Marybeth

## 22.3   Predicates

The simplest predicates are properties of individuals. They are things you can say about an object. Here are some examples of English predicates:

> \_\_\_\_\_ is a dog
> \_\_\_\_\_ is a member of Monty Python
> A piano fell on \_\_\_\_\_

In general, you can think about predicates as things which combine with singular terms to make sentences. Conversely, you can start with sentences and make predicates out of them by removing terms. Consider the sentence, 'Vinnie borrowed the family car from Nunzio.' By removing a singular term, we can obtain any of three different predicates:

> \_\_\_\_\_ borrowed the family car from Nunzio
> Vinnie borrowed \_\_\_\_\_ from Nunzio
> Vinnie borrowed the family car from \_\_\_\_\_

In FOL, PREDICATES are capital letters $A$ through $Z$, with or without subscripts. We might write a symbolization key for predicates thus:

> $A(x)$: \_\_\_\_\_$_x$ is angry
> $H(x)$: \_\_\_\_\_$_x$ is happy

(Why the subscripts on the gaps? We will return to this in §24.)

If we combine our two symbolization keys, we can start to symbolize some English sentences that use these names and predicates in combination. For example, consider the English sentences:

1. Elsa is angry.

2. Gregor and Marybeth are angry.

3. If Elsa is angry, then so are Gregor and Marybeth.

Sentence 1 is straightforward: we symbolize it by '$A(e)$'.

Sentence 2: this is a conjunction of two simpler sentences. The simple sentences can be symbolized just by '$A(g)$' and '$A(m)$'. Then we help ourselves to our resources from TFL, and symbolize the entire sentence by '$A(g) \land A(m)$'. This illustrates an important point: FOL has all of the truth-functional connectives of TFL.

Sentence 3: this is a conditional, whose antecedent is sentence 1 and whose consequent is sentence 2, so we can symbolize this with '$A(e) \to (A(g) \land A(m))$'.

## 22.4  Quantifiers

We are now ready to introduce quantifiers. Consider these sentences:

4. Everyone is happy.

5. Someone is angry.

It might be tempting to symbolize sentence 4 as '$H(e) \land H(g) \land H(m)$'. Yet this would only say that Elsa, Gregor, and Marybeth are happy. We want to say that *everyone* is happy, even those with no names. In order to do this, we introduce the '$\forall$' symbol. This is called the UNIVERSAL QUANTIFIER.

A quantifier must always be followed by a VARIABLE. In FOL, variables are italic lowercase letters '$s$' through '$z$', with or without subscripts. So we might symbolize sentence 4 as '$\forall x\, H(x)$'. The variable '$x$' is serving as a kind of placeholder. The expression '$\forall x$' intuitively means that you can pick anyone and put them in as '$x$'. The subsequent '$H(x)$' indicates, of that thing you picked out, that it is happy.

It should be pointed out that there is no special reason to use '$x$' rather than some other variable. The sentences '$\forall x\, H(x)$',

'$\forall y\, H(y)$', '$\forall z\, H(z)$', and '$\forall x_5 H(x_5)$' use different variables, but they will all be logically equivalent.

To symbolize sentence 5, we introduce another new symbol: the EXISTENTIAL QUANTIFIER, '$\exists$'. Like the universal quantifier, the existential quantifier requires a variable. Sentence 5 can be symbolized by '$\exists x\, A(x)$'. Whereas '$\forall x\, A(x)$' is read naturally as 'for all $x$, $x$ is angry', '$\exists x\, A(x)$' is read naturally as 'there is something, $x$, such that $x$ is angry'. Once again, the variable is a kind of placeholder; we could just as easily have symbolized sentence 5 by '$\exists z\, A(z)$', '$\exists w_{256} A(w_{256})$', or whatever.

Some more examples will help. Consider these further sentences:

6. No one is angry.
7. There is someone who is not happy.
8. Not everyone is happy.

Sentence 6 can be paraphrased as, 'It is not the case that someone is angry'. We can then symbolize it using negation and an existential quantifier: '$\neg \exists x\, A(x)$'. Yet sentence 6 could also be paraphrased as, 'Everyone is not angry'. With this in mind, it can be symbolized using negation and a universal quantifier: '$\forall x\, \neg A(x)$'. Both of these are acceptable symbolizations. Indeed, it will transpire that, in general, $\forall x\, \neg \mathcal{A}$ is logically equivalent to $\neg \exists x\, \mathcal{A}$. (Notice that we have here returned to the practice of using '$\mathcal{A}$' as a metavariable, from §8.) Symbolizing a sentence one way, rather than the other, might seem more 'natural' in some contexts, but it is not much more than a matter of taste.

Sentence 7 is most naturally paraphrased as, 'There is some $x$, such that $x$ is not happy'. This then becomes '$\exists x\, \neg H(x)$'. Of course, we could equally have written '$\neg \forall x\, H(x)$', which we would naturally read as 'it is not the case that everyone is happy'. That too would be a perfectly adequate symbolization of sentence 8.

## 22.5  Domains

Given the symbolization key we have been using, '$\forall x\, H(x)$' symbolizes 'Everyone is happy'. Who is included in this *everyone*? When we use sentences like this in English, we usually do not mean everyone now alive on the Earth. We certainly do not mean everyone who was ever alive or who will ever live. We usually mean something more modest: everyone now in the building, everyone enrolled in the ballet class, or whatever.

In order to eliminate this ambiguity, we will need to specify a DOMAIN. The domain is the collection of things that we are talking about. So if we want to talk about people in Chicago, we define the domain to be people in Chicago. We write this at the beginning of the symbolization key, like this:

domain: people in Chicago

The quantifiers *range over* the domain. Given this domain, '$\forall x$' is to be read roughly as 'Every person in Chicago is such that...' and '$\exists x$' is to be read roughly as 'Some person in Chicago is such that...'.

In FOL, the domain must always include at least one thing. Moreover, in English we can legitimately infer 'something is angry' from 'Gregor is angry'. In FOL, then, we will want to be able to infer '$\exists x\, A(x)$' from '$A(g)$'. So we will insist that each name must pick out exactly one thing in the domain. If we want to name people in places beside Chicago, then we need to include those people in the domain.

> A domain must have *at least* one member. Every name must pick out *exactly* one member of the domain, but a member of the domain may be picked out by one name, many names, or none at all.

Even allowing for a domain with just one member can produce some strange results. Suppose we have this as a symbolization key:

domain: the Eiffel Tower
$P(x)$: _____$x$ is in Paris.

The sentence $\forall x\, P(x)$ might be paraphrased in English as 'Everything is in Paris.' Yet that would be misleading. It means that everything *in the domain* is in Paris. This domain contains only the Eiffel Tower, so with this symbolization key $\forall x\, P(x)$ just means that the Eiffel Tower is in Paris.

## Non-referring terms

In FOL, each name must pick out exactly one member of the domain. A name cannot refer to more than one thing—it is a *singular* term. Each name must still pick out *something*. This is connected to a classic philosophical problem: the so-called problem of non-referring terms.

Medieval philosophers typically used sentences about the *chimera* to exemplify this problem. Chimera is a mythological creature; it does not really exist. Consider these two sentences:

9. Chimera is angry.
10. Chimera is not angry.

It is tempting just to define a name to mean 'chimera.' The symbolization key would look like this:

domain: creatures on Earth
$A(x)$: _____$x$ is angry.
$c$: chimera

We could then symbolize sentence 9 as $A(c)$ and sentence 10 as $\neg A(c)$.

Problems will arise when we ask whether these sentences are true or false.

One option is to say that sentence 9 is not true, because there is no chimera. If sentence 9 is false because it talks about a nonexistent thing, then sentence 10 is false for the same reason. Yet this would mean that $A(c)$ and $\neg A(c)$ would both be false. Given the truth conditions for negation, this cannot be the case.

Since we cannot say that they are both false, what should we do? Another option is to say that sentence 9 is *meaningless* because it talks about a non-existent thing. So $A(c)$ would be a meaningful expression in FOL for some interpretations but not for others. Yet this would make our formal language hostage to particular interpretations. Since we are interested in logical form, we want to consider the logical force of a sentence like $A(c)$ apart from any particular interpretation. If $A(c)$ were sometimes meaningful and sometimes meaningless, we could not do that.

This is the *problem of non-referring terms*, and we will return to it later (see p. 243.) The important point for now is that each name of FOL *must* refer to something in the domain, although the domain can contain any things we like. If we want to symbolize arguments about mythological creatures, then we must define a domain that includes them. This option is important if we want to consider the logic of stories. We can symbolize a sentence like 'Sherlock Holmes lived at 221B Baker Street' by including fictional characters like Sherlock Holmes in our domain.

# CHAPTER 23

# *Sentences with one quantifier*

We now have all of the pieces of FOL. Symbolizing more complicated sentences is just a matter of knowing how to combine predicates, names, quantifiers, and connectives. There is a knack to this, and there is no substitute for practice.

## 23.1 Common quantifier phrases

Consider these sentences:

1. Every coin in my pocket is a quarter.
2. Some coin on the table is a dime.
3. Not all the coins on the table are dimes.
4. None of the coins in my pocket are dimes.

In providing a symbolization key, we need to specify a domain. Since we are talking about coins in my pocket and on the table, the domain must at least contain all of those coins. Since we are not talking about anything besides coins, we let the domain be all coins. Since we are not talking about any specific coins, we do not need to deal with any names. So here is our key:

domain: all coins
$P(x)$: _____$_x$ is in my pocket
$T(x)$: _____$_x$ is on the table
$Q(x)$: _____$_x$ is a quarter
$D(x)$: _____$_x$ is a dime

Sentence 1 is most naturally symbolized using a universal quantifier. The universal quantifier says something about everything in the domain, not just about the coins in my pocket. Sentence 1 can be paraphrased as 'for any coin, *if* that coin is in my pocket *then* it is a quarter'. So we can symbolize it as '$\forall x(P(x) \rightarrow Q(x))$'.

Since sentence 1 is about coins that are both in my pocket *and* that are quarters, it might be tempting to symbolize it using a conjunction. However, the sentence '$\forall x(P(x) \wedge Q(x))$' would symbolize the sentence 'every coin is both a quarter and in my pocket'. This obviously means something very different than sentence 1. And so we see:

> A sentence can be symbolized as $\forall x(\mathcal{F}(x) \rightarrow \mathcal{G}(x))$ if it can be paraphrased in English as 'every $F$ is $G$'.

Sentence 2 is most naturally symbolized using an existential quantifier. It can be paraphrased as 'there is some coin which is both on the table and which is a dime'. So we can symbolize it as '$\exists x(T(x) \wedge D(x))$'.

Notice that we needed to use a conditional with the universal quantifier, but we used a conjunction with the existential quantifier. Suppose we had instead written '$\exists x(T(x) \rightarrow D(x))$'. That would mean that there is some object in the domain of which '$(T(x) \rightarrow D(x))$' is true. Recall that, in TFL, $\mathcal{A} \rightarrow \mathcal{B}$ is logically equivalent (in TFL) to $\neg\mathcal{A} \vee \mathcal{B}$. This equivalence will also hold in FOL. So '$\exists x(T(x) \rightarrow D(x))$' is true if there is some object in the domain, such that '$(\neg T(x) \vee D(x))$' is true of that object. That is, '$\exists x(T(x) \rightarrow D(x))$' is true if some coin is *either* not on the table *or* is a dime. Of course there is a coin that is not on the table: there are coins in lots of other places. So it is *very easy* for '$\exists x(T(x) \rightarrow D(x))$' to be true. A conditional will usually be the natural connective to use with a universal quantifier, but a conditional within the scope of an existential quantifier tends to say something very weak indeed. As a general rule of thumb, do not put conditionals in the scope of existential quantifiers unless you are sure that you need one.

> A sentence can be symbolized as $\exists x(\mathscr{F}(x) \wedge \mathscr{G}(x))$ if it can be paraphrased in English as 'some $F$ is $G$'.

Sentence 3 can be paraphrased as, 'It is not the case that every coin on the table is a dime'. So we can symbolize it by '$\neg\forall x(T(x) \rightarrow D(x))$'. You might look at sentence 3 and paraphrase it instead as, 'Some coin on the table is not a dime'. You would then symbolize it by '$\exists x(T(x) \wedge \neg D(x))$'. Although it is probably not immediately obvious yet, these two sentences are logically equivalent. (This is due to the logical equivalence between $\neg\forall x\, \mathscr{A}$ and $\exists x \neg\mathscr{A}$, mentioned in §22, along with the equivalence between $\neg(\mathscr{A} \rightarrow \mathscr{B})$ and $\mathscr{A} \wedge \neg\mathscr{B}$.)

Sentence 4 can be paraphrased as, 'It is not the case that there is some dime in my pocket'. This can be symbolized by '$\neg\exists x(P(x) \wedge D(x))$'. It might also be paraphrased as, 'Everything in my pocket is a non-dime', and then could be symbolized by '$\forall x(P(x) \rightarrow \neg D(x))$'. Again the two symbolizations are logically equivalent; both are correct symbolizations of sentence 4.

> A sentence that can be paraphrased as 'no $F$ is $G$' can be symbolized as $\neg\exists x(\mathscr{F}(x) \wedge \mathscr{G}(x))$ and also as $\forall x(\mathscr{F}(x) \rightarrow \neg\mathscr{G}(x))$.

Finally, consider 'only', as in:

5. Only dimes are on the table.

How should we symbolize this? A good strategy is to consider when the sentence would be false. If we are saying that only dimes are on the table, we are excluding all the cases where something on the table is a non-dime. So we can symbolize the sentence the same way we would symbolize 'No non-dimes are on the table.' Remembering the lesson we just learned, and symbolizing '$x$ is a non-dime' as '$\neg D(x)$', the possible symbolizations are: '$\neg\exists x(T(x) \land \neg D(x))$', or alternatively: '$\forall x(T(x) \to \neg\neg D(x))$'. Since double negations cancel out, the second is just as good as '$\forall x(T(x) \to D(x))$'. In other words, 'Only dimes are on the table' and 'Everything on the table is a dime' are symbolized the same way.

---

A sentence that can be paraphrased as 'only $F$s are $G$s' can be symbolized as $\neg\exists x(\mathcal{G}(x) \land \neg\mathcal{F}(x))$ and also as $\forall x(\mathcal{G}(x) \to \mathcal{F}(x))$.

---

## 23.2 Empty predicates

In §22, we emphasized that a name must pick out exactly one object in the domain. However, a predicate need not apply to anything in the domain. A predicate that applies to nothing in the domain is called an EMPTY PREDICATE. This is worth exploring.

Suppose we want to symbolize these two sentences:

6. Every monkey knows sign language
7. Some monkey knows sign language

It is possible to write the symbolization key for these sentences in this way:

domain: animals
$M(x)$: _____$_x$ is a monkey.
$S(x)$: _____$_x$ knows sign language.

Sentence 6 can now be symbolized by '$\forall x(M(x) \to S(x))$'. Sentence 7 can be symbolized as '$\exists x(M(x) \land S(x))$'.

It is tempting to say that sentence 6 *entails* sentence 7. That is, we might think that it is impossible that every monkey knows sign language unless some monkey knows sign language. But this would be a mistake. It is possible for the sentence '$\forall x(M(x) \rightarrow S(x))$' to be true even though the sentence '$\exists x(M(x) \wedge S(x))$' is false.

How can this be? The answer comes from considering whether these sentences would be true or false *if there were no monkeys.* If there were no monkeys at all (in the domain), then '$\forall x(M(x) \rightarrow S(x))$' would be *vacuously* true: take any monkey you like—it knows sign language! But if there were no monkeys at all (in the domain), then '$\exists x(M(x) \wedge S(x))$' would be false.

Another example will help to bring this home. Suppose we extend the above symbolization key, by adding:

$R(x)$: _____$x$ is a refrigerator

Now consider the sentence '$\forall x(R(x) \rightarrow M(x))$'. This symbolizes 'every refrigerator is a monkey'. This sentence is true, given our symbolization key, which is counterintuitive, since we (presumably) do not want to say that there are a whole bunch of refrigerator monkeys. It is important to remember, though, that '$\forall x(R(x) \rightarrow M(x))$' is true iff any member of the domain that is a refrigerator is a monkey. Since the domain is *animals,* there are no refrigerators in the domain. Again, then, the sentence is *vacuously* true.

If you were actually dealing with the sentence 'All refrigerators are monkeys', then you would most likely want to include kitchen appliances in the domain. Then the predicate '$R$' would not be empty and the sentence '$\forall x(R(x) \rightarrow M(x))$' would be false.

> When $\mathscr{F}$ is an empty predicate, any sentence $\forall x(\mathscr{F}(x) \rightarrow \ldots)$ is vacuously true.

## 23.3 Picking a domain

The appropriate symbolization of an English language sentence in FOL will depend on the symbolization key. Choosing a key can be difficult. Suppose we want to symbolize the English sentence:

    8. Every rose has a thorn.

We might offer this symbolization key:

    $R(x)$: _____$x$ is a rose
    $T(x)$: _____$x$ has a thorn

It is tempting to say that sentence 8 should be symbolized as '$\forall x(R(x) \to T(x))$', but we have not yet chosen a domain. If the domain contains all roses, this would be a good symbolization. Yet if the domain is merely *things on my kitchen table*, then '$\forall x(R(x) \to T(x))$' would only come close to covering the fact that every rose *on my kitchen table* has a thorn. If there are no roses on my kitchen table, the sentence would be trivially true. This is not what we want. To symbolize sentence 8 adequately, we need to include all the roses in the domain, but now we have two options.

First, we can restrict the domain to include all roses but *only* roses. Then sentence 8 can, if we like, be symbolized with '$\forall x \, T(x)$'. This is true iff everything in the domain has a thorn; since the domain is just the roses, this is true iff every rose has a thorn. By restricting the domain, we have been able to symbolize our English sentence with a very short sentence of FOL. So this approach can save us trouble, if every sentence that we want to deal with is about roses.

Second, we can let the domain contain things besides roses: rhododendrons; rats; rifles; whatevers, and we will certainly need to include a more expansive domain if we simultaneously want to symbolize sentences like:

    9. Every cowboy sings a sad, sad song.

Our domain must now include both all the roses (so that we can symbolize sentence 8) and all the cowboys (so that we can symbolize sentence 9). So we might offer the following symbolization key:

domain: people and plants
$C(x)$: _____$_x$ is a cowboy
$S(x)$: _____$_x$ sings a sad, sad song
$R(x)$: _____$_x$ is a rose
$T(x)$: _____$_x$ has a thorn

Now we will have to symbolize sentence 8 with '$\forall x(R(x) \rightarrow T(x))$', since '$\forall x\, T(x)$' would symbolize the sentence 'every person or plant has a thorn'. Similarly, we will have to symbolize sentence 9 with '$\forall x(C(x) \rightarrow S(x))$'.

In general, the universal quantifier can be used to symbolize the English expression 'everyone' if the domain only contains people. If there are people and other things in the domain, then 'everyone' must be treated as 'every person'.

## 23.4   The utility of paraphrase

When symbolizing English sentences in FOL, it is important to understand the structure of the sentences you want to symbolize. What matters is the final symbolization in FOL, and sometimes you will be able to move from an English language sentence directly to a sentence of FOL. Other times, it helps to paraphrase the sentence one or more times. Each successive paraphrase should move from the original sentence closer to something that you can easily symbolize directly in FOL.

For the next several examples, we will use this symbolization key:

domain: people
$B(x)$: _____$_x$ is a bassist.
$R(x)$: _____$_x$ is a rock star.

$k$: Kim Deal

Now consider these sentences:

10. If Kim Deal is a bassist, then she is a rock star.
11. If a person is a bassist, then she is a rock star.

The same words appear as the consequent in sentences 10 and 11 ('... she is a rock star'), but they mean very different things. To make this clear, it often helps to paraphrase the original sentences, removing pronouns.

Sentence 10 can be paraphrased as, 'If Kim Deal is a bassist, then *Kim Deal* is a rockstar'. This can obviously be symbolized as '$B(k) \rightarrow R(k)$'.

Sentence 11 must be paraphrased differently: 'If a person is a bassist, then *that person* is a rock star'. This sentence is not about any particular person, so we need a variable. As an intermediate step, we can paraphrase this as, 'For any person x, if x is a bassist, then x is a rockstar'. Now this can be symbolized as '$\forall x(B(x) \rightarrow R(x))$'. This is the same sentence we would have used to symbolize 'Everyone who is a bassist is a rock star'. On reflection, that is surely true iff sentence 11 is true, as we would hope.

Consider these further sentences:

12. If anyone is a bassist, then Kim Deal is a rock star.
13. If anyone is a bassist, then she is a rock star.

The same words appear as the antecedent in sentences 12 and 13 ('If anyone is a bassist...'), but it can be tricky to work out how to symbolize these two uses. Again, paraphrase will come to our aid.

Sentence 12 can be paraphrased, 'If there is at least one bassist, then Kim Deal is a rock star'. It is now clear that this is a conditional whose antecedent is a quantified expression; so we can symbolize the entire sentence with a conditional as the main logical operator: '$\exists x B(x) \rightarrow R(k)$'.

Sentence 13 can be paraphrased, 'For all people $x$, if $x$ is a bassist, then $x$ is a rock star'. Or, in more natural English, it can be paraphrased by 'All bassists are rock stars'. It is best symbolized as '$\forall x(B(x) \rightarrow R(x))$', just like sentence 11.

The moral is that the English words 'any' and 'anyone' should typically be symbolized using quantifiers, and if you are having a hard time determining whether to use an existential or a universal quantifier, try paraphrasing the sentence with an English sentence that uses words *besides* 'any' or 'anyone'.

## 23.5   Quantifiers and scope

Continuing the example, suppose we want to symbolize these sentences:

14. If everyone is a bassist, then Lars is a bassist
15. Everyone is such that, if they are a bassist, then Lars is a bassist.

To symbolize these sentences, we will have to add a new name to the symbolization key, namely:

  $l$: Lars

Sentence 14 is a conditional, whose antecedent is 'everyone is a bassist', so we will symbolize it with '$\forall x\, B(x) \rightarrow B(l)$'. This sentence is *necessarily* true: if *everyone* is indeed a bassist, then take any one you like—for example Lars—and he will be a bassist.

Sentence 15, by contrast, might best be paraphrased by 'every person $x$ is such that, if $x$ is a bassist, then Lars is a bassist'. This is symbolized by '$\forall x(B(x) \rightarrow B(l))$'. This sentence is false; Kim Deal is a bassist. So '$B(k)$' is true. Suppose that Lars is not a bassist (say, he's a drummer instead), so '$B(l)$' is false. Accordingly, '$B(k) \rightarrow B(l)$' will be false, so '$\forall x(B(x) \rightarrow B(l))$' will be false as well.

In short, '$\forall x B(x) \rightarrow B(l)$' and '$\forall x(B(x) \rightarrow B(l))$' are very different sentences. We can explain the difference in terms of the *scope* of the quantifier. The scope of quantification is very much like the scope of negation, which we considered when discussing TFL, and it will help to explain it in this way.

In the sentence '$\neg B(k) \to B(l)$', the scope of '$\neg$' is just the antecedent of the conditional. We are saying something like: if '$B(k)$' is false, then '$B(l)$' is true. Similarly, in the sentence '$\forall x B(x) \to B(l)$', the scope of '$\forall x$' is just the antecedent of the conditional. We are saying something like: if '$B(x)$' is true of *everything*, then '$B(l)$' is also true.

In the sentence '$\neg(B(k) \to B(l))$', the scope of '$\neg$' is the entire sentence. We are saying something like: '$(B(k) \to B(l))$' is false. Similarly, in the sentence '$\forall x(B(x) \to B(l))$', the scope of '$\forall x$' is the entire sentence. We are saying something like: '$(B(x) \to B(l))$' is true of *everything*.

The moral of the story is simple. When you are using conditionals, be very careful to make sure that you have sorted out the scope correctly.

## Ambiguous predicates

Suppose we just want to symbolize this sentence:

16. Adina is a skilled surgeon.

Let the domain be people, let $K(x)$ mean '$x$ is a skilled surgeon', and let $a$ mean Adina. Sentence 16 is simply $K(a)$.

Suppose instead that we want to symbolize this argument:

> The hospital will only hire a skilled surgeon. All surgeons are greedy. Billy is a surgeon, but is not skilled. Therefore, Billy is greedy, but the hospital will not hire him.

We need to distinguish being a *skilled surgeon* from merely being a *surgeon*. So we define this symbolization key:

domain: people
  $G(x)$: _____$x$ is greedy.

$H(x)$:  The hospital will hire _____$x$.
$R(x)$:  _____$x$ is a surgeon.
$K(x)$:  _____$x$ is skilled.
    $b$:  Billy

Now the argument can be symbolized in this way:

$$\forall x \big[\neg(R(x) \land K(x)) \rightarrow \neg H(x)\big]$$
$$\forall x (R(x) \rightarrow G(x))$$
$$R(b) \land \neg K(b)$$
$$\therefore\ G(b) \land \neg H(b)$$

Next suppose that we want to symbolize this argument:

Carol is a skilled surgeon and a tennis player. Therefore, Carol is a skilled tennis player.

If we start with the symbolization key we used for the previous
argument, we could add a predicate (let $T(x)$ mean '$x$ is a tennis
player') and a name (let $c$ mean Carol).  Then the argument
becomes:

$$(R(c) \land K(c)) \land T(c)$$
$$\therefore\ T(c) \land K(c)$$

This symbolization is a disaster!  It takes what in English is a
terrible argument and symbolizes it as a valid argument in FOL.
The problem is that there is a difference between being *skilled as
a surgeon* and *skilled as a tennis player*. Symbolizing this argument
correctly requires two separate predicates, one for each type of
skill. If we let $K_1(x)$ mean '$x$ is skilled as a surgeon' and $K_2(x)$
mean '$x$ is skilled as a tennis player,' then we can symbolize the
argument in this way:

$$(R(c) \land K_1(c)) \land T(c)$$
$$\therefore\ T(c) \land K_2(c)$$

Like the English language argument it symbolizes, this is invalid.

The moral of these examples is that you need to be careful of symbolizing predicates in an ambiguous way. Similar problems can arise with predicates like *good*, *bad*, *big*, and *small*. Just as skilled surgeons and skilled tennis players have different skills, big dogs, big mice, and big problems are big in different ways.

Is it enough to have a predicate that means '*x* is a skilled surgeon', rather than two predicates '*x* is skilled' and '*x* is a surgeon'? Sometimes. As sentence 16 shows, sometimes we do not need to distinguish between skilled surgeons and other surgeons.

Must we always distinguish between different ways of being skilled, good, bad, or big? No. As the argument about Billy shows, sometimes we only need to talk about one kind of skill. If you are symbolizing an argument that is just about dogs, it is fine to define a predicate that means '*x* is big.' If the domain includes dogs and mice, however, it is probably best to make the predicate mean '*x* is big for a dog.'

## Practice exercises

**A.** Here are the syllogistic figures identified by Aristotle and his successors, along with their medieval names:

1. **Barbara.** All G are F. All H are G. So: All H are F
2. **Celarent.** No G are F. All H are G. So: No H are F
3. **Ferio.** No G are F. Some H is G. So: Some H is not F
4. **Darii.** All G are F. Some H is G. So: Some H is F.
5. **Camestres.** All F are G. No H are G. So: No H are F.
6. **Cesare.** No F are G. All H are G. So: No H are F.
7. **Baroko.** All F are G. Some H is not G. So: Some H is not F.
8. **Festino.** No F are G. Some H are G. So: Some H is not F.
9. **Datisi.** All G are F. Some G is H. So: Some H is F.
10. **Disamis.** Some G is F. All G are H. So: Some H is F.
11. **Ferison.** No G are F. Some G is H. So: Some H is not F.
12. **Bokardo.** Some G is not F. All G are H. So: Some H is not F.
13. **Camenes.** All F are G. No G are H So: No H is F.

14. **Dimaris.** Some F is G. All G are H. So: Some H is F.
15. **Fresison.** No F are G. Some G is H. So: Some H is not F.

Symbolize each argument in FOL.

**B.** Using the following symbolization key:

domain: people
    $K(x)$: _____$_x$ knows the combination to the safe
    $S(x)$: _____$_x$ is a spy
    $V(x)$: _____$_x$ is a vegetarian
      $h$: Hofthor
      $i$: Ingmar

symbolize the following sentences in FOL:

1. Neither Hofthor nor Ingmar is a vegetarian.
2. No spy knows the combination to the safe.
3. No one knows the combination to the safe unless Ingmar does.
4. Hofthor is a spy, but no vegetarian is a spy.

**C.** Using this symbolization key:

domain: all animals
    $A(x)$: _____$_x$ is an alligator.
    $M(x)$: _____$_x$ is a monkey.
    $R(x)$: _____$_x$ is a reptile.
    $Z(x)$: _____$_x$ lives at the zoo.
      $a$: Amos
      $b$: Bouncer
      $c$: Cleo

symbolize each of the following sentences in FOL:

1. Amos, Bouncer, and Cleo all live at the zoo.
2. Bouncer is a reptile, but not an alligator.
3. Some reptile lives at the zoo.
4. Every alligator is a reptile.

5. Any animal that lives at the zoo is either a monkey or an alligator.
6. There are reptiles which are not alligators.
7. If any animal is an reptile, then Amos is.
8. If any animal is an alligator, then it is a reptile.

**D**. For each argument, write a symbolization key and symbolize the argument in FOL.

1. Willard is a logician. All logicians wear funny hats. So Willard wears a funny hat
2. Nothing on my desk escapes my attention. There is a computer on my desk. As such, there is a computer that does not escape my attention.
3. All my dreams are black and white. Old TV shows are in black and white. Therefore, some of my dreams are old TV shows.
4. Neither Holmes nor Watson has been to Australia. A person could see a kangaroo only if they had been to Australia or to a zoo. Although Watson has not seen a kangaroo, Holmes has. Therefore, Holmes has been to a zoo.
5. No one expects the Spanish Inquisition. No one knows the troubles I've seen. Therefore, anyone who expects the Spanish Inquisition knows the troubles I've seen.
6. All babies are illogical. Nobody who is illogical can manage a crocodile. Berthold is a baby. Therefore, Berthold is unable to manage a crocodile.

# CHAPTER 24

# *Multiple generality*

So far, we have only considered sentences that require one-place predicates and one quantifier. The full power of FOL really comes out when we start to use many-place predicates and multiple quantifiers. For this insight, we largely have Gottlob Frege (1879) to thank, but also C. S. Peirce.

## 24.1 Many-placed predicates

All of the predicates that we have considered so far concern properties that objects might have. Those predicates have one gap in them, and to make a sentence, we simply need to slot in one term. They are ONE-PLACE predicates.

However, other predicates concern the *relation* between two things. Here are some examples of relational predicates in English:

_____ loves _____
_____ is to the left of _____
_____ is in debt to _____

These are TWO-PLACE predicates. They need to be filled in with two terms in order to make a sentence. Conversely, if we start with an English sentence containing many singular terms, we can remove two singular terms, to obtain different two-place predicates. Consider the sentence 'Vinnie borrowed the family car from Nunzio'. By deleting two singular terms, we can obtain any of three different two-place predicates

> Vinnie borrowed _____ from _____
> _____ borrowed the family car from _____
> _____ borrowed _____ from Nunzio

and by removing all three singular terms, we obtain a THREE-PLACE predicate:

> _____ borrowed _____ from _____

Indeed, there is no in principle upper limit on the number of places that our predicates may contain.

## 24.2  Mind the gap(s)!

We have used the same symbol, '_____', to indicate a gap formed by deleting a term from a sentence. However, as Frege emphasised, these are *different* gaps. To obtain a sentence, we can fill them in with the same term, but we can equally fill them in with different terms, and in various different orders. The following are three perfectly perfectly good sentences, obtained by filling in the gaps in '_____ loves _____' in different ways; but they all have distinctively different meanings:

1. Karl loves Imre.
2. Imre loves Karl.
3. Karl loves Karl.

The point is that we need to keep track of the gaps in predicates, so that we can keep track of how we are filling them in. To keep track of the gaps, we assign them variables. Suppose we want to symbolize the preceding sentences. Then I might start with the following representation key:

domain: people
     $i$: Imre
     $k$: Karl
  $L(x,y)$: \_\_\_\_\_$_x$ loves \_\_\_\_\_$_y$

Sentence 1 will be symbolized by '$L(k,i)$', sentence 2 will be symbolized by '$L(i,k)$', and sentence 3 will be symbolised by '$L(k,k)$'. Here are a few more sentences that we can symbolize with the same key:

4. Imre loves himself.
5. Karl loves Imre, but not vice versa.
6. Karl is loved by Imre.

Sentence 4 can be paraphrased as 'Imre loves Imre', and so symbolised by '$L(i,i)$'. Sentence 5 is a conjunction. We can paraphrase it as 'Karl loves Imre, and Imre does not love Karl', and so symbolise it as '$L(k,i) \land \neg L(i,k)$'. Sentence 6 can be paraphrased by 'Imre loves Karl', and so symbolised as '$L(i,k)$'. In this last case, of course, we have lots the difference in *tone* between the active and passive voice; but we have at least preserved the truth conditions.

But the relationship between 'Imre loves Karl' and 'Karl is loved by Imre' highlights something important. To see what, suppose we add another entry to our symbolization key:

  $M(x,y)$: \_\_\_\_\_$_y$ loves \_\_\_\_\_$_x$

The entry for '$M$' uses exactly the same English word—'loves'— as the entry for '$L$'. *But the gaps have been swapped around!* (Just look closely at the subscripts.) And this *matters*.

To explain: when we see a sentence like '$L(k,i)$', we are being told to take the *first* name (i.e., '$k$') and associate its value (i.e., Karl) with the gap labelled '$x$', then take the *second* name (i.e.,

'$i$') and associate its value (i.e., Imre) with the gap labelled '$y$', and so come up with: *Karl loves Imre.* The sentence '$M(i,k)$' also tells us to take the *first* name (i.e., '$i$') and plug its value into the gap labelled '$x$', and take the *second* name (i.e., '$k$') and plug its value into the gap labelled '$y$', and so come up with: *Imre loves Karl.*

So, '$L(i,k)$' and '$M(k,i)$' both symbolize 'Imre loves Karl', whereas '$L(k,i)$' and '$M(i,k)$' both symbolize 'Karl loves Imre'. Since love can be unrequited, these are different claims.

One last example might be helpful. Suppose we add this to our symbolisation key:

$P(x,y)$: _____$_x$ prefers _____$_x$ to _____$_y$

Now the sentence '$P(i,k)$' symbolises 'Imre prefers Imre to Karl', and '$P(k,i)$' symbolises 'Karl prefers Karl to Imre'. And note that we could have achieved the same effect, if we had instead specified:

$P(x,y)$: _____$_x$ prefers themselves to _____$_y$

In any case, the overall moral of this is simple. *When dealing with predicates with more than one place, pay careful attention to the order of the gaps!*

## 24.3 The order of quantifiers

Consider the sentence 'everyone loves someone'. This is potentially ambiguous. It might mean either of the following:

7. For every person x, there is some person that x loves
8. There is some particular person whom every person loves

Sentence 7 can be symbolized by '$\forall x \exists y\, L(x,y)$', and would be true of a love-triangle. For example, suppose that our domain of discourse is restricted to Imre, Juan and Karl. Suppose also that Karl loves Imre but not Juan, that Imre loves Juan but not Karl, and that Juan loves Karl but not Imre. Then sentence 7 is true.

Sentence 8 is symbolized by '$\exists y \forall x\, L(x,y)$'. Sentence 8 is *not* true in the situation just described. Again, suppose that our domain of discourse is restricted to Imre, Juan and Karl. Then all of Juan, Imre and Karl must converge on (at least) one object of love.

The point of the example is to illustrate that the order of the quantifiers matters a great deal. Indeed, to switch them around is called a *quantifier shift fallacy*. Here is an example, which comes up in various forms throughout the philosophical literature:

> For every person, there is some truth they cannot know. ($\forall\exists$)
> ∴ There is some particular truth that no person can know. ($\exists\forall$)

This argument form is obviously invalid. It's just as bad as:[1]

> Every dog has its day.                                    ($\forall\exists$)
> ∴ There is a day for all the dogs.                        ($\exists\forall$)

The order of quantifiers is also important in definitions in mathematics. For instance, there is a big difference between pointwise and uniform continuity of functions:

▷ A function $f$ is *pointwise continuous* if

$$\forall\epsilon\forall x\forall y\exists\delta(|x-y| < \delta \rightarrow |F(x) - f(y)| < \epsilon)$$

▷ A function $f$ is *uniformly continuous* if

$$\forall\epsilon\exists\delta\forall x\forall y(|x-y| < \delta \rightarrow |F(x) - f(y)| < \epsilon)$$

The moral is simple: *take great care with the order of your quantifiers!*.

---

[1] Thanks to Rob Trueman for the example.

## 24.4  Stepping-stones to symbolization

As we are starting to see, symbolization in FOL can become a bit tricky. So, when symbolizing a complex sentence, you should lay down several stepping-stones. As usual, the idea is best illustrated by example. Consider this symbolisation key:

domain: people and dogs
  $D(x)$: _____$x$ is a dog
  $F(x,y)$: _____$x$ is a friend of _____$y$
  $O(x,y)$: _____$x$ owns _____$y$
      $g$: Geraldo

Now let's try to symbolize these sentences:

9. Geraldo is a dog owner.
10. Someone is a dog owner.
11. All of Geraldo's friends are dog owners.
12. Every dog owner is a friend of a dog owner.
13. Every dog owner's friend owns a dog of a friend.

Sentence 9 can be paraphrased as, 'There is a dog that Geraldo owns'. This can be symbolized by '$\exists x(D(x) \land O(g,x))$'.

Sentence 10 can be paraphrased as, 'There is some y such that y is a dog owner'. Dealing with part of this, we might write '$\exists y(y$ is a dog owner)'. Now the fragment we have left as '$y$ is a dog owner' is much like sentence 9, except that it is not specifically about Geraldo. So we can symbolize sentence 10 by:

$$\exists y \exists x(D(x) \land O(y,x))$$

We should pause to clarify something here. In working out how to symbolize the last sentence, we wrote down '$\exists y(y$ is a dog owner)'. To be very clear: this is *neither* an FOL sentence *nor* an English sentence: it uses bits of FOL ('$\exists$', '$y$') and bits of English ('dog owner'). It is really is *just a stepping-stone* on the way to symbolizing the entire English sentence with a FOL sentence. You should regard it as a bit of rough-working-out, on a par with the doodles that you might absent-mindedly draw in the margin of this book, whilst you are concentrating fiercely on some problem.

Sentence 11 can be paraphrased as, 'Everyone who is a friend of Geraldo is a dog owner'. Using our stepping-stone tactic, we might write

$$\forall x\big[F(x,g) \rightarrow x \text{ is a dog owner}\big]$$

Now the fragment that we have left to deal with, '$x$ is a dog owner', is structurally just like sentence 9. However, it would be a mistake for us simply to write

$$\forall x\big[F(x,g) \rightarrow \exists x(D(x) \wedge O(x,x))\big]$$

for we would here have a *clash of variables*. The scope of the universal quantifier, '$\forall x$', is the entire conditional, so the '$x$' in '$D(x)$' should be governed by that, but '$D(x)$' also falls under the scope of the existential quantifier '$\exists x$', so the '$x$' in '$D(x)$' should be governed by that. Now confusion reigns: which '$x$' are we talking about? Suddenly the sentence becomes ambiguous (if it is even meaningful at all), and logicians hate ambiguity. The broad moral is that a single variable cannot serve two quantifier-masters simultaneously.

To continue our symbolization, then, we must choose some different variable for our existential quantifier. What we want is something like:

$$\forall x\big[F(x,g) \rightarrow \exists z(D(z) \wedge O(x,z))\big]$$

This adequately symbolizes sentence 11.

Sentence 12 can be paraphrased as 'For any $x$ that is a dog owner, there is a dog owner who $x$ is a friend of'. Using our stepping-stone tactic, this becomes

$$\forall x\big[x \text{ is a dog owner} \rightarrow \exists y(y \text{ is a dog owner} \wedge F(x,y))\big]$$

Completing the symbolization, we end up with

$$\forall x\big[\exists z(D(z) \wedge O(x,z)) \rightarrow \exists y\big(\exists z(D(z) \wedge O(y,z)) \wedge F(x,y)\big)\big]$$

Note that we have used the same letter, '$z$', in both the antecedent and the consequent of the conditional, but that these are governed by two different quantifiers. This is ok: there is no clash here, because it is clear which quantifier that variable falls under. We might graphically represent the scope of the quantifiers thus:

$$\underbrace{\forall x \Big[ \underbrace{\exists z(D(z) \wedge O(x,z))}_{\text{scope of 1st '}\exists z\text{'}} \rightarrow \overbrace{\exists y (\underbrace{\exists z(D(z) \wedge O(y,z))}_{\text{scope of 2nd '}\exists z\text{'}} \wedge F(x,y))}^{\text{scope of '}\exists y\text{'}} \Big]}_{\text{scope of '}\forall x\text{'}}$$

This shows that no variable is being forced to serve two masters simultaneously.

Sentence 13 is the trickiest yet. First we paraphrase it as 'For any $x$ that is a friend of a dog owner, $x$ owns a dog which is also owned by a friend of $x$'. Using our stepping-stone tactic, this becomes:

$\forall x \big[ x$ is a friend of a dog owner $\rightarrow$

$\qquad\qquad x$ owns a dog which is owned by a friend of $x \big]$

Breaking this down a bit more:

$\forall x \big[ \exists y(F(x,y) \wedge y$ is a dog owner$) \rightarrow$

$\qquad\qquad \exists y(D(y) \wedge O(x,y) \wedge y$ is owned by a friend of $x) \big]$

And a bit more:

$\forall x \big[ \exists y(F(x,y) \wedge \exists z(D(z) \wedge O(y,z))) \rightarrow$

$\qquad\qquad \exists y(D(y) \wedge O(x,y) \wedge \exists z(F(z,x) \wedge O(z,y))) \big]$

And we are done!

## 24.5   Supressed quantifiers

Logic can often help to get clear on the meanings of English claims, especially where the quantifiers are left implicit or their order is ambiguous or unclear. The clarity of expression and thinking afforded by FOL can give you a significant advantage in argument, as can be seen in the following takedown by British political philosopher Mary Astell (1666–1731) of her contemporary, the theologian William Nicholls. In Discourse IV: The Duty of Wives to their Husbands of his *The Duty of Inferiors towards their Superiors, in Five Practical Discourses* (London 1701), Nicholls argued that women are naturally inferior to men. In the preface to the 3rd edition of her treatise *Some Reflections upon Marriage, Occasion'd by the Duke and Duchess of Mazarine's Case; which is also considered,* Astell responded as follows:

> 'Tis true, thro' Want of Learning, and of that Superior Genius which Men as Men lay claim to, she [Astell] was ignorant of the *Natural Inferiority* of our Sex, which our Masters lay down as a Self-Evident and Fundamental Truth. She saw nothing in the Reason of Things, to make this either a Principle or a Conclusion, but much to the contrary; it being Sedition at least, if not Treason to assert it in this Reign.
>
> For if by the Natural Superiority of their Sex, they mean that *every* Man is by Nature superior to *every* Woman, which is the obvious meaning, and that which must be stuck to if they would speak Sense, it wou'd be a Sin in *any* Woman to have Dominion over *any* Man, and the greatest Queen ought not to command but to obey her Footman, because no Municipal Laws can supersede or change the Law of Nature; so that if the Dominion of the Men be such, the *Salique Law*,[2] as unjust as *English Men* have ever

---

[2]The Salique law was the common law of France which prohibited the crown be passed on to female heirs.

thought it, ought to take place over all the Earth, and the most glorious Reigns in the *English, Danish, Castilian*, and other Annals, were wicked Violations of the Law of Nature!

If they mean that *some* Men are superior to *some* Women this is no great Discovery; had they turn'd the Tables they might have seen that *some* Women are Superior to *some* Men. Or had they been pleased to remember their Oaths of Allegiance and Supremacy, they might have known that *One* Woman is superior to *All* the Men in these Nations, or else they have sworn to very little purpose.[3] And it must not be suppos'd, that their Reason and Religion wou'd suffer them to take Oaths, contrary to the Laws of Nature and Reason of things.[4]

We can symbolize the different interpretations Astell offers of Nicholls' claim that men are superior to women: He either meant that every man is superior to every woman, i.e.,

$$\forall x(M(x) \to \forall y(W(y) \to S(x,y)))$$

or that some men are superior to some women,

$$\exists x(M(x) \land \exists y(W(y) \land S(x,y))).$$

The latter is true, but so is

$$\exists y(W(y) \land \exists x(M(x) \land S(y,x))).$$

(some women are superior to some men), so that would be "no great discovery." In fact, since the Queen is superior to all her subjects, it's even true that some woman is superior to every man, i.e.,

$$\exists y(W(y) \land \forall x(M(x) \to S(y,x))).$$

---

[3]In 1706, England was ruled by Queen Anne.

[4]Mary Astell, *Reflections upon Marriage*, 1706 Preface, iii–iv, and Mary Astell, *Political Writings*, ed. Patricia Springborg, Cambridge University Press, 1996, 9–10.

But this is incompatible with the "obvious meaning" of Nicholls' claim, i.e., the first reading. So what Nicholls claims amounts to treason against the Queen!

## Practice exercises

**A.** Using this symbolization key:

domain: all animals
$A(x)$: \_\_\_\_\_$x$ is an alligator
$M(x)$: \_\_\_\_\_$x$ is a monkey
$R(x)$: \_\_\_\_\_$x$ is a reptile
$Z(x)$: \_\_\_\_\_$x$ lives at the zoo
$L(x,y)$: \_\_\_\_\_$x$ loves \_\_\_\_\_$y$
    $a$: Amos
    $b$: Bouncer
    $c$: Cleo

symbolize each of the following sentences in FOL:

1. If Cleo loves Bouncer, then Bouncer is a monkey.
2. If both Bouncer and Cleo are alligators, then Amos loves them both.
3. Cleo loves a reptile.
4. Bouncer loves all the monkeys that live at the zoo.
5. All the monkeys that Amos loves love him back.
6. Every monkey that Cleo loves is also loved by Amos.
7. There is a monkey that loves Bouncer, but sadly Bouncer does not reciprocate this love.

**B.** Using the following symbolization key:

domain: all animals
$D(x)$: \_\_\_\_\_$x$ is a dog
$S(x)$: \_\_\_\_\_$x$ likes samurai movies
$L(x,y)$: \_\_\_\_\_$x$ is larger than \_\_\_\_\_$y$
    $r$: Rave

$h$: Shane
$d$: Daisy

symbolize the following sentences in FOL:

1. Rave is a dog who likes samurai movies.
2. Rave, Shane, and Daisy are all dogs.
3. Shane is larger than Rave, and Daisy is larger than Shane.
4. All dogs like samurai movies.
5. Only dogs like samurai movies.
6. There is a dog that is larger than Shane.
7. If there is a dog larger than Daisy, then there is a dog larger than Shane.
8. No animal that likes samurai movies is larger than Shane.
9. No dog is larger than Daisy.
10. Any animal that dislikes samurai movies is larger than Rave.
11. There is an animal that is between Rave and Shane in size.
12. There is no dog that is between Rave and Shane in size.
13. No dog is larger than itself.
14. Every dog is larger than some dog.
15. There is an animal that is smaller than every dog.
16. If there is an animal that is larger than any dog, then that animal does not like samurai movies.

**C.** Using the symbolization key given, symbolize each English-language sentence into FOL.

domain: candies
   $C(x)$: _____$_x$ has chocolate in it.
   $M(x)$: _____$_x$ has marzipan in it.
   $S(x)$: _____$_x$ has sugar in it.
   $T(x)$: Boris has tried _____$_x$.
$B(x,y)$: _____$_x$ is better than _____$_y$.

1. Boris has never tried any candy.
2. Marzipan is always made with sugar.

3. Some candy is sugar-free.
4. The very best candy is chocolate.
5. No candy is better than itself.
6. Boris has never tried sugar-free chocolate.
7. Boris has tried marzipan and chocolate, but never together.
8. Any candy with chocolate is better than any candy without it.
9. Any candy with chocolate and marzipan is better than any candy that lacks both.

**D.** Using the following symbolization key:

domain: people and dishes at a potluck
  $R(x)$: \_\_\_\_\_$_x$ has run out.
  $T(x)$: \_\_\_\_\_$_x$ is on the table.
  $F(x)$: \_\_\_\_\_$_x$ is food.
  $P(x)$: \_\_\_\_\_$_x$ is a person.
 $L(x,y)$: \_\_\_\_\_$_x$ likes \_\_\_\_\_$_y$.
    $e$: Eli
    $f$: Francesca
    $g$: the guacamole

symbolize the following English sentences in FOL:

1. All the food is on the table.
2. If the guacamole has not run out, then it is on the table.
3. Everyone likes the guacamole.
4. If anyone likes the guacamole, then Eli does.
5. Francesca only likes the dishes that have run out.
6. Francesca likes no one, and no one likes Francesca.
7. Eli likes anyone who likes the guacamole.
8. Eli likes anyone who likes the people that he likes.
9. If there is a person on the table already, then all of the food must have run out.

**E.** Using the following symbolization key:

domain: people

$D(x)$: \_\_\_\_\_$_x$ dances ballet.
$F(x)$: \_\_\_\_\_$_x$ is female.
$M(x)$: \_\_\_\_\_$_x$ is male.
$C(x,y)$: \_\_\_\_\_$_x$ is a child of \_\_\_\_\_$_y$.
$S(x,y)$: \_\_\_\_\_$_x$ is a sibling of \_\_\_\_\_$_y$.

      $e$: Elmer
      $j$: Jane
      $p$: Patrick

symbolize the following sentences in FOL:

1. All of Patrick's children are ballet dancers.
2. Jane is Patrick's daughter.
3. Patrick has a daughter.
4. Jane is an only child.
5. All of Patrick's sons dance ballet.
6. Patrick has no sons.
7. Jane is Elmer's niece.
8. Patrick is Elmer's brother.
9. Patrick's brothers have no children.
10. Jane is an aunt.
11. Everyone who dances ballet has a brother who also dances ballet.
12. Every woman who dances ballet is the child of someone who dances ballet.

# CHAPTER 25

# *Identity*

Consider this sentence:

1. Pavel owes money to everyone

Let the domain be people; this will allow us to symbolize 'everyone' with a universal quantifier. Offering the symbolization key:

$O(x,y)$: _____$x$ owes money to _____$y$
    $p$: Pavel

we can symbolize sentence 1 by '$\forall x\, O(p,x)$'. But this has a (perhaps) odd consequence. It requires that Pavel owes money to every member of the domain (whatever the domain may be). The domain certainly includes Pavel. So this entails that Pavel owes money to himself. And maybe we did not want to say that. Maybe we meant to leave it open if Pavel owes money to himself, something we could have expressed more precisely by using either on of the following:

2. Pavel owes money to everyone *else*
3. Pavel owes money to everyone *other than* Pavel

But we do not have any way for dealing with the italicised words yet. The solution is to add another symbol to FOL.

## 25.1   Adding identity

The symbol '=' will be a two-place predicate. Since it will have a special meaning, we shall write it a bit differently: we put it *between* two terms, rather than out front. (This should also be familiar; consider a mathematical equation like $\frac{1}{2} = 0.5$.) And the special meaning for '=' is given by the fact that we *always* adopt the following symbolization key:

$x = y$: \_\_\_\_\_$_x$ is identical to \_\_\_\_\_$_y$

This does not mean *merely* that the objects in question are indistinguishable, or that all of the same things are true of them. Rather, it means that the objects in question are *the very same* object.

To put this to use, suppose we want to symbolize this sentence:

4. Pavel is Mister Checkov.

Let us add to our symbolization key:

$c$: Mister Checkov

Now sentence 4 can be symbolized as '$p = c$'. This tells us that the names '$p$' and '$c$' both name the same thing.

We can also now deal with sentences 2 and 3. Both of these sentences can be paraphrased as 'Everyone who is not Pavel is owed money by Pavel'. Paraphrasing some more, we get: 'For all $x$, if $x$ is not Pavel, then $x$ is owed money by Pavel'. Now that we are armed with our new identity symbol, we can symbolize this as '$\forall x(\neg x = p \rightarrow O(p,x))$'.

This last sentence contains the formula '$\neg x = p$'. That might look a bit strange, because the symbol that comes immediately after the '$\neg$' is a variable, rather than a predicate, but this is not a problem. We are simply negating the entire formula, '$x = p$'.

## 25.2  'Only' and 'except'

In addition to sentences that use the word 'else', and 'other than', identity is helpful when symbolizing some sentences that contain the words 'only', and 'except'. Consider:

5. Only Pavel owes money to Hikaru.

Let '$h$' name Hikaru. Plausibly, sentence 5 is true if, and only if, both of the following conditions hold:

6. Pavel owes money to Hikaru.
7. Noone who is not Pavel owes money to Hikaru.

Sentence 7 can be symbolized by any one of:

$$\neg\exists x(\neg x = p \wedge O(x,h)),$$
$$\forall x(\neg x = p \rightarrow \neg O(x,h)),$$
$$\forall x(O(x,h) \rightarrow x = p).$$

Thus, we can symbolize sentence 5 as the conjunction of one of the above with the symbolization of 6, '$O(p,h)$', or more compactly using '$\leftrightarrow$' as '$\forall x(O(x,h) \leftrightarrow x = p)$'.

8. Everyone except Pavel owes money to Hikaru.

Sentence 8 can be treated similarly, although now of course Pavel does *not* owe Hikaru money. We can paraphrase it as 'Everyone who is not Pavel owes Hikaru money, and Pavel does not'. Consequently, it can be symbolized as, '$\forall x(\neg x = p \rightarrow O(x,h)) \wedge \neg O(p,h)$', or more concisely, '$\forall x(\neg x = p \leftrightarrow O(x,h))$'. Other locutions akin to 'except' such as 'but' or 'besides' (as used in 'noone but Pavel' or 'someone besides Hikaru') can be treated in similary ways.

The above treatment of so-called "exceptives" is not uncontentious. Some linguists think that sentence 8 does not entail that Pavel doesn't owe Hikaru money, and so the symbolization should just be '$\forall x(\neg x = p \rightarrow O(x,h))$'. There are also uses of 'except' that clearly do not have that entailment, especially in mathematical writing. For instance, you may read in a calculus textbook that "the function $f$ is defined everywhere except possibly at $a$". That means only that for every point $x$ other than $a$, $f$ is defined at $x$. It is not required that $f$ is undefined at $a$; it's left open whether $f$ is or is not defined at $a$.

## 25.3 There are at least...

We can also use identity to say how many things there are of a particular kind. For example, consider these sentences:

9. There is at least one apple
10. There are at least two apples
11. There are at least three apples

We will use the symbolization key:

$A(x)$: _____$x$ is an apple

Sentence 9 does not require identity. It can be adequately symbolized by '$\exists x\, A(x)$': There is an apple; perhaps many, but at least one.

It might be tempting to also symbolize sentence 10 without identity. Yet consider the sentence '$\exists x \exists y (A(x) \land A(y))$'. Roughly, this says that there is some apple $x$ in the domain and some apple $y$ in the domain. Since nothing precludes these from being one and the same apple, this would be true even if there were only one apple. In order to make sure that we are dealing with *different* apples, we need an identity predicate. Sentence 10 needs to say that the two apples that exist are not identical, so it can be symbolized by '$\exists x \exists y ((A(x) \land A(y)) \land \neg x = y)$'.

Sentence 11 requires talking about three different apples. Now we need three existential quantifiers, and we need to make sure that each will pick out something different:

$$\exists x \exists y \exists z [((A(x) \land A(y)) \land A(z)) \land ((\neg x = y \land \neg y = z) \land \neg x = z)].$$

Note that it is *not* enough to use '$\neg x = y \land \neg y = z$' to symbolize '$x$, $y$, and $z$ are all different.' For that would be true if $x$ and $y$ were different, but $x = z$. In general, to say that $x_1, \ldots, x_n$ are all different, we must have a conjunction of $\neg x_i = x_j$ for every different pair $i$ and $j$.

## 25.4 There are at most...

Now consider these sentences:

12. There is at most one apple
13. There are at most two apples

Sentence 12 can be paraphrased as, 'It is not the case that there are at least *two* apples'. This is just the negation of sentence 10:

$$\neg \exists x \exists y [(A(x) \land A(y)) \land \neg x = y]$$

But sentence 12 can also be approached in another way. It means that if you pick out an object and it's an apple, and then you pick out an object and it's also an apple, you must have picked out the same object both times. With this in mind, it can be symbolized by

$$\forall x \forall y [(A(x) \land A(y)) \rightarrow x = y]$$

The two sentences will turn out to be logically equivalent.

Similarly, sentence 13 can be approached in two equivalent ways. It can be paraphrased as, 'It is not the case that there are *three* or more distinct apples', so we can offer:

$$\neg \exists x \exists y \exists z [((A(x) \land A(y)) \land A(z)) \land ((\neg x = y \land \neg x = z) \land \neg y = z)]$$

Alternatively we can read it as saying that if you pick out an apple, and an apple, and an apple, then you will have picked out (at least) one of these objects more than once. Thus:

$$\forall x \forall y \forall z [((A(x) \land A(y)) \land A(z)) \rightarrow ((x = y \lor x = z) \lor y = z)]$$

## 25.5   There are exactly...

We can now consider precise of numerical quantity, like:

14. There is exactly one apple.
15. There are exactly two apples.
16. There are exactly three apples.

Sentence 14 can be paraphrased as, 'There is *at least* one apple and there is *at most* one apple'. This is just the conjunction of sentence 9 and sentence 12. So we can offer:

$$\exists x A(x) \land \forall x \forall y \big[ (A(x) \land A(y)) \to x = y \big]$$

But it is perhaps more straightforward to paraphrase sentence 14 as, 'There is a thing $x$ which is an apple, and everything which is an apple is just $x$ itself'. Thought of in this way, we offer:

$$\exists x \big[ A(x) \land \forall y (A(y) \to x = y) \big]$$

Similarly, sentence 15 may be paraphrased as, 'There are *at least* two apples, and there are *at most* two apples'. Thus we could offer

$$\exists x \exists y ((A(x) \land A(y)) \land \neg x = y) \land$$
$$\forall x \forall y \forall z \big[ ((A(x) \land A(y)) \land A(z)) \to ((x = y \lor x = z) \lor y = z) \big]$$

More efficiently, though, we can paraphrase it as 'There are at least two different apples, and every apple is one of those two apples'. Then we offer:

$$\exists x \exists y \big[ ((A(x) \land A(y)) \land \neg x = y) \land \forall z (A(z) \to (x = z \lor y = z)) \big]$$

Finally, consider these sentence:

17. There are exactly two things
18. There are exactly two objects

It might be tempting to add a predicate to our symbolization key, to symbolize the English predicate '_____ is a thing' or '_____ is an object', but this is unnecessary. Words like 'thing' and 'object' do not sort wheat from chaff: they apply trivially to everything, which is to say, they apply trivially to every thing. So we can symbolize either sentence with either of the following:

$$\exists x \exists y \neg x = y \land \neg \exists x \exists y \exists z((\neg x = y \land \neg y = z) \land \neg x = z)$$
$$\exists x \exists y \left[ \neg x = y \land \forall z(x = z \lor y = z) \right]$$

## Practice exercises

**A.** Consider the sentence,

19. Every officer except Pavel owes money to Hikaru.

Symbolize this sentence, using '$F(x)$' for '_____$x$ is an officer'. Are you confident that your symbolization is true if, and only if, sentence 19 is true? What happens if every officer owes money to Hikaru, Pavel does not, but Pavel isn't an officer?

**B.** Explain why:

- '$\exists x \forall y(A(y) \leftrightarrow x = y)$' is a good symbolization of 'there is exactly one apple'.
- '$\exists x \exists y \left[ \neg x = y \land \forall z(A(z) \leftrightarrow (x = z \lor y = z)) \right]$' is a good symbolization of 'there are exactly two apples'.

# CHAPTER 26

# *Sentences of FOL*

We know how to represent English sentences in FOL. The time has finally come to define the notion of a *sentence* of FOL.

## 26.1 Expressions

There are six kinds of symbols in FOL:

**Predicates** $A, B, C, \ldots, Z$, or with subscripts, as needed: $A_1, B_1, Z_1, A_2, A_{25}, J_{375}, \ldots$

**Names** $a, b, c, \ldots, r$, or with subscripts, as needed $a_1, b_{224}, h_7, m_{32}, \ldots$

**Variables** $s, t, u, v, w, x, y, z$, or with subscripts, as needed $x_1, y_1, z_1, x_2, \ldots$

**Connectives** $\neg, \wedge, \vee, \rightarrow, \leftrightarrow$

**Brackets** ( , )

**Quantifiers** $\forall, \exists$

We define an EXPRESSION OF FOL as any string of symbols of FOL. Take any of the symbols of FOL and write them down, in any order, and you have an expression.

## 26.2  Terms and formulas

In §6, we went straight from the statement of the vocabulary of TFL to the definition of a sentence of TFL. In FOL, we will have to go via an intermediary stage: via the notion of a FORMULA. The intuitive idea is that a formula is any sentence, or anything which can be turned into a sentence by adding quantifiers out front. But this intuitive idea will take some time to unpack.

We start by defining the notion of a term.

> A TERM is any name or any variable.

So, here are some terms:

$$a, b, x, x_1 x_2, y, y_{254}, z$$

Next we need to define atomic formulas.

> 1. Any sentence letter is an atomic formula.
>
> 2. If $\mathcal{R}$ is an $n$-place predicate and $t_1, t_2, \ldots, t_n$ are terms, then $\mathcal{R}(t_1, t_2, \ldots, t_n)$ is an atomic formula.
>
> 3. If $t_1$ and $t_2$ are terms, then $t_1 = t_2$ is an atomic formula.
>
> 4. Nothing else is an atomic formula.

Note that we consider sentence letters also formulas of FOL, so every sentence of TFL is also a formula of FOL.

The use of script letters here follows the conventions laid down in §8. So, '$\mathcal{R}$' is not itself a predicate of FOL. Rather, it is a symbol of our metalanguage (augmented English) that we use to talk about any predicate of FOL. Similarly, '$t_1$' is not a term of FOL, but a symbol of the metalanguage that we can use to talk about any term of FOL. So, where '$F$' is a one-place predicate, '$G$' is a three-place predicate, and '$S$' is a six-place predicate, here are some atomic formulas:

| | |
|---|---|
| $D$ | $F(a)$ |
| $x = a$ | $G(x, a, y)$ |
| $a = b$ | $G(a, a, a)$ |
| $F(x)$ | $S(x_1, x_2, a, b, y, x_1)$ |

Once we know what atomic formulas are, we can offer recursion clauses to define arbitrary formulas. The first few clauses are exactly the same as for TFL.

1. Every atomic formula is a formula.

2. If $\mathscr{A}$ is a formula, then $\neg\mathscr{A}$ is a formula.

3. If $\mathscr{A}$ and $\mathscr{B}$ are formulas, then $(\mathscr{A} \wedge \mathscr{B})$ is a formula.

4. If $\mathscr{A}$ and $\mathscr{B}$ are formulas, then $(\mathscr{A} \vee \mathscr{B})$ is a formula.

5. If $\mathscr{A}$ and $\mathscr{B}$ are formulas, then $(\mathscr{A} \rightarrow \mathscr{B})$ is a formula.

6. If $\mathscr{A}$ and $\mathscr{B}$ are formulas, then $(\mathscr{A} \leftrightarrow \mathscr{B})$ is a formula.

7. If $\mathscr{A}$ is a formula and $x$ is a variable, then $\forall x\, \mathscr{A}$ is a formula.

8. If $\mathscr{A}$ is a formula and $x$ is a variable, then $\exists x\, \mathscr{A}$ is a formula.

9. Nothing else is a formula.

So, assuming again that '$F$' is a one-place predicate, '$G$' is a three-place predicate and '$S$' is a six place-predicate, here are some formulas you can build this way:

$$F(x)$$
$$G(a,y,z)$$
$$S(y,z,y,a,y,x)$$
$$(G(a,y,z) \rightarrow S(y,z,y,a,y,x))$$
$$\forall z(G(a,y,z) \rightarrow S(y,z,y,a,y,x))$$
$$F(x) \wedge \forall z(G(a,y,z) \rightarrow S(y,z,y,a,y,x))$$
$$\exists y(F(x) \wedge \forall z(G(a,y,z) \rightarrow S(y,z,y,a,y,x)))$$
$$\forall x \exists y(F(x) \wedge \forall z(G(a,y,z) \rightarrow S(y,z,y,a,y,x)))$$

We can now give a formal definition of scope, which incorporates the definition of the scope of a quantifier. Here we follow the case of TFL, though we note that a logical operator can be either a connective or a quantifier:

---

The MAIN LOGICAL OPERATOR in a formula is the operator that was introduced most recently, when that formula was constructed using the recursion rules.

The SCOPE of a logical operator in a formula is the subformula for which that operator is the main logical operator.

---

So we can graphically illustrate the scope of the quantifiers in the preceding example thus:

$$
\begin{array}{c}
\text{scope of `}\forall x\text{'} \\
\text{scope of `}\exists y\text{'} \\
\text{scope of `}\forall z\text{'} \\
\forall x\, \exists y(F(x) \leftrightarrow \forall z(G(a,y,z) \rightarrow S(y,z,y,a,y,x)))
\end{array}
$$

## 26.3 Sentences and free variables

Recall that we are largely concerned in logic with assertoric sentences: sentences that can be either true or false. Many formulas are not sentences. Consider the following symbolization key:

domain: people
$L(x,y)$: _____$_x$ loves _____$_y$
    $b$: Boris

Consider the atomic formula '$L(z,z)$'. All atomic formula are formulas, so '$L(z,z)$' is a formula, but can it be true or false? You might think that it will be true just in case the person named by '$z$' loves themself, in the same way that '$L(b,b)$' is true just in case Boris (the person named by '$b$') loves himself. *However, '$z$' is a variable, and does not name anyone or any thing.*

   Of course, if we put an existential quantifier out front, obtaining '$\exists z L(z,z)$', then this would be true iff someone loves themselves. Equally, if we wrote '$\forall z L(z,z)$', this would be true iff everyone loves themselves. The point is that we need a quantifier to tell us how to deal with a variable.

   Let's make this idea precise.

> An occurrence of a variable $x$ is BOUND iff it falls within the scope of either $\forall x$ or $\exists x$. An occurrence of a variable which is not bound is FREE.

   For example, consider the formula

$$(\forall x(E(x) \lor D(y)) \to \exists z(E(x) \to L(z,x)))$$

The scope of the universal quantifier '$\forall x$' is '$\forall x(E(x) \lor D(y))$', so the first '$x$' is bound by the universal quantifier. However, the second and third occurrence of '$x$' are free. Equally, the '$y$' is free. The scope of the existential quantifier '$\exists z$' is '$(E(x) \to L(z,x))$', so '$z$' is bound.

   Finally we can say the following.

> A SENTENCE of FOL is any formula of FOL that contains
> no free variables.

## 26.4 Bracketing conventions

We will adopt the same notational conventions governing brackets that we did for TFL (see §6 and §11.3.) First, we may omit
the outermost brackets of a formula. Second, we may use square
brackets, '[' and ']', in place of brackets to increase the readability
of formulas.

   Sentences of FOL used in our examples can become quite
cumbersome, and so we also introduce a convention to deal with
conjunctions and disjunctions of more than two sentences. We
stipulate that $A_1 \land A_2 \land \cdots \land A_n$ and $A_1 \lor A_2 \lor \cdots \lor A_n$ are to be
interpreted as, respectively:

$$(\ldots (A_1 \land A_2) \land \cdots \land A_n)$$
$$(\ldots (A_1 \lor A_2) \lor \cdots \lor A_n)$$

In practice, this just means that you are allowed to leave out
parentheses in long conjucntions and disjunctions. But remember
that (unless they are the outermost parentheses of the sentence)
you must still enclose the entire conjucntion or disjunction in
parentheses. Also, you cannot mix conjunctions and disjunctions
with each other or with other connectives. So the following are
still not allowed, and would be ambiguous if they were:

$$A \lor B \land C \land D$$
$$B \lor C \to D$$

## 26.5 Superscripts on predicates

Above, we said that an $n$-place predicate followed by $n$ terms is
an atomic formula. But there is a small issue with this definition:
the symbols we use for predicates do not, themselves, indicate

how many places the predicate has. Indeed, in some places in this book, we have used the letter '$G$' as a one-place predicate; in other places we have used it as a three-place predicate. So, unless we state explicitly whether we want to use '$G$' as a one-place predicate or as a three place predicate, it is *indeterminate* whether '$G(a)$' is an atomic formula or not.

There is an easy way to avoid this, which many books adopt. Instead of saying that our predicates are just capital letters (with numerical subscripts as necessary), we could say that they are capital letters *with numerical superscripts* (and with numerical subscripts as necessary). The purpose of the superscript would be to say explicitly how many places the predicate has. On this approach, '$G^1$' would be a one-place predicate, and '$G^3$' would be an (entirely different) three places predicate. They would need to have different entries in any symbolisation key. And '$G^1(a)$' would be an atomic formula, whereas '$G^3(a)$' would not; likewise '$G^3(a,b,c)$' would be an atomic formula, and '$G^1(a,b,c)$' would not.

So, we *could* add superscripts to all our predicates. This would have the advantage of making certain things completely explicit. However, it would have the disadvantage of making our formulas much harder to read; the superscripts would distract the eye. So, we will not bother to make this change. Our predicates will remain *without* superscripts. (And, in practice, any book which includes superscripts almost immediately stops including them!)

However, this leaves open a possibility of ambiguity. So, when any ambiguity could arise—in practice, very rarely—you should say, explicitly, how many places your predicate(s) have.

## Practice exercises

**A**. Identify which variables are bound and which are free.

1. $\exists x\, L(x,y) \wedge \forall y\, L(y,x)$
2. $\forall x\, A(x) \wedge B(x)$
3. $\forall x(A(x) \wedge B(x)) \wedge \forall y(C(x) \wedge D(y))$

4. $\forall x \exists y [R(x,y) \rightarrow (J(z) \wedge K(x))] \vee R(y,x)$

5. $\forall x_1 (M(x_2) \leftrightarrow L(x_2,x_1)) \wedge \exists x_2\, L(x_3,x_2)$

# CHAPTER 27

# *Definite descriptions*

Consider sentences like:

1. Nick is the traitor.
2. The traitor went to Cambridge.
3. The traitor is the deputy

These are definite descriptions: they are meant to pick out a *unique* object. They should be contrasted with *indefinite* descriptions, such as 'Nick is *a* traitor'. They should equally be contrasted with *generics*, such as '*The* whale is a mammal' (when it's inappropriate to ask *which* whale). The question we face is: how should we deal with definite descriptions in FOL?

## 27.1 Treating definite descriptions as terms

One option would be to introduce new names whenever we come across a definite description. This is probably not a great idea. We know that *the* traitor—whoever it is—is indeed *a* traitor. We want to preserve that information in our symbolization.

A second option would be to use a *new* definite description operator, such as '$\imath$'. The idea would be to symbolize 'the $F$' as

'$\imath x\, F(x)$' (think 'the $x$ such that $F(x)$'); or to symbolize 'the $G$' as '$\imath x\, G(x)$', etc. Expressions of the form $\imath x\, \mathcal{A}(x)$ would then behave like names. If we were to follow this path, we could use the following symbolization key:

domain: people
    $T(x)$: _____$x$ is a traitor
    $D(x)$: _____$x$ is a deputy
    $C(x)$: _____$x$ went to Cambridge
       $n$: Nick

Then, we could symbolize sentence 1 with '$n = \imath x\, T(x)$', sentence 2 with '$C(\imath x\, T(x))$', and sentence 3 with '$\imath x\, T(x) = \imath x\, D(x)$'.

However, it would be nice if we didn't have to add a new symbol to FOL. And we might be able to make do without one.

## 27.2 Russell's analysis

Bertrand Russell offered an analysis of definite descriptions. Very briefly put, he observed that, when we say 'the $F$' in the context of a definite description, our aim is to pick out the *one and only* thing that is $F$ (in the appropriate context). Thus Russell analysed the notion of a definite description as follows:[1]

> the $F$ is $G$ **iff** there is at least one $F$, *and*
>
> there is at most one $F$, *and*
>
> every $F$ is $G$

Note a very important feature of this analysis: *'the' does not appear on the right-side of the equivalence.* Russell is aiming to provide an understanding of definite descriptions in terms that do not presuppose them.

Now, one might worry that we can say 'the table is brown' without implying that there is one and only one table in the universe. But this is not (yet) a fantastic counterexample to Russell's

---

[1] Bertrand Russell, 'On Denoting', 1905, *Mind 14*, pp. 479–93; also Russell, *Introduction to Mathematical Philosophy*, 1919, London: Allen and Unwin, ch. 16.

analysis. The domain of discourse is likely to be restricted by context (e.g., to salient objects in my vicinity).

If we accept Russell's analysis of definite descriptions, then we can symbolize sentences of the form 'the $F$ is $G$' using our strategy for numerical quantification in FOL. After all, we can deal with the three conjuncts on the right-hand side of Russell's analysis as follows:

$$\exists x F(x) \land \forall x \forall y((F(x) \land F(y)) \to x = y) \land \forall x(F(x) \to G(x))$$

In fact, we could express the same point rather more crisply, by recognizing that the first two conjuncts just amount to the claim that there is *exactly* one $F$, and that the last conjunct tells us that that object is $G$. So, equivalently, we could offer:

$$\exists x\big[(F(x) \land \forall y(F(y) \to x = y)) \land G(x)\big]$$

Using these sorts of techniques, we can now symbolize sentences 1–3 without using any new-fangled fancy operator, such as '$\imath$'.

Sentence 1 is exactly like the examples we have just considered. So we would symbolize it by

$$\exists x\big[T(x) \land \forall y(T(y) \to x = y) \land x = n\big].$$

Sentence 2 poses no problems either:

$$\exists x\big[T(x) \land \forall y(T(y) \to x = y) \land C(x)\big].$$

Sentence 3 is a little trickier, because it links two definite descriptions. But, deploying Russell's analysis, it can be paraphrased by 'there is exactly one traitor, $x$, and there is exactly one deputy, $y$, and $x = y$'. So we can symbolize it by:

$$\exists x \exists y\big([T(x) \land \forall z(T(z) \to x = z)] \land \\ [D(y) \land \forall z(D(z) \to y = z)] \land x = y\big)$$

Note that the formula '$x = y$' must fall within the scope of both quantifiers!

## 27.3   Empty definite descriptions

One of the nice features of Russell's analysis is that it allows us to handle *empty* definite descriptions neatly.

France has no king at present. Now, if we were to introduce a name, '$k$', to name the present King of France, then everything would go wrong: remember from §22 that a name must always pick out some object in the domain, and whatever we choose as our domain, it will contain no present kings of France.

Russell's analysis neatly avoids this problem. Russell tells us to treat definite descriptions using predicates and quantifiers, instead of names. Since predicates can be empty (see §23), this means that no difficulty now arises when the definite description is empty.

Indeed, Russell's analysis helpfully highlights two ways to go wrong in a claim involving a definite description. To adapt an example from Stephen Neale (1990),[2] suppose Alex claims:

4. I am dating the present king of France.

Using the following symbolization key:

$a$: Alex
$K(x)$: _____$x$ is a present king of France
$D(x,y)$: _____$x$ is dating _____$y$

(Note that the symbolization key speaks of *a* present King of France, not *the* present King of France; i.e., it employs indefinite, rather than definite, description.) Sentence 4 would be symbolized by '$\exists x\big[(K(x) \land \forall y(K(y) \to x = y)) \land D(a,x)\big]$'. Now, this can be false in (at least) two ways, corresponding to these two different sentences:

5. There is noone who is both the present King of France and such that he and Alex are dating.

---

[2]Neale, *Descriptions*, 1990, Cambridge: MIT Press.

6. There is a unique present King of France, but Alex is not dating him.

Sentence 5 might be paraphrased by 'It is not the case that: the present King of France and Alex are dating'. It will then be symbolized by '$\neg\exists x[(K(x) \land \forall y(K(y) \rightarrow x = y)) \land D(a,x)]$'. We might call this *outer* negation, since the negation governs the entire sentence. Note that the sentence is true if there is no present King of France.

Sentence 6 can be symbolized by '$\exists x[(K(x) \land \forall y(K(y) \rightarrow x = y)) \land \neg D(a,x)]$'. We might call this *inner* negation, since the negation occurs within the scope of the definite description. Note that its truth requires that there is a present King of France, albeit one who is not dating Alex.

## 27.4  Possessives, 'both', 'neither'

We can use Russell's analysis of definite descriptions also to deal with singular possessive constructions in English. For instance, 'Smith's murderer' means something like 'the person who murdered Smith', i.e., it is a disguised definite description. On Russell's analysis, the sentence

7. Smith's murderer is insane.

can be false in one of three ways. It can be false because the one person who murdered Smith is not, in fact, insane. But it can also be false if the definite description is empty, namely if either no-one murdered Smith (e.g., if Smith met with an unfortunate accident) or if more than one person murdered Smith.

To symbolize sentences containing singular possessives such as 'Smith's murderer' you should paraphrase them using an explicit definite description, e.g., 'The person who murdered Smith is insane' and then symbolize it according to Russell's analysis. In our case, we would use the symbolization key:

Domain: people

$I(x)$: _____$x$ is insane
$M(x,y)$: _____$x$ murdered _____$y$
    $s$: Smith

Our symbolization then reads, '$\exists x[M(x,s) \land \forall y(M(y,s) \rightarrow x = y) \land I(x)]$'.

Two other determiners that we can extend Russell's analysis to are 'both' and 'neither'. To say 'both $F$s are $G$' is to say that there are exactly two $F$s, and each of them is $G$. To say that 'neither $F$ is $G$', is to also say that there are exactly two $F$s, and neither of them is $G$. In FOL, the symbolizations would read, respectively,

$$\exists x \exists y \big[ F(x) \land F(y) \land \neg x = y \land$$
$$\forall z(F(z) \rightarrow (x = z \lor y = z)) \land G(x) \land G(y) \big]$$
$$\exists x \exists y \big[ F(x) \land F(y) \land \neg x = y \land$$
$$\forall z(F(z) \rightarrow (x = z \lor y = z)) \land \neg G(x) \land \neg G(y) \big]$$

Compare these symbolizations with the symbolizations of 'exactly two $F$s are $G$s' from section 25.5, i.e., of 'there are exactly two things that are both $F$ and $G$':

$$\exists x \exists y \big[ (F(x) \land G(x)) \land (F(y) \land G(y)) \land \neg x = y \land$$
$$\forall z((F(z) \land G(z)) \rightarrow (x = z \lor y = z)) \big]$$

The difference between the symbolization of this and that of 'both $F$s are $G$s' lies in the antecedent of the conditional. For 'exactly two $F$s are $G$s', we only require that there are no $F$s *that are also $G$s* other than $x$ and $y$, whereas for 'both $F$s are $G$s', there cannot be any $F$s, whether they are $G$s or not, other than $x$ and $y$. In other words, 'both $F$s are $G$s' implies that exactly two $F$s are $G$s. However, 'exactly two $F$s are $G$s' does not imply that both $F$s are $G$s (there might be a third $F$ which isn't a $G$).

## 27.5 The adequacy of Russell's analysis

How good is Russell's analysis of definite descriptions? This question has generated a substantial philosophical literature, but we will restrict ourselves to two observations.

One worry focusses on Russell's treatment of empty definite descriptions. If there are no $F$s, then on Russell's analysis, both 'the $F$ is $G$' is and 'the $F$ is non-$G$' are false. P.F. Strawson suggested that such sentences should not be regarded as false, exactly, but involve *presupposition failure*, and so need to be treated as *neither* true *nor* false.[3]

If we agree with Strawson here, we will need to revise our logic. For, in our logic, there are only two truth values (True and False), and every sentence is assigned exactly one of these truth values.

But there is room to disagree with Strawson. Strawson is appealing to some linguistic intuitions, but it is not clear that they are very robust. For example: isn't it just *false*, not 'gappy', that Tim is dating the present King of France?

Keith Donnellan raised a second sort of worry, which (very roughly) can be brought out by thinking about a case of mistaken identity.[4] Two men stand in the corner: a very tall man drinking what looks like a gin martini; and a very short man drinking what looks like a pint of water. Seeing them, Malika says:

8. The gin-drinker is very tall!

Russell's analysis will have us render Malika's sentence as:

8'. There is exactly one gin-drinker [in the corner], and whoever is a gin-drinker [in the corner] is very tall.

Now suppose that the very tall man is actually drinking *water* from a martini glass; whereas the very short man is drinking a

---

[3]P.F. Strawson, 'On Referring', 1950, *Mind 59*, pp. 320–34.

[4]Keith Donnellan, 'Reference and Definite Descriptions', 1966, *Philosophical Review 77*, pp. 281–304.

pint of (neat) gin. By Russell's analysis, Malika has said something false, but don't we want to say that Malika has said something *true*?

Again, one might wonder how clear our intuitions are on this case. We can all agree that Malika intended to pick out a particular man, and say something true of him (that he was tall). On Russell's analysis, she actually picked out a different man (the short one), and consequently said something false of him. But maybe advocates of Russell's analysis only need to explain *why* Malika's intentions were frustrated, and so why she said something false. This is easy enough to do: Malika said something false because she had false beliefs about the men's drinks; if Malika's beliefs about the drinks had been true, then she would have said something true.[5]

To say much more here would lead us into deep philosophical waters. That would be no bad thing, but for now it would distract us from the immediate purpose of learning formal logic. So, for now, we will stick with Russell's analysis of definite descriptions, when it comes to putting things into FOL. It is certainly the best that we can offer, without significantly revising our logic, and it is quite defensible as an analysis.

## Practice exercises

**A**. Using the following symbolization key:

domain: people
$K(x)$:  _____$x$ knows the combination to the safe.
$S(x)$:  _____$x$ is a spy.
$V(x)$:  _____$x$ is a vegetarian.
$T(x,y)$:  _____$x$ trusts _____$y$.
    $h$: Hofthor

---

[5]Interested parties should read Saul Kripke, 'Speaker Reference and Semantic Reference', 1977, in French et al (eds.), *Contemporary Perspectives in the Philosophy of Language*, Minneapolis: University of Minnesota Press, pp. 6-27.

*i*: Ingmar

symbolize the following sentences in FOL:

1. Hofthor trusts a vegetarian.
2. Everyone who trusts Ingmar trusts a vegetarian.
3. Everyone who trusts Ingmar trusts someone who trusts a vegetarian.
4. Only Ingmar knows the combination to the safe.
5. Ingmar trusts Hofthor, but no one else.
6. The person who knows the combination to the safe is a vegetarian.
7. The person who knows the combination to the safe is not a spy.

**B.** Using the following symbolization key:

domain: cards in a standard deck
$B(x)$: _____$_x$ is black.
$C(x)$: _____$_x$ is a club.
$D(x)$: _____$_x$ is a deuce.
$J(x)$: _____$_x$ is a jack.
$M(x)$: _____$_x$ is a man with an axe.
$O(x)$: _____$_x$ is one-eyed.
$W(x)$: _____$_x$ is wild.

symbolize each sentence in FOL:

1. All clubs are black cards.
2. There are no wild cards.
3. There are at least two clubs.
4. There is more than one one-eyed jack.
5. There are at most two one-eyed jacks.
6. There are two black jacks.
7. There are four deuces.
8. The deuce of clubs is a black card.
9. One-eyed jacks and the man with the axe are wild.

10. If the deuce of clubs is wild, then there is exactly one wild card.
11. The man with the axe is not a jack.
12. The deuce of clubs is not the man with the axe.

**C.** Using the following symbolization key:

domain: animals in the world
    $B(x)$: \_\_\_\_\_$_x$ is in Farmer Brown's field.
    $H(x)$: \_\_\_\_\_$_x$ is a horse.
    $P(x)$: \_\_\_\_\_$_x$ is a Pegasus.
    $W(x)$: \_\_\_\_\_$_x$ has wings.

symbolize the following sentences in FOL:

1. There are at least three horses in the world.
2. There are at least three animals in the world.
3. There is more than one horse in Farmer Brown's field.
4. There are three horses in Farmer Brown's field.
5. There is a single winged creature in Farmer Brown's field; any other creatures in the field must be wingless.
6. The Pegasus is a winged horse.
7. The animal in Farmer Brown's field is not a horse.
8. The horse in Farmer Brown's field does not have wings.

**D.** In this chapter, we symbolized 'Nick is the traitor' by '$\exists x(T(x) \wedge \forall y(T(y) \rightarrow x = y) \wedge x = n)$'. Explain why these would be equally good symbolisations:

- $T(n) \wedge \forall y(T(y) \rightarrow n = y)$
- $\forall y(T(y) \leftrightarrow y = n)$

# CHAPTER 28

# *Ambiguity*

In chapter 7 we discussed the fact that sentences of English can be ambiguous, and pointed out that sentences of TFL are not. One important application of this fact is that the structural ambiguity of English sentences can often, and usefully, be straightened out using different symbolizations. One common source of ambiguity is *scope ambiguity*, where the English sentence does not make it clear which logical word is supposed to be in the scope of which other. Multiple interpretations are possible. In FOL, every connective and quantifier has a well-determined scope, and so whether or not one of them occurs in the scope of another in a given sentence of FOL is always determined.

For instance, consider the English idiom,

1. Everything that glitters is not gold.

If we think of this sentence as of the form 'every $F$ is not $G$' where $F(x)$ symbolizes '_____$_x$ glitters' and $G(x)$ is '_____$_x$ is gold', we would symbolize it as:

$$\forall x(F(x) \to \neg G(x)),$$

in other words, we symbolize it the same way as we would 'Nothing that glitters is gold'. But the idiom does not mean that! It means that one should not assume that just because something glitters, it is gold; not everything that appears valuable is in fact

valuable. To capture the actual meaning of the idiom, we would
have to symbolize it instead as we would 'Not everything that
glitters is gold', i.e., in the following way:

$$\neg\forall x(F(x) \to G(x))$$

Compare the first of these with the previous symbolization: again
we see that the difference in the two meanings of the ambiguous
sentence lies in whether the '¬' is in the scope of the '∀' (in the
first symbolization) or '∀' is in the scope of '¬' (in the second).

Of course we can alternatively symbolize the two readings
using existential quantifiers as well:

$$\neg\exists x(F(x) \wedge G(x))$$
$$\exists x(F(x) \wedge \neg G(x))$$

In chapter 23 we discussed how to symbolize sentences involving 'only'. Consider the sentence:

2. Only young cats are playful.

According to our schema, we would symbolize it this way:

$$\forall x(P(x) \to (Y(x) \wedge C(x)))$$

The meaning of this sentence of FOL is something like, 'If an
animal is playful, it is a young cat'. (Assuming that the domain
is animals, of course.) This is probably not what's intended in
uttering sentence 2, however. It's more likely that we want to say
that old cats are not playful. In other words, what we mean to say
is that if something is a cat and playful, it must be young. This
would be symbolized as:

$$\forall x((C(x) \wedge P(x)) \to Y(x))$$

There is even a third reading! Suppose we're talking about young
animals and their characteristics. And suppose you wanted to say
that of all the young animals, only the cats are playful. You could
symbolize this reading as:

$$\forall x((Y(x) \land P(x)) \to C(x))$$

Each of the last two readings can be made salient in English by placing the stress appropriately. For instance, to suggest the last reading, you would say 'Only young *cats* are playful', and to get the other reading you would say 'Only *young* cats are playful'. The very first reading can be indicate by stressing both 'young' and 'cats': 'Only *young cats* are playful' (but not old cats, or dogs of any age).

In sections 24.3 and 24.5 we discussed the importance of the order of quantifiers. This is relevant here because, in English, the order of quantifiers is sometimes not completely determined. When both universal ('all') and existential ('some', 'a') quantifiers are involved, this can result in scope ambiguities. Consider:

3. Everyone went to see a movie.

This sentence is ambiguous. In one interpretatation, it means that there is a single movie that everyone went to see. In the other, it means that everyone went to see some movie or other, but not necessarily the same one. The two readings can be symbolized, respectively, by

$$\exists x(M(x) \land \forall y(P(y) \to S(y,x)))$$
$$\forall y(P(y) \to \exists x(M(x) \land S(y,x)))$$

We assume here that the domain contains (at least) people and movies, and the symbolization key,

$P(y)$: _____$_y$ is a person,
$M(x)$: _____$_x$ is a movie
$S(y,x)$: _____$_y$ went to see _____$_x$.

In the first reading, we say that the existential quantifier has *wide scope* (and its scope contains the universal quantifier, which has *narrow scope*), and the other way round in the second.

In chapter 27, we encountered another scope ambiguity, arising from definite descriptions interacting with negation. Consider Russell's own example:

4. The King of France is not bald.

If the definite description has wide scope, and we are interpreting the 'not' as an 'inner' negation (as we said before), sentence 4 is interpreted to assert the existence of a single King of France, to whom we are ascribing non-baldness. In this reading, it is symbolized as '$\exists x\big[K(x) \wedge \forall y(K(y) \to x = y)) \wedge \neg B(x)\big]$'. In the other reading, the 'not' denies the sentence 'The King of France is bald', and we would symbolize it as: '$\neg\exists x\big[K(x) \wedge \forall y(K(y) \to x = y)) \wedge B(x)\big]$'. In the first case, we say that the definite description has wide scope and in the second that it has narrow scope.

## Practice exercises

**A**. Each of the following sentences is ambiguous. Provide a symbolization key for each, and symbolize all readings.

1. Noone likes a quitter.
2. CSI found only red hair at the scene.
3. Smith's murderer hasn't been arrested.

**B**. Russell gave the following example in his paper 'On Denoting':

> I have heard of a touchy owner of a yacht to whom a guest, on first seeing it, remarked, 'I thought your yacht was larger than it is'; and the owner replied, 'No, my yacht is not larger than it is'.

Explain what's going on.

# PART VI

# *Interpretations*

# CHAPTER 29

# *Extensionality*

Recall that TFL is a truth-functional language. Its connectives are all truth-functional, and *all* that we can do with TFL is key sentences to particular truth values. We can do this *directly*. For example, we might stipulate that the TFL sentence '*P*' is to be true. Alternatively, we can do this *indirectly*, offering a symbolization key, e.g.:

> *P*: Big Ben is in London

But recall from §10 that this is *just* a means of specifying '*P*'s truth value; the symbolization key statement amounts to something like the following stipulation:

- The TFL sentence '*P*' is true iff Big Ben is in London

And we emphasised in §10 that TFL cannot handle differences in meaning that go beyond mere differences in truth value.

## 29.1   Symbolizing versus translating

FOL has some similar limitations. It gets beyond mere truth values, since it enables us to split up sentences into terms, predicates and quantifiers. This enables us to consider what is *true of* some particular object, or of some or all objects. *But that's it.*

To unpack this a bit, consider this symbolization key:

$C(x)$: _____$_x$ teaches Logic III in Calgary

This stipulation does not carry the *meaning* of the English predicate across into our FOL predicate. We are simply stipulating something like this:

- '$C(x)$' and '_____$_x$ teaches Logic III in Calgary' are to be *true of* exactly the same things.

So, in particular:

- '$C(x)$' is to be true of exactly those things which teach Logic III in Calgary (whatever those things might be).

This is an indirect way of stipulating which things a predicate is true of.

Alternatively, we can stipulate predicate extensions directly. For example, we can stipulate that '$C(x)$' is to be true of Richard Zach, and Richard Zach alone. As it happens, this direct stipulation would have the same effect as the indirect stipulation, since Richard, and Richard alone, teaches Logic III in Calgary. Note, however, that the English predicates '_____ is Richard Zach' and '_____ teaches Logic III in Calgary' have very different meanings!

The point is that FOL has no resources for dealing with nuances of meaning. When we interpret FOL, all we are considering is what the predicates are true of, regardless of whether we specify these things directly or indirectly. The things a predicate is true of are known as the EXTENSION of that predicate. We say that FOL is an EXTENSIONAL LANGUAGE because FOL does not represent differences of meaning between predicates that have the same extension.

This is why we speak of *symbolizing* English sentences in FOL. It is doubtful that we are *translating* English into FOL, for translation should preserve meaning.

## 29.2   Extensions

We can stipulate directly what predicates are to be true of. And our stipulations can be as arbitrary as we like. For example, we could stipulate that '$H(x)$' should be true of, and only of, the following objects:

Justin Trudeau

the number $\pi$

every top-F key on every piano ever made

Armed with this interpretation of '$H(x)$', suppose we now add to our symbolization key:

$j$: Justin Trudeau
$a$: Angela Merkel
$p$: the number $\pi$

Then '$H(j)$' and '$H(p)$' will both be true, on this interpretation, but '$H(a)$' will be false, since Angela Merkel was not among the stipulated objects.

This process of explicit stipulation is sometimes described as stipulating the *extension* of a predicate. Note that, in the stipulation we just gave, the objects we listed have nothing particularly in common. This doesn't matter. Logic doesn't care about what we humans (at a particular moment) think 'naturally go together'; to logic, all objects are on an equal footing.

Any well-defined collection of objects is a potential extension of a one-place predicate. The example above shows one way of stipulating the extension of '$H(x)$' by *enumeration*, i.e., we simply list the objects in the extension of '$H(x)$'. We can also stipulate the extension, as we have also already seen, by giving an English predicate, such as '_____$_x$ teaches Logic III at Calgary' or '_____$_x$ is an even integer between 3 and 9'. The latter would specify an extension consisting of, and only of, 4, 6, and 8.

Note that some predicates of English, such as '_____$_x$ is a round square', are not true of anything. In this case we say the extension of the predicate is *empty*. We do allow empty extensions, and we can stipulate that the extension of a '$H(x)$' is to be empty simply by not listing any members. (It may be odd to consider collections of no things, but logic is odd this way sometimes.)

## 29.3   Many-place predicates

All of this is quite easy to understand when it comes to one-place predicates, but it gets messier when we deal with two-place predicates. Consider a symbolization key like:

$L(x,y)$: _____$x$ loves _____$y$

Given what we said above, this symbolization key should be read as saying:

- '$L(x,y)$' and '_____$x$ loves _____$y$' are to be true of exactly the same things

So, in particular:

- '$L(x,y)$' is to be true of x and y (in that order) iff x loves y.

It is important that we insist upon the order here, since love—famously—is not always reciprocated. (Note that 'x' and 'y' on the right here are symbols of augmented English, and that they are being *used*. By contrast, 'x' and 'y' in '$L(x,y)$' are symbols of FOL, and they are being *mentioned*.)

That is an indirect stipulation. What about a direct stipulation? This is also tricky. If we *simply* list objects that fall under '$L(x,y)$', we will not know whether they are the lover or the beloved (or both). We have to find a way to include the order in our explicit stipulation.

To do this, we can specify that two-place predicates are true of *pairs* of objects, where the order of the pair is important. Thus we might stipulate that '$B(x,y)$' is to be true of, and only of, the following pairs of objects:

⟨Lenin, Marx⟩
⟨de Beauvoir, Sartre⟩
⟨Sartre, de Beauvoir⟩

Here the angle-brackets keep us informed concerning order. Suppose we now add the following stipulations:

  $l$:  Lenin
 $m$:  Marx
  $b$:  de Beauvoir
  $r$:  Sartre

Then '$B(l,m)$' will be true, since ⟨Lenin, Marx⟩ is in our explicit list, but '$B(m,l)$' will be false, since ⟨Marx, Lenin⟩ is not in our list. However, both '$B(b,r)$' and '$B(r,b)$' will be true, since both ⟨de Beauvoir, Sartre⟩ and ⟨Sartre, de Beauvoir⟩ are in our explicit list.

To make these ideas more precise, we would need to develop some very elementary *set theory*. Set theory has formal apparatus which allows us to deal with extensions, ordered pairs, and so forth. However, set theory is not covered in this book. So I shall leave these ideas at an imprecise level. Nevertheless, the general idea should be clear.

## 29.4   Semantics for identity

Identity is a special predicate of FOL. We write it a bit differently than other two-place predicates: '$x = y$' instead of '$I(x,y)$' (for example). More important, though, its interpretation is fixed, once and for all.

If two names refer to the same object, then swapping one name for another will not change the truth value of any sentence. So, in particular, if '$a$' and '$b$' name the same object, then all of the following will be true:

$$A(a) \leftrightarrow A(b)$$
$$B(a) \leftrightarrow B(b)$$
$$R(a,a) \leftrightarrow R(b,b)$$
$$R(a,a) \leftrightarrow R(a,b)$$
$$R(c,a) \leftrightarrow R(c,b)$$
$$\forall x\, R(x,a) \leftrightarrow \forall x\, R(x,b)$$

Some philosophers have believed the reverse of this claim. That is, they have believed that when exactly the same sentences (not containing '=') are true of $a$ and $b$, then $a$ and $b$ are the very same object. This is a highly controversial philosophical claim—sometimes called the *identity of indiscernibles*—and our logic will not subscribe to it; we allow that exactly the same things might be true of two *distinct* objects.

To bring this out, consider the following interpretation:

domain: P.D. Magnus, Tim Button
   $a$: P.D. Magnus
   $b$: Tim Button
   • For every primitive predicate we care to consider, that predicate is true of *nothing*.

Suppose '$A$' is a one-place predicate; then '$A(a)$' is false and '$A(b)$' is false, so '$A(a) \leftrightarrow A(b)$' is true. Similarly, if '$R$' is a two-place predicate, then '$R(a,a)$' is false and '$R(a,b)$' is false, so that '$R(a,a) \leftrightarrow R(a,b)$' is true. And so it goes: every atomic sentence not involving '=' is false, so every biconditional linking such sentences is true. For all that, Tim Button and P.D. Magnus are two distinct people, not one and the same!

## 29.5 Interpretations

We defined a VALUATION in TFL as any assignment of truth and falsity to sentence letters. In FOL, we are going to define an

INTERPRETATION as consisting of four things:

- the specification of a domain
- for each sentence letter we care to consider, a truth value
- for each name that we care to consider, an assignment of exactly one object within the domain
- for each predicate that we care to consider (apart from '='), a specification of what things (in what order) the predicate is to be true of. (We don't need to specify an interpretation of '=', since it has a *fixed* interpretation.)

The symbolization keys that we considered in Part V consequently give us one very convenient way to present an interpretation. We will continue to use them in this chapter. Following the discussion of §29.2, we now also allow extensions specified by enumerations on the right side, e.g.,

domain: heads of state, numbers
  $H(x)$: Justin Trudeau, Angela Merkel, $\pi$

is a perfectly good way of specifying an interpretation, as is

domain: 0, 1, 2
  $L(x,y)$: $\langle 0,1 \rangle$, $\langle 0, 2 \rangle$, $\langle 1, 2 \rangle$

We could have specified the same extension (on this particular domain) by giving the English predicate '_____$x$ is less than _____$y$'.

However, it is sometimes also convenient to present an interpretation *diagrammatically*. To illustrate (literally): suppose we want to consider just a single two-place predicate, '$R(x,y)$'. Then we can represent it just by drawing an arrow between two objects, and stipulate that '$R(x,y)$' is to hold of $x$ and $y$ just in case there is an arrow running from $x$ to $y$ in our diagram. As an example, we might offer:

This diagram could be used to describe an interpretation whose domain is the first four positive whole numbers, and which interprets '$R(x,y)$' as being true of and only of:

$$\langle 1, 2\rangle, \langle 2, 3\rangle, \langle 3, 4\rangle, \langle 4, 1\rangle, \langle 1, 3\rangle$$

Equally we might offer this diagram:

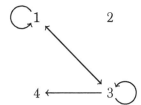

The interpretation specified by this diagram can also be given by listing what's in the domain and in the extension of '$R(x,y)$':

domain: 1, 2, 3, 4
$R(x,y)$: $\langle 1, 3\rangle, \langle 3, 1\rangle, \langle 3, 4\rangle, \langle 1, 1\rangle, \langle 3, 3\rangle$

If we wanted, we could make our diagrams more complex. For example, we could add names as labels for particular objects. Equally, to symbolize the extension of a one-place predicate, we might simply draw a circle around some particular objects and stipulate that the thus encircled objects (and only them) are to fall under the predicate '$H(x)$', say. To specify multiple predicates we could use colored (or dashed, dotted) lines for arrows and circles.

## CHAPTER 30

# *Truth in FOL*

We have introduced you to interpretations. Since, among other things, they tell us which predicates are true of which objects, they will provide us with an account of the truth of atomic sentences. However, we now need to say, precisely, what it is for an arbitrary FOL sentence to be true or false in an interpretation.

We know from §26 that there are three kinds of sentence in FOL:

- atomic sentences
- sentences whose main logical operator is a sentential connective
- sentences whose main logical operator is a quantifier

We need to explain truth for all three kinds of sentence.

We will provide a completely general explanation in this section. However, to try to keep the explanation comprehensible, we will, at several points, use the following interpretation:

domain: all people born before 2000CE
     $a$: Aristotle
     $b$: Beyoncé
  $P(x)$: _____$_x$ is a philosopher
$R(x,y)$: _____$_x$ was born before _____$_y$

This will be our *go-to example* in what follows.

## 30.1   Atomic sentences

The truth of atomic sentences should be fairly straightforward. For sentence letters, the interpretation specifies if it is true or false. The sentence '$P(a)$' should be true just in case '$P(x)$' is true of '$a$'. Given our go-to interpretation, this is true iff Aristotle is a philosopher. Aristotle is a philosopher. So the sentence is true. Equally, '$P(b)$' is false on our go-to interpretation.

Likewise, on this interpretation, '$R(a,b)$' is true iff the object named by '$a$' was born before the object named by '$b$'. Well, Aristotle was born before Beyoncé. So '$R(a,b)$' is true. Equally, '$R(a,a)$' is false: Aristotle was not born before Aristotle.

Dealing with atomic sentences, then, is very intuitive. When $\mathscr{R}$ is an $n$-place predicate and $a_1$, $a_2$, ..., $a_n$ are names,

> The sentence $\mathscr{R}(a_1, a_2, \ldots, a_n)$ is true in an interpretation **iff**
> $\mathscr{R}$ is true of the objects named by $a_1$, $a_2$, ..., $a_n$ (in that order) in that interpretation.

Recall, though, that there is a special kind of atomic sentence: two names connected by an identity sign constitute an atomic sentence. This kind of atomic sentence is also easy to handle. Where $a$ and $b$ are any names,

> $a = b$ is true in an interpretation **iff**
> $a$ and $b$ name the very same object in that interpretation

So in our go-to interpretation, '$a = b$' is false, since Aristotle is distinct from Beyoncé.

## 30.2   Sentential connectives

We saw in §26 that FOL sentences can be built up from simpler ones using the truth-functional connectives that were familiar from TFL. The rules governing these truth-functional connectives are *exactly* the same as they were when we considered TFL. Here they are:

$\mathcal{A} \land \mathcal{B}$ is true in an interpretation **iff**
both $\mathcal{A}$ is true and $\mathcal{B}$ is true in that interpretation

$\mathcal{A} \lor \mathcal{B}$ is true in an interpretation **iff**
either $\mathcal{A}$ is true or $\mathcal{B}$ is true in that interpretation

$\neg\mathcal{A}$ is true in an interpretation **iff**
$\mathcal{A}$ is false in that interpretation

$\mathcal{A} \to \mathcal{B}$ is true in an interpretation **iff**
either $\mathcal{A}$ is false or $\mathcal{B}$ is true in that interpretation

$\mathcal{A} \leftrightarrow \mathcal{B}$ is true in an interpretation **iff**
$\mathcal{A}$ has the same truth value as $\mathcal{B}$ in that interpretation

This presents the very same information as the characteristic truth tables for the connectives; it just does so in a slightly different way. Some examples will probably help to illustrate the idea. (Make sure you understand them!) On our go-to interpretation:

- '$a = a \land P(a)$' is true
- '$R(a,b) \land P(b)$' is false because, although '$R(a,b)$' is true, '$P(b)$' is false
- '$a = b \lor P(a)$' is true
- '$\neg a = b$' is true
- '$P(a) \land \neg(a = b \land R(a,b))$' is true, because '$P(a)$' is true and '$a = b$' is false

Make sure you understand these examples.

## 30.3 When the main logical operator is a quantifier

The exciting innovation in FOL, though, is the use of *quantifiers*, but expressing the truth conditions for quantified sentences is a bit more fiddly than one might first expect.

Here is a naïve first thought. We want to say that '$\forall x\, F(x)$' is true iff '$F(x)$' is true of everything in the domain. This should not be too problematic: our interpretation will specify directly what '$F(x)$' is true of.

Unfortunately, this naïve thought is not general enough. For example, we want to be able to say that '$\forall x \exists y\, L(x,y)$' is true just in case (speaking roughly) '$\exists y\, L(x,y)$' is true of everything in the domain. But our interpretation does not *directly* specify what '$\exists y\, L(x,y)$' is true of. Instead, whether or not this is true of something should follow just from the interpretation of the predicate '$L$', the domain, and the meanings of the quantifiers.

So here is a second naïve thought. We might try to say that '$\forall x \exists y\, L(x,y)$' is to be true in an interpretation iff $\exists y\, L(a,y)$ is true for *every* name $a$ that we have included in our interpretation. Similarly, we might try to say that $\exists y\, L(a,y)$ is true just in case $L(a,b)$ is true for *some* name $b$ that we have included in our interpretation.

Unfortunately, this is not right either. To see this, observe that our go-to interpretation only interprets *two* names, '$a$' and '$b$'. But the domain—all people born before the year 2000CE—contains many more than two people. (And we have no intention of trying to correct for this by naming *all* of them!)

So here is a third thought. (And this thought is not naïve, but correct.) Although it is not the case that we have named *everyone*, each person *could* have been given a name. So we should focus on this possibility of extending an interpretation by adding a new name. We will offer a few examples of how this might work, centring on our go-to interpretation, and we will then present the formal definition.

In our go-to interpretation, '$\exists x\, R(b,x)$' should be true. After all, in the domain, there is certainly someone who was born after Beyoncé. Lady Gaga is one of those people. Indeed, if we were to extend our go-to interpretation—temporarily, mind—by adding the name '$c$' to refer to Lady Gaga, then '$R(b,c)$' would be true on this extended interpretation. This, surely, should suffice to make '$\exists x\, R(b,x)$' true on the original go-to interpretation.

In our go-to interpretation, '$\exists x(P(x) \land R(x,a))$' should also be true. After all, in the domain, there is certainly someone who was both a philosopher and born before Aristotle. Socrates is one such person. Indeed, if we were to extend our go-to interpretation by letting a new name, '$c$', denote Socrates, then '$W(c) \land R(c,a)$' would be true on this extended interpretation. Again, this should surely suffice to make '$\exists x(P(x) \land R(x,a))$' true on the original go-to interpretation.

In our go-to interpretation, '$\forall x \exists y\, R(x,y)$' should be false. After all, consider the last person born in the year 1999. We don't know who that was, but if we were to extend our go-to interpretation by letting a new name, '$d$', denote that person, then we would not be able to find anyone else in the domain to denote with some further new name, perhaps '$e$', in such a way that '$R(d,e)$' would be true. Indeed, no matter *whom* we named with '$e$', '$R(d,e)$' would be false. This observation is surely sufficient to make '$\exists y\, R(d,y)$' *false* in our extended interpretation, which in turn is surely sufficient to make '$\forall x \exists y\, R(x,y)$' false on the original go-to interpretation.

If you have understood these three examples, that's what matters. It provides the basis for a formal definition of truth for quantified sentences.

Strictly speaking, though, we still need to *give* that definition. The result, sadly, is a bit ugly, and requires a few new definitions. Brace yourself!

Suppose that $\mathcal{A}$ is a formula containing at least one occurrence of the variable $x$, and that $x$ is free in $\mathcal{A}$. We will write this thus:

$$\mathcal{A}(\ldots x \ldots x \ldots)$$

Suppose also that $c$ is a name. Then we will write:

$$\mathscr{A}(\ldots c \ldots c \ldots)$$

for the formula we obtain by replacing *every* occurrence of $x$ in $\mathscr{A}$ with $c$. The resulting formula is called a SUBSTITUTION INSTANCE of $\forall x \mathscr{A}$ and $\exists x \mathscr{A}$. Also, $c$ is called the INSTANTIATING NAME. So:

$$\exists x (R(e,x) \leftrightarrow F(x))$$

is a substitution instance of

$$\forall y \exists x (R(y,x) \leftrightarrow F(x))$$

with the instantiating name '$e$' and instantiated variable '$y$'.

Our interpretation will include a specification of which names correspond to which objects in the domain. Take any object in the domain, say, $d$, and a name $c$ which is not already assigned by the interpretation. If our interpretation is **I**, then we can consider the interpretation $\mathbf{I}[d/c]$ which is just like **I** except it *also* assigns the name $c$ to the object $d$. Then we can say that $d$ SATISFIES the formula $\mathscr{A}(\ldots x \ldots x \ldots)$ in the interpretation **I** if, and only if, $\mathscr{A}(\ldots c \ldots c \ldots)$ is true in $\mathbf{I}[d/c]$. (If $d$ satisfies $\mathscr{A}(\ldots x \ldots x \ldots)$ we also say that $\mathscr{A}(\ldots x \ldots x \ldots)$ is *true of $d$*.)

---

The interpretation $\mathbf{I}[d/c]$ is just like the interpretation **I** except it also assigns the name $c$ to the object $d$.

An object $d$ SATISFIES $\mathscr{A}(\ldots x \ldots x \ldots)$ in interpretation **I** **iff** $\mathscr{A}(\ldots c \ldots c \ldots)$ is true in $\mathbf{I}[d/c]$.

---

So, for instance, Socrates satisfies the formula $P(x)$ since $P(c)$ is true in the interpretation $\mathbf{I}[\text{Socrates}/c]$, i.e., the interpretation:

domain: all people born before 2000CE
    $a$: Aristotle
    $b$: Beyoncé
    $c$: Socrates

$P(x)$: _____$_x$ is a philosopher
$R(x,y)$: _____$_x$ was born before _____$_y$

Armed with this notation, the rough idea is as follows. The sentence $\forall x \mathcal{A}(\ldots x \ldots x \ldots)$ will be true in **I** iff, for any object $d$ in the domain, $\mathcal{A}(\ldots c \ldots c \ldots)$ is true in $\mathbf{I}[d/c]$, i.e., no matter what object (in the domain) we name with $c$. In other words, $\forall x \mathcal{A}(\ldots x \ldots x \ldots)$ is true iff every object in the domain satisfies $\mathcal{A}(\ldots x \ldots x \ldots)$. Similarly, the sentence $\exists x \mathcal{A}$ will be true iff there is *some* object that satisifes $\mathcal{A}(\ldots x \ldots x \ldots)$, i.e., $\mathcal{A}(\ldots c \ldots c \ldots)$ true in $\mathbf{I}[d/c]$ for some object $d$.

> $\forall x \mathcal{A}(\ldots x \ldots x \ldots)$ is true in an interpretation **iff** every object in the domain satisfies $\mathcal{A}(\ldots x \ldots x \ldots)$.
>
> $\exists x \mathcal{A}(\ldots x \ldots x \ldots)$ is true in an interpretation **iff** at least one object in the domain satisfies $\mathcal{A}(\ldots x \ldots x \ldots)$.

To be clear: all this is doing is formalizing (very pedantically) the intuitive idea expressed on the previous page. The result is a bit ugly, and the final definition might look a bit opaque. Hopefully, though, the *spirit* of the idea is clear.

## 30.4  Satisfaction of formulas

The concept of an object satisfying a formula with a free variable can also be extended to formulas with more than one free variable. If we have a formula $\mathcal{A}(x,y)$ with two free variables $x$ and $y$, then we can say that a pair of objects $\langle a,b \rangle$ satisfies $\mathcal{A}(x,y)$ iff $\mathcal{A}(c,d)$ is true in the interpretation extended by two names $c$ and $d$, where $c$ names $a$ and $d$ names $b$. So, for instance, $\langle \text{Socrates}, \text{Plato} \rangle$ satisfies $R(x,y)$ since $R(c,d)$ is true in the interpretation:

domain:  all people born before 2000CE
      $a$: Aristotle

$b$: Beyoncé

$c$: Socrates

$d$: Plato

$P(x)$: _____$x$ is a philosopher

$R(x,y)$: _____$x$ was born before _____$y$

For atomic formulas, the objects, pairs of objects, etc., that satisfy them are exactly the extension of the predicate given in the interpretation. But the notion of satisfaction also applies to non-atomic formulas, e.g., the formula $P(x) \land R(x,b)$ is satisfied by all philosophers born before Beyoncé. It even applies to formulas involving quantifiers, e.g., $P(x) \land \neg \exists y(P(y) \land R(y,x))$ is satisfied by all people who are philosophers and for whom it is true that no philosopher was born before them—in other words, it is true of the first philosopher.

By considering formulas (possibly involving quantifiers) with two free variables, we can express relations for which we do not have dedicated predicate symbols in our interpretation or symbolization key. Consider the formula $R(x,y)$. It expresses the relation '_____$x$ was born before _____$y$', since that is how we have specified its extension. What happens if we switch the variables, i.e., consider '$R(y,x)$'? A pair of objects $\langle y,x \rangle$ in the domain (i.e., people) satisfies $R(y,x)$ if, and only if, the reverse pair $\langle x,y \rangle$ satisfies $R(x,y)$. In other words, $R(y,x)$ expresses the relation '_____$x$ was born *after* _____$y$'. Or suppose we add to our interpretation a predicate for 'teacher of'.

$T(x,y)$: _____$x$ was a teacher of _____$y$

Then the formula '$\exists z(T(z,x) \land T(z,y))$' is satisfied by x and y if, and only if, some person z was a teacher of both x and y, i.e., it expresses '_____$x$ and _____$y$ have a teacher in common'. Similarly, '$\forall z(T(x,z) \leftrightarrow T(y,z))$' expresses '_____$x$ and _____$y$ taught the same people'.

## Practice exercises

**A.** Consider the following interpretation:

- The domain comprises only Corwin and Benedict
- '$A(x)$' is to be true of both Corwin and Benedict
- '$B(x)$' is to be true of Benedict only
- '$N(x)$' is to be true of no one
- '$c$' is to refer to Corwin

Determine whether each of the following sentences is true or false in that interpretation:

1. $B(c)$
2. $A(c) \leftrightarrow \neg N(c)$
3. $N(c) \rightarrow (A(c) \vee B(c))$
4. $\forall x\, A(x)$
5. $\forall x \neg B(x)$
6. $\exists x (A(x) \wedge B(x))$
7. $\exists x (A(x) \rightarrow N(x))$
8. $\forall x (N(x) \vee \neg N(x))$
9. $\exists x\, B(x) \rightarrow \forall x\, A(x)$

**B.** Consider the following interpretation:

- The domain comprises only Lemmy, Courtney and Eddy
- '$G(x)$' is to be true of Lemmy, Courtney and Eddy.
- '$H(x)$' is to be true of and only of Courtney
- '$M(x)$' is to be true of and only of Lemmy and Eddy
- '$c$' is to refer to Courtney
- '$e$' is to refer to Eddy

Determine whether each of the following sentences is true or false in that interpretation:

1. $H(c)$
2. $H(e)$
3. $M(c) \vee M(e)$

4. $G(c) \lor \neg G(c)$
5. $M(c) \rightarrow G(c)$
6. $\exists x\, H(x)$
7. $\forall x\, H(x)$
8. $\exists x\, \neg M(x)$
9. $\exists x (H(x) \land G(x))$
10. $\exists x (M(x) \land G(x))$
11. $\forall x (H(x) \lor M(x))$
12. $\exists x\, H(x) \land \exists x\, M(x)$
13. $\forall x (H(x) \leftrightarrow \neg M(x))$
14. $\exists x\, G(x) \land \exists x \neg G(x)$
15. $\forall x \exists y (G(x) \land H(y))$

**C.** Following the diagram conventions introduced at the end of §29, consider the following interpretation:

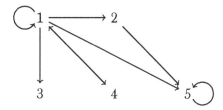

Determine whether each of the following sentences is true or false in that interpretation:

1. $\exists x\, R(x,x)$
2. $\forall x\, R(x,x)$
3. $\exists x \forall y\, R(x,y)$
4. $\exists x \forall y\, R(y,x)$
5. $\forall x \forall y \forall z ((R(x,y) \land R(y,z)) \rightarrow R(x,z))$
6. $\forall x \forall y \forall z ((R(x,y) \land R(x,z)) \rightarrow R(y,z))$
7. $\exists x \forall y\, \neg R(x,y)$
8. $\forall x (\exists y\, R(x,y) \rightarrow \exists y\, R(y,x))$
9. $\exists x \exists y (\neg x = y \land R(x,y) \land R(y,x))$
10. $\exists x \forall y (R(x,y) \leftrightarrow x = y)$
11. $\exists x \forall y (R(y,x) \leftrightarrow x = y)$

12. $\exists x \exists y (\neg x = y \land R(x,y) \land \forall z (R(z,x) \leftrightarrow y = z))$

# CHAPTER 31

# *Semantic concepts*

Defining truth in FOL was quite fiddly. But now that we are done, we can define various other central logical notions. These definitions will look very similar to those for TFL, from §12. However, remember that they concern *interpretations*, rather than valuations.

We will use the symbol '⊨' for FOL much as we did for TFL. So:

$$\mathscr{A}_1, \mathscr{A}_2, \ldots, \mathscr{A}_n \vDash \mathscr{C}$$

means that there is no interpretation in which all of $\mathscr{A}_1$, $\mathscr{A}_2$, ..., $\mathscr{A}_n$ are true and in which $\mathscr{C}$ is false. Derivatively,

$$\vDash \mathscr{A}$$

means that $\mathscr{A}$ is true in every interpretation.

The other logical notions also have corresponding definitions in FOL:

▷ An FOL sentence $\mathscr{A}$ is a VALIDITY iff $\mathscr{A}$ is true in every interpretation; i.e., $\vDash \mathscr{A}$.

▷ $\mathscr{A}$ is a CONTRADICTION iff $\mathscr{A}$ is false in every interpretation; i.e., $\vDash \neg \mathscr{A}$.

▷ $\mathcal{A}_1, \mathcal{A}_2, \ldots \mathcal{A}_n \therefore \mathcal{C}$ is VALID IN FOL iff there is no interpretation in which all of the premises are true and the conclusion is false; i.e., $\mathcal{A}_1, \mathcal{A}_2, \ldots \mathcal{A}_n \vDash \mathcal{C}$. It is INVALID IN FOL otherwise.

▷ Two FOL sentences $\mathcal{A}$ and $\mathcal{B}$ are EQUIVALENT iff they are true in exactly the same interpretations as each other; i.e., both $\mathcal{A} \vDash \mathcal{B}$ and $\mathcal{B} \vDash \mathcal{A}$.

▷ The FOL sentences $\mathcal{A}_1, \mathcal{A}_2, \ldots, \mathcal{A}_n$ are JOINTLY SATISFIABLE iff some interpretation makes all of them true. They are JOINTLY UNSATISFIABLE iff there is no such interpretation.

# CHAPTER 32

# *Using interpretations*

## 32.1 Validities and contradictions

Suppose we want to show that '$\exists x\, A(x,x) \to B(d)$' is *not* a validity. This requires showing that the sentence is not true in every interpretation; i.e., that it is false in some interpretation. If we can provide just one interpretation in which the sentence is false, then we will have shown that the sentence is not a validity.

In order for '$\exists x\, A(x,x) \to B(d)$' to be false, the antecedent ('$\exists x\, A(x,x)$') must be true, and the consequent ('$B(d)$') must be false. To construct such an interpretation, we start by specifying a domain. Keeping the domain small makes it easier to specify what the predicates will be true of, so we will start with a domain that has just one member. For concreteness, let's say it is *just* the city of Paris.

domain: Paris

The name '$d$' must refer to something in the domain, so we have no option but:

    $d$: Paris

Recall that we want '$\exists x\, A(x,x)$' to be true, so we want all members of the domain to be paired with themselves in the extension of '$A$'. We can just offer:

$A(x,y)$: _____$x$ is identical with _____$y$

Now '$A(d,d)$' is true, so it is surely true that '$\exists x\, A(x,x)$'. Next, we want '$B(d)$' to be false, so the referent of '$d$' must not be in the extension of '$B$'. We might simply offer:

$B(x)$: _____$x$ is in Germany

Now we have an interpretation where '$\exists x\, A(x,x)$' is true, but where '$B(d)$' is false. So there is an interpretation where '$\exists x\, A(x,x) \to B(d)$' is false. So '$\exists x\, A(x,x) \to B(d)$' is not a validity.

We can just as easily show that '$\exists x A(x,x) \to B(d)$' is not a contradiction. We need only specify an interpretation in which '$\exists x A(x,x) \to B(d)$' is true; i.e., an interpretation in which either '$\exists x\, A(x,x)$' is false or '$B(d)$' is true. Here is one:

domain: Paris
   $d$: Paris
$A(x,y)$: _____$x$ is identical with _____$y$
 $B(x)$: _____$x$ is in France

This shows that there is an interpretation where '$\exists x A(x,x) \to B(d)$' is true. So '$\exists x\, A(x,x) \to B(d)$' is not a contradiction.

> To show that $\mathcal{A}$ is not a validity, it suffices to find an interpretation where $\mathcal{A}$ is false.
> To show that $\mathcal{A}$ is not a contradiction, it suffices to find an interpretation where $\mathcal{A}$ is true.

## 32.2  Logical equivalence

Suppose we want to show that '$\forall x\, S(x)$' and '$\exists x\, S(x)$' are not logically equivalent. We need to construct an interpretation in which the two sentences have different truth values; we want one of them to be true and the other to be false. We start by specifying a domain. Again, we make the domain small so that we can specify extensions easily. In this case, we will need at least two objects. (If we chose a domain with only one member, the two sentences would end up with the same truth value. In order to see why, try constructing some partial interpretations with one-member domains.) For concreteness, let's take:

domain: Ornette Coleman, Miles Davis

We can make '$\exists x\, S(x)$' true by including something in the extension of '$S$', and we can make '$\forall x\, S(x)$' false by leaving something out of the extension of '$S$'. For concreteness, let's say:

$S(x)$: _____$_x$ plays saxophone

Now '$\exists x\, S(x)$' is true, because '$S(x)$' is true of Ornette Coleman. Slightly more precisely, extend our interpretation by allowing '$c$' to name Ornette Coleman. '$S(c)$' is true in this extended interpretation, so '$\exists x\, S(x)$' was true in the original interpretation. Similarly, '$\forall x\, S(x)$' is false, because '$S(x)$' is false of Miles Davis. Slightly more precisely, extend our interpretation by allowing '$d$' to name Miles Davis, and '$S(d)$' is false in this extended interpretation, so '$\forall x\, S(x)$' was false in the original interpretation. We have provided a counter-interpretation to the claim that '$\forall x\, S(x)$' and '$\exists x\, S(x)$' are logically equivalent.

> To show that $\mathcal{A}$ and $\mathcal{B}$ are not logically equivalent, it suffices to find an interpretation where one is true and the other is false.

## 32.3  Validity, entailment and satisfiability

To test for validity, entailment, or satisfiability, we typically need to produce interpretations that determine the truth value of several sentences simultaneously.

Consider the following argument in FOL:

$$\exists x(G(x) \to G(a)) \therefore \exists x\, G(x) \to G(a)$$

To show that this is invalid, we must make the premise true and the conclusion false. The conclusion is a conditional, so to make it false, the antecedent must be true and the consequent must be false. Clearly, our domain must contain two objects. Let's try:

domain: Karl Marx, Ludwig von Mises
 $G(x)$: \_\_\_\_\_$_x$ hated communism
  $a$: Karl Marx

Given that Marx wrote *The Communist Manifesto*, '$G(a)$' is plainly false in this interpretation. But von Mises famously hated communism, so '$\exists x\, G(x)$' is true in this interpretation. Hence '$\exists x\, G(x) \to G(a)$' is false, as required.

Does this interpretation make the premise true? Yes it does! Note that '$G(a) \to G(a)$' is true. (Indeed, it is a validity.) But then certainly '$\exists x(G(x) \to G(a))$' is true, so the premise is true, and the conclusion is false, in this interpretation. The argument is therefore invalid.

In passing, note that we have also shown that '$\exists x(G(x) \to G(a))$' does *not* entail '$\exists x\, G(x) \to G(a)$', i.e., that $\exists x(G(x) \to G(a)) \nvDash \exists x G(x) \to G(a)$. Equally, we have shown that the sentences '$\exists x(G(x) \to G(a))$' and '$\neg(\exists x\, G(x) \to G(a))$' are jointly satisfiable.

Let's consider a second example. Consider:

$$\forall x \exists y\, L(x,y) \therefore \exists y \forall x\, L(x,y)$$

Again, we want to show that this is invalid. To do this, we must make the premises true and the conclusion false. Here is a suggestion:

domain: Canadian citizens currently in a domestic partnership
   with another Canadian citizen
 $L(x,y)$: \_\_\_\_\_$_x$ is in a domestic partnership with \_\_\_\_\_$_y$

The premise is clearly true on this interpretation. Anyone in the domain is a Canadian citizen in a domestic partnership with some other Canadian citizen. That other citizen will also, then, be in the domain. So for everyone in the domain, there will be someone (else) in the domain with whom they are in a domestic partnership. Hence '$\forall x \exists y\, L(x,y)$' is true. However, the conclusion is clearly false, for that would require that there is some single person who is in a domestic partnership with everyone in the domain, and there is no such person, so the argument is invalid. We observe immediately that the sentences '$\forall x \exists y\, L(x,y)$' and '$\neg \exists y \forall x\, L(x,y)$' are jointly satisfiable and that '$\forall x \exists y\, L(x,y)$' does not entail '$\exists y \forall x\, L(x,y)$'.

For our third example, we'll mix things up a bit. In §29, we described how we can present some interpretations using diagrams. For example:

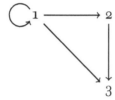

Using the conventions employed in §29, the domain of this interpretation is the first three positive whole numbers, and '$R(x,y)$' is true of x and y just in case there is an arrow from x to y in our diagram. Here are some sentences that the interpretation makes true:

- '$\forall x \exists y\, R(y,x)$'
- '$\exists x \forall y\, R(x,y)$'                                   witness 1
- '$\exists x \forall y (R(y,x) \leftrightarrow x = y)$'                    witness 1
- '$\exists x \exists y \exists z ((\neg y = z \wedge R(x,y)) \wedge R(z,x))$'    witness 2
- '$\exists x \forall y\, \neg R(x,y)$'                               witness 3
- '$\exists x (\exists y\, R(y,x) \wedge \neg \exists y\, R(x,y))$'            witness 3

This immediately shows that all of the preceding six sentences are jointly satisfiable. We can use this observation to generate *invalid* arguments, e.g.:

$$\forall x \exists y\, R(y,x), \exists x \forall y\, R(x,y) \therefore \forall x \exists y\, R(x,y)$$
$$\exists x \forall y\, R(x,y), \exists x \forall y \neg R(x,y) \therefore \neg \exists x \exists y \exists z(\neg y = z \wedge (R(x,y) \wedge R(z,x)))$$

and many more besides.

---

If some interpretation makes all of $\mathcal{A}_1, \mathcal{A}_2, \ldots, \mathcal{A}_n$ true and $\mathcal{C}$ is false, then:

- $\mathcal{A}_1, \mathcal{A}_2, \ldots, \mathcal{A}_n \therefore \mathcal{C}$ is *invalid*; and
- $\mathcal{A}_1, \mathcal{A}_2, \ldots, \mathcal{A}_n \nvDash \mathcal{C}$; and
- And $\mathcal{A}_1, \mathcal{A}_2, \ldots, \mathcal{A}_n, \neg \mathcal{C}$ are jointly satisfiable.

---

An interpretation which refutes a claim—to logical truth, say, or to entailment—is called a *counter-interpretation*, or a *counter-model*.

We'll close this section, though, with a caution about the relationship between (in)validity and (non)entailment. Recall FOL's limitations: it is is an extensional language; it ignores issues of vagueness; and it cannot handle cases of validity for 'special reasons'. To take one illustration of these issues, consider this natural-language argument:

> Every fox is cute.
> ∴ All vixens are cute.

This is valid: necessarily every vixen is a fox, so it is impossible for the premise to be true and the conclusion false. Now, we might sensibly symbolize the argument as follows:

$$\forall x(F(x) \rightarrow C(x)) \therefore \forall x(V(x) \rightarrow C(x))$$

However, it is easy to find counter-models which show that $\forall x(F(x) \rightarrow C(x)) \nvDash \forall x(V(x) \rightarrow C(x))$. (*Exercise*: find one.) So, it would be *wrong* to infer that the English argument is *invalid*, just because there is a counter-model to the relevant *FOL-entailment*.

The general moral is this. If you want to infer from the absence of an entailment in FOL to the invalidity of some English argument, then you need to argue that nothing important is lost in the way you have symbolized the English argument.

## Practice exercises

**A.** Show that each of the following is neither a validity nor a contradiction:

1. $D(a) \wedge D(b)$
2. $\exists x\, T(x, h)$
3. $P(m) \wedge \neg \forall x\, P(x)$
4. $\forall z\, J(z) \leftrightarrow \exists y\, J(y)$
5. $\forall x(W(x, m, n) \vee \exists y L(x, y))$
6. $\exists x(G(x) \rightarrow \forall y\, M(y))$
7. $\exists x(x = h \wedge x = i)$

**B.** Show that the following pairs of sentences are not logically equivalent.

1. $J(a),\ K(a)$
2. $\exists x\, J(x),\ J(m)$
3. $\forall x\, R(x, x),\ \exists x\, R(x, x)$
4. $\exists x\, P(x) \rightarrow Q(c),\ \exists x(P(x) \rightarrow Q(c))$
5. $\forall x(P(x) \rightarrow \neg Q(x)),\ \exists x(P(x) \wedge \neg Q(x))$
6. $\exists x(P(x) \wedge Q(x)),\ \exists x(P(x) \rightarrow Q(x))$
7. $\forall x(P(x) \rightarrow Q(x)),\ \forall x(P(x) \wedge Q(x))$
8. $\forall x \exists y\, R(x, y),\ \exists x \forall y\, R(x, y)$
9. $\forall x \exists y\, R(x, y),\ \forall x \exists y\, R(y, x)$

**C.** Show that the following sentences are jointly satisfiable:

1. $M(a), \neg N(a), P(a), \neg Q(a)$
2. $L(e, e), L(e, g), \neg L(g, e), \neg L(g, g)$
3. $\neg(M(a) \wedge \exists x\, A(x)), M(a) \vee F(a), \forall x(F(x) \rightarrow A(x))$
4. $M(a) \vee M(b), M(a) \rightarrow \forall x \neg M(x)$

5. $\forall y\, G(y), \forall x(G(x) \rightarrow H(x)), \exists y \neg I(y)$
6. $\exists x(B(x) \vee A(x)), \forall x \neg C(x), \forall x\big[(A(x) \wedge B(x)) \rightarrow C(x)\big]$
7. $\exists x\, X(x), \exists x\, Y(x), \forall x(X(x) \leftrightarrow \neg Y(x))$
8. $\forall x(P(x) \vee Q(x)), \exists x \neg(Q(x) \wedge P(x))$
9. $\exists z(N(z) \wedge O(z,z)), \forall x \forall y(O(x,y) \rightarrow O(y,x))$
10. $\neg \exists x \forall y\, R(x,y), \forall x \exists y\, R(x,y)$
11. $\neg R(a,a), \forall x(x = a \vee R(x,a))$
12. $\forall x \forall y \forall z\big[(x = y \vee y = z) \vee x = z\big], \exists x \exists y\, \neg x = y$
13. $\exists x \exists y((Z(x) \wedge Z(y)) \wedge x = y), \neg Z(d), d = e$

**D.** Show that the following arguments are invalid:

1. $\forall x(A(x) \rightarrow B(x)) \therefore \exists x\, B(x)$
2. $\forall x(R(x) \rightarrow D(x)), \forall x(R(x) \rightarrow F(x)) \therefore \exists x(D(x) \wedge F(x))$
3. $\exists x(P(x) \rightarrow Q(x)) \therefore \exists x\, P(x)$
4. $N(a) \wedge N(b) \wedge N(c) \therefore \forall x\, N(x)$
5. $R(d,e), \exists x\, R(x,d) \therefore R(e,d)$
6. $\exists x(E(x) \wedge F(x)), \exists x\, F(x) \rightarrow \exists x\, G(x) \therefore \exists x(E(x) \wedge G(x))$
7. $\forall x\, O(x,c), \forall x\, O(c,x) \therefore \forall x\, O(x,x)$
8. $\exists x(J(x) \wedge K(x)), \exists x \neg K(x), \exists x \neg J(x) \therefore \exists x(\neg J(x) \wedge \neg K(x))$
9. $L(a,b) \rightarrow \forall x\, L(x,b), \exists x\, L(x,b) \therefore L(b,b)$
10. $\forall x(D(x) \rightarrow \exists y\, T(y,x)) \therefore \exists y \exists z\, \neg y = z$

# CHAPTER 33

# *Reasoning about all interpretations*

## 33.1 Validities and contradictions

We can show that a sentence is *not* a validity just by providing one carefully specified interpretation: an interpretation in which the sentence is false. To show that something *is* a validity, on the other hand, it would not be enough to construct ten, one hundred, or even a thousand interpretations in which the sentence is true. A sentence is only a validity if it is true in *every* interpretation, and there are infinitely many interpretations. We need to reason about all of them, and we cannot do this by dealing with them one by one!

Sometimes, we can reason about all interpretations fairly easily. For example, we can offer a relatively simple argument that '$R(a,a) \vee \neg R(a,a)$' is a validity:

> Any relevant interpretation will give '$R(a,a)$' a truth value. If '$R(a,a)$' is true in an interpretation, then

'$R(a,a) \lor \neg R(a,a)$' is true in that interpretation. If '$R(a,a)$' is false in an interpretation, then $\neg R(a,a)$ is true, and so '$R(a,a) \lor \neg R(a,a)$' is true in that interpretation. These are the only alternatives. So '$R(a,a) \lor \neg R(a,a)$' is true in every interpretation. Therefore, it is a validity.

This argument is valid, of course, and its conclusion is true. However, it is not an argument in FOL. Rather, it is an argument in English *about* FOL: it is an argument in the metalanguage.

Note another feature of the argument. Since the sentence in question contained no quantifiers, we did not need to think about how to interpret '$a$' and '$R$'; the point was just that, however we interpreted them, '$R(a,a)$' would have some truth value or other. (We could ultimately have given the same argument concerning TFL sentences.)

Let's have another example. The sentence '$\forall x(R(x,x) \lor \neg R(x,x))$' should obviously be a validity. However, saying *precisely* why is quite tricky. We cannot say that '$R(x,x) \lor \neg R(x,x)$' is true in every interpretation, since '$R(x,x) \lor \neg R(x,x)$' is not even a *sentence* of FOL (remember that '$x$' is a variable, not a name). Instead, we should say something like this:

Consider some arbitrary interpretation. $\forall x(R(x,x) \lor \neg R(x,x))$ is true in our interpretation iff $R(x,x) \lor \neg R(x,x)$ is satisfied by every object of its domain. Consider some arbitrary member of the domain, which, for convenience, we will call Fred. Either Fred satisfies $R(x,x)$ or it does not. If Fred satisfies '$R(x,x)$', then Fred also satisfies '$R(x,x) \lor \neg R(x,x)$'. If Fred does not satisfy '$R(x,x)$', it *does* satisfy '$\neg R(x,x)$' and so also '$R(x,x) \lor \neg R(x,x)$'.[1] So either way, Fred satisfies '$R(x,x) \lor \neg R(x,x)$'. Since there was nothing special about Fred—we might have

---

[1] We use here the fact that the truth conditions for connectives also apply to satisfaction: $a$ satisfies $\mathcal{A}(x) \lor \mathcal{B}(x)$ iff $a$ satisfies $\mathcal{A}(x)$ or $\mathcal{B}(x)$, etc.

chosen any object—we see that every object in the do-
main satisfies '$R(x,x) \lor \neg R(x,x)$'. So '$\forall x(R(x,x) \lor$
$\neg R(x,x))$' is true in our interpretation. But we
chose our interpretation arbitrarily, so '$\forall x(R(x,x) \lor$
$\neg R(x,x))$' is true in every interpretation. It is therefore a validity.

This is quite longwinded, but, as things stand, there is no alternative. In order to show that a sentence is a validity, we must
reason about *all* interpretations.

## 33.2  Other cases

Similar points hold of other cases too. Thus, we must reason
about all interpretations if we want to show:

- that a sentence is a contradiction; for this requires that it is
  false in *every* interpretation.
- that two sentences are logically equivalent; for this requires
  that they have the same truth value in *every* interpretation.
- that some sentences are jointly unsatisfiable; for this requires that there is no interpretation in which all of those
  sentences are true together; i.e. that, in *every* interpretation,
  at least one of those sentences is false.
- that an argument is valid; for this requires that the conclusion is true in *every* interpretation where the premises are
  true.
- that some sentences entail another sentence.

The problem is that, with the tools available to you so far, reasoning about all interpretations is a serious challenge! For a final
example, here is a perfectly obvious entailment:

$$\forall x(H(x) \land J(x)) \vDash \forall x\, H(x)$$

After all, if everything is both $H$ and $J$, then everything is $H$. But
we can only establish the entailment by considering what must

be true in every interpretation in which the premise is true. To show this, we would have to reason as follows:

> Consider an arbitrary interpretation in which '$\forall x(H(x) \land J(x))$' is true. It follows that '$H(x) \land J(x)$' is satisfied by every object in this interpretation. '$H(x)$' will, then, also be satisfied by every object.[2] So it must be that '$\forall x\, H(x)$' is true in the interpretation. We've assumed nothing about the interpretation except that it was one in which '$\forall x(H(x) \land J(x))$' is true. So any interpretation in which '$\forall x(H(x) \land J(x))$' is true is one in which '$\forall x\, H(x)$' is true.

Even for a simple entailment like this one, the reasoning is somewhat complicated. For more complicated entailments, the reasoning can be extremely torturous.

The following table summarises whether a single interpretation or counter-interpretation suffices, or whether we must reason about all interpretations.

|  | **Yes** | **No** |
|---|---|---|
| validity? | all interpretations | one counter-interpretation |
| contradiction? | all interpretations | one counter-interpretation |
| equivalent? | all interpretations | one counter-interpretation |
| satisfiable? | one interpretation | all interpretations |
| valid? | all interpretations | one counter-interpretation |
| entailment? | all interpretations | one counter-interpretation |

You might want to compare this table with the table at the end of §14. The key difference resides in the fact that TFL concerns truth tables, whereas FOL concerns interpretations. This difference is deeply important, since each truth-table only ever has finitely many lines, so that a complete truth table is a relatively tractable object. By contrast, there are infinitely many interpretations for any given sentence(s), so that reasoning about all interpretations can be a deeply tricky business.

---

[2]Here again we make use of the fact that any object that satisfies $\mathscr{A}(x) \land \mathscr{B}(x)$ must satisfy both $\mathscr{A}(x)$ and $\mathscr{B}(x)$.

# PART VII

# *Natural deduction for FOL*

# CHAPTER 34

# *Basic rules for FOL*

The language of FOL makes use of all of the connectives of TFL. So proofs in FOL will use all of the basic and derived rules from Part IV. We will also use the proof-theoretic notions (particularly, the symbol '⊢') introduced there. However, we will also need some new basic rules to govern the quantifiers, and to govern the identity sign.

## 34.1 Universal elimination

From the claim that everything is $F$, you can infer that any particular thing is $F$. You name it; it's $F$. So the following should be fine:

$$
\begin{array}{ll}
1 & \forall x\, R(x,x,d) \\
\hline
2 & R(a,a,d) \qquad \forall \text{E } 1
\end{array}
$$

We obtained line 2 by dropping the universal quantifier and replacing every instance of '$x$' with '$a$'. Equally, the following should be allowed:

$$1 \quad \forall x \, R(x,x,d)$$
$$2 \quad R(d,d,d) \qquad \forall E \ 1$$

We obtained line 2 here by dropping the universal quantifier and replacing every instance of '*x*' with '*d*'. We could have done the same with any other name we wanted.

This motivates the universal elimination rule ($\forall$E):

$$m \quad \forall x \, \mathcal{A}(\dots x \dots x \dots)$$
$$\mathcal{A}(\dots c \dots c \dots) \qquad \forall E \ m$$

The notation here was introduced in §30. The point is that you can obtain any *substitution instance* of a universally quantified formula: replace every instance of the quantified variable with any name you like.

We should emphasize that (as with every elimination rule) you can only apply the $\forall$E rule when the universal quantifier is the main logical operator. So the following is *banned*:

$$1 \quad \forall x \, B(x) \rightarrow B(k)$$
$$2 \quad B(b) \rightarrow B(k) \qquad \text{naughy attempt to invoke } \forall E \ 1$$

This is illegitimate, since '$\forall x$' is not the main logical operator in line 1. (If you need a reminder as to why this sort of inference should be banned, reread §23.)

## 34.2 Existential introduction

From the claim that some particular thing is $F$, you can infer that something is $F$. So we ought to allow:

$$1 \quad R(a,a,d)$$
$$2 \quad \exists x \, R(a,a,x) \qquad \exists I \ 1$$

Here, we have replaced the name '*d*' with a variable '*x*', and then existentially quantified over it. Equally, we would have allowed:

$$
\begin{array}{l|l}
1 & R(a,a,d) \\
\hline
2 & \exists x\, R(x,x,d) \quad \exists\text{I } 1
\end{array}
$$

Here we have replaced both instances of the name '*a*' with a variable, and then existentially generalised. But we do not need to replace *both* instances of a name with a variable: if Narcissus loves himself, then there is someone who loves Narcissus. So we also allow:

$$
\begin{array}{l|l}
1 & R(a,a,d) \\
\hline
2 & \exists x\, R(x,a,d) \quad \exists\text{I } 1
\end{array}
$$

Here we have replaced *one* instance of the name '*a*' with a variable, and then existentially generalised. These observations motivate our introduction rule, although to explain it, we will need to introduce some new notation.

Where $\mathcal{A}$ is a sentence containing the name $c$, we can emphasize this by writing '$\mathcal{A}(\ldots c \ldots c \ldots)$'. We will write '$\mathcal{A}(\ldots x \ldots c \ldots)$' to indicate any formula obtained by replacing *some or all* of the instances of the name $c$ with the variable $x$. Armed with this, our introduction rule is:

$$
\begin{array}{l|l}
m & \mathcal{A}(\ldots c \ldots c \ldots) \\
  & \exists x\, \mathcal{A}(\ldots x \ldots c \ldots) \quad \exists\text{I } m \\
\end{array}
$$

$x$ must not occur in $\mathcal{A}(\ldots c \ldots c \ldots)$

The constraint is included to guarantee that any application of the rule yields a sentence of FOL. Thus the following is allowed:

| | | |
|---|---|---|
| 1 | $R(a,a,d)$ | |
| 2 | $\exists x\, R(x,a,d)$ | $\exists$I 1 |
| 3 | $\exists y \exists x\, R(x,y,d)$ | $\exists$I 2 |

But this is banned:

| | | |
|---|---|---|
| 1 | $R(a,a,d)$ | |
| 2 | $\exists x\, R(x,a,d)$ | $\exists$I 1 |
| 3 | $\exists x\, \exists x\, R(x,x,d)$ | naughty attempt to invoke $\exists$I 2 |

since the expression on line 3 contains clashing variables, and so is not a sentence of FOL.

## 34.3 Empty domains

The following proof combines our two new rules for quantifiers:

| | | |
|---|---|---|
| 1 | $\forall x\, F(x)$ | |
| 2 | $F(a)$ | $\forall$E 1 |
| 3 | $\exists x\, F(x)$ | $\exists$I 2 |

Could this be a bad proof? If anything exists at all, then certainly we can infer that something is $F$, from the fact that everything is $F$. But what if *nothing* exists at all? Then it is surely vacuously true that everything is $F$; however, it does not following that something is $F$, for there is nothing to *be* $F$. So if we claim that, as a matter of logic alone, '$\exists x\, F(x)$' follows from '$\forall x\, F(x)$', then we are claiming that, as a matter of *logic alone*, there is something rather than nothing. This might strike us as a bit odd.

Actually, we are already committed to this oddity. In §22, we stipulated that domains in FOL must have at least one member. We then defined a validity (of FOL) as a sentence which is true in every interpretation. Since '$\exists x\, x = x$' will be true in every interpretation, this *also* had the effect of stipulating that it is a matter of logic that there is something rather than nothing.

Since it is far from clear that logic should tell us that there must be something rather than nothing, we might well be cheating a bit here.

If we refuse to cheat, though, then we pay a high cost. Here are three things that we want to hold on to:

- $\forall x\, F(x) \vdash F(a)$: after all, that was $\forall$E.
- $F(a) \vdash \exists x\, F(x)$: after all, that was $\exists$I.
- the ability to copy-and-paste proofs together: after all, reasoning works by putting lots of little steps together into rather big chains.

If we get what we want on all three counts, then we have to countenance that $\forall x F x \vdash \exists x\, F(x)$. So, if we get what we want on all three counts, the proof system alone tells us that there is something rather than nothing. And if we refuse to accept that, then we have to surrender one of the three things that we want to hold on to!

Before we start thinking about which to surrender, we might want to ask how *much* of a cheat this is. Granted, it may make it harder to engage in theological debates about why there is something rather than nothing. But the rest of the time, we will get along just fine. So maybe we should just regard our proof system (and FOL, more generally) as having a very slightly limited purview. If we ever want to allow for the possibility of *nothing*, then we will have to cast around for a more complicated proof system. But for as long as we are content to ignore that possibility, our proof system is perfectly in order. (As, similarly, is the stipulation that every domain must contain at least one object.)

## 34.4 Universal introduction

Suppose you had shown of each particular thing that it is F (and that there are no other things to consider). Then you would be justified in claiming that everything is F. This would motivate the following proof rule. If you had established each and every single substitution instance of '$\forall x\, F(x)$', then you can infer '$\forall x\, F(x)$'.

Unfortunately, that rule would be utterly unusable. To establish each and every single substitution instance would require proving '$F(a)$', '$F(b)$', ..., '$F(j_2)$', ..., '$F(r_{79002})$', ..., and so on. Indeed, since there are infinitely many names in FOL, this process would never come to an end. So we could never apply that rule. We need to be a bit more cunning in coming up with our rule for introducing universal quantification.

A solution will be inspired by considering:

$$\forall x\, F(x) \therefore \forall y\, F(y)$$

This argument should *obviously* be valid. After all, alphabetical variation ought to be a matter of taste, and of no logical consequence. But how might our proof system reflect this? Suppose we begin a proof thus:

| | | |
|---|---|---|
| 1 | $\forall x\, F(x)$ | |
| 2 | $F(a)$ | $\forall$E 1 |

We have proved '$F(a)$'. And, of course, nothing stops us from using the same justification to prove '$F(b)$', '$F(c)$', ..., '$F(j_2)$', ..., '$F(r_{79002})$', ..., and so on until we run out of space, time, or patience. But reflecting on this, we see that there is a way to prove $Fc$, for any name $c$. And if we can do it for *any* thing, we should surely be able to say that '$F$' is true of *everything*. This therefore justifies us in inferring '$\forall y\, F(y)$', thus:

$$1 \quad \forall x\, F(x)$$

$$2 \quad F(a) \qquad \forall \text{E } 1$$

$$3 \quad \forall y\, F(y) \qquad \forall \text{I } 2$$

The crucial thought here is that '*a*' was just some *arbitrary* name. There was nothing special about it—we might have chosen any other name—and still the proof would be fine. And this crucial thought motivates the universal introduction rule (∀I):

$$m \quad \mathcal{A}(\ldots c \ldots c \ldots)$$

$$\forall x\, \mathcal{A}(\ldots x \ldots x \ldots) \qquad \forall \text{I } m$$

*c* must not occur in any undischarged assumption
*x* must not occur in $\mathcal{A}(\ldots c \ldots c \ldots)$

A crucial aspect of this rule, though, is bound up in the first constraint. This constraint ensures that we are always reasoning at a sufficiently general level. To see the constraint in action, consider this terrible argument:

> Everyone loves Kylie Minogue; therefore everyone loves themselves.

We might symbolize this obviously invalid inference pattern as:

$$\forall x\, L(x,k) \; \therefore \; \forall x\, L(x,x)$$

Now, suppose we tried to offer a proof that vindicates this argument:

$$1 \quad \forall x\, L(x,k)$$

$$2 \quad L(k,k) \qquad \forall \text{E } 1$$

$$3 \quad \forall x\, L(x,x) \qquad \text{naughty attempt to invoke } \forall \text{I } 2$$

This is not allowed, because '$k$' occurred already in an undischarged assumption, namely, on line 1. The crucial point is that, if we have made any assumptions about the object we are working with, then we are not reasoning generally enough to license ∀I.

Although the name may not occur in any *undischarged* assumption, it may occur in a *discharged* assumption. That is, it may occur in a subproof that we have already closed. For example, this is just fine:

| 1 | | $G(d)$ | |
|---|---|---|---|
| 2 | | $G(d)$ | R 1 |
| 3 | $G(d) \rightarrow G(d)$ | | →I 1–2 |
| 4 | $\forall z(G(z) \rightarrow G(z))$ | | ∀I 3 |

This tells us that '$\forall z(G(z) \rightarrow G(z))$' is a *theorem*. And that is as it should be.

We should emphasise one last point. As per the conventions of §30.3, the use of ∀I requires that we are replacing *every* instance of the name $c$ in $\mathcal{A}(\ldots x \ldots x \ldots)$ with the variable $x$. If we only replace *some* names and not others, we end up 'proving' silly things. For example, consider the argument:

> Everyone is as old as themselves; so everyone is as old as Judi Dench.

We might symbolise this as follows:

$$\forall x\, O(x,x) \therefore \forall x\, O(x,d)$$

But now suppose we tried to *vindicate* this terrible argument with the following:

| 1 | $\forall x\, O(x,x)$ | |
|---|---|---|
| 2 | $O(d,d)$ | ∀E 1 |
| 3 | $\forall x\, O(x,d)$ | naughty attempt to invoke ∀I 2 |

Fortunately, our rules do not allow for us to do this: the attempted proof is banned, since it doesn't replace *every* occurrence of '*d*' in line 2 with an '*x*'.

## 34.5   Existential elimination

Suppose we know that *something* is $F$. The problem is that simply knowing this does not tell us which thing is $F$. So it would seem that from '$\exists x\, F(x)$' we cannot immediately conclude '$F(a)$', '$F(e_{23})$', or any other substitution instance of the sentence. What can we do?

Suppose we know that something is $F$, and that everything which is $F$ is also $G$. In (almost) natural English, we might reason thus:

> Since something is $F$, there is some particular thing which is an $F$. We do not know anything about it, other than that it's an $F$, but for convenience, let's call it 'Becky'. So: Becky is $F$. Since everything which is $F$ is $G$, it follows that Becky is $G$. But since Becky is $G$, it follows that something is $G$. And nothing depended on which object, exactly, Becky was. So, something is $G$.

We might try to capture this reasoning pattern in a proof as follows:

$$1 \quad \exists x\, F(x)$$

$$2 \quad \forall x(F(x) \rightarrow G(x))$$

$$3 \quad \boxed{F(b)}$$

$$4 \quad F(b) \rightarrow G(b) \qquad \forall E\ 2$$

$$5 \quad G(b) \qquad \rightarrow E\ 4,\ 3$$

$$6 \quad \exists x\, G(x) \qquad \exists I\ 5$$

$$7 \quad \exists x\, G(x) \qquad \exists E\ 1,\ 3\text{--}6$$

Breaking this down: we started by writing down our assumptions. At line 3, we made an additional assumption: '$F(b)$'. This was just a substitution instance of '$\exists x\, F(x)$'. On this assumption, we established '$\exists x\, G(x)$'. Note that we had made no *special* assumptions about the object named by '$b$'; we had *only* assumed that it satisfies '$F(x)$'. So nothing depends upon which object it is. And line 1 told us that *something* satisfies '$F(x)$', so our reasoning pattern was perfectly general. We can discharge the specific assumption '$F(b)$', and simply infer '$\exists x\, G(x)$' on its own.

Putting this together, we obtain the existential elimination rule ($\exists E$):

$$m \quad \exists x\, \mathscr{A}(\dots x \dots x \dots)$$

$$i \quad \boxed{\mathscr{A}(\dots c \dots c \dots)}$$

$$j \quad \mathscr{B}$$

$$\mathscr{B} \qquad \qquad \exists E\ m,\ i\text{--}j$$

$c$ must not occur in any assumption undischarged before line $i$

$c$ must not occur in $\exists x\, \mathscr{A}(\dots x \dots x \dots)$

$c$ must not occur in $\mathscr{B}$

As with universal introduction, the constraints are extremely important. To see why, consider the following terrible argument:

Tim Button is a lecturer. Someone is not a lecturer.
So Tim Button is both a lecturer and not a lecturer.

We might symbolize this obviously invalid inference pattern as follows:

$$L(b), \exists x \, \neg L(x) \therefore L(b) \wedge \neg L(b)$$

Now, suppose we tried to offer a proof that vindicates this argument:

| | |
|---|---|
| 1 | $L(b)$ |
| 2 | $\exists x \, \neg L(x)$ |
| 3 | $\quad \neg L(b)$ |
| 4 | $\quad L(b) \wedge \neg L(b)$    $\wedge$I 1, 3 |
| 5 | $L(b) \wedge \neg L(b)$      naughty attempt |
| | to invoke $\exists$E 2, 3–4 |

The last line of the proof is not allowed. The name that we used in our substitution instance for '$\exists x \, \neg L(x)$' on line 3, namely '$b$', occurs in line 4. The this would be no better:

| | |
|---|---|
| 1 | $L(b)$ |
| 2 | $\exists x \, \neg L(x)$ |
| 3 | $\quad \neg L(b)$ |
| 4 | $\quad L(b) \wedge \neg L(b)$    $\wedge$I 1, 3 |
| 5 | $\quad \exists x (L(x) \wedge \neg L(x))$    $\exists$I 4 |
| 6 | $\exists x (L(x) \wedge \neg L(x))$    naughty attempt |
| | to invoke $\exists$E 2, 3–5 |

The last line is still not allowed. For the name that we used in our substitution instance for '$\exists x \neg L(x)$', namely '$b$', occurs in an undischarged assumption, namely line 1.

The moral of the story is this. *If you want to squeeze information out of an existential quantifier, choose a new name for your substitution instance.* That way, you can guarantee that you meet all the constraints on the rule for $\exists$E.

## Practice exercises

**A.** Explain why these two 'proofs' are *incorrect*. Also, provide interpretations which would invalidate the fallacious argument forms the 'proofs' enshrine:

| 1 | $\forall x\, R(x,x)$ | |
|---|---|---|
| 2 | $R(a,a)$ | $\forall$E 1 |
| 3 | $\forall y\, R(a,y)$ | $\forall$I 2 |
| 4 | $\forall x\, \forall y\, R(x,y)$ | $\forall$I 3 |

| 1 | $\forall x\, \exists y\, R(x,y)$ | |
|---|---|---|
| 2 | $\exists y\, R(a,y)$ | $\forall$E 1 |
| 3 | $R(a,a)$ | |
| 4 | $\exists x\, R(x,x)$ | $\exists$I 3 |
| 5 | $\exists x\, R(x,x)$ | $\exists$E 2, 3–4 |

**B.** The following three proofs are missing their citations (rule and line numbers). Add them, to turn them into bona fide proofs.

1.

1 | $\forall x \exists y (R(x,y) \vee R(y,x))$

2 | $\forall x \neg R(m,x)$

3 | $\exists y (R(m,y) \vee R(y,m))$

4 | $\quad R(m,a) \vee R(a,m)$

5 | $\quad \neg R(m,a)$

6 | $\quad R(a,m)$

7 | $\quad \exists x\, R(x,m)$

8 | $\exists x\, R(x,m)$

2.

1 | $\forall x(\exists y\, L(x,y) \rightarrow \forall z\, L(z,x))$

2 | $L(a,b)$

3 | $\exists y\, L(a,y) \rightarrow \forall z L(z,a)$

4 | $\exists y\, L(a,y)$

5 | $\forall z\, L(z,a)$

6 | $L(c,a)$

7 | $\exists y\, L(c,y) \rightarrow \forall z\, L(z,c)$

8 | $\exists y\, L(c,y)$

9 | $\forall z\, L(z,c)$

10 | $L(c,c)$

11 | $\forall x\, L(x,x)$

3.

| | | |
|---|---|---|
| 1 | $\forall x(J(x) \rightarrow K(x))$ | |
| 2 | $\exists x \forall y\, L(x,y)$ | |
| 3 | $\forall x\, J(x)$ | |
| 4 | | $\forall y\, L(a,y)$ |
| 5 | | $L(a,a)$ |
| 6 | | $J(a)$ |
| 7 | | $J(a) \rightarrow K(a)$ |
| 8 | | $K(a)$ |
| 9 | | $K(a) \wedge L(a,a)$ |
| 10 | | $\exists x(K(x) \wedge L(x,x))$ |
| 11 | $\exists x(K(x) \wedge L(x,x))$ | |

**C.** In §23 problem A, we considered fifteen syllogistic figures of Aristotelian logic. Provide proofs for each of the argument forms. NB: You will find it *much* easier if you symbolize (for example) 'No F is G' as '$\forall x(F(x) \rightarrow \neg G(x))$'.

**D.** Aristotle and his successors identified other syllogistic forms which depended upon 'existential import'. Symbolize each of these argument forms in FOL and offer proofs.

1. **Barbari.** Something is H. All G are F. All H are G. So: Some H is F
2. **Celaront.** Something is H. No G are F. All H are G. So: Some H is not F
3. **Cesaro.** Something is H. No F are G. All H are G. So: Some H is not F.
4. **Camestros.** Something is H. All F are G. No H are G. So: Some H is not F.

5. **Felapton**. Something is G. No G are F. All G are H. So: Some H is not F.
6. **Darapti**. Something is G. All G are F. All G are H. So: Some H is F.
7. **Calemos**. Something is H. All F are G. No G are H. So: Some H is not F.
8. **Fesapo**. Something is G. No F is G. All G are H. So: Some H is not F.
9. **Bamalip**. Something is F. All F are G. All G are H. So: Some H are F.

**E.** Provide a proof of each claim.

1. $\vdash \forall x\, F(x) \to \forall y (F(y) \wedge F(y))$
2. $\forall x(A(x) \to B(x)), \exists x\, A(x) \vdash \exists x\, B(x)$
3. $\forall x(M(x) \leftrightarrow N(x)), M(a) \wedge \exists x\, R(x,a) \vdash \exists x\, N(x)$
4. $\forall x \forall y\, G(x,y) \vdash \exists x\, G(x,x)$
5. $\vdash \forall x\, R(x,x) \to \exists x \exists y\, R(x,y)$
6. $\vdash \forall y \exists x(Q(y) \to Q(x))$
7. $N(a) \to \forall x(M(x) \leftrightarrow M(a)), M(a), \neg M(b) \vdash \neg N(a)$
8. $\forall x \forall y(G(x,y) \to G(y,x)) \vdash \forall x \forall y(G(x,y) \leftrightarrow G(y,x))$
9. $\forall x(\neg M(x) \vee L(j,x)), \forall x(B(x) \to L(j,x)), \forall x(M(x) \vee B(x)) \vdash \forall x\, L(j,x)$

**F.** Write a symbolization key for the following argument, symbolize it, and prove it:

> There is someone who likes everyone who likes everyone that she likes. Therefore, there is someone who likes herself.

**G.** Show that each pair of sentences is provably equivalent.

1. $\forall x(A(x) \to \neg B(x)), \neg \exists x(A(x) \wedge B(x))$
2. $\forall x(\neg A(x) \to B(d)), \forall x\, A(x) \vee B(d)$
3. $\exists x\, P(x) \to Q(c), \forall x(P(x) \to Q(c))$

**H**. For each of the following pairs of sentences: If they are provably equivalent, give proofs to show this. If they are not, construct an interpretation to show that they are not logically equivalent.

1. $\forall x\, P(x) \rightarrow Q(c), \forall x(P(x) \rightarrow Q(c))$
2. $\forall x\, \forall y\, \forall z\, B(x,y,z), \forall x\, B(x,x)x$
3. $\forall x\, \forall y\, D(x,y), \forall y\, \forall x\, D(x,y)$
4. $\exists x\, \forall y\, D(x,y), \forall y\, \exists x\, D(x,y)$
5. $\forall x(R(c,a) \leftrightarrow R(x,a)), R(c,a) \leftrightarrow \forall x\, R(x,a)$

**I**. For each of the following arguments: If it is valid in FOL, give a proof. If it is invalid, construct an interpretation to show that it is invalid.

1. $\exists y\, \forall x\, R(x,y) \therefore \forall x\, \exists y\, R(x,y)$
2. $\forall x\, \exists y\, R(x,y) \therefore \exists y\, \forall x\, R(x,y)$
3. $\exists x(P(x) \wedge \neg Q(x)) \therefore \forall x(P(x) \rightarrow \neg Q(x))$
4. $\forall x(S(x) \rightarrow T(a)), S(d) \therefore T(a)$
5. $\forall x(A(x) \rightarrow B(x)), \forall x(B(x) \rightarrow C(x)) \therefore \forall x(A(x) \rightarrow C(x))$
6. $\exists x(D(x) \vee E(x)), \forall x(D(x) \rightarrow F(x)) \therefore \exists x(D(x) \wedge F(x))$
7. $\forall x\, \forall y(R(x,y) \vee R(y,x)) \therefore R(j,j)$
8. $\exists x\, \exists y(R(x,y) \vee R(y,x)) \therefore R(j,j)$
9. $\forall x\, P(x) \rightarrow \forall x\, Q(x), \exists x\, \neg P(x) \therefore \exists x\, \neg Q(x)$
10. $\exists x\, M(x) \rightarrow \exists x\, N(x), \neg\exists x\, N(x) \therefore \forall x\, \neg M(x)$

# CHAPTER 35

# *Proofs with quantifiers*

In §17 we discussed strategies for constructing proofs using the basic rules of natural deduction for TFL. The same principles apply to the rules for the quantifiers. If we want to prove a quantifier sentence $\forall x\, \mathcal{A}(x)$ or $\exists x\, \mathcal{A}(x)$. We can work backward by justifying the sentence we want by $\forall$I or $\exists$I and trying to find a proof of the corresponding premise of that rule. And to work forward from a quantified sentence, we apply $\forall$E or $\exists$E, as the case may be.

Specifically, suppose you want to prove $\forall x\, \mathcal{A}(x)$. To do so using $\forall$I, we would need a proof of $\mathcal{A}(c)$ for some name $c$ which does not occur in any undischarged assumption. To apply the corresponding strategy, i.e., to construct a proof of $\forall x\, \mathcal{A}(x)$ by working backward, is thus to write $\mathcal{A}(c)$ above it and then to continue to try to find a proof of that sentence.

$$
\begin{array}{ll}
& \vdots \\
n & \mathcal{A}(c) \\
n+1 & \forall x\, \mathcal{A}(x) \qquad \forall\text{I } n
\end{array}
$$

$\mathcal{A}(c)$ is obtained from $\mathcal{A}(x)$ by replacing every free occurrence of $x$ in $\mathcal{A}(x)$ by $c$. For this to work, $c$ must satisfy the special condition. We can ensure that it does by always picking a name that does not already occur in the proof constructed so far. (Of course, it will occur in the proof we end up constructing—just not in an assumption that is undischarged at line $n + 1$.)

To work backward from a sentence $\exists x\, \mathcal{A}(x)$ we similarly write a sentence above it that can serve as a justification for an application of the $\exists$I rule, i.e., a sentence of the form $\mathcal{A}(c)$.

$$
\begin{array}{c|ll}
 & \;\vdots & \\
n & \mathcal{A}(c) & \\
n+1 & \exists x\, \mathcal{A}(x) & \exists\text{I } n
\end{array}
$$

This looks just like what we would do if we were working backward from a universally quantified sentence. The difference is that whereas for $\forall$I we have to pick a name $c$ which does not occur in the proof (so far), for $\exists$I we may and in general must pick a name $c$ which already occurs in the proof. Just like in the case of $\lor$I, it is often not clear which $c$ will work out, and so to avoid having to backtrack you should work backward from existentially quantified sentences only when all other strategies have been applied.

By contrast, working *forward* from sentences $\exists x\, \mathcal{A}(x())$ generally always works and you won't have to backtrack. Working forward from an existentially quantified sentence takes into account not just $\exists x\, \mathcal{A}(x)$ but also whatever sentence $\mathcal{B}$ you would like to prove. It requires that you set up a subproof above $\mathcal{B}$, wherein $\mathcal{B}$ is the last line, and a substitution instance $\mathcal{A}(c)$ of $\exists x\, \mathcal{A}(x)$ as the assumption. In order to ensure that the condition on $c$ that governs $\exists$E is satisfied, chose a name $c$ which does not already occur in the proof.

$$
\begin{array}{c|l}
 & \vdots \\
m & \exists x\, \mathcal{A}(x) \\
 & \vdots \\
n & \quad \mathcal{A}(c) \\
 & \quad \vdots \\
k & \quad \mathcal{B} \\
k+1 & \mathcal{B} \qquad\qquad \exists\mathrm{E}\; m,\, n\text{--}k
\end{array}
$$

You'll then continue with the goal of proving $\mathcal{B}$, but now inside a subproof in which you have an additional sentence to work with, namely $\mathcal{A}(c)$.

Lastly, working forward from $\forall x\, \mathcal{A}(x)$ means that you can always write down $\mathcal{A}(c)$ and justify it using $\forall$E, for any name $c$. Of course, you wouldn't want to do that willy-nilly. Only certain names $c$ will help in your task of proving whatever goal sentence you are working on. So, like working backward from $\exists x\, \mathcal{A}(x)$, you should work forward from $\forall x\, \mathcal{A}(x)$ only after all other strategies have been applied.

Let's consider as an example the argument $\forall x(A(x) \rightarrow B) \therefore \exists x\, A(x) \rightarrow B$. To start constructing a proof, we write the premise at the top and the conclusion at the bottom.

$$
\begin{array}{c|l}
1 & \forall x(A(x) \rightarrow B) \\
 & \vdots \\
n & \exists x\, A(x) \rightarrow B
\end{array}
$$

The strategies for connectives of TFL still apply, and you should apply them in the same order: first work backward from conditionals, negated sentences, conjunctions, and now also universal quantifiers, then forward from disjunctions and now existential quantifiers, and only then try to apply →E, ¬E, ∨I, ∀E, or ∃I. In our case, that means, working backward from the conclusion:

| | |
|---|---|
| 1 | $\forall x(A(x) \rightarrow B)$ |
| 2 | $\exists x\, A(x)$ |
| | ⋮ |
| $n-1$ | $B$ |
| $n$ | $\exists x\, A(x) \rightarrow B$      →I 2–$(n-1)$ |

Our next step should be to work forward from $\exists x\, A(x)$ on line 2. For that, we have to pick a name not already in our proof. Since no names appear, we can pick any name, say '$d$'

| | |
|---|---|
| 1 | $\forall x(A(x) \rightarrow B)$ |
| 2 | $\exists x\, A(x)$ |
| 3 | $A(d)$ |
| | ⋮ |
| $n-2$ | $B$ |
| $n-1$ | $B$          ∃E 2, 3–$(n-2)$ |
| $n$ | $\exists x\, A(x) \rightarrow B$      →I 2–$(n-1)$ |

Now we've exhausted our primary strategies, and it is time to work forward from the premise $\forall x(A(x) \rightarrow B)$. Applying ∀E means we can justify any instance of $A(c) \rightarrow B$, regardless of what $c$ we choose. Of course, we'll do well to choose $d$, since that will give us $A(d) \rightarrow B$. Then we can apply →E to justify $B$, finishing the proof.

| | | |
|---|---|---|
| 1 | $\forall x(A(x) \rightarrow B)$ | |
| 2 | $\exists x\, A(x)$ | |
| 3 | $A(d)$ | |
| 4 | $A(d) \rightarrow B$ | $\forall$E 1 |
| 5 | $B$ | $\rightarrow$E 4, 3 |
| 6 | $B$ | $\exists$E 2, 3–5 |
| 7 | $\exists x\, A(x) \rightarrow B$ | $\rightarrow$I 2–6 |

Now let's construct a proof of the converse. We begin with

| | |
|---|---|
| 1 | $\exists x\, A(x) \rightarrow B$ |
| | $\vdots$ |
| $n$ | $\forall x(A(x) \rightarrow B)$ |

Note that the premise is a conditional, not an existentially quantified sentence, so we should not (yet) work forward from it. Working backward from the conclusion, $\forall x(A(x) \rightarrow B)$, leads us to look for a proof of $A(d) \rightarrow B$:

| | |
|---|---|
| 1 | $\exists x\, A(x) \rightarrow B$ |
| | $\vdots$ |
| $n-1$ | $A(d) \rightarrow B$ |
| $n$ | $\forall x(A(x) \rightarrow B)$    $\forall$I $n-1$ |

And working backward from $A(d) \rightarrow B$ means we should set up a subproof with $A(d)$ as an assumption and $B$ as the last line:

$$
\begin{array}{ll}
1 & \exists x\, A(x) \to B \\[6pt]
2 & \quad A(d) \\[6pt]
& \quad \vdots \\[6pt]
n-2 & \quad B \\[6pt]
n-1 & A(d) \to B \qquad \to\text{I } 2\text{-}(n-2) \\[6pt]
n & \forall x(A(x) \to B) \quad \forall \text{I } n-1
\end{array}
$$

Now we can work forward from the premise on line 1. That's a conditional, and its consequent happens to be the sentence $B$ we are trying to justify. So we should look for a proof of its antecedent, $\exists x\, A(x)$. Of course, that is now readily available, by $\exists$I from line 2, and we're done:

$$
\begin{array}{lll}
1 & \exists x\, A(x) \to B & \\[6pt]
2 & \quad A(d) & \\[6pt]
3 & \quad \exists x\, A(x) & \exists \text{I } 2 \\[6pt]
4 & \quad B & \to\text{E } 1,\, 3 \\[6pt]
5 & A(d) \to B & \to\text{I } 2\text{-}4 \\[6pt]
6 & \forall x(A(x) \to B) & \forall \text{I } 5
\end{array}
$$

## Practice exercises

**A.** Use the strategies to find proofs for each of the following arguments and theorems:

  1. $A \to \forall x\, B(x) \,\therefore\, \forall x(A \to B(x))$
  2. $\exists x(A \to B(x)) \,\therefore\, A \to \exists x\, B(x)$
  3. $\forall x(A(x) \land B(x)) \leftrightarrow (\forall x\, A(x) \land \forall x\, B(x))$
  4. $\exists x(A(x) \lor B(x)) \leftrightarrow (\exists x\, A(x) \lor \exists x\, B(x))$
  5. $A \lor \forall x\, B(x)) \,\therefore\, \forall x(A \lor B(x))$

6. $\forall x(A(x) \rightarrow B) \therefore \exists x\, A(x) \rightarrow B$
7. $\exists x(A(x) \rightarrow B) \therefore \forall x\, A(x) \rightarrow B$
8. $\forall x(A(x) \rightarrow \exists y\, A(y))$

Use only the basic rules of TFL in addition to the basic quantifier rules.

**B.** Use the strategies to find proofs for each of the following arguments and theorems:

1. $\forall x\, R(x,x) \therefore \forall x\, \exists y\, R(x,y)$
2. $\forall x\, \forall y\, \forall z[(R(x,y) \wedge R(y,z)) \rightarrow R(x,z)]$
   $\therefore \forall x\, \forall y[R(x,y) \rightarrow \forall z(R(y,z) \rightarrow R(x,z))]$
3. $\forall x\, \forall y\, \forall z[(R(x,y) \wedge R(y,z)) \rightarrow R(x,z)],$
   $\forall x\, \forall y(R(x,y) \rightarrow R(y,x))$
   $\therefore \forall x\, \forall y\, \forall z[(R(x,y) \wedge R(x,z)) \rightarrow R(y,z)]$
4. $\forall x\, \forall y(R(x,y) \rightarrow R(y,x))$
   $\therefore \forall x\, \forall y\, \forall z[(R(x,y) \wedge R(x,z)) \rightarrow \exists u(R(y,u) \wedge R(z,u))]$
5. $\neg\exists x\, \forall y(A(x,y) \leftrightarrow \neg A(y,y))$

**C.** Use the strategies to find proofs for each of the following arguments and theorems:

1. $\forall x\, A(x) \rightarrow B \therefore \exists x(A(x) \rightarrow B)$
2. $A \rightarrow \exists x\, B(x) \therefore \exists x(A \rightarrow B(x))$
3. $\forall x(A \vee B(x)) \therefore A \vee \forall x\, B(x)$
4. $\exists x(A(x) \rightarrow \forall y\, A(y))$
5. $\exists x(\exists y\, A(y) \rightarrow A(x))$

These require the use of IP. Use only the basic rules of TFL in addition to the basic quantifier rules.

# CHAPTER 36

# *Conversion of quantifiers*

In this section, we will add some additional rules to the basic rules of the previous section. These govern the interaction of quantifiers and negation.

In §22, we noted that $\neg\exists x \mathcal{A}$ is logically equivalent to $\forall x \neg\mathcal{A}$. We will add some rules to our proof system that govern this. In particular, we add:

$$
\begin{array}{r|l}
m & \forall x \neg\mathcal{A} \\
 & \\
 & \neg\exists x \, \mathcal{A} \quad\quad \text{CQ } m
\end{array}
$$

and

$$
\begin{array}{r|l}
m & \neg\exists x \, \mathcal{A} \\
 & \\
 & \forall x \neg\mathcal{A} \quad\quad \text{CQ } m
\end{array}
$$

Equally, we add:

$$m \quad | \quad \exists x \, \neg \mathscr{A}$$

$$\neg \forall x \, \mathscr{A} \quad \text{CQ } m$$

and

$$m \quad | \quad \neg \forall x \, \mathscr{A}$$

$$\exists x \, \neg \mathscr{A} \quad \text{CQ } m$$

## Practice exercises

**A.** Show in each case that the sentences are inconsistent:

1. $S(a) \to T(m), T(m) \to S(a), T(m) \land \neg S(a)$
2. $\neg \exists x \, R(x,a), \forall x \, \forall y \, R(y,x)$
3. $\neg \exists x \, \exists y \, L(x,y), L(a,a)$
4. $\forall x(P(x) \to Q(x)), \forall z(P(z) \to R(z)), \forall y \, P(y), \neg Q(a) \land \neg R(b)$

**B.** Show that each pair of sentences is provably equivalent:

1. $\forall x(A(x) \to \neg B(x)), \neg \exists x(A(x) \land B(x))$
2. $\forall x(\neg A(x) \to B(d)), \forall x \, A(x) \lor B(d)$

**C.** In §23, we considered what happens when we move quantifiers 'across' various logical operators. Show that each pair of sentences is provably equivalent:

1. $\forall x(F(x) \land G(a)), \forall x \, F(x) \land G(a)$
2. $\exists x(F(x) \lor G(a)), \exists x \, F(x) \lor G(a)$
3. $\forall x(G(a) \to F(x)), G(a) \to \forall x \, F(x)$
4. $\forall x(F(x) \to G(a)), \exists x \, F(x) \to G(a)$
5. $\exists x(G(a) \to F(x)), G(a) \to \exists x \, F(x)$
6. $\exists x(F(x) \to G(a)), \forall x \, F(x) \to G(a)$

NB: the variable '$x$' does not occur in '$G(a)$'. When all the quantifiers occur at the beginning of a sentence, that sentence is said to be in *prenex normal form*. These equivalences are sometimes called *prenexing rules*, since they give us a means for putting any sentence into prenex normal form.

## CHAPTER 37

# *Rules for identity*

In §29, we mentioned the philosophically contentious thesis of the *identity of indiscernibles*. This is the claim that objects which are indiscernible in every way are, in fact, identical to each other. It was also mentioned that we will not subscribe to this thesis. It follows that, no matter how much you learn about two objects, we cannot prove that they are identical. That is unless, of course, you learn that the two objects are, in fact, identical, but then the proof will hardly be very illuminating.

The general point, though, is that *no sentences* which do not already contain the identity predicate could justify an inference to '$a = b$'. So our identity introduction rule cannot allow us to infer to an identity claim containing two *different* names.

However, every object is identical to itself. No premises, then, are required in order to conclude that something is identical to itself. So this will be the identity introduction rule:

$$c = c \quad =\text{I}$$

Notice that this rule does not require referring to any prior lines of the proof. For any name $c$, you can write $c = c$ on any point, with only the =I rule as justification.

Our elimination rule is more fun. If you have established '$a = b$', then anything that is true of the object named by '$a$' must also be true of the object named by '$b$'. For any sentence with '$a$' in it, you can replace some or all of the occurrences of '$a$' with '$b$' and produce an equivalent sentence. For example, from '$R(a,a)$' and '$a = b$', you are justified in inferring '$R(a,b)$', '$R(b,a)$' or '$R(b,b)$'. More generally:

$$
\begin{array}{r|l}
m & a = b \\[4pt]
n & \mathcal{A}(\ldots a \ldots a \ldots) \\[4pt]
 & \mathcal{A}(\ldots b \ldots a \ldots) \quad \text{=E } m, n
\end{array}
$$

The notation here is as for ∃I. So $\mathcal{A}(\ldots a \ldots a \ldots)$ is a formula containing the name $a$, and $\mathcal{A}(\ldots b \ldots a \ldots)$ is a formula obtained by replacing one or more instances of the name $a$ with the name $b$. Lines $m$ and $n$ can occur in either order, and do not need to be adjacent, but we always cite the statement of identity first. Symmetrically, we allow:

$$
\begin{array}{r|l}
m & a = b \\[4pt]
n & \mathcal{A}(\ldots b \ldots b \ldots) \\[4pt]
 & \mathcal{A}(\ldots a \ldots b \ldots) \quad \text{=E } m, n
\end{array}
$$

This rule is sometimes called *Leibniz's Law*, after Gottfried Leibniz.

To see the rules in action, we will prove some quick results. First, we will prove that identity is *symmetric*:

| | | | |
|---|---|---|---|
| 1 | | $a = b$ | |
| 2 | | $a = a$ | =I |
| 3 | | $b = a$ | =E 1, 2 |
| 4 | $a = b \rightarrow b = a$ | | →I 1–3 |
| 5 | $\forall y(a = y \rightarrow y = a)$ | | ∀I 4 |
| 6 | $\forall x\, \forall y(x = y \rightarrow y = x)$ | | ∀I 5 |

We obtain line 3 by replacing one instance of '$a$' in line 2 with an instance of '$b$'; this is justified given '$a = b$'.

Second, we will prove that identity is *transitive*:

| | | | |
|---|---|---|---|
| 1 | | $a = b \wedge b = c$ | |
| 2 | | $a = b$ | ∧E 1 |
| 3 | | $b = c$ | ∧E 1 |
| 4 | | $a = c$ | =E 2, 3 |
| 5 | $(a = b \wedge b = c) \rightarrow a = c$ | | →I 1–4 |
| 6 | $\forall z((a = b \wedge b = z) \rightarrow a = z)$ | | ∀I 5 |
| 7 | $\forall y\, \forall z((a = y \wedge y = z) \rightarrow a = z)$ | | ∀I 6 |
| 8 | $\forall x\, \forall y \forall z((x = y \wedge y = z) \rightarrow x = z)$ | | ∀I 7 |

We obtain line 4 by replacing '$b$' in line 3 with '$a$'; this is justified given '$a = b$'.

## Practice exercises

**A.** Provide a proof of each claim.

1. $P(a) \vee Q(b), Q(b) \rightarrow b = c, \neg P(a) \vdash Q(c)$
2. $m = n \vee n = o, A(n) \vdash A(m) \vee A(o)$

3. $\forall x\; x = m, R(m,a) \vdash \exists x\, R(x,x)$
4. $\forall x \forall y (R(x,y) \to x = y) \vdash R(a,b) \to R(b,a)$
5. $\neg\exists x \neg x = m \vdash \forall x \forall y (P(x) \to P(y))$
6. $\exists x\, J(x), \exists x\, \neg J(x) \vdash \exists x \exists y\, \neg x = y$
7. $\forall x (x = n \leftrightarrow M(x)), \forall x (O(x) \lor \neg M(x)) \vdash O(n)$
8. $\exists x\, D(x), \forall x (x = p \leftrightarrow D(x)) \vdash D(p)$
9. $\exists x \big[ (K(x) \land \forall y (K(y) \to x = y)) \land B(x) \big], Kd \vdash B(d)$
10. $\vdash P(a) \to \forall x (P(x) \lor \neg x = a)$

**B.** Show that the following are provably equivalent:

- $\exists x \big( [F(x) \land \forall y (F(y) \to x = y)] \land x = n \big)$
- $F(n) \land \forall y (F(y) \to n = y)$

And hence that both have a decent claim to symbolize the English sentence 'Nick is the $F$'.

**C.** In §25, we claimed that the following are logically equivalent symbolizations of the English sentence 'there is exactly one $F$':

- $\exists x\, F(x) \land \forall x \forall y \big[ (F(x) \land F(y)) \to x = y \big]$
- $\exists x \big[ F(x) \land \forall y (F(y) \to x = y) \big]$
- $\exists x \forall y (F(y) \leftrightarrow x = y)$

Show that they are all provably equivalent. (*Hint*: to show that three claims are provably equivalent, it suffices to show that the first proves the second, the second proves the third and the third proves the first; think about why.)

**D.** Symbolize the following argument

> There is exactly one $F$. There is exactly one $G$. Nothing is both $F$ and $G$. So: there are exactly two things that are either $F$ or $G$.

And offer a proof of it.

# CHAPTER 38

# *Derived rules*

As in the case of TFL, we first introduced some rules for FOL as basic (in §34), and then added some further rules for conversion of quantifiers (in §36). In fact, the CQ rules should be regarded as *derived* rules, for they can be derived from the *basic* rules of §34. (The point here is as in §20.) Here is a justification for the first CQ rule:

| | | |
|---|---|---|
| 1 | $\forall x\,\neg A(x)$ | |
| 2 | $\exists x\,A(x)$ | |
| 3 | $A(c)$ | |
| 4 | $\neg A(c)$ | $\forall$E 1 |
| 5 | $\bot$ | $\neg$E 4, 3 |
| 6 | $\bot$ | $\exists$E 2, 3–5 |
| 7 | $\neg\exists x\,A(x)$ | $\neg$I 2–6 |

Here is a justification of the third CQ rule:

$$
\begin{array}{ll}
1 \quad \exists x \, \neg A(x) & \\
2 \quad\quad \forall x \, A(x) & \\
3 \quad\quad\quad \neg A(c) & \\
4 \quad\quad\quad A(c) & \forall\text{E } 2 \\
5 \quad\quad\quad \bot & \neg\text{E } 3, 4 \\
6 \quad\quad \bot & \exists\text{E } 1, 3\text{--}5 \\
7 \quad \neg\forall x \, A(x) & \neg\text{I } 2\text{--}6
\end{array}
$$

This explains why the CQ rules can be treated as derived. Similar justifications can be offered for the other two CQ rules.

## Practice exercises

**A.** Offer proofs which justify the addition of the second and fourth CQ rules as derived rules.

# CHAPTER 39

# *Proofs and semantics*

We have used two different turnstiles in this book. This:

$$\mathcal{A}_1, \mathcal{A}_2, \ldots, \mathcal{A}_n \vdash \mathcal{C}$$

means that there is some proof which ends with $\mathcal{C}$ and whose only undischarged assumptions are among $\mathcal{A}_1, \mathcal{A}_2, \ldots, \mathcal{A}_n$. This is a *proof-theoretic notion*. By contrast, this:

$$\mathcal{A}_1, \mathcal{A}_2, \ldots, \mathcal{A}_n \vDash \mathcal{C}$$

means that no valuation (or interpretation) makes all of $\mathcal{A}_1, \mathcal{A}_2, \ldots, \mathcal{A}_n$ true and $\mathcal{C}$ false. This concerns assignments of truth and falsity to sentences. It is a *semantic notion*.

It cannot be emphasized enough that these are different notions. But we can emphasize it a bit more: *They are different notions.*

Once you have internalised this point, continue reading.

Although our semantic and proof-theoretic notions are different, there is a deep connection between them. To explain this connection, we will start by considering the relationship between validities and theorems.

324

To show that a sentence is a theorem, you need only produce a proof. Granted, it may be hard to produce a twenty line proof, but it is not so hard to check each line of the proof and confirm that it is legitimate; and if each line of the proof individually is legitimate, then the whole proof is legitimate. Showing that a sentence is a validity, though, requires reasoning about all possible interpretations. Given a choice between showing that a sentence is a theorem and showing that it is a validity, it would be easier to show that it is a theorem.

Contrawise, to show that a sentence is *not* a theorem is hard. We would need to reason about all (possible) proofs. That is very difficult. However, to show that a sentence is not a validity, you need only construct an interpretation in which the sentence is false. Granted, it may be hard to come up with the interpretation; but once you have done so, it is relatively straightforward to check what truth value it assigns to a sentence. Given a choice between showing that a sentence is not a theorem and showing that it is not a validity, it would be easier to show that it is not a validity.

Fortunately, *a sentence is a theorem if and only if it is a validity*. As a result, if we provide a proof of $\mathcal{A}$ on no assumptions, and thus show that $\mathcal{A}$ is a theorem, i.e., $\vdash \mathcal{A}$, we can legitimately infer that $\mathcal{A}$ is a validity, i.e., $\vDash \mathcal{A}$. Similarly, if we construct an interpretation in which $\mathcal{A}$ is false and thus show that it is not a validity, i.e., $\nvDash \mathcal{A}$, it follows that $\mathcal{A}$ is not a theorem, i.e., $\nvdash \mathcal{A}$.

More generally, we have the following powerful result:

$$\mathcal{A}_1, \mathcal{A}_2, \ldots, \mathcal{A}_n \vdash \mathcal{B} \text{ \textbf{iff} } \mathcal{A}_1, \mathcal{A}_2, \ldots, \mathcal{A}_n \vDash \mathcal{B}$$

This shows that, whilst provability and entailment are *different* notions, they are extensionally equivalent. As such:

- An argument is *valid* iff *the conclusion can be proved from the premises*.
- A sentence is a *validity* iff it is a *theorem*.
- Two sentences are *equivalent* iff they are *provably equivalent*.
- Sentences are *jointly satisfiable* iff they are *jointly consistent*.

For this reason, you can pick and choose when to think in terms of proofs and when to think in terms of valuations/interpretations, doing whichever is easier for a given task. The table on the next page summarises which is (usually) easier.

It is intuitive that provability and semantic entailment should agree. But—let us repeat this—do not be fooled by the similarity of the symbols '⊨' and '⊢'. These two symbols have very different meanings. The fact that provability and semantic entailment agree is not an easy result to come by.

In fact, demonstrating that provability and semantic entailment agree is, very decisively, the point at which introductory logic becomes intermediate logic.

| | Yes | No |
|---|---|---|
| Is $\mathcal{A}$ a **validity**? | give a proof which shows $\vdash \mathcal{A}$ | give an interpretation in which $\mathcal{A}$ is false |
| Is $\mathcal{A}$ a **contradiction**? | give a proof which shows $\vdash \neg\mathcal{A}$ | give an interpretation in which $\mathcal{A}$ is true |
| Are $\mathcal{A}$ and $\mathcal{B}$ **equivalent**? | give two proofs, one for $\mathcal{A} \vdash \mathcal{B}$ and one for $\mathcal{B} \vdash \mathcal{A}$ | give an interpretation in which $\mathcal{A}$ and $\mathcal{B}$ have different truth values |
| Are $\mathcal{A}_1, \mathcal{A}_2, \ldots, \mathcal{A}_n$ **jointly satisfiable**? | give an interpretation in which all of $\mathcal{A}_1, \mathcal{A}_2, \ldots, \mathcal{A}_n$ are true | prove a contradiction from assumptions $\mathcal{A}_1, \mathcal{A}_2, \ldots, \mathcal{A}_n$ |
| Is $\mathcal{A}_1, \mathcal{A}_2, \ldots, \mathcal{A}_n \therefore \mathcal{C}$ **valid**? | give a proof with assumptions $\mathcal{A}_1, \mathcal{A}_2, \ldots, \mathcal{A}_n$ and concluding with $\mathcal{C}$ | give an interpretation in which each of $\mathcal{A}_1, \mathcal{A}_2, \ldots, \mathcal{A}_n$ is true and $\mathcal{C}$ is false |

# PART VIII

# *Modal logic*

# CHAPTER 40

# *Introducing modal logic*

Modal logic (ML) is the logic of *modalities*, ways in which a statement can be true. *Necessity* and *possibility* are two such modalities: a statement can be true, but it can also be necessarily true (true no matter how the world might have been). For instance, logical truths are not just true because of some accidental feature of the world, but true come what may. A possible statement may not actually be true, but it might have been true. We use □ to express necessity, and ◇ to express possibility. So you can read □𝒜 as *It is necessarily the case that 𝒜*, and ◇𝒜 as *It is possibly the case that 𝒜*.

There are lots of different kinds of necessity. It is *humanly impossible* for me to run at 100mph. Given the sorts of creatures that we are, no human can do that. But still, it isn't *physically impossible* for me to run that fast. We haven't got the technology to do it yet, but it is surely physically possible to swap my biological legs for robotic ones which could run at 100mph. By contrast, it is physically impossible for me to run faster than the speed of light. The laws of physics forbid any object from accelerating up to that speed. But even that isn't *logically* impossible. It isn't a contradiction to imagine that the laws of physics might have been different, and that they might have allowed objects to move faster than light.

Which kind of modality does ML deal with? *All of them!* ML is a very flexible tool. We start with a basic set of rules that govern □ and ◇, and then add more rules to fit whatever kind of modality we are interested in. In fact, ML is so flexible that we do not even have to think of □ and ◇ as expressing *necessity* and *possibility*. We might instead read □ as expressing *provability*, so that □𝒜 means *It is provable that 𝒜*, and ◇𝒜 means *It is not refutable that 𝒜*. Similarly, we can interpret □ to mean *S knows that 𝒜* or *S believes that 𝒜*. Or we might read □ as expressing *moral obligation*, so that □𝒜 means *It is morally obligatory that 𝒜*, and ◇𝒜 means *It is morally permissible that 𝒜*. All we would need to do is cook up the right rules for these different readings of □ and ◇.

A modal formula is one that includes modal operators such as □ and ◇. Depending on the interpretation we assign to □ and ◇, different modal formulas will be provable or valid. For instance, □𝒜 → 𝒜 might say that "if 𝒜 is necessary, it is true," if □ is interpreted as necessity. It might express "if 𝒜 is known, then it is true," if □ expresses known truth. Under both these interpretations, □𝒜 → 𝒜 is valid: All necessary propositions are true come what may, so are true in the actual world. And if a proposition is known to be true, it must be true (one can't know something that's false). However, when □ is interpreted as "it is believed that" or "it ought to be the case that," □𝒜 → 𝒜 is not valid: We can believe false propositions. Not every proposition that ought to be true is in fact true, e.g., "Every murderer will be brought to justice." This *ought* to be true, but it isn't.

We will consider different kinds of systems of ML. They differ in the rules of proof allowed, and in the semantics we use to define our logical notions. The different systems we'll consider are called **K**, **T**, **S4**, and **S5**. **K** is the basic system; everything that is valid or provable in **K** is also provable in the others. But there are some things that **K** does not prove, such as the formula $\Box A \to A$ for sentence letter $A$. So **K** is not an appropriate modal logic for necessity and possibility (where □𝒜 → 𝒜 should be provable).

This is provable in the system **T**, so **T** is more appropriate when dealing with necessity and possibiliity, but less apropriate when dealing with belief or obligation, since then $\Box\mathcal{A} \to \mathcal{A}$ should *not* (always) be provable. The perhaps best system of ML for necessity and possibility, and in any case the most widely accepted, is the strongest of the systems we consider, **S5**.

## 40.1 The Language of ML

In order to do modal logic, we have to do two things. First, we want to learn how to prove things in ML. Second, we want to see how to construct interpretations for ML. But before we can do either of these things, we need to explain how to construct sentences in ML.

The language of ML is an extension of TFL. We could have started with FOL, which would have given us Quantified Modal Logic (QML). QML is much more powerful than ML, but it is also much, much more complicated. So we are going to keep things simple, and start with TFL.

Just like TFL, ML starts with an infinite stock of *atoms*. These are written as capital letters, with or without numerical subscripts: $A$, $B$, $\ldots A_1$, $B_1$, $\ldots$ We then take all of the rules about how to make sentences from TFL, and add two more for $\Box$ and $\Diamond$:

(1) Every atom of ML is a sentence of ML.

(2) If $\mathcal{A}$ is a sentence of ML, then $\neg\mathcal{A}$ is a sentence of ML.

(3) If $\mathcal{A}$ and $\mathcal{B}$ are sentences of ML, then $(\mathcal{A} \wedge \mathcal{B})$ is a sentence of ML.

(4) If $\mathcal{A}$ and $\mathcal{B}$ are sentences of ML, then $(\mathcal{A} \vee \mathcal{B})$ is a sentence of ML.

(5) If $\mathcal{A}$ and $\mathcal{B}$ are sentences of ML, then $(\mathcal{A} \to \mathcal{B})$ is a sentence of ML.

(6) If $\mathscr{A}$ and $\mathscr{B}$ are sentences of ML, then $(\mathscr{A} \leftrightarrow \mathscr{B})$ is a sentence of ML.

(7) If $\mathscr{A}$ is a sentence of ML, then $\Box\mathscr{A}$ is a sentence of ML.

(8) If $\mathscr{A}$ is a sentence of ML, then $\Diamond\mathscr{A}$ is a sentence of ML.

(9) Nothing else is a sentence of ML.

Here are some examples of ML sentences:

$A, \; P \vee Q, \; \Box A, \; C \vee \Box D, \; \Box\Box(A \rightarrow R), \; \Box\Diamond(S \wedge (Z \leftrightarrow (\Box W \vee \Diamond Q)))$

# CHAPTER 41

# *Natural deduction for ML*

Now that we know how to make sentences in ML, we can look at how to *prove* things in ML. We will use ⊢ to express provability. So $\mathscr{A}_1, \mathscr{A}_2, \ldots \mathscr{A}_n$ ⊢ $\mathscr{C}$ means that $\mathscr{C}$ can be proven from $\mathscr{A}_1, \mathscr{A}_2, \ldots \mathscr{A}_n$. However, we will be looking at a number of different systems of ML, and so it will be useful to add a subscript to indicate which system we are working with. So for example, if we want to say that we can prove $\mathscr{C}$ from $\mathscr{A}_1, \mathscr{A}_2, \ldots \mathscr{A}_n$ *in system* **K**, we will write: $\mathscr{A}_1, \mathscr{A}_2, \ldots \mathscr{A}_n$ ⊢$_\mathbf{K}$ $\mathscr{C}$.

## 41.1   System K

We start with a particularly simple system called **K**, in honour of the philosopher and logician Saul Kripke. **K** includes all of the natural deduction rules from TFL, including the derived rules as well as the basic ones. **K** then adds a special kind of subproof, plus two new basic rules for □.

333

The special kind of subproof looks like an ordinary subproof, except it has a □ in its assumption line instead of a formula. We call them *strict subproofs*—they allow as to reason and prove things about alternate possibilities. What we can prove inside a strict subproof holds in any alternate possibility, in particular, in alternate possibilities where the assumptions in force in our proof may not hold. In a strict subproofs, all assumptions are disregarded, and we are not allowed to appeal to any lines outside the strict subproof (except as allowed by the modal rules given below).

The □I rule allows us to derive a formula □$\mathcal{A}$ if we can derive $\mathcal{A}$ inside a strict subproof. It is our fundamental method of introducing □ into proofs. The basic idea is simple enough: if $\mathcal{A}$ is a theorem, then □$\mathcal{A}$ should be a theorem too. (Remember that to call $\mathcal{A}$ a theorem is to say that we can prove $\mathcal{A}$ without relying on any undischarged assumptions.)

Suppose we wanted to prove □$(A \rightarrow A)$. The first thing we need to do is prove that $A \rightarrow A$ is a theorem. You already know how to do that using TFL. You simply present a proof of $A \rightarrow A$ which doesn't start with any premises, like this:

$$
\begin{array}{ll}
1 \quad \big| \quad A \\
2 \quad \big| \quad A \qquad \text{R } 1 \\
3 \quad A \rightarrow A \qquad \rightarrow\text{I } 1\text{--}2
\end{array}
$$

But to apply □I, we need to have proven the formula inside a strict subproof. Since our proof of $A \rightarrow A$ makes use of no assumptions at all, this is possible.

$$
\begin{array}{ll}
1 \quad \big| \quad \square \\
2 \quad \big| \quad \big| \quad A \\
3 \quad \big| \quad \big| \quad A \qquad \text{R } 2 \\
4 \quad \big| \quad A \rightarrow A \qquad \rightarrow\text{I } 2\text{--}3 \\
5 \quad \square(A \rightarrow A) \qquad \square\text{I } 1\text{--}4
\end{array}
$$

$$
\begin{array}{c|c}
m & \phantom{x}\Box \\[1em]
n & \phantom{x}\mathcal{A} \\[1em]
& \Box\mathcal{A} \qquad \Box\text{I } m\text{--}n
\end{array}
$$

No line above line $m$ may be cited by any rule within the strict subproof begun at line $m$ unless the rule explicitly allows it.

It is essential to emphasise that in strict subproof you cannot use any rule which appeals to anything you proved outside of the strict subproof. There are exceptions, e.g., the $\Box$E rule below. These rules will explicitly state that they can be used inside strict subproofs and cite lines outside the strict subproof. This restriction is essential, otherwise we would get terrible results. For example, we could provide the following proof to vindicate $A \therefore \Box A$:

$$
\begin{array}{r|l}
1 & A \\[0.5em]
2 & \quad \Box \\[0.5em]
3 & \quad A \qquad \text{incorrect use of R 1} \\[0.5em]
4 & \Box A \qquad \Box\text{I 2--3}
\end{array}
$$

This is not a legitimate proof, because at line 3 we appealed to line 1, even though line 1 comes before the beginning of the strict subproof at line 2.

We said above that a strict subproof allows us to reason about arbitrary alternate possible situations. What can be proved in a strict subproof holds in all alternate possible situations, and so is necessary. This is the idea behind the $\Box$I rule. On the other hand, if we've assumed that something is necessary, we have therewith assumed that it is true in all alternate possbile situations. Hence, we have the rule $\Box$E:

$$
\begin{array}{c|c}
m & \Box\mathcal{A} \\
 & \\
 & \quad\begin{array}{|c}
 \Box \\
 \hline
\end{array} \\
n & \quad\ \mathcal{A} \qquad \Box\text{E } m
\end{array}
$$

$\Box$E can only be applied if line $m$ (containing $\Box A$) lies *outside* of the strict subproof in which line $n$ falls, and this strict subproof is not itself part of a strict subproof not containing $m$.

$\Box$E allows you to assert $\mathcal{A}$ inside a strict subproof if you have $\Box\mathcal{A}$ outside the strict subproof. The restriction means that you can only do this in the first strict subproof, you cannot apply the $\Box$E rule inside a nested strict subproof. So the following is not allowed:

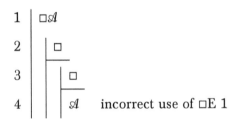

The incorrect use of $\Box$E on line 4 violates the condition, because although line 1 lies outside the strict subproof in which line 4 falls, the strict subproof containing line 4 lies inside the strict subproof beginning on line 2 which does not contain line 1.

Let's begin with an example.

$$
\begin{array}{r|ll}
1 & \square A & \\
2 & \square B & \\
\hline
3 & \quad\square & \\
4 & \quad A & \square\text{E }1 \\
5 & \quad B & \square\text{E }2 \\
6 & \quad A \wedge B & \wedge\text{I }4,\,5 \\
7 & \square(A \wedge B) & \square\text{I }3\text{--}7
\end{array}
$$

We can also mix regular subproofs and strict subproofs:

$$
\begin{array}{r|ll}
1 & \square(A \to B) & \\
2 & \quad \square A & \\
\hline
3 & \quad\quad \square & \\
4 & \quad\quad A & \square\text{E }2 \\
5 & \quad\quad A \to B & \square\text{E }1 \\
6 & \quad\quad B & \to\text{E }4,\,5 \\
7 & \quad \square B & \\
8 & \square A \to \square B & \to\text{I }2\text{--}7
\end{array}
$$

This is called the *Distribution Rule*, because it tells us that $\square$ 'distributes' over $\to$.

The rules $\square$I and $\square$E look simple enough, and indeed **K** is a very simple system! But **K** is more powerful than you might have thought. You can prove a fair few things in it.

## 41.2 Possibility

In the last subsection, we looked at all of the basic rules for **K**. But you might have noticed that all of these rules were about necessity, □, and none of them were about possibility, ◇. That's because we can *define* possibility in terms of necessity:

$$\Diamond \mathcal{A} =_{df} \neg\Box\neg\mathcal{A}$$

In other words, to say that $\mathcal{A}$ is *possibly true*, is to say that $\mathcal{A}$ is *not necessarily false*. As a result, it isn't really essential to add a ◇, a special symbol for possibility, into system **K**. Still, the system will be *much* easier to use if we do, and so we will add the following definitional rules:

$$
\begin{array}{c|l}
m & \neg\Box\neg\mathcal{A} \\[1em]
 & \Diamond\mathcal{A} \qquad \text{Def}\Diamond\ m \\[2em]
m & \Diamond\mathcal{A} \\[1em]
 & \neg\Box\neg\mathcal{A} \qquad \text{Def}\Diamond\ m
\end{array}
$$

Importantly, you should not think of these rules as any real addition to **K**: they just record the way that ◇ is defined in terms of □.

If we wanted, we could leave our rules for **K** here. But it will be helpful to add some *Modal Conversion* rules, which give us some more ways of flipping between □ and ◇:

$$
\begin{array}{c|l}
m & \neg\Box\mathcal{A} \\[4pt]
  & \Diamond\neg\mathcal{A} \qquad \text{MC } m
\end{array}
$$

$$
\begin{array}{c|l}
m & \Diamond\neg\mathcal{A} \\[4pt]
  & \neg\Box\mathcal{A} \qquad \text{MC } m
\end{array}
$$

$$
\begin{array}{c|l}
m & \neg\Diamond\mathcal{A} \\[4pt]
  & \Box\neg\mathcal{A} \qquad \text{MC } m
\end{array}
$$

$$
\begin{array}{c|l}
m & \Box\neg\mathcal{A} \\[4pt]
  & \neg\Diamond\mathcal{A} \qquad \text{MC } m
\end{array}
$$

These Modal Conversion Rules are also no addition to the power of **K**, because they can be derived from the basic rules, along with the definition of $\Diamond$.

In system **K**, using Def$\Diamond$ (or the modal conversion rules), one can prove $\Diamond A \leftrightarrow \neg\Box\neg A$. When laying out system **K**, we started with $\Box$ as our primitive modal symbol, and then defined $\Diamond$ in terms of it. But if we had preferred, we could have started with $\Diamond$ as our primitive, and then defined $\Box$ as follows: $\Box\mathcal{A} =_{df} \neg\Diamond\neg\mathcal{A}$. There is, then, no sense in which necessity is somehow more *fundamental* than possibility. Necessity and possibility are exactly as fundamental as each other.

## 41.3   System T

So far we have focussed on **K**, which is a very simple modal system. **K** is so weak that it will not even let you prove $\mathcal{A}$ from $\Box\mathcal{A}$. But if we are thinking of $\Box$ as expressing *necessity*, then we will want to be able to make this inference: if $\mathcal{A}$ is *necessarily true*, then it must surely be *true*!

This leads us to a new system, **T**, which we get by adding the following rule to **K**:

$$
\begin{array}{r|ll}
m & \Box\mathcal{A} & \\
\\
n & \mathcal{A} & \textbf{RT } m
\end{array}
$$

The line $n$ on which rule **RT** is applied must *not* lie in a strict subproof that begins after line $m$.

The restriction on rule **T** is in a way the opposite of the restriction on $\Box$E: you can *only* use $\Box$E in a nested strict subproof, but you cannot use **T** in a nested strict subproof.

We can prove things in **T** which we could not prove in **K**, e.g., $\Box A \to A$.

## 41.4   System S4

**T** allows you to strip away the necessity boxes: from $\Box\mathcal{A}$, you may infer $\mathcal{A}$. But what if we wanted to add extra boxes? That is, what if we wanted to go from $\Box\mathcal{A}$ to $\Box\Box\mathcal{A}$? Well, that would be no problem, if we had proved $\Box\mathcal{A}$ by applying $\Box$I to a strict subproof of $\mathcal{A}$ which itself does not use $\Box$E. In that case, $\mathcal{A}$ is a tautology, and by nesting the strict subproof inside another strict subproof and applying $\Box$I again, we can prove $\Box\Box\mathcal{A}$. For example, we could prove $\Box\Box(P \to P)$ like this:

| | | | |
|---|---|---|---|
| 1 | $\Box$ | | |
| 2 | | $\Box$ | |
| 3 | | | $P$ | |
| 4 | | | $P$ | R 3 |
| 5 | | $P \to P$ | | $\to$I 3–4 |
| 6 | $\Box(P \to P)$ | | $\Box$I 2–5 |
| 7 | $\Box\Box(P \to P)$ | | $\Box$I 1–6 |

But what if we didn't prove $\Box\mathcal{A}$ in this restricted way, but used $\Box$E inside the strict subproof of $\mathcal{A}$. If we put that strict subproof inside another strict subproof, the requirement of rule $\Box$E to not cite a line containing $\Box\mathcal{A}$ which lies in another strict subproof that has not yet concluded, is violated. Or what if $\Box\mathcal{A}$ were just an assumption we started our proof with? Could we infer $\Box\Box\mathcal{A}$ then? Not in **T**, we couldn't. And this might well strike you as a limitation of **T**, at least if we are reading $\Box$ as expressing *necessity*. It seems intuitive that if $\mathcal{A}$ is necessarily true, then it couldn't have *failed* to be necessarily true.

This leads us to another new system, **S4**, which we get by adding the following rule to **T**:

$$
\begin{array}{l|l}
m & \Box A \\
\\
  & \quad\begin{array}{|l} \Box \\ \hline \end{array} \\
  & \quad\;\Box \\
n & \quad\;\Box A \quad \text{R4 } m
\end{array}
$$

Note that **R4** can only be applied if line $m$ (containing $\Box A$) lies outside of the strict subproof in which line $n$ falls, and this strict subproof is not itself part of a strict subproof not containing $m$.

Rule **R4** looks just like $\Box$E, except that instead of yielding $A$ from $\Box A$ it yields $\Box A$ inside a strict subproof. The restriction is the same, however: **R4** allows us to "import" $\Box A$ into a strict subproof, but not into a strict subproof itself nested inside a strict subproof. However, if that is necessary, an additional application of **R4** would have the same result.

Now we can prove even more results. For instance:

$$
\begin{array}{l|l}
1 & \quad\begin{array}{|l} \Box A \end{array} \\
2 & \quad\;\;\begin{array}{|l} \Box \\ \hline \end{array} \\
3 & \quad\;\;\Box A \qquad \text{R4 } 1 \\
4 & \quad\Box\Box A \qquad \Box\text{I } 2\text{--}3 \\
5 & \Box A \rightarrow \Box\Box A \quad \rightarrow\text{I } 1\text{--}6
\end{array}
$$

Similarly, we can prove $\Diamond\Diamond A \rightarrow \Diamond A$. This shows us that as well as letting us *add* extra *boxes*, **S4** lets us *delete* extra *diamonds*: from $\Diamond\Diamond A$, you can always infer $\Diamond A$.

## 41.5  System S5

In **S4**, we can always add a box in front of another box. But **S4** does not automatically let us add a box in front of a *diamond*.

That is, **S4** does not generally permit the inference from $\Diamond\mathcal{A}$ to $\Box\Diamond\mathcal{A}$. But again, that might strike you as a shortcoming, at least if you are reading $\Box$ and $\Diamond$ as expressing *necessity* and *possibility*. It seems intuitive that if $\mathcal{A}$ is possibly true, then it couldn't have *failed* to be possibly true.

This leads us to our final modal system, **S5**, which we get by adding the following rule to **S4**:

$$
\begin{array}{c|ll}
m & \neg\Box\mathcal{A} & \\
  & \quad\begin{array}{|l} \Box \\ \hline \end{array} & \\
n & \quad \neg\Box\mathcal{A} & \text{R5 } m \\
\end{array}
$$

Rule **R5** can only be applied if line $m$ (containing $\neg\Box\mathcal{A}$) lies outside of the strict subproof in which line $n$ falls, and this strict subproof is not itself part of a strict subproof not containing line $m$.

This rule allows us to show, for instance, that $\Diamond\Box A \vdash_{\text{S5}} \Box A$:

$$
\begin{array}{c|ll}
1 & \Diamond\Box A & \\
2 & \neg\Box\neg\Box A & \text{Def}\Diamond\ 1 \\
3 & \quad \neg\Box A & \\
4 & \quad\quad \Box & \\
5 & \quad\quad \neg\Box A & \text{R5 } 3 \\
6 & \quad \Box\neg\Box A & \Box\text{I } 4\text{–}5 \\
7 & \quad \bot & \neg\text{E } 2, 6 \\
8 & \Box A & \text{IP } 3\text{–}7 \\
\end{array}
$$

So, as well as adding boxes in front of diamonds, we can also delete diamonds in front of boxes.

We got **S5** just by adding the rule **R5** rule to **S4**. In fact, we could have added rule **R5** to **T** alone, and leave out rule **R4**). Everything we can prove by rule **R4** can also be proved using **RT** together with **R5**. For instance, here is a proof that shows $\Box A \vdash_{S5} \Box\Box A$ without using **R4**:

| | | |
|---|---|---|
| 1 | $\Box A$ | |
| 2 | $\Box\neg\Box A$ | |
| 3 | $\neg\Box A$ | **RT** 2 |
| 4 | $\bot$ | $\neg$E 1, 3 |
| 5 | $\neg\Box\neg\Box A$ | $\neg$I 2–4 |
| 6 | $\Box$ | |
| 7 | $\neg\Box A$ | |
| 8 | $\Box$ | |
| 9 | $\neg\Box A$ | **R5** 7 |
| 10 | $\Box\neg\Box A$ | $\Box$I 8–9 |
| 11 | $\neg\Box\neg\Box A$ | **R5** 5 |
| 12 | $\bot$ | $\neg$E 10, 11 |
| 13 | $\Box A$ | IP 7–12 |
| 14 | $\Box\Box A$ | $\Box$I 6–13 |

**S5** is *strictly stronger* than **S4**: there are things which can be proved in **S5**, but not in **S4** (e.g., $\Diamond\Box A \rightarrow \Box A$).

The important point about **S5** can be put like this: if you have a long string of boxes and diamonds, in any combination whatsoever, you can delete all but the last of them. So for example, $\Diamond\Box\Diamond\Diamond\Box\Box\Diamond\Box A$ can be simplified down to just $\Box A$.

## Practice exercises

**A.** Provide proofs for the following:

1. $\Box(A \land B) \vdash_K \Box A \land \Box B$
2. $\Box A \land \Box B \vdash_K \Box(A \land B)$
3. $\Box A \lor \Box B \vdash_K \Box(A \lor B)$
4. $\Box(A \leftrightarrow B) \vdash_K \Box A \leftrightarrow \Box B$

**B.** Provide proofs for the following (without using Modal Conversion!):

1. $\neg \Box A \vdash_K \Diamond \neg A$
2. $\Diamond \neg A \vdash_K \neg \Box A$
3. $\neg \Diamond A \vdash_K \Box \neg A$
4. $\Box \neg A \vdash_K \neg \Diamond A$

**C.** Provide proofs of the following (and now feel free to use Modal Conversion!):

1. $\Box(A \to B), \Diamond A \vdash_K \Diamond B$
2. $\Box A \vdash_K \neg \Diamond \neg A$
3. $\neg \Diamond \neg A \vdash_K \Box A$

**D.** Provide proofs for the following:

1. $P \vdash_T \Diamond P$
2. $\vdash_T (A \land B) \lor (\neg \Box A \lor \neg \Box B)$

**E.** Provide proofs for the following:

1. $\Box(\Box A \to B), \Box(\Box B \to C), \Box A \vdash_{S4} \Box \Box C$
2. $\Box A \vdash_{S4} \Box(\Box A \lor B)$
3. $\Diamond \Diamond A \vdash_{S4} \Diamond A$

**F.** Provide proofs in **S5** for the following:

1. $\neg \Box \neg A, \Diamond B \vdash_{S5} \Box(\Diamond A \land \Diamond B)$
2. $A \vdash_{S5} \Box \Diamond A$
3. $\Diamond \Diamond A \vdash_{S5} \Diamond A$

# CHAPTER 42

# *Semantics for ML*

So far, we have focussed on laying out various systems of Natural Deduction for ML. Now we will look at the *semantics* for ML. A semantics for a language is a method for assigning truth-values to the sentences in that language. So a semantics for ML is a method for assigning truth-values to the sentences of ML.

## 42.1   Interpretations of ML

The big idea behind the semantics for ML is this. In ML, sentences are not just true or false, full stop. A sentence is true or false *at a given possible world*, and a single sentence may well be true at some worlds and false at others. We then say that $\Box \mathcal{A}$ is true iff $\mathcal{A}$ is true at *every* world, and $\Diamond \mathcal{A}$ is true iff $\mathcal{A}$ is true at *some* world.

That's the big idea, but we need to refine it and make it more precise. To do this, we need to introduce the idea of an *interpretation* of ML. The first thing you need to include in an interpretation is a collection of *possible worlds*. Now, at this point you might well want to ask: What exactly is a possible world? The intuitive idea is that a possible world is another way that this world could

346

have been. But what exactly does that mean? This is an excellent philosophical question, and we will look at it in a lot of detail later. But we do not need to worry too much about it right now. As far as the formal logic goes, possible worlds can be anything you like. All that matters is that you supply each interpretation with a non-empty collection of things labelled POSSIBLE WORLDS.

Once you have chosen your collection of possible worlds, you need to find some way of determining which sentences of ML are true at which possible worlds. To do that, we need to introduce the notion of a *valuation function*. Those of you who have studied some maths will already be familiar with the general idea of a function. But for those of you who haven't, a function is a mathematical entity which maps arguments to values. That might sound a little bit abstract, but some familiar examples will help. Take the function $x+1$. This is a function which takes in a number as argument, and then spits out the next number as value. So if you feed in the number 1 as an argument, the function $x+1$ will spit out the number 2 as a value; if you feed in 2, it will spit out 3; if you feed in 3, it will spit out 4 ... Or here is another example: the function $x+y$. This time, you have to feed two arguments into this function if you want it to return a value: if you feed in 2 and 3 as your arguments, it spits out 5; if you feed in 1003 and 2005, it spits out 3008; and so on.

A valuation function for ML takes in a sentence and a world as its arguments, and then returns a truth-value as its value. So if $v$ is a valuation function and $w$ is a possible world, $v_w(\mathcal{A})$ is whatever truth-value $v$ maps $\mathcal{A}$ and $w$ to: if $v_w(\mathcal{A}) = F$, then $\mathcal{A}$ is false at world $w$ on valuation $v$; if $v_w(\mathcal{A}) = T$, then $\mathcal{A}$ is true at world $w$ on valuation $v$.

These valuation functions are allowed to map any *atomic* sentence to any truth-value at any world. But there are rules about which truth-values more complex sentences get assigned at a world. Here are the rules for the connectives from TFL:

(1) $v_w(\neg\mathcal{A}) = T$ iff: $v_w(\mathcal{A}) = F$

(2) $v_w(\mathcal{A} \wedge \mathcal{B}) = T$ iff: $v_w(\mathcal{A}) = T$ and $v_w(\mathcal{B}) = T$

(3) $v_w(\mathcal{A} \vee \mathcal{B}) = T$ iff: $v_w(\mathcal{A}) = T$ or $v_w(\mathcal{B}) = T$, or both

(4) $v_w(\mathcal{A} \rightarrow \mathcal{B}) = T$ iff: $v_w(\mathcal{A}) = F$ or $v_w(\mathcal{B}) = T$, or both

(5) $v_w(\mathcal{A} \leftrightarrow \mathcal{B}) = T$ iff: $v_w(\mathcal{A}) = T$ and $v_w(\mathcal{B}) = T$, or $v_w(\mathcal{A}) = F$ and $v_w(\mathcal{B}) = F$

So far, these rules should all look very familiar. Essentially, they all work exactly like the truth-tables for TFL. The only difference is that these truth-table rules have to be applied over and over again, to one world at a time.

But what are the rules for the new modal operators, □ and ◇? The most obvious idea would be to give rules like these:

$$v_w(\Box\mathcal{A}) = T \text{ iff } \forall w'(v_{w'}(\mathcal{A}) = T)$$

$$v_w(\Diamond\mathcal{A}) = T \text{ iff } \exists w'(v_{w'}(\mathcal{A}) = T)$$

This is just the fancy formal way of writing out the idea that □$\mathcal{A}$ is true at $w$ just in case $\mathcal{A}$ is true at *every* world, and ◇$\mathcal{A}$ is true at $w$ just in case $\mathcal{A}$ is true at *some* world.

However, while these rules are nice and simple, they turn out not to be quite as useful as we would like. As we mentioned, ML is meant to be a very flexible tool. It is meant to be a general framework for dealing with lots of different kinds of necessity. As a result, we want our semantic rules for □ and ◇ to be a bit less rigid. We can do this by introducing another new idea: *accessibility relations*.

An accessibility relation, $R$, is a relation between possible worlds. Roughly, to say that $Rw_1w_2$ (in English: world $w_1$ *accesses* world $w_2$) is to say that $w_2$ is possible *relative to* $w_1$. In other words, by introducing accessibility relations, we open up the idea that a given world might be possible relative to some worlds but not others. This turns out to be a *very* fruitful idea when studying modal systems. We can now give the following semantic rules for □ and ◇:

(6) $v_{w_1}(\Box\mathcal{A}) = T$ iff $\forall w_2(Rw_1w_2 \rightarrow v_{w_2}(\mathcal{A}) = T)$

(7) $v_{w_1}(\Diamond \mathcal{A}) = T$ iff $\exists w_2(Rw_1w_2 \land v_{w_2}(\mathcal{A}) = T)$

Or in plain English: $\Box \mathcal{A}$ is true in world $w_1$ iff $\mathcal{A}$ is true in every world that is possible relative to $w_1$; and $\Diamond \mathcal{A}$ is true in world $w_1$ iff $\mathcal{A}$ is true in some world that is possible relative to $w_1$.

So, there we have it. An interpretation for ML consists of three things: a collection of possible worlds, $W$; an accessibility relation, $R$; and a valuation function, $v$. The collection of 'possible worlds' can really be a collection of anything you like. It really doesn't matter, so long as $W$ isn't empty. (For many purposes, it is helpful just to take a collection of numbers to be your collection of worlds.) And for now, at least, $R$ can be any relation between the worlds in $W$ that you like. It could be a relation which every world in $W$ bears to every world in $W$, or one which no world bears to any world, or anything in between. And lastly, $v$ can map any atomic sentence of ML to any truth-value at any world. All that matters is that it follows the rules (1)–(7) when it comes to the more complex sentences.

Let's look at an example. It is often helpful to present interpretations of ML as diagrams, like this:

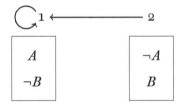

Here is how to read the interpretation off from this diagram. It contains just two worlds, 1 and 2. The arrows between the worlds indicate the accessibility relation. So 1 and 2 both access 1, but neither 1 nor 2 accesses 2. The boxes at each world let us know which atomic sentences are true at each world: $A$ is true at 1 but false at 2; $B$ is false at 1 but true at 2. You may only write an atomic sentence or the negation of an atomic sentence into one of these boxes. We can figure out what truth-values the more complex sentences get at each world from that. For example, on this interpretation all of the following sentences are true at $w_1$:

$$A \wedge \neg B, B \rightarrow A, \Diamond A, \Box \neg B$$

If you don't like thinking diagrammatically, then you can also present an interpretation like this:

$W$: 1, 2

$R$: $\langle 1, 1 \rangle, \langle 2, 1 \rangle$

$$v_1(A) = T, v_2(B) = F, v_2(A) = F, v_2(B) = T$$

You will get the chance to cook up some interpretations of your own shortly, when we start looking at *counter-interpretations*.

## 42.2 A Semantics for System K

We can now extend all of the semantic concepts of TFL to cover ML:

> ▷ $\mathcal{A}_1, \mathcal{A}_2, \ldots \mathcal{A}_n \therefore \mathcal{C}$ is MODALLY VALID iff there is no world in any interpretation at which $\mathcal{A}_1, \mathcal{A}_2, \ldots \mathcal{A}_n$ are all true and $\mathcal{C}$ is false.
>
> ▷ $\mathcal{A}$ is a MODAL TRUTH iff $\mathcal{A}$ is true at every world in every interpretation.
>
> ▷ $\mathcal{A}$ is a MODAL CONTRADICTION iff $\mathcal{A}$ is false at every world in every interpretation.
>
> ▷ $\mathcal{A}$ is MODALLY SATISFIABLE iff $\mathcal{A}$ is true at some world in some interpretation.

(From now on we will drop the explicit 'modal' qualifications, since they can be taken as read.)

We can also extend our use of $\vDash$. However, we need to add subscripts again, just as we did with $\vdash$. So, when we want to say that $\mathcal{A}_1, \mathcal{A}_2, \ldots \mathcal{A}_n \therefore \mathcal{C}$ is valid, we will write: $\mathcal{A}_1, \mathcal{A}_2, \ldots \mathcal{A}_n \vDash_\mathbf{K} \mathcal{C}$.

Let's get more of a feel for this semantics by presenting some counter-interpretations. Consider the following (false) claim:

$$\neg A \vDash_\mathbf{K} \neg \Diamond A$$

In order to present a counter-interpretation to this claim, we need to cook up an interpretation which makes $\neg A$ true at some world $w$, and $\neg \Diamond A$ false at $w$. Here is one such interpretation, presented diagrammatically:

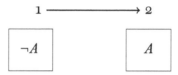

It is easy to see that this will work as a counter-interpretation for our claim. First, $\neg A$ is true at world 1. And second, $\neg \Diamond A$ is false at 1: $A$ is true at 2, and 2 is accessible from 1. So there is some world in this interpretation where $\neg A$ is true and $\neg \Diamond A$ is false, so it is not the case that $\neg A \vDash_\mathbf{K} \neg \Diamond A$.

Why did we choose the subscript **K**? Well, it turns out that there is an important relationship between system **K** and the definition of validity we have just given. In particular, we have the following two results:

  ▷ If $\mathcal{A}_1, \mathcal{A}_2, \ldots \mathcal{A}_n \vdash_\mathbf{K} \mathcal{C}$, then $\mathcal{A}_1, \mathcal{A}_2, \ldots \mathcal{A}_n \vDash_\mathbf{K} \mathcal{C}$

  ▷ If $\mathcal{A}_1, \mathcal{A}_2, \ldots \mathcal{A}_n \vDash_\mathbf{K} \mathcal{C}$, then $\mathcal{A}_1, \mathcal{A}_2, \ldots \mathcal{A}_n \vdash_\mathbf{K} \mathcal{C}$

The first result is known as a *soundness* result, since it tells us that the rules of **K** are good, sound rules: if you can vindicate an argument by giving a proof for it using system **K**, then that argument really is valid. The second result is known as a *completeness* result, since it tells us that the rules of **K** are broad enough to capture all of the valid arguments: if an argument is valid, then it will be possible to offer a proof in **K** which vindicates it.

Now, it is one thing to state these results, quite another to prove them. However, we will not try to prove them here. But the idea behind the proof of soundness will perhaps make clearer how strict subproofs work.

In a strict subproof, we are not allowed to make use of any information from outside the strict subproof, except what we import into the strict subproof using □E. If we've assumed or proved □$\mathscr{A}$, by □E, we can used $\mathscr{A}$ inside a strict subproof. And in **K**, that is the only way to import a formula into a strict subproof. So everything that can be proved inside a strict subproof must follow from formulas $\mathscr{A}$ where outside the strict subproof we have □$\mathscr{A}$. Let's imagine that we are reasoning about what's true in a possible world in some interpretation. If we know that □$\mathscr{A}$ is true in that possible world, we know that $\mathscr{A}$ is true in all accessible worlds. So, everything proved inside a strict subproof is true in all accessible possible worlds. That is why □I is a sound rule.

## 42.3 A Semantics for System T

A few moments ago, we said that system **K** is sound and complete. Where does that leave the other modal systems we looked at, namely **T**, **S4** and **S5**? Well, they are all *unsound*, relative to the definition of validity we gave above. For example, all of these systems allow us to infer $A$ from □$A$, even though □$A \nvDash_{\mathbf{K}} A$.

Does that mean that these systems are a waste of time? Not at all! These systems are only unsound *relative to the definition of validity we gave above*. (Or to use symbols, they are unsound relative to $\vDash_{\mathbf{K}}$.) So when we are dealing with these stronger modal systems, we just need to modify our definition of validity to fit. This is where accessibility relations come in really handy.

When we introduced the idea of an accessibility relation, we said that it could be any relation between worlds that you like: you could have it relating every world to every world, no world to any world, or anything in between. That is how we were thinking of accessibility relations in our definition of $\vDash_K$. But if we wanted, we could start putting some restrictions on the accessibility relation. In particular, we might insist that it has to be *reflexive*:

  ▷ $\forall w R w w$

In English: every world accesses itself. Or in terms of relative possibility: every world is possible relative to itself. If we imposed this restriction, we could introduce a new consequence relation, $\vDash_T$, as follows:

> $\mathscr{A}_1, \mathscr{A}_2, \ldots \mathscr{A}_n \vDash_T \mathscr{C}$ iff there is no world in any interpretation *which has a reflexive accessibility relation*, at which $\mathscr{A}_1, \mathscr{A}_2, \ldots \mathscr{A}_n$ are all true and $\mathscr{C}$ is false

We have attached the **T** subscript to $\vDash$ because it turns out that system **T** is sound and complete relative to this new definition of validity:

  ▷ If $\mathscr{A}_1, \mathscr{A}_2, \ldots \mathscr{A}_n \vdash_T \mathscr{C}$, then $\mathscr{A}_1, \mathscr{A}_2, \ldots \mathscr{A}_n \vDash_T \mathscr{C}$

  ▷ If $\mathscr{A}_1, \mathscr{A}_2, \ldots \mathscr{A}_n \vDash_T \mathscr{C}$, then $\mathscr{A}_1, \mathscr{A}_2, \ldots \mathscr{A}_n \vdash_T \mathscr{C}$

As before, we will not try to prove these soundness and completeness results. However, it is relatively easy to see how insisting that the accessibility relation must be reflexive will vindicate the RT rule:

> $$m \quad \Big| \quad \Box\mathscr{A}$$
> $$\quad \Big| \quad \mathscr{A} \qquad \textbf{RT } m$$

To see this, just imagine trying to cook up a counter-interpretation to this claim:

$$\Box\mathscr{A} \vDash_T \mathscr{A}$$

We would need to construct a world, $w$, at which $\Box\mathcal{A}$ was true, but $\mathcal{A}$ was false. Now, if $\Box\mathcal{A}$ is true at $w$, then $\mathcal{A}$ must be true at every world $w$ accesses. But since the accessibility relation is reflexive, $w$ accesses $w$. So $\mathcal{A}$ must be true at $w$. But now $\mathcal{A}$ must be true *and* false at $w$. Contradiction!

## 42.4   A Semantics for S4

How else might we tweak our definition of validity? Well, we might also stipulate that the accessibility relation has to be *transitive*:

▷ $\forall w_1 \forall w_2 \forall w_3((Rw_1w_2 \wedge Rw_2w_3) \to Rw_1w_3)$

In English: if $w_1$ accesses $w_2$, and $w_2$ accesses $w_3$, then $w_1$ accesses $w_3$. Or in terms of relative possibility: if $w_3$ is possible relative to $w_2$, and $w_2$ is possible relative to $w_1$, then $w_3$ is possible relative to $w_1$. If we added this restriction on our accessibility relation, we could introduce a new consequence relation, $\vDash_{S4}$, as follows:

> $\mathcal{A}_1, \mathcal{A}_2, \dots \mathcal{A}_n \vDash_{S4} \mathcal{C}$ iff there is no world in any interpretation *which has a reflexive and transitive accessibility relation*, at which $\mathcal{A}_1, \mathcal{A}_2, \dots \mathcal{A}_n$ are all true and $\mathcal{C}$ is false

We have attached the **S4** subscript to $\vDash$ because it turns out that system **S4** is sound and complete relative to this new definition of validity:

▷ If $\mathcal{A}_1, \mathcal{A}_2, \dots \mathcal{A}_n \vdash_{S4} \mathcal{C}$, then $\mathcal{A}_1, \mathcal{A}_2, \dots \mathcal{A}_n \vDash_{S4} \mathcal{C}$

▷ If $\mathcal{A}_1, \mathcal{A}_2, \dots \mathcal{A}_n \vDash_{S4} \mathcal{C}$, then $\mathcal{A}_1, \mathcal{A}_2, \dots \mathcal{A}_n \vdash_{S4} \mathcal{C}$

As before, we will not try to prove these soundness and completeness results. However, it is relatively easy to see how insisting that the accessibility relation must be transitive will vindicate the **S4** rule:

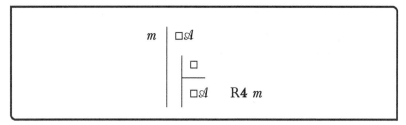

The idea behind strict subproofs, remember, is that they are ways to prove things that must be true in all accessible worlds. So the **R4** rule means that whenever $\Box\mathcal{A}$ is true, $\Box\mathcal{A}$ must also be true in every accessible world. In other words, we must have $\Box\mathcal{A} \vDash_{\mathbf{S4}} \Box\Box\mathcal{A}$.

To see this, just imagine trying to cook up a counter-interpretation to this claim:

$$\Box\mathcal{A} \vDash_{\mathbf{S4}} \Box\Box\mathcal{A}$$

We would need to construct a world, $w_1$, at which $\Box\mathcal{A}$ was true, but $\Box\Box\mathcal{A}$ was false. Now, if $\Box\Box\mathcal{A}$ is false at $w_1$, then $w_1$ must access some world, $w_2$, at which $\Box\mathcal{A}$ is false. Equally, if $\Box\mathcal{A}$ is false at $w_2$, then $w_2$ must access some world, $w_3$, at which $\mathcal{A}$ is false. We just said that $w_1$ accesses $w_2$, and $w_2$ accesses $w_3$. So since we are now insisting that the accessibility relation be transitive, $w_1$ must access $w_3$. And as $\Box\mathcal{A}$ is true at $w_1$, and $w_3$ is accessible from $w_1$, it follows that $\mathcal{A}$ must be true at $w_3$. So $\mathcal{A}$ is true *and* false at $w_3$. Contradiction!

## 42.5   A Semantics for S5

Let's put one more restriction on the accessibility relation. This time, let's insist that it must also be *symmetric*:

▷   $\forall w_1 \forall w_2 (Rw_1w_2 \rightarrow Rw_2w_1)$

In English: if $w_1$ accesses $w_2$, then $w_2$ accesses $w_1$. Or in terms of relative possibility: if $w_2$ is possible relative to $w_1$, then $w_1$ is possible relative to $w_2$. Logicians call a relation that is reflexive, symmetric, and transitive an *equivalence* relation. We can now define a new consequence relation, $\vDash_{S5}$, as follows:

$\mathcal{A}_1, \mathcal{A}_2, \ldots \mathcal{A}_n \vDash_{S5} \mathcal{C}$ iff there is no world in any interpretation *whose accessibility relation is an equivalence relation*, at which $\mathcal{A}_1, \mathcal{A}_2, \ldots \mathcal{A}_n$ are all true and $\mathcal{C}$ is false

We have attached the **S5** subscript to $\vDash$ because it turns out that system **S5** is sound and complete relative to this new definition of validity:

 ▷ If $\mathcal{A}_1, \mathcal{A}_2, \ldots \mathcal{A}_n \vdash_{S5} \mathcal{C}$, then $\mathcal{A}_1, \mathcal{A}_2, \ldots \mathcal{A}_n \vDash_{S5} \mathcal{C}$

 ▷ If $\mathcal{A}_1, \mathcal{A}_2, \ldots \mathcal{A}_n \vDash_{S5} \mathcal{C}$, then $\mathcal{A}_1, \mathcal{A}_2, \ldots \mathcal{A}_n \vdash_{S5} \mathcal{C}$

As before, we will not try to prove these soundness and completeness results here. However, it is relatively easy to see how insisting that the accessibility relation must be an equivalence relation will vindicate the R5 rule:

$$
\begin{array}{l|l}
m & \neg\Box\mathcal{A} \\
& \quad\begin{array}{|l} \Box \\ \hline \neg\Box\mathcal{A} \quad\quad \text{R5 } m \end{array}
\end{array}
$$

The rule says that if $\mathcal{A}$ is not necessary, i.e., false in some accessible world, it is also not necessary in any accessible possible world, i.e., we have $\neg\Box\mathcal{A} \vdash_{S5} \Box\neg\Box\mathcal{A}$.

To see this, just imagine trying to cook up a counter-interpretation to this claim:

$$\neg\Box\mathcal{A} \vDash_{S5} \Box\neg\Box\mathcal{A}$$

We would need to construct a world, $w_1$, at which $\neg\Box\mathcal{A}$ was true, but $\Box\neg\Box\mathcal{A}$ was false. Now, if $\neg\Box\mathcal{A}$ is true at $w_1$, then $w_1$ must access some world, $w_2$, at which $\mathcal{A}$ is false. Equally, if $\Box\neg\Box\mathcal{A}$ is false at $w_1$, then $w_1$ must access some world, $w_3$, at which $\neg\Box\mathcal{A}$ is false. Since we are now insisting that the accessibility relation is an equivalence relation, and hence symmetric, we can infer that $w_3$ accesses $w_1$. Thus, $w_3$ accesses $w_1$, and $w_1$ accesses $w_2$. Again, since we are now insisting that the accessibility relation is an equivalence relation, and hence transitive, we can infer that $w_3$ accesses $w_2$. But earlier we said that $\neg\Box\mathcal{A}$ is false at $w_3$, which implies that $\mathcal{A}$ is true at every world which $w_3$ accesses. So $\mathcal{A}$ is true *and* false at $w_2$. Contradiction!

In the definition of $\vDash_{S5}$, we stipulated that the accessibility relation must be an equivalence relation. But it turns out that there is another way of getting a notion of validity fit for **S5**. Rather than stipulating that the accessibility relation be an equivalence relation, we can instead stipulate that it be a *universal* relation:

   ▷  $\forall w_1 \forall w_2 R w_1 w_2$

In English: every world accesses every world. Or in terms of relative possibility: every world is possible relative to every world. Using this restriction on the accessibility relation, we could have defined $\vDash_{S5}$ like this:

> $\mathcal{A}_1, \mathcal{A}_2, \ldots \mathcal{A}_n \vDash_{S5} \mathcal{C}$ iff there is no world in any interpretation *which has a universal accessibility relation*, at which $\mathcal{A}_1, \mathcal{A}_2, \ldots \mathcal{A}_n$ are all true and $\mathcal{C}$ is false.

If we defined $\vDash_{S5}$ like this, we would still get the same soundness and completeness results for **S5**. What does this tell us? Well, it means that if we are dealing with a notion of necessity according to which *every* world is possible relative to *every* world, then we should use **S5**. What is more, most philosophers assume that the notions of necessity that they are most concerned with, like *logical necessity* and *metaphysical necessity*, are of exactly this kind. So **S5** is the modal system that most philosophers use most of the time.

## Practice exercises

**A**. Present counter-interpretations to the following false claims:

1. $\neg P \vDash_\mathbf{K} \neg \Diamond P$
2. $\Box(P \lor Q) \vDash_\mathbf{K} \Box P \lor \Box Q$
3. $\vDash_\mathbf{K} \neg\Box(A \land \neg A)$
4. $\Box A \vDash_\mathbf{K} A$

**B**. Present counter-interpretations to the following false claims:

1. $\Diamond A \vDash_\mathbf{S4} \Box \Diamond A$
2. $\Diamond A, \Box(\Diamond A \to B) \vDash_\mathbf{S4} \Box B$

**C**. Present counter-interpretations to the following false claims:

1. $\Box(M \to O), \Diamond M \vDash_\mathbf{T} O$
2. $\Box A \vDash_\mathbf{T} \Box\Box A$

## Further reading

Modal logic is a large subfield of logic. We have only scratched the surface. If you want to learn more about modal logic, here are some textbooks you might consult.

▷ Hughes, G. E., & Cresswell, M. J. (1996). *A New Introduction to Modal Logic*, Oxford: Routledge.

▷ Priest, G. (2008). *An Introduction to Non-Classical Logic*, 2nd ed., Cambridge: Cambridge University Press.

▷ Garson, J. W. (2013). *Modal Logic for Philosophers*, 2nd ed., Cambridge: Cambridge University Press.

None of these authors formulate their modal proof systems in quite the way we did, but the closest formulation is given by Garson.

# PART IX

# *Metatheory*

# CHAPTER 43

# *Normal forms*

## 43.1 Disjunctive normal form

Sometimes it is useful to consider sentences of a particularly simple form. For instance, we might consider sentences in which ¬ only attaches to atomic sentences, or those which are combinations of atomic sentences and negated atomic sentences using only ∧. A relatively general but still simple form is that where a sentence is a disjunction of conjunctions of atomic or negated atomic sentences. When such a sentence is constructed, we start with atomic sentences, then (perhaps) attach negations, then (perhaps) combine using ∧, and finally (perhaps) combine using ∨.

Let's say that a sentence is in DISJUNCTIVE NORMAL FORM *iff* it meets all of the following conditions:

(DNF1)  No connectives occur in the sentence other than negations, conjunctions and disjunctions;

(DNF2)  Every occurrence of negation has minimal scope (i.e. any '¬' is immediately followed by an atomic sentence);

(DNF3)  No disjunction occurs within the scope of any conjunction.

360

So, here are are some sentences in disjunctive normal form:

$$A$$
$$(A \land \neg B \land C)$$
$$(A \land B) \lor (A \land \neg B)$$
$$(A \land B) \lor (A \land B \land C \land \neg D \land \neg E)$$
$$A \lor (C \land \neg P_{234} \land P_{233} \land Q) \lor \neg B$$

Note that we have here broken one of the maxims of this book and *temporarily* allowed ourselves to employ the relaxed bracketing-conventions that allow conjunctions and disjunctions to be of arbitrary length. These conventions make it easier to see when a sentence is in disjunctive normal form. We will continue to help ourselves to these relaxed conventions, without further comment.

To further illustrate the idea of disjunctive normal form, we will introduce some more notation. We write '$\pm\mathcal{A}$' to indicate that $\mathcal{A}$ is an atomic sentence which may or may not be prefaced with an occurrence of negation. Then a sentence in disjunctive normal form has the following shape:

$$(\pm\mathcal{A}_1 \land \ldots \land \pm\mathcal{A}_i) \lor (\pm\mathcal{A}_{i+1} \land \ldots \land \pm\mathcal{A}_j) \lor \ldots \lor (\pm\mathcal{A}_{m+1} \land \ldots \land \pm\mathcal{A}_n)$$

We now know what it is for a sentence to be in disjunctive normal form. The result that we are aiming at is:

> **Disjunctive Normal Form Theorem.** For any sentence, there is an equivalent sentence in disjunctive normal form.

Henceforth, we will abbreviate 'Disjunctive Normal Form' by 'DNF'.

## 43.2 Proof of DNF theorem via truth tables

Our first proof of the DNF Theorem employs truth tables. We will first illustrate the technique for finding an equivalent sentence in DNF, and then turn this illustration into a rigorous proof.

Let's suppose we have some sentence, $\mathcal{S}$, which contains three atomic sentences, '$A$', '$B$' and '$C$'. The very first thing to do is fill out a complete truth table for $\mathcal{S}$. Maybe we end up with this:

| $A$ | $B$ | $C$ | $\mathcal{S}$ |
|---|---|---|---|
| T | T | T | T |
| T | T | F | F |
| T | F | T | T |
| T | F | F | F |
| F | T | T | F |
| F | T | F | F |
| F | F | T | T |
| F | F | F | T |

As it happens, $\mathcal{S}$ is true on four lines of its truth table, namely lines 1, 3, 7 and 8. Corresponding to each of those lines, we will write down four sentences, whose only connectives are negations and conjunctions, where every negation has minimal scope:

1. '$A \wedge B \wedge C$'          which is true on line 1 (and only then)
2. '$A \wedge \neg B \wedge C$'          which is true on line 3 (and only then)
3. '$\neg A \wedge \neg B \wedge C$'          which is true on line 7 (and only then)
4. '$\neg A \wedge \neg B \wedge \neg C$'          which is true on line 8 (and only then)

We now combine all of these conjunctions using $\vee$, like so:

$$(A \wedge B \wedge C) \vee (A \wedge \neg B \wedge C) \vee (\neg A \wedge \neg B \wedge C) \vee (\neg A \wedge \neg B \wedge \neg C)$$

This gives us a sentence in DNF which is true on exactly those lines where one of the disjuncts is true, i.e. it is true on (and only on) lines 1, 3, 7, and 8. So this sentence has exactly the same truth table as $\mathcal{S}$. So we have a sentence in DNF that is logically equivalent to $\mathcal{S}$, which is exactly what we wanted!

Now, the strategy that we just adopted did not depend on the specifics of $\mathcal{S}$; it is perfectly general. Consequently, we can use it to obtain a simple proof of the DNF Theorem.

Pick any arbitrary sentence, $\mathcal{S}$, and let $\mathcal{A}_1, \ldots, \mathcal{A}_n$ be the atomic sentences that occur in $\mathcal{S}$. To obtain a sentence in DNF that is logically equivalent $S$, we consider $S$'s truth table. There are two cases to consider:

1. *$S$ is false on every line of its truth table.* Then, $S$ is a contradiction. In that case, the contradiction $(\mathscr{A}_1 \wedge \neg\mathscr{A}_1)$ is in DNF and logically equivalent to $S$.

2. *$S$ is true on at least one line of its truth table.* For each line $i$ of the truth table, let $\mathscr{B}_i$ be a conjunction of the form

$$(\pm\mathscr{A}_1 \wedge \ldots \wedge \pm\mathscr{A}_n)$$

where the following rules determine whether or not to include a negation in front of each atomic sentence:

$\mathscr{A}_m$ is a conjunct of $\mathscr{B}_i$ *iff* $\mathscr{A}_m$ is true on line $i$

$\neg\mathscr{A}_m$ is a conjunct of $\mathscr{B}_i$ *iff* $\mathscr{A}_m$ is false on line $i$

Given these rules, $\mathscr{B}_i$ is true on (and only on) line $i$ of the truth table which considers all possible valuations of $\mathscr{A}_1, \ldots, \mathscr{A}_n$ (i.e. $S$'s truth table).

Next, let $i_1$, $i_2$, ..., $i_m$ be the numbers of the lines of the truth table where $S$ is *true*. Now let $\mathscr{D}$ be the sentence:

$$\mathscr{B}_{i_1} \vee \mathscr{B}_{i_2} \vee \ldots \vee \mathscr{B}_{i_m}$$

Since $S$ is true on at least one line of its truth table, $\mathscr{D}$ is indeed well-defined; and in the limiting case where $S$ is true on exactly one line of its truth table, $\mathscr{D}$ is just $\mathscr{B}_{i_1}$, for some $i_1$.

By construction, $\mathscr{D}$ is in DNF. Moreover, by construction, for each line $i$ of the truth table: $S$ is true on line $i$ of the truth table *iff* one of $\mathscr{D}$'s disjuncts (namely, $\mathscr{B}_i$) is true on, and only on, line $i$. Hence $S$ and $\mathscr{D}$ have the same truth table, and so are logically equivalent.

These two cases are exhaustive and, either way, we have a sentence in DNF that is logically equivalent to $\mathcal{S}$.

So we have proved the DNF Theorem. Before we say any more, though, we should immediately flag that we are hereby returning to the austere definition of a (TFL) sentence, according to which we can assume that any conjunction has exactly two conjuncts, and any disjunction has exactly two disjuncts.

## 43.3  Conjunctive normal form

So far in this chapter, we have discussed *disjunctive* normal form. It may not come as a surprise to hear that there is also such a thing as *conjunctive normal form* (CNF).

The definition of CNF is exactly analogous to the definition of DNF. So, a sentence is in CNF *iff* it meets all of the following conditions:

(CNF1)  No connectives occur in the sentence other than negations, conjunctions and disjunctions;

(CNF2)  Every occurrence of negation has minimal scope;

(CNF3)  No conjunction occurs within the scope of any disjunction.

Generally, then, a sentence in CNF looks like this

$$(\pm\mathcal{A}_1 \vee \ldots \vee \pm\mathcal{A}_i) \wedge (\pm\mathcal{A}_{i+1} \vee \ldots \vee \pm\mathcal{A}_j) \wedge \ldots \wedge (\pm\mathcal{A}_{m+1} \vee \ldots \vee \pm\mathcal{A}_n)$$

where each $\mathcal{A}_k$ is an atomic sentence.

We can now prove another normal form theorem:

> **Conjunctive Normal Form Theorem.** For any sentence, there is an equivalent sentence in conjunctive normal form.

Given a TFL sentence, $\mathcal{S}$, we begin by writing down the complete truth table for $\mathcal{S}$.

If $\mathcal{S}$ is *true* on every line of the truth table, then $\mathcal{S}$ and $(\mathcal{A}_1 \vee \neg\mathcal{A}_1)$ are logically equivalent.

If $\mathcal{S}$ is *false* on at least one line of the truth table then, for every line on the truth table where $\mathcal{S}$ is false, write down a disjunction $(\pm\mathcal{A}_1 \vee \ldots \vee \pm\mathcal{A}_n)$ which is *false* on (and only on) that line. Let $\mathcal{C}$ be the conjunction of all of these disjuncts; by construction, $\mathcal{C}$ is in CNF and $\mathcal{S}$ and $\mathcal{C}$ are logically equivalent.

## Practice exercises

**A.** Consider the following sentences:

1. $(A \rightarrow \neg B)$
2. $\neg(A \leftrightarrow B)$
3. $(\neg A \vee \neg(A \wedge B))$
4. $(\neg(A \rightarrow B) \wedge (A \rightarrow C))$
5. $(\neg(A \vee B) \leftrightarrow ((\neg C \wedge \neg A) \rightarrow \neg B))$
6. $((\neg(A \wedge \neg B) \rightarrow C) \wedge \neg(A \wedge D))$

For each sentence, find an equivalent sentence in DNF and one in CNF.

# CHAPTER 44

# *Functional completeness*

Of our connectives, ¬ attaches to a single sentence, and the others all combine exactly two sentences. We may also introduce the idea of an *n*-place connective. For example, we could consider a three-place connective, '♡', and stipulate that it is to have the following characteristic truth table:

| $A$ | $B$ | $C$ | $♡(A, B, C)$ |
|-----|-----|-----|-----|
| T | T | T | F |
| T | T | F | T |
| T | F | T | T |
| T | F | F | F |
| F | T | T | F |
| F | T | F | T |
| F | F | T | F |
| F | F | F | F |

Probably this new connective would not correspond with any natural English expression (at least not in the way that '∧' corresponds with 'and'). But a question arises: if we wanted to employ a connective with this characteristic truth table, must we add a *new* connective to TFL? Or can we get by with the connectives

366

we *already have* (as we can for the connective 'neither…nor' for instance)?

Let us make this question more precise. Say that some connectives are JOINTLY FUNCTIONALLY COMPLETE *iff*, for any possible truth table, there is a sentence containing only those connectives with that truth table.

The general point is, when we are armed with some jointly functionally complete connectives, no characteristic truth table lies beyond our grasp. And in fact, we are in luck.

---

**Functional Completeness Theorem.** The connectives of TFL are jointly functionally complete. Indeed, the following pairs of connectives are jointly functionally complete:

    1. '¬' and '∨'
    2. '¬' and '∧'
    3. '¬' and '→'

---

Given any truth table, we can use the method of proving the DNF Theorem (or the CNF Theorem) via truth tables from chapter 43, to write down a scheme which has the same truth table. For example, employing the truth table method for proving the DNF Theorem, we find that the following scheme has the same characteristic truth table as $\heartsuit(A, B, C)$, above:

$$(A \wedge B \wedge \neg C) \vee (A \wedge \neg B \wedge C) \vee (\neg A \wedge B \wedge \neg C)$$

It follows that the connectives of TFL are jointly functionally complete. We now prove each of the subsidiary results.

*Subsidiary Result 1: functional completeness of '¬' and '∨'.* Observe that the scheme that we generate, using the truth table method of proving the DNF Theorem, will only contain the connectives '¬', '∧' and '∨'. So it suffices to show that there is an equivalent scheme which contains only '¬' and '∨'. To demonstrate this, we simply consider that

$$(\mathscr{A} \wedge \mathscr{B}) \quad \text{and} \quad \neg(\neg\mathscr{A} \vee \neg\mathscr{B})$$

are logically equivalent.

*Subsidiary Result 2: functional completeness of '¬' and '∧'.* Exactly as in Subsidiary Result 1, making use of the fact that

$$(\mathscr{A} \vee \mathscr{B}) \quad \text{and} \quad \neg(\neg\mathscr{A} \wedge \neg\mathscr{B})$$

are logically equivalent.

*Subsidiary Result 3: functional completeness of '¬' and '→'.* Exactly as in Subsidiary Result 1, making use of these equivalences instead:

$$(\mathscr{A} \vee \mathscr{B}) \quad \text{and} \quad (\neg\mathscr{A} \rightarrow \mathscr{B})$$
$$(\mathscr{A} \wedge \mathscr{B}) \quad \text{and} \quad \neg(\mathscr{A} \rightarrow \neg\mathscr{B})$$

Alternatively, we could simply rely upon one of the other two subsidiary results, and (repeatedly) invoke only one of these two equivalences.

In short, there is never any *need* to add new connectives to TFL. Indeed, there is already some redundancy among the connectives we have: we could have made do with just two connectives, if we had been feeling really austere.

## 44.1   Individually functionally complete connectives

In fact, some two-place connectives are *individually* functionally complete. These connectives are not standardly included in TFL, since they are rather cumbersome to use. But their existence shows that, if we had wanted to, we could have defined a truth-functional language that was functionally complete, which contained only a single primitive connective.

The first such connective we will consider is '↑', which has the following characteristic truth table.

| $\mathcal{A}$ | $\mathcal{B}$ | $\mathcal{A} \uparrow \mathcal{B}$ |
|:---:|:---:|:---:|
| T | T | F |
| T | F | T |
| F | T | T |
| F | F | T |

This is often called 'the Sheffer stroke', after Henry Sheffer, who used it to show how to reduce the number of logical connectives in Russell and Whitehead's *Principia Mathematica*.[1] (In fact, Charles Sanders Peirce had anticipated Sheffer by about 30 years, but never published his results, and the Polish philosopher Erward Stamm published the same result two years before Sheffer.)[2] It is quite common, as well, to call it 'nand', since its characteristic truth table is the negation of the truth table for '∧'.

> '↑' is functionally complete all by itself.

The functional completeness Theorem tells us that '¬' and '∨' are jointly functionally complete. So it suffices to show that, given any scheme which contains only those two connectives, we can rewrite it as an equivalent scheme which contains only '↑'. As in the proof of the subsidiary cases of the functional completeness Theorem, then, we simply apply the following equivalences:

$$\neg \mathcal{A} \quad \text{and} \quad (\mathcal{A} \uparrow \mathcal{A})$$
$$(\mathcal{A} \vee \mathcal{B}) \quad \text{and} \quad ((\mathcal{A} \uparrow \mathcal{A}) \uparrow (\mathcal{B} \uparrow \mathcal{B}))$$

to the Subsidiary Result 1.

Similarly, we can consider the connective '↓':

---

[1] Sheffer, 'A Set of Five Independent Postulates for Boolean Algebras, with application to logical constants,' (1913, *Transactions of the American Mathematical Society* 14.4)

[2] See Peirce, 'A Boolian Algebra with One Constant', which dates to c. 1880, Peirce's *Collected Papers*, 4.264–5, and Stamm, "Beitrag zur Algebra der Logik," *Monatshefte für Mathematik und Physik* 22 (1911): 137–49.

| $\mathcal{A}$ | $\mathcal{B}$ | $\mathcal{A} \downarrow \mathcal{B}$ |
|:---:|:---:|:---:|
| T | T | F |
| T | F | F |
| F | T | F |
| F | F | T |

This is sometimes called the 'Peirce arrow' (Peirce himself called it 'ampheck'). More often, though, it is called 'nor', since its characteristic truth table is the negation of '∨', that is, of 'neither ... nor ...'.

> '↓' is functionally complete all by itself.

As in the previous result for ↑, although invoking the equivalences:

$$\neg\mathcal{A} \quad \text{and} \quad (\mathcal{A} \downarrow \mathcal{A})$$
$$(\mathcal{A} \wedge \mathcal{B}) \quad \text{and} \quad ((\mathcal{A} \downarrow \mathcal{A}) \downarrow (\mathcal{B} \downarrow \mathcal{B}))$$

and Subsidiary Result 2.

## 44.2 Failures of functional completeness

In fact, the *only* two-place connectives which are individually functionally complete are '↑' and '↓'. But how would we show this? More generally, how can we show that some connectives are *not* jointly functionally complete?

The obvious thing to do is to try to find some truth table which we *cannot* express, using just the given connectives. But there is a bit of an art to this.

To make this concrete, let's consider the question of whether '∨' is functionally complete all by itself. After a little reflection, it should be clear that it is not. In particular, it should be clear that any scheme which only contains disjunctions cannot have the same truth table as negation, i.e.:

| $\mathcal{A}$ | $\neg\mathcal{A}$ |
|:---:|:---:|
| T | F |
| F | T |

The intuitive reason, why this should be so, is simple: the top line of the desired truth table needs to have the value False; but the top line of any truth table for a scheme which *only* contains $\vee$ will always be True. The same is true for $\wedge$, $\rightarrow$, and $\leftrightarrow$.

> '$\vee$', '$\wedge$', '$\rightarrow$', and '$\leftrightarrow$' are not functionally complete by themselves.

In fact, the following is true:

> The *only* two-place connectives that are functionally complete by themselves are '$\uparrow$' and '$\downarrow$'.

This is of course harder to prove than for the primitive connectives. For instance, the "exclusive or" connective does not have a T in the first line of its characteristic truth table, and so the method used above no longer suffices to show that it cannot express all truth tables. It is also harder to show that, e.g., '$\leftrightarrow$' and '$\neg$' *together* are not functionally complete.

# CHAPTER 45

# *Proving equivalences*

## 45.1   Substitutability of equivalents

Recall from §12.2 that $\mathcal{P}$ and $\mathcal{Q}$ are equivalent (in TFL) iff, for every valuation, their truth values agree. We have seen many examples of this and used both truth tables and natural dedcution proofs to establish such equivalences. In chapter 43 we've even proved that ever sentence of TFL is equivalent to one in conjunctive and one in disjunctive normal form. If $\mathcal{P}$ and $\mathcal{Q}$ are equivalent, they always have the same truth value, either one entails the other, and from either one you can prove the other.

Equivalent sentences are not the same, of course: the sentences $\neg\neg A$ and $A$ may always have the same truth value, but the first starts with the '$\neg$' symbol while the second doesn't. But you may wonder if it's always true that we can replace one of a pair of equivalent sentences by the other, and the results will be equivalent, too. For instance, consider $\neg\neg A \to B$ and $A \to B$. The second results from the first by replacing '$\neg\neg A$' by '$A$'. And these two sentences are also equivalent.

This is a general fact, and it is not hard to see why it is true. In any valuation, we compute the truth value of a sentence "from

372

the inside out." So when it comes to determining the truth value of '$\neg\neg A \to B$', we first compute the truth value of '$\neg\neg A$', and the truth value of the overall sentence then just depends on that truth value (true or false, as the case may be) and the rest of the sentence (the truth value of '$B$' and the truth table for '$\to$'). But since '$\neg\neg A$' are equivalent, they always have the same truth value in a given valuation—hence, replacing '$\neg\neg A$' by '$A$' cannot change the truth value of the overall sentence. The same of course is true for any other sentence equivalent to '$\neg\neg A$', say, '$A \land (A \lor A)$'.

To state the result in general, let's use the notation $\mathcal{R}(\mathcal{P})$ to mean a sentence which contains the sentence $\mathcal{P}$ as a part. Then by $\mathcal{R}(\mathcal{Q})$ we mean the result of replacing the occurrence of $\mathcal{P}$ by the sentence $\mathcal{Q}$. For instance, if $\mathcal{P}$ is the sentence letter '$A$', $\mathcal{Q}$ is the sentence '$\neg\neg A$', and $\mathcal{R}(\mathcal{P})$ is '$A \to B$', then $\mathcal{R}(\mathcal{Q})$ is '$\neg\neg A \to B$'.

> If $\mathcal{P}$ and $\mathcal{Q}$ are equivalent, then so are $\mathcal{R}(\mathcal{P})$ and $\mathcal{R}(\mathcal{Q})$.

It follows from this fact that any sentence of the form $\mathcal{R}(\mathcal{P}) \leftrightarrow \mathcal{R}(\mathcal{Q})$, where $\mathcal{P}$ and $\mathcal{Q}$ are equivalent, is a tautology. However, the proofs in natural deduction will be wildly different for different $\mathcal{R}$. (As an exercise, give proofs that show that

$$\vdash (\neg\neg P \to Q) \leftrightarrow (P \to Q) \text{ and}$$
$$\vdash (\neg\neg P \land Q) \leftrightarrow (P \land Q)$$

and compare the two.)

Here is another fact: if two sentences $\mathcal{P}$ and $\mathcal{Q}$ are equivalent, and you replace some sentence letter in both $\mathcal{P}$ and $\mathcal{Q}$ by the same sentence $\mathcal{R}$, the results are also equivalent. For instance, if you replace '$A$' in both '$A \land B$' and '$B \land A$' by, say, '$\neg C$', you get '$\neg C \land B$' and '$B \land \neg C$', and those are equivalent. We can record this, too:

> Equivalence is preserved under replacement of sentence
> letters, i.e., if $\mathscr{P}(A)$ and $\mathbb{Q}(A)$ both contain the sentence
> letter '$A$' and are equivalent, then the sentences $\mathscr{P}(\mathscr{R})$ and
> $\mathbb{Q}(\mathscr{R})$ (resulting by replacing '$A$' by $\mathscr{R}$ in both) are also
> equivalent.

This means that once we have shown that two sentence are
equivalent (e.g., '$\neg\neg A$' and '$A$', or '$A \wedge B$' and '$B \wedge A$') we know
that all their common "instances" are also equivalent. Note that
we do not immediately get this from a truth table or a natural
deduction proof. E.g., a truth table that shows that '$\neg\neg A$' and '$A$'
are equivalent does *not* also show that '$\neg\neg(B \rightarrow C)$' and '$B \rightarrow C$'
are equivalent: the former needs just 2 lines, the latter 4.

## 45.2   Chains of equivalences

When you want to verify that two sentences are equivalent, you
can of course do a truth table, or look for a formal proof. But
there is a simpler method, based on the principle of substitutabil-
ity of equivalents we just discussed: Armed with a small catalog of
simple equivalences, replace parts of your first sentence by equivalent parts, and repeat until you reach your second sentence.

This method of showing sentences equivalent is underwritten
by the two facts from the previous section. The first fact tells us
that *if*, say, $\neg\neg\mathscr{P}$ and $\mathscr{P}$ are equivalent (for any sentence $\mathscr{P}$), then
replacing $\neg\neg\mathscr{P}$ in a sentence by $\mathscr{P}$ results in an equivalent sentence. The second fact tells us *that* $\neg\neg\mathscr{P}$ and $\mathscr{P}$ are always equivalent, for any sentence $\mathscr{P}$. (A simple truth table shows that '$\neg\neg A$'
and '$A$' are equivalent.) By the second fact we know that when-
ever we replace '$A$' in both '$\neg\neg A$' and '$A$' by some sentence $\mathscr{P}$, we
get equivalent results. In other words, from the fact that '$\neg\neg A$'
and '$A$' are equivalent and the second fact, we can conclude that,
for any sentence $\mathscr{P}$, $\neg\neg\mathscr{P}$ and $\mathscr{P}$ are equivalent.

Let's give an example. By De Morgan's Laws, the following

pairs of sentences are equivalent:

$$\neg(A \wedge B) \text{ and } (\neg A \vee \neg B)$$
$$\neg(A \vee B) \text{ and } (\neg A \wedge \neg B)$$

This can be verified by constructing two truth tables, or four natural deduction proofs that show:

$$\neg(A \wedge B) \vdash (\neg A \vee \neg B)$$
$$(\neg A \vee \neg B) \vdash \neg(A \wedge B)$$
$$\neg(A \vee B) \vdash (\neg A \wedge \neg B)$$
$$(\neg A \wedge \neg B) \vdash \neg(A \vee B)$$

By the second fact, *any* pairs of sentences of the following forms are equivalent:

$$\neg(\mathcal{P} \wedge \mathcal{Q}) \text{ and } (\neg\mathcal{P} \vee \neg\mathcal{Q})$$
$$\neg(\mathcal{P} \vee \mathcal{Q}) \text{ and } (\neg\mathcal{P} \wedge \neg\mathcal{Q})$$

Now consider the sentence '$\neg(R \vee (S \wedge T))$'. We will find an equivalent sentence in which all '$\neg$' signs attach directly to sentence letters. In the first step, we consider this as a sentence of the form $\neg(\mathcal{P} \vee \mathcal{Q})$—then $\mathcal{P}$ is the sentence '$R$' and $\mathcal{Q}$ is '$(S \wedge T)$'. Since $\neg(\mathcal{P} \vee \mathcal{Q})$ is equivalent to $(\neg\mathcal{P} \wedge \neg\mathcal{Q})$ (by the second of De Morgan's Laws) we can replace the entire sentence by $(\neg\mathcal{P} \wedge \neg\mathcal{Q})$. In this case (where $\mathcal{P}$ is '$R$' and $\mathcal{Q}$ is '$(S \wedge T)$') we obtain '$(\neg R \wedge \neg(S \wedge T))$'. This new sentence contains as a part the sentence '$\neg(S \wedge T)$'. It is of the form $\neg(\mathcal{P} \wedge \mathcal{Q})$, except now $\mathcal{P}$ is the sentence letter '$S$' and $\mathcal{Q}$ is '$T$'. By De Morgan's Law (the first one this time), this is equivalent to $(\neg\mathcal{P} \vee \neg\mathcal{Q})$, or in this specific case, to '$(\neg S \vee \neg T)$'. So we can replace the part '$\neg(S \wedge T)$' by '$(\neg S \vee \neg T)$'. This now results in the sentence '$(\neg R \wedge (\neg S \vee \neg T))$', in which the '$\neg$' symbols all attach directly to sentence letters. We've "pushed" the negations inwards as far as possible. We can record such a chain of equivalences by listing the individual steps, and recording, just as we do in natural deduction, which basic equivalence we use in each case:

$$\neg(\boxed{R} \lor \boxed{(S \land T)})$$

$$(\neg\boxed{R} \land \neg\boxed{(S \land T)}) \qquad\qquad \text{DeM}$$

$$(\neg(R \land \boxed{\neg(\boxed{S} \land \boxed{T})}))$$

$$(\neg(R \land \boxed{(\neg\boxed{S} \lor \neg\boxed{T})})) \qquad\qquad \text{DeM}$$

We've highlighted the sentence replaced, and those matching the $\mathcal{P}$ and $\mathcal{Q}$ in De Morgan's Laws for clarity, but this is not necessary, and we won't keep doing it.

In table 45.1 we've given a list of basic equivalences you can use for such chains of equivalences. The labels abbreviate the customary name for the respective logical laws: double negation (DN), De Morgan (DeM), commutativity (Comm), distributivity (Dist), associativity (Assoc), idempotence (Id), and absorption (Abs).

## 45.3   Finding equivalent normal forms

In chapter 43 we showed that every sentence of TFL is equivalent to one in disjunctive normal form (DNF) and to one in conjunctive normal form (CNF). We did this by giving a method to construct a sentences in DNF or CNF equivalent to the original sentence by first constructing a truth table, and then "reading off" a sentence in DNF or CNF from the truth table. This method has two drawbacks. The first one is that the resulting sentences in DNF or CNF are not always the shortest ones. The second one is that the method itself becomes hard to apply when the sentence you start with contains more than a handful of sentence letters (since the truth table for a sentence with $n$ sentence letters has $2^n$ lines).

We can use chains of equivalences as an alternative method: To find a sentence in DNF, we can successively apply basic equiv-

$$\neg\neg\mathcal{P} \Leftrightarrow \mathcal{P} \qquad \text{(DN)}$$

$$(\mathcal{P} \to \mathcal{Q}) \Leftrightarrow (\neg\mathcal{P} \vee \mathcal{Q}) \qquad \text{(Cond)}$$
$$\neg(\mathcal{P} \to \mathcal{Q}) \Leftrightarrow (\mathcal{P} \wedge \neg\mathcal{Q})$$

$$(\mathcal{P} \leftrightarrow \mathcal{Q}) \Leftrightarrow ((\mathcal{P} \to \mathcal{Q}) \wedge (\mathcal{Q} \to \mathcal{P})) \qquad \text{(Bicond)}$$

$$\neg(\mathcal{P} \wedge \mathcal{Q}) \Leftrightarrow (\neg\mathcal{P} \vee \neg\mathcal{Q}) \qquad \text{(DeM)}$$
$$\neg(\mathcal{P} \vee \mathcal{Q}) \Leftrightarrow (\neg\mathcal{P} \wedge \neg\mathcal{Q})$$

$$(\mathcal{P} \vee \mathcal{Q}) \Leftrightarrow (\mathcal{Q} \vee \mathcal{P}) \qquad \text{(Comm)}$$
$$(\mathcal{P} \wedge \mathcal{Q}) \Leftrightarrow (\mathcal{Q} \wedge \mathcal{P})$$

$$(\mathcal{P} \wedge (\mathcal{Q} \vee \mathcal{R})) \Leftrightarrow ((\mathcal{P} \wedge \mathcal{Q}) \vee (\mathcal{P} \wedge \mathcal{R})) \qquad \text{(Dist)}$$
$$(\mathcal{P} \vee (\mathcal{Q} \wedge \mathcal{R})) \Leftrightarrow ((\mathcal{P} \vee \mathcal{Q}) \wedge (\mathcal{P} \vee \mathcal{R}))$$
$$(\mathcal{P} \vee (\mathcal{Q} \vee \mathcal{R})) \Leftrightarrow ((\mathcal{P} \vee \mathcal{Q}) \vee \mathcal{R}) \qquad \text{(Assoc)}$$
$$(\mathcal{P} \wedge (\mathcal{Q} \wedge \mathcal{R})) \Leftrightarrow ((\mathcal{P} \wedge \mathcal{Q}) \wedge \mathcal{R})$$

$$(\mathcal{P} \vee \mathcal{P}) \Leftrightarrow \mathcal{P} \qquad \text{(Id)}$$
$$(\mathcal{P} \wedge \mathcal{P}) \Leftrightarrow \mathcal{P}$$

$$(\mathcal{P} \wedge (\mathcal{P} \vee \mathcal{Q})) \Leftrightarrow \mathcal{P} \qquad \text{(Abs)}$$
$$(\mathcal{P} \vee (\mathcal{P} \wedge \mathcal{Q})) \Leftrightarrow \mathcal{P}$$

$$(\mathcal{P} \wedge (\mathcal{Q} \vee \neg\mathcal{Q})) \Leftrightarrow \mathcal{P} \qquad \text{(Simp)}$$
$$(\mathcal{P} \vee (\mathcal{Q} \wedge \neg\mathcal{Q})) \Leftrightarrow \mathcal{P}$$

$$(\mathcal{P} \vee (\mathcal{Q} \vee \neg\mathcal{Q})) \Leftrightarrow (\mathcal{Q} \vee \neg\mathcal{Q})$$
$$(\mathcal{P} \wedge (\mathcal{Q} \wedge \neg\mathcal{Q})) \Leftrightarrow (\mathcal{Q} \wedge \neg\mathcal{Q})$$

*Table 45.1: Basic equivalences*

alences until we have found an equivalent sentence that is in DNF. Recall the conditions a sentence in DNF must satisfy:

(DNF1)  No connectives occur in the sentence other than negations, conjunctions and disjunctions;

(DNF2)  Every occurrence of negation has minimal scope (i.e., any '¬' is immediately followed by an atomic sentence);

(DNF3)  No disjunction occurs within the scope of any conjunction.

Condition (DNF1) says that we must remove all '→' and '↔' symbols from a sentence. This is what the basic equivalences (Cond) and (Bicond) are good for. For instance, suppose we start with the sentence

$$\neg(A \land \neg C) \land (\neg A \to \neg B).$$

We can get rid of the '→' by using (Cond). In this case $\mathcal{P}$ is '¬$A$' and $\mathbb{Q}$ is '¬$B$'. We get:

$$\neg(A \land \neg C) \land (\neg\neg A \lor \neg B) \qquad\qquad \text{Cond}$$

The double negation can be removed, since '¬¬$A$' is equivalent to '$A$':

$$\neg(A \land \neg C) \land (A \lor \neg B) \qquad\qquad \text{DN}$$

Now condition (DNF1) is satisfied: our sentence contains only '¬', '∧', and '∨'. Condition (DNF2) says that we must find a way to have all '¬'s apply immediately to sentence letters. But in the first conjunct it doesn't. To ensure (DNF2) is satisfied, we use De Morgan's Laws and the double negation (DN) law as many times as needed.

$$(\neg A \lor \neg\neg C) \land (A \lor \neg B) \qquad\qquad \text{DeM}$$
$$(\neg A \lor C) \land (A \lor \neg B) \qquad\qquad \text{DN}$$

The resulting sentence is now in CNF—it is a conjunction of disjunctions of sentence letters and negated sentence letters. But we want a sentence in DNF, i.e., a sentence in which (DNF3) is satisfied: no '$\lor$' occurs in the scope of an '$\land$'. We use the distributive laws (Dist) to ensure this. The last sentence is of the form $\mathscr{P} \land (\mathscr{Q} \lor \mathscr{R})$, where $\mathscr{P}$ is '$(\neg A \lor C)$', $\mathscr{Q}$ is '$A$', and $\mathscr{R}$ is '$\neg B$'. By applying (Dist) once we get:

$$((\neg A \lor C) \land A)) \lor ((\neg A \lor C) \land \neg B) \qquad \text{Dist}$$

This looks worse, but if we keep going, it's going to look better! The two disjuncts almost look like we can apply (Dist) again, except the '$\lor$' is on the wrong side. This is what commutativity (Comm) is good for. let's apply it to '$(\neg A \lor C) \land A$':

$$(A \land (\neg A \lor C)) \lor ((\neg A \lor C) \land \neg B) \qquad \text{Comm}$$

We can apply (Dist) again to the resulting part, '$A \land (\neg A \lor C)$':

$$((A \land \neg A) \lor (A \land C)) \lor ((\neg A \lor C) \land \neg B) \qquad \text{Dist}$$

Now in the left half, no '$\lor$' is in the scope of an '$\land$'. Let's apply the same principles to the right half:

$$((A \land \neg A) \lor (A \land C)) \lor (\neg B \land (\neg A \lor C)) \qquad \text{Comm}$$
$$((A \land \neg A) \lor (A \land C)) \lor ((\neg B \land \neg A) \lor (\neg B \land C)) \qquad \text{Dist}$$

Our sentence is now in DNF! But we can simplify it a bit: '$(A \land \neg A)$' is a contradiction in TFL, i.e., it is always false. And if you combine something that's always false using '$\lor$' with a sentence $\mathscr{P}$, you get something equivalent to just $\mathscr{P}$. This is the second of the simplification (Simp) rules.

$$((A \land C) \lor (A \land \neg A)) \lor ((\neg B \land \neg A) \lor (\neg B \land C)) \qquad \text{Comm}$$
$$(A \land C) \lor ((\neg B \land \neg A) \lor (\neg B \land C)) \qquad \text{Simp}$$

The final result is still in DNF, but a bit simpler still. It is also much simpler than the DNF we would have obtained by the method of chapter 43. In fact, the sentence we started with could have been the $\mathcal{S}$ of §43.2—it has exactly the truth table used as an example there. The DNF we found there (on p. 362), was (with all necessary brackets):

$$((((A \wedge B) \wedge C) \vee ((A \wedge \neg B) \wedge C)) \vee ((\neg A \wedge \neg B) \wedge C)) \vee ((\neg A \wedge \neg B) \wedge \neg C).$$

## Practice exercises

**A.** Consider the following sentences:

1. $(A \to \neg B)$
2. $\neg(A \leftrightarrow B)$
3. $(\neg A \vee \neg(A \wedge B))$
4. $(\neg(A \to B) \wedge (A \to C))$
5. $(\neg(A \vee B) \leftrightarrow ((\neg C \wedge \neg A) \to \neg B))$
6. $((\neg(A \wedge \neg B) \to C) \wedge \neg(A \wedge D))$

For each sentence, find an equivalent sentence in DNF and one in CNF by giving a chain of equivalences. Use (Id), (Abs), and (Simp) to simplify your sentences as much as possible.

# CHAPTER 46

# *Soundness*

In this chapter we relate TFL's semantics to its natural deduction *proof system* (as defined in Part IV). We will prove that the formal proof system is safe: you can only prove sentences from premises from which they actually follow. Intuitively, a formal proof system is sound iff it does not allow you to prove any invalid arguments. This is obviously a highly desirable property. It tells us that our proof system will never lead us astray. Indeed, if our proof system were not sound, then we would not be able to trust our proofs. The aim of this chapter is to prove that our proof system is sound.

Let's make the idea more precise. We'll abbreviate a list of sentences using the greek letter Γ ('gamma'). A formal proof system is SOUND (relative to a given semantics) *iff*, whenever there is a formal proof of 𝒞 from assumptions among Γ, then Γ genuinely entails 𝒞 (given that semantics). Otherwise put, to prove that TFL's proof system is sound, we need to prove the following

> **Soundness Theorem.** For any sentences Γ and 𝒞: if Γ ⊢ 𝒞, then Γ ⊨ 𝒞

To prove this, we will check each of the rules of TFL's proof system individually. We want to show that no application of those rules ever leads us astray. Since a proof just involves repeated application of those rules, this will show that no proof ever leads

381

us astray. Or at least, that is the general idea.

To begin with, we must make the idea of 'leading us astray' more precise. Say that a line of a proof is SHINY iff the assumptions on which that line depends entail the sentence on that line.[1] To illustrate the idea, consider the following:

| | | |
|---|---|---|
| 1 | $F \to (G \land H)$ | |
| 2 | $F$ | |
| 3 | $G \land H$ | $\to$E 1, 2 |
| 4 | $G$ | $\land$E 3 |
| 5 | $F \to G$ | $\to$I 2–4 |

Line 1 is shiny iff $F \to (G \land H) \vDash F \to (G \land H)$. You should be easily convinced that line 1 is, indeed, shiny! Similarly, line 4 is shiny iff $F \to (G \land H), F \vDash G$. Again, it is easy to check that line 4 is shiny. As is every line in this TFL-proof. We want to show that this is no coincidence. That is, we want to prove:

**Shininess Lemma.** Every line of every TFL-proof is shiny.

Then we will know that we have never gone astray, on any line of a proof. Indeed, given the Shininess Lemma, it will be easy to prove the Soundness Theorem:

*Proof.* Suppose $\Gamma \vdash \mathscr{C}$. Then there is a TFL-proof, with $\mathscr{C}$ appearing on its last line, whose only undischarged assumptions are among $\Gamma$. The Shininess Lemma tells us that every line on every TFL-proof is shiny. So this last line is shiny, i.e. $\Gamma \vDash \mathscr{C}$. QED

It remains to prove the Shininess Lemma.

To do this, we observe that every line of any TFL-proof is obtained by applying some rule. So what we want to show is that no application of a rule of TFL's proof system will lead us astray.

---

[1]The word 'shiny' is not standard among logicians.

More precisely, say that a rule of inference is RULE-SOUND *iff* for all TFL-proofs, if we obtain a line on a TFL-proof by applying that rule, and every earlier line in the TFL-proof is shiny, then our new line is also shiny. What we need to show is that *every* rule in TFL's proof system is rule-sound.

We will do this in the next section. But having demonstrated the rule-soundness of every rule, the Shininess Lemma will follow immediately:

*Proof.* Fix any line, line $n$, on any TFL-proof. The sentence written on line $n$ must be obtained using a formal inference rule which is rule-sound. This is to say that, if every earlier line is shiny, then line $n$ itself is shiny. Hence, by strong induction on the length of TFL-proofs, every line of every TFL-proof is shiny. QED

Note that this proof appeals to a principle of strong induction on the length of TFL-proofs. This is the first time we have seen that principle, and you should pause to confirm that it is, indeed, justified.

It remains to show that every rule is rule-sound. This is not difficult, but it is time-consuming, since we need to check each rule individually, and TFL's proof system has plenty of rules! To speed up the process marginally, we will introduce a convenient abbreviation: '$\Delta_i$' ('delta') will abbreviate the assumptions (if any) on which line $i$ depends in our TFL-proof (context will indicate which TFL-proof we have in mind).

> Introducing an assumption is rule-sound.

If $\mathcal{A}$ is introduced as an assumption on line $n$, then $\mathcal{A}$ is among $\Delta_n$, and so $\Delta_n \vDash \mathcal{A}$.

> $\wedge$I is rule-sound.

*Proof.* Consider any application of $\wedge$I in any TFL-proof, i.e., something like:

$$
\begin{array}{c|ll}
i & \mathcal{A} & \\
& & \\
j & \mathcal{B} & \\
& & \\
n & \mathcal{A} \wedge \mathcal{B} & \wedge\text{I } i, j
\end{array}
$$

To show that $\wedge$I is rule-sound, we assume that every line before line $n$ is shiny; and we aim to show that line $n$ is shiny, i.e. that $\Delta_n \vDash \mathcal{A} \wedge \mathcal{B}$.

So, let $v$ be any valuation that makes all of $\Delta_n$ true.

We first show that $v$ makes $\mathcal{A}$ true. To prove this, note that all of $\Delta_i$ are among $\Delta_n$. By hypothesis, line $i$ is shiny. So any valuation that makes all of $\Delta_i$ true makes $\mathcal{A}$ true. Since $v$ makes all of $\Delta_i$ true, it makes $\mathcal{A}$ true too.

We can similarly see that $v$ makes $\mathcal{B}$ true.

So $v$ makes $\mathcal{A}$ true and $v$ makes $\mathcal{B}$ true. Consequently, $v$ makes $\mathcal{A} \wedge \mathcal{B}$ true. So any valuation that makes all of the sentences among $\Delta_n$ true also makes $\mathcal{A} \wedge \mathcal{B}$ true. That is: line $n$ is shiny. QED

All of the remaining lemmas establishing rule-soundness will have, essentially, the same structure as this one did.

$\wedge$E is rule-sound.

*Proof.* Assume that every line before line $n$ on some TFL-proof is shiny, and that $\wedge$E is used on line $n$. So the situation is:

$$
\begin{array}{c|ll}
i & \mathcal{A} \wedge \mathcal{B} & \\
& & \\
n & \mathcal{A} & \wedge\text{E } i
\end{array}
$$

(or perhaps with $\mathcal{B}$ on line $n$ instead; but similar reasoning will apply in that case). Let $v$ be any valuation that makes all of $\Delta_n$ true. Note that all of $\Delta_i$ are among $\Delta_n$. By hypothesis, line $i$ is shiny. So any valuation that makes all of $\Delta_i$ true makes $\mathcal{A} \wedge \mathcal{B}$ true. So $v$ makes $\mathcal{A} \wedge \mathcal{B}$ true, and hence makes $\mathcal{A}$ true. So $\Delta_n \vDash \mathcal{A}$. QED

> $\lor$I is rule-sound.

We leave this as an exercise.

> $\lor$E is rule-sound.

*Proof.* Assume that every line before line $n$ on some TFL-proof is shiny, and that $\land$E is used on line $n$. So the situation is:

$$
\begin{array}{c|l}
m & \mathscr{A} \lor \mathscr{B} \\[4pt]
i & \quad \big| \; \mathscr{A} \\[4pt]
j & \quad \big| \; \mathscr{C} \\[4pt]
k & \quad \big| \; \mathscr{B} \\[4pt]
l & \quad \big| \; \mathscr{C} \\[4pt]
n & \mathscr{C} \qquad \lor\text{E } m,\, i\text{--}j,\, k\text{--}l
\end{array}
$$

Let $v$ be any valuation that makes all of $\Delta_n$ true. Note that all of $\Delta_m$ are among $\Delta_n$. By hypothesis, line $m$ is shiny. So any valuation that makes $\Delta_n$ true makes $\mathscr{A} \lor \mathscr{B}$ true. So in particular, $v$ makes $\mathscr{A} \lor \mathscr{B}$ true, and hence either $v$ makes $\mathscr{A}$ true, or $v$ makes $\mathscr{B}$ true. We now reason through these two cases:

*Case 1: $v$ makes $\mathscr{A}$ true.* All of $\Delta_i$ are among $\Delta_n$, with the possible exception of $\mathscr{A}$. Since $v$ makes all of $\Delta_n$ true, and also makes $\mathscr{A}$ true, $v$ makes all of $\Delta_i$ true. Now, by assumption, line $j$ is shiny; so $\Delta_j \vDash \mathscr{C}$. But the sentences $\Delta_i$ are just the sentences $\Delta_j$, so $\Delta_i \vDash \mathscr{C}$. So, any valuation that makes all of $\Delta_i$ true makes $\mathscr{C}$ true. But $v$ is just such a valuation. So $v$ makes $\mathscr{C}$ true.

*Case 2: $v$ makes $\mathscr{B}$ true.* Reasoning in exactly the same way, considering lines $k$ and $l$, $v$ makes $\mathscr{C}$ true.

Either way, $v$ makes $\mathscr{C}$ true. So $\Delta_n \vDash \mathscr{C}$. QED

---

¬E is rule-sound.

---

*Proof.* Assume that every line before line $n$ on some TFL-proof is shiny, and that ¬E is used on line $n$. So the situation is:

$$
\begin{array}{ll}
i & \mathcal{A} \\
\\
j & \neg\mathcal{A} \\
\\
n & \bot \qquad \text{¬E } i, j
\end{array}
$$

Note that all of $\Delta_i$ and all of $\Delta_j$ are among $\Delta_n$. By hypothesis, lines $i$ and $j$ are shiny. So any valuation which makes all of $\Delta_n$ true would have to make both $\mathcal{A}$ and $\neg\mathcal{A}$ true. But no valuation can do that. So no valuation makes all of $\Delta_n$ true. So $\Delta_n \vDash \bot$, vacuously. QED

---

X is rule-sound.

---

We leave this as an exercise.

---

¬I is rule-sound.

---

*Proof.* Assume that every line before line $n$ on some TFL-proof is shiny, and that ¬I is used on line $n$. So the situation is:

$$
\begin{array}{ll}
i & \quad \mathcal{A} \\
\\
j & \quad \bot \\
\\
n & \neg\mathcal{A} \qquad \text{¬I } i\text{--}j
\end{array}
$$

Let $v$ be any valuation that makes all of $\Delta_n$ true. Note that all of $\Delta_n$ are among $\Delta_i$, with the possible exception of $\mathcal{A}$ itself. By hypothesis, line $j$ is shiny. But no valuation can make '$\bot$' true, so no valuation can make all of $\Delta_j$ true. Since the sentences $\Delta_i$ are just the sentences $\Delta_j$, no valuation can make all of $\Delta_i$ true.

Since $v$ makes all of $\Delta_n$ true, it must therefore make $\mathcal{A}$ false, and so make $\neg\mathcal{A}$ true. So $\Delta_n \vDash \neg\mathcal{A}$. QED

> IP, $\rightarrow$I, $\rightarrow$E, $\leftrightarrow$I, and $\leftrightarrow$E are all rule-sound.

We leave these as exercises.

This establishes that all the basic rules of our proof system are rule-sound. Finally, we show:

> All of the derived rules of our proof system are rule-sound.

*Proof.* Suppose that we used a derived rule to obtain some sentence, $\mathcal{A}$, on line $n$ of some TFL-proof, and that every earlier line is shiny. Every use of a derived rule can be replaced (at the cost of long-windedness) with multiple uses of basic rules. That is to say, we could have used basic rules to write $\mathcal{A}$ on some line $n+k$, without introducing any further assumptions. So, applying our individual results that all basic rules are rule-sound several times ($k+1$ times, in fact), we can see that line $n+k$ is shiny. Hence the derived rule is rule-sound. QED

And that's that! We have shown that every rule—basic or otherwise—is rule-sound, which is all that we required to establish the Shininess Lemma, and hence the Soundness Theorem.

But it might help to round off this chapter if we repeat my informal explanation of what we have done. A formal proof is just a sequence—of arbitrary length—of applications of rules. We have shown that any application of any rule will not lead you astray. It follows (by induction) that no formal proof will lead you astray. That is: our proof system is sound.

## Practice exercises

**A.** Complete the Lemmas left as exercises in this chapter. That is, show that the following are rule-sound:

   1. $\vee$I. (*Hint*: this is similar to the case of $\wedge$E.)

2. X. (*Hint*: this is similar to the case of ¬E.)
3. →I. (*Hint*: this is similar to ∨E.)
4. →E.
5. IP. (*Hint*: this is similar to the case of ¬I.)

# Appendices

# APPENDIX A

# *Symbolic notation*

## 1.1 Alternative nomenclature

**Truth-functional logic**. TFL goes by other names. Sometimes it is called *sentential logic*, because it deals fundamentally with sentences. Sometimes it is called *propositional logic*, on the idea that it deals fundamentally with propositions. We have stuck with *truth-functional logic*, to emphasize the fact that it deals only with assignments of truth and falsity to sentences, and that its connectives are all truth-functional.

**First-order logic**. FOL goes by other names. Sometimes it is called *predicate logic*, because it allows us to apply predicates to objects. Sometimes it is called *quantified logic*, because it makes use of quantifiers.

**Formulas**. Some texts call formulas *well-formed formulas*. Since 'well-formed formula' is such a long and cumbersome phrase, they then abbreviate this as *wff*. This is both barbarous and unnecessary (such texts do not countenance 'ill-formed formulas'). We have stuck with 'formula'.

In §6, we defined *sentences* of TFL. These are also sometimes called 'formulas' (or 'well-formed formulas') since in TFL, unlike FOL, there is no distinction between a formula and a sentence.

**Valuations**.    Some texts call valuations *truth-assignments*, or *truth-value assignments*.

*n*-**place predicates**.    We have chosen to call predicates 'one-place', 'two-place', 'three-place', etc. Other texts respectively call them 'monadic', 'dyadic', 'triadic', etc. Still other texts call them 'unary', 'binary', 'ternary', etc.

**Names**.    In FOL, we have used '$a$', '$b$', '$c$', for names. Some texts call these 'constants'. Other texts do not mark any difference between names and variables in the syntax. Those texts focus simply on whether the symbol occurs *bound* or *unbound*.

**Domains**.    Some texts describe a domain as a 'domain of discourse', or a 'universe of discourse'.

## 1.2   Alternative symbols

In the history of formal logic, different symbols have been used at different times and by different authors. Often, authors were forced to use notation that their printers could typeset. This appendix presents some common symbols, so that you can recognize them if you encounter them in an article or in another book.

**Negation**.    Two commonly used symbols are the *hoe*, '$\neg$', and the *swung dash* or *tilda*, '$\sim$.' In some more advanced formal systems it is necessary to distinguish between two kinds of negation; the distinction is sometimes represented by using both '$\neg$' and '$\sim$'. Older texts sometimes indicate negation by a line over the formula being negated, e.g., $\overline{A \wedge B}$. Some texts use '$x \neq y$' to abbreviate '$\neg x = y$'.

**Disjunction.**   The symbol '∨' is typically used to symbolize inclusive disjunction. One etymology is from the Latin word 'vel', meaning 'or'.

**Conjunction.**   Conjunction is often symbolized with the *ampersand*, '&'. The ampersand is a decorative form of the Latin word 'et', which means 'and'. (Its etymology still lingers in certain fonts, particularly in italic fonts; thus an italic ampersand might appear as '*&*'.) This symbol is commonly used in natural English writing (e.g. 'Smith & Sons'), and so even though it is a natural choice, many logicians use a different symbol to avoid confusion between the object and metalanguage: as a symbol in a formal system, the ampersand is not the English word '&'. The most common choice now is '∧', which is a counterpart to the symbol used for disjunction. Sometimes a single dot, '·', is used. In some older texts, there is no symbol for conjunction at all; '*A* and *B*' is simply written '*AB*'.

**Material Conditional.**   There are two common symbols for the material conditional: the *arrow*, '→', and the *horseshoe*, '⊃'.

**Material Biconditional.**   The *double-headed arrow*, '↔', is used in systems that use the arrow to represent the material conditional. Systems that use the horseshoe for the conditional typically use the *triple bar*, '≡', for the biconditional.

**Quantifiers.**   The universal quantifier is typically symbolized as a rotated 'A', and the existential quantifier as a rotated, 'E'. In some texts, there is no separate symbol for the universal quantifier. Instead, the variable is just written in parentheses in front of the formula that it binds. For example, they might write '$(x)P(x)$' where we would write '$\forall x\, P(x)$'.

These alternative typographies are summarised below:

| | |
|---:|:---|
| negation | ¬, ~ |
| conjunction | ∧, &, • |
| disjunction | ∨ |
| conditional | →, ⊃ |
| biconditional | ↔, ≡ |
| universal quantifier | $\forall x$, $(x)$ |

## Polish notation

This section briefly discusses sentential logic in Polish notation, a system of notation introduced in the late 1920s by the Polish logician Jan Łukasiewicz.

Lower case letters are used as sentence letters. The capital letter $N$ is used for negation. $A$ is used for disjunction, $K$ for conjunction, $C$ for the conditional, $E$ for the biconditional. ('$A$' is for alternation, another name for logical disjunction. '$E$' is for equivalence.)

In Polish notation, a binary connective is written *before* the two sentences that it connects. For example, the sentence $A \wedge B$ of TFL would be written $Kab$ in Polish notation.

The sentences $\neg A \rightarrow B$ and $\neg(A \rightarrow B)$ are very different; the main logical operator of the first is the conditional, but the main connective of the second is negation. In TFL, we show this by putting parentheses around the conditional in the second sentence. In Polish notation, parentheses are never required. The left-most connective is always the main connective. The first sentence would simply be written $CNab$ and the second $NCab$.

This feature of Polish notation means that it is possible to evaluate sentences simply by working through the symbols from right to left. If you were constructing a truth table for $NKab$, for example, you would first consider the truth-values assigned to $b$ and $a$, then consider their conjunction, and then negate the result. The general rule for what to evaluate next in TFL is not nearly so simple. In TFL, the truth table for $\neg(A \wedge B)$ requires looking at $A$ and $B$, then looking in the middle of the sentence at the conjunction, and then at the beginning of the sentence at the negation. Because the order of operations can be specified more mechanically in Polish notation, variants of Polish notation are used as the internal structure for many computer programming languages.

# *Alternative proof systems*

In formulating our natural deduction system, we treated certain rules of natural deduction as *basic*, and others as *derived*. However, we could equally well have taken various different rules as basic or derived. We will illustrate this point by considering some alternative treatments of disjunction, negation, and the quantifiers. We will also explain why we have made the choices that we have.

## 2.1  Alternative disjunction elimination

Some systems take DS as their basic rule for disjunction elimination. Such systems can then treat the ∨E rule as a derived rule. For they might offer the following proof scheme:

| $m$ | $\mathcal{A} \vee \mathcal{B}$ | |
| $i$ | $\quad\mathcal{A}$ | |
| $j$ | $\quad\mathcal{C}$ | |
| $k$ | $\quad\mathcal{B}$ | |
| $l$ | $\quad\mathcal{C}$ | |
| $n$ | $\mathcal{A} \to \mathcal{C}$ | $\to$I $i$–$j$ |
| $n+1$ | $\mathcal{B} \to \mathcal{C}$ | $\to$I $k$–$l$ |
| $n+2$ | $\quad\neg\mathcal{C}$ | |
| $n+3$ | $\quad\quad\mathcal{A}$ | |
| $n+4$ | $\quad\quad\mathcal{C}$ | $\to$E $n+3$, $n$ |
| $n+5$ | $\quad\quad\bot$ | $\neg$E $n+2$, $n+4$ |
| $n+6$ | $\quad\neg\mathcal{A}$ | $\neg$I $n+3$–$n+5$ |
| $n+7$ | $\quad\mathcal{B}$ | DS $m$, $n+6$ |
| $n+8$ | $\quad\mathcal{C}$ | $\to$E $n+7$, $n+1$ |
| $n+9$ | $\quad\bot$ | $\neg$E $n+2$, $n+8$ |
| $n+10$ | $\mathcal{C}$ | IP $n+2$–$n+9$ |

So why did we choose to take $\vee$E as basic, rather than DS?[1] Our reasoning is that DS involves the use of '$\neg$' in the statement of the rule. It is in some sense 'cleaner' for our disjunction elimination rule to avoid mentioning *other* connectives.

---

[1]P.D. Magnus's original version of this book went the other way.

## 2.2 Alternative negation rules

Some systems take the following rule as their basic negation introduction rule:

$$
\begin{array}{ll}
m & \quad \mathcal{A} \\
& \quad \overline{\phantom{x}} \\
n-1 & \quad \mathcal{B} \\
n & \quad \neg\mathcal{B} \\
& \neg\mathcal{A} \qquad \neg\text{I*} \; m\text{--}n
\end{array}
$$

and a corresponding version of the rule we called IP as their basic negation elimination rule:

$$
\begin{array}{ll}
m & \quad \neg\mathcal{A} \\
& \quad \overline{\phantom{x}} \\
n-1 & \quad \mathcal{B} \\
n & \quad \neg\mathcal{B} \\
& \mathcal{A} \qquad \neg\text{E*} \; m\text{--}n
\end{array}
$$

Using these two rules, we could we could have avoided all use of the symbol '$\perp$' altogether.[2] The resulting system would have had fewer rules than ours.

Another way to deal with negation is to use either LEM or DNE as a basic rule and introduce IP as a derived rule. Typically, in such a system the rules are given different names, too. E.g., sometimes what we call ¬E is called $\perp$I, and what we call X is called $\perp$E.[3]

So why did we chose our rules for negation and contradiction?

Our first reason is that adding the symbol '$\perp$' to our natural deduction system makes proofs considerably easier to work with. For instance, in our system it's always clear what the conclusion

---

[2]Again, P.D. Magnus's original version of this book went the other way.

[3]The version of this book due to Tim Button goes this route and replaces IP with LEM, which he calls TND, for "tertium non datur."

of a subproof is: the sentence on the last line, e.g. $\bot$ in IP or $\neg$I. In $\neg$I* and $\neg$E*, subproofs have two conclusions, so you can't check at one glance if an application of them is correct.

Our second reason is that a lot of fascinating philosophical discussion has focussed on the acceptability or otherwise of indirect proof IP (equivalently, excluded middle, i.e. LEM, or double negation elimination DNE) and explosion (i.e. X). By treating these as separate rules in the proof system, you will be in a better position to engage with that philosophical discussion. In particular: having invoked these rules explicitly, it would be much easier for us to know what a system which lacked these rules would look like.

This discussion, and in fact the vast majority of mathematical study on applications of natural deduction proofs beyond introductory courses, makes reference to a different version of natural deduction. This version was invented by Gerhard Gentzen in 1935 as refined by Dag Prawitz in 1965. Our set of basic rules coincides with theirs. In other words, the rules we use are those that are standard in philosophical and mathematical discussion of natural deduction proofs outside of introductory courses.

## 2.3  Alternative quantification rules

An alternative approach to the quantifiers is to take as basic the rules for $\forall$I and $\forall$E from §34, and also two CQ rule which allow us to move from $\forall x \neg \mathcal{A}$ to $\neg \exists x \mathcal{A}$ and vice versa.[4]

Taking only these rules as basic, we could have derived the $\exists$I and $\exists$E rules provided in §34. To derive the $\exists$I rule is fairly simple. Suppose $\mathcal{A}$ contains the name $c$, and contains no instances of the variable $x$, and that we want to do the following:

---

[4]Warren Goldfarb follows this line in *Deductive Logic*, 2003, Hackett Publishing Co.

$$m \quad | \quad \mathcal{A}(\ldots c \ldots c \ldots)$$

$$k \quad | \quad \exists x \mathcal{A}(\ldots x \ldots c \ldots)$$

This is not yet permitted, since in this new system, we do not have the ∃I rule. We can, however, offer the following:

| | | |
|---|---|---|
| $m$ | $\mathcal{A}(\ldots c \ldots c \ldots)$ | |
| $m+1$ | $\neg \exists x \mathcal{A}(\ldots x \ldots c \ldots)$ | |
| $m+2$ | $\forall x \neg \mathcal{A}(\ldots x \ldots c \ldots)$ | CQ $m+1$ |
| $m+3$ | $\neg \mathcal{A}(\ldots c \ldots c \ldots)$ | ∀E $m+2$ |
| $m+4$ | $\bot$ | ¬E $m+3$, $m$ |
| $m+5$ | $\exists x \mathcal{A}(\ldots x \ldots c \ldots)$ | IP $m+1$–$m+4$ |

To derive the ∃E rule is rather more subtle. This is because the ∃E rule has an important constraint (as, indeed, does the ∀I rule), and we need to make sure that we are respecting it. So, suppose we are in a situation where we *want* to do the following:

| | | |
|---|---|---|
| $m$ | $\exists x \mathcal{A}(\ldots x \ldots x \ldots)$ | |
| $i$ | $\mathcal{A}(\ldots c \ldots c \ldots)$ | |
| $j$ | $\mathcal{B}$ | |
| $k$ | $\mathcal{B}$ | |

where $c$ does not occur in any undischarged assumptions, or in $\mathcal{B}$, or in $\exists x \mathcal{A}(\ldots x \ldots x \ldots)$. Ordinarily, we would be allowed to use the ∃E rule; but we are not here assuming that we have access to this rule as a basic rule. Nevertheless, we could offer the following, more complicated derivation:

| $m$ | $\exists x \mathcal{A}(\ldots x \ldots x \ldots)$ | |
|---|---|---|
| $i$ | $\quad \mathcal{A}(\ldots c \ldots c \ldots)$ | |
| $j$ | $\quad \mathcal{B}$ | |
| $k$ | $\mathcal{A}(\ldots c \ldots c \ldots) \to \mathcal{B}$ | $\to$I $i$–$j$ |
| $k+1$ | $\quad \neg \mathcal{B}$ | |
| $k+2$ | $\quad \neg \mathcal{A}(\ldots c \ldots c \ldots)$ | MT $k, k+1$ |
| $k+3$ | $\quad \forall x \neg \mathcal{A}(\ldots x \ldots x \ldots)$ | $\forall$I $k+2$ |
| $k+4$ | $\quad \neg \exists x \mathcal{A}(\ldots x \ldots x \ldots)$ | CQ $k+3$ |
| $k+5$ | $\quad \bot$ | $\neg$E $k+4, m$ |
| $k+6$ | $\mathcal{B}$ | IP $k+1$–$k+5$ |

We are permitted to use $\forall$I on line $k+3$ because $c$ does not occur in any undischarged assumptions or in $\mathcal{B}$. The entries on lines $k+4$ and $k+1$ contradict each other, because $c$ does not occur in $\exists x \mathcal{A}(\ldots x \ldots x \ldots)$.

Armed with these derived rules, we could now go on to derive the two remaining CQ rules, exactly as in §38.

So, why did we start with all of the quantifier rules as basic, and then derive the CQ rules?

Our first reason is that it seems more intuitive to treat the quantifiers as on a par with one another, giving them their own basic rules for introduction and elimination.

Our second reason relates to the discussion of alternative negation rules. In the derivations of the rules of $\exists$I and $\exists$E that we have offered in this section, we invoked IP. But, as we mentioned earlier, IP is a contentious rule. So, if we want to move to a system which abandons IP, but which still allows us to use existential quantifiers, we will want to take the introduction and elimination rules for the quantifiers as basic, and take the CQ rules as derived. (Indeed, in a system without IP, LEM, and

DNE, we will be *unable* to derive the CQ rule which moves from $\neg \forall x \mathcal{A}$ to $\exists x \neg \mathcal{A}$.)

# *Quick reference*

## 3.1 Characteristic truth tables

| $\mathscr{A}$ | $\neg\mathscr{A}$ |
|---|---|
| T | F |
| F | T |

| $\mathscr{A}$ | $\mathscr{B}$ | $\mathscr{A} \land \mathscr{B}$ | $\mathscr{A} \lor \mathscr{B}$ | $\mathscr{A} \rightarrow \mathscr{B}$ | $\mathscr{A} \leftrightarrow \mathscr{B}$ |
|---|---|---|---|---|---|
| T | T | T | T | T | T |
| T | F | F | T | F | F |
| F | T | F | T | T | F |
| F | F | F | F | T | T |

## 3.2 Symbolization

### SENTENTIAL CONNECTIVES

| | |
|---|---|
| It is not the case that $P$ | $\neg P$ |
| Either $P$ or $Q$ | $(P \vee Q)$ |
| Neither $P$ nor $Q$ | $\neg(P \vee Q)$ or $(\neg P \wedge \neg Q)$ |
| Both $P$ and $Q$ | $(P \wedge Q)$ |
| If $P$ then $Q$ | $(P \rightarrow Q)$ |
| $P$ only if $Q$ | $(P \rightarrow Q)$ |
| $P$ if and only if $Q$ | $(P \leftrightarrow Q)$ |
| $P$ unless $Q$ | $(P \vee Q)$ |

### PREDICATES

| | |
|---|---|
| All $F$s are $G$s | $\forall x(F(x) \rightarrow G(x))$ |
| Some $F$s are $G$s | $\exists x(F(x) \wedge G(x))$ |
| Not all $F$s are $G$s | $\neg\forall x(F(x) \rightarrow G(x))$ or $\exists x(F(x) \wedge \neg G(x))$ |
| No $F$s are $G$s | $\forall x(F(x) \rightarrow \neg G(x))$ or $\neg\exists x(F(x) \wedge G(x))$ |
| Only $F$s are $G$s | $\forall x(G(x) \rightarrow F(x))$ $\neg\exists x(\neg F(x) \wedge G(x))$ |

### IDENTITY

| | |
|---|---|
| Only $c$ is $G$ | $\forall x(G(x) \leftrightarrow x = c)$ |
| Everything other than $c$ is $G$ | $\forall x(\neg x = c \rightarrow G(x))$ |
| Everything except $c$ is $G$ | $\forall x(\neg x = c \leftrightarrow G(x))$ |
| The $F$ is $G$ | $\exists x(F(x) \wedge \forall y(F(y) \rightarrow x = y) \wedge G(x))$ |
| It is not the case that the $F$ is $G$ | $\neg\exists x(F(x) \wedge \forall y(F(y) \rightarrow x = y) \wedge G(x))$ |
| The $F$ is non-$G$ | $\exists x(F(x) \wedge \forall y(F(y) \rightarrow x = y) \wedge \neg G(x))$ |

## 3.3 Using identity to symbolize quantities

**There are at least _____ $F$s.**

one   $\exists x \, F(x)$

two   $\exists x_1 \exists x_2 (F(x_1) \wedge F(x_2) \wedge \neg x_1 = x_2)$

three   $\exists x_1 \exists x_2 \exists x_3 (F(x_1) \wedge F(x_2) \wedge F(x_3) \wedge$
$\neg x_1 = x_2 \wedge \neg x_1 = x_3 \wedge \neg x_2 = x_3)$

four   $\exists x_1 \exists x_2 \exists x_3 \exists x_4 (F(x_1) \wedge F(x_2) \wedge F(x_3) \wedge F(x_4) \wedge$
$\neg x_1 = x_2 \wedge \neg x_1 = x_3 \wedge \neg x_1 = x_4 \wedge$
$\neg x_2 = x_3 \wedge \neg x_2 = x_4 \wedge \neg x_3 = x_4)$

$n$   $\exists x_1 \ldots \exists x_n (F(x_1) \wedge \ldots \wedge F(x_n) \wedge$
$\neg x_1 = x_2 \wedge \ldots \wedge \neg x_{n-1} = x_n)$

**There are at most _____ $F$s.**

One way to say 'there are at most $n$ $F$s' is to put a negation sign in front of the symbolization for 'there are at least $n + 1$ $F$s'.   Equivalently, we can offer:

one   $\forall x_1 \forall x_2 [(F(x_1) \wedge F(x_2)) \rightarrow x_1 = x_2]$

two   $\forall x_1 \forall x_2 \forall x_3 [(F(x_1) \wedge F(x_2) \wedge F(x_3)) \rightarrow$
$(x_1 = x_2 \vee x_1 = x_3 \vee x_2 = x_3)]$

three   $\forall x_1 \forall x_2 \forall x_3 \forall x_4 [(F(x_1) \wedge F(x_2) \wedge F(x_3) \wedge F(x_4)) \rightarrow$
$(x_1 = x_2 \vee x_1 = x_3 \vee x_1 = x_4 \vee$
$x_2 = x_3 \vee x_2 = x_4 \vee x_3 = x_4)]$

$n$   $\forall x_1 \ldots \forall x_{n+1} [(F(x_1) \wedge \ldots \wedge F(x_{n+1})) \rightarrow$
$(x_1 = x_2 \vee \ldots \vee x_n = x_{n+1})]$

**There are exactly _____ $F$s.**

One way to say 'there are exactly $n$ $F$s' is to conjoin two of the symbolizations above and say 'there are at least $n$ $F$s and there are at most $n$ $F$s.' The following equivalent formulas are shorter:

zero   $\forall x \, \neg F(x)$

one   $\exists x \big[ F(x) \wedge \forall y (F(y) \rightarrow x = y) \big]$

two   $\exists x_1 \exists x_2 \big[ F(x_1) \wedge F(x_2) \wedge$
$\neg x_1 = x_2 \wedge \forall y \big( F(y) \rightarrow (y = x_1 \vee y = x_2) \big) \big]$

three   $\exists x_1 \exists x_2 \exists x_3 \big[ F(x_1) \wedge F(x_2) \wedge F(x_3) \wedge$
$\neg x_1 = x_2 \wedge \neg x_1 = x_3 \wedge \neg x_2 = x_3 \wedge$
$\forall y \big( F(y) \rightarrow (y = x_1 \vee y = x_2 \vee y = x_3) \big) \big]$

$n$   $\exists x_1 \ldots \exists x_n \big[ F(x_1) \wedge \ldots \wedge F(x_n) \wedge$
$\neg x_1 = x_2 \wedge \ldots \wedge \neg x_{n-1} = x_n \wedge$
$\forall y \big( F(y) \rightarrow (y = x_1 \vee \ldots \vee y = x_n) \big) \big]$

## 3.4   Basic deduction rules for TFL

### Reiteration

$$
\begin{array}{c|l}
m & \mathcal{A} \\
  & \\
  & \mathcal{A} \quad \text{R } m
\end{array}
$$

### Conjunction

$$
\begin{array}{c|l}
m & \mathcal{A} \\
n & \mathcal{B} \\
  & \mathcal{A} \wedge \mathcal{B} \quad \wedge\text{I } m, n
\end{array}
$$

$$
\begin{array}{c|l}
m & \mathcal{A} \wedge \mathcal{B} \\
  & \mathcal{A} \quad\quad \wedge\text{E } m
\end{array}
$$

$$
\begin{array}{c|l}
m & \mathcal{A} \wedge \mathcal{B} \\
  & \mathcal{B} \quad\quad \wedge\text{E } m
\end{array}
$$

### Conditional

$$
\begin{array}{c|l}
i & \quad \mathcal{A} \\
j & \quad \mathcal{B} \\
  & \mathcal{A} \rightarrow \mathcal{B} \quad \rightarrow\text{I } i\text{--}j
\end{array}
$$

$$
\begin{array}{c|l}
m & \mathcal{A} \rightarrow \mathcal{B} \\
n & \mathcal{A} \\
  & \mathcal{B} \quad\quad \rightarrow\text{E } m, n
\end{array}
$$

### Negation

$$
\begin{array}{c|l}
i & \quad \mathcal{A} \\
j & \quad \bot \\
  & \neg\mathcal{A} \quad \neg\text{I } i\text{--}j
\end{array}
$$

$$
\begin{array}{c|l}
m & \neg\mathcal{A} \\
n & \mathcal{A} \\
  & \bot \quad\quad \neg\text{E } m, n
\end{array}
$$

### Indirect proof

$$
\begin{array}{c|l}
i & \quad \neg\mathcal{A} \\
j & \quad \bot \\
  & \mathcal{A} \quad\quad \text{IP } i\text{--}j
\end{array}
$$

### Explosion

$$
\begin{array}{c|l}
m & \bot \\
  & \mathcal{A} \quad \text{X } m
\end{array}
$$

## Disjunction

$$
\begin{array}{ll}
m & \mathscr{A} \\
& \mathscr{A} \vee \mathscr{B} \qquad \vee\text{I } m
\end{array}
$$

$$
\begin{array}{ll}
m & \mathscr{A} \\
& \mathscr{B} \vee \mathscr{A} \qquad \vee\text{I } m
\end{array}
$$

$$
\begin{array}{ll}
m & \mathscr{A} \vee \mathscr{B} \\
i & \quad \mathscr{A} \\
j & \quad \mathscr{C} \\
k & \quad \mathscr{B} \\
l & \quad \mathscr{C} \\
& \mathscr{C} \qquad \vee\text{E } m,\ i\text{--}j,\ k\text{--}l
\end{array}
$$

## Biconditional

$$
\begin{array}{ll}
i & \quad \mathscr{A} \\
j & \quad \mathscr{B} \\
k & \quad \mathscr{B} \\
l & \quad \mathscr{A} \\
& \mathscr{A} \leftrightarrow \mathscr{B} \qquad \leftrightarrow\text{I } i\text{--}j,\ k\text{--}l
\end{array}
$$

$$
\begin{array}{ll}
m & \mathscr{A} \leftrightarrow \mathscr{B} \\
n & \mathscr{A} \\
& \mathscr{B} \qquad \leftrightarrow\text{E } m,\ n
\end{array}
$$

$$
\begin{array}{ll}
m & \mathscr{A} \leftrightarrow \mathscr{B} \\
n & \mathscr{B} \\
& \mathscr{A} \qquad \leftrightarrow\text{E } m,\ n
\end{array}
$$

## 3.5   Derived rules for TFL

### Disjunctive syllogism

$$
\begin{array}{ll}
m & \mathcal{A} \vee \mathcal{B} \\[4pt]
n & \neg\mathcal{A} \\[4pt]
 & \mathcal{B} \qquad \text{DS } m, n
\end{array}
$$

$$
\begin{array}{ll}
m & \mathcal{A} \vee \mathcal{B} \\[4pt]
n & \neg\mathcal{B} \\[4pt]
 & \mathcal{A} \qquad \text{DS } m, n
\end{array}
$$

### Modus Tollens

$$
\begin{array}{ll}
m & \mathcal{A} \rightarrow \mathcal{B} \\[4pt]
n & \neg\mathcal{B} \\[4pt]
 & \neg\mathcal{A} \qquad \text{MT } m, n
\end{array}
$$

### Double-negation elimination

$$
\begin{array}{ll}
m & \neg\neg\mathcal{A} \\[4pt]
 & \mathcal{A} \qquad \text{DNE } m
\end{array}
$$

### Excluded middle

$$
\begin{array}{ll}
i & \quad \mathcal{A} \\[4pt]
j & \quad \mathcal{B} \\[4pt]
k & \quad \neg\mathcal{A} \\[4pt]
l & \quad \mathcal{B} \\[4pt]
 & \mathcal{B} \qquad \text{LEM } i\text{--}j,\ k\text{--}l
\end{array}
$$

### De Morgan Rules

$$
\begin{array}{ll}
m & \neg(\mathcal{A} \vee \mathcal{B}) \\[4pt]
 & \neg\mathcal{A} \wedge \neg\mathcal{B} \qquad \text{DeM } m
\end{array}
$$

$$
\begin{array}{ll}
m & \neg\mathcal{A} \wedge \neg\mathcal{B} \\[4pt]
 & \neg(\mathcal{A} \vee \mathcal{B}) \qquad \text{DeM } m
\end{array}
$$

$$
\begin{array}{ll}
m & \neg(\mathcal{A} \wedge \mathcal{B}) \\[4pt]
 & \neg\mathcal{A} \vee \neg\mathcal{B} \qquad \text{DeM } m
\end{array}
$$

$$
\begin{array}{ll}
m & \neg\mathcal{A} \vee \neg\mathcal{B} \\[4pt]
 & \neg(\mathcal{A} \wedge \mathcal{B}) \qquad \text{DeM } m
\end{array}
$$

## 3.6  Basic deduction rules for FOL

### Universal elimination

$$
m \quad \forall x \mathcal{A}(\ldots x \ldots x \ldots)
$$

$$
\mathcal{A}(\ldots c \ldots c \ldots) \qquad \forall\text{E } m
$$

### Existential introduction

$$
m \quad \mathcal{A}(\ldots c \ldots c \ldots)
$$

$$
\exists x \mathcal{A}(\ldots x \ldots c \ldots) \qquad \exists\text{I } m
$$

$x$ must not occur in
$\mathcal{A}(\ldots c \ldots c \ldots)$

### Universal introduction

$$
m \quad \mathcal{A}(\ldots c \ldots c \ldots)
$$

$$
\forall x \mathcal{A}(\ldots x \ldots x \ldots) \qquad \forall\text{I } m
$$

$c$ must not occur in any
undischarged assumption

$x$ must not occur in
$\mathcal{A}(\ldots c \ldots c \ldots)$

### Existential elimination

$$
m \quad \exists x \mathcal{A}(\ldots x \ldots x \ldots)
$$

$$
i \quad \mathcal{A}(\ldots c \ldots c \ldots)
$$

$$
j \quad \mathcal{B}
$$

$$
\mathcal{B} \qquad \exists\text{E } m,\, i\text{–}j
$$

$c$ must not occur in any
undischarged assumption, in
$\exists x \mathcal{A}(\ldots x \ldots x \ldots)$, or in $\mathcal{B}$

### Identity introduction

$$
c = c \qquad =\text{I}
$$

### Identity elimination

$$
m \quad a = b
$$

$$
n \quad \mathcal{A}(\ldots a \ldots a \ldots)
$$

$$
\mathcal{A}(\ldots b \ldots a \ldots) \qquad =\text{E } m,\, n
$$

$$
m \quad a = b
$$

$$
n \quad \mathcal{A}(\ldots b \ldots b \ldots)
$$

$$
\mathcal{A}(\ldots a \ldots b \ldots) \qquad =\text{E } m,\, n
$$

## 3.7  Derived rules for FOL

$m$ | $\forall x \neg \mathcal{A}$

   | $\neg \exists x \mathcal{A}$    CQ $m$

$m$ | $\neg \exists x \mathcal{A}$

   | $\forall x \neg \mathcal{A}$    CQ $m$

$m$ | $\exists x \neg \mathcal{A}$

   | $\neg \forall x \mathcal{A}$    CQ $m$

$m$ | $\neg \forall x \mathcal{A}$

   | $\exists x \neg \mathcal{A}$    CQ $m$

## 3.8 Rules for chains of equivalences

$$\neg\neg\mathscr{P} \Leftrightarrow \mathscr{P} \qquad \text{(DN)}$$

$$(\mathscr{P} \rightarrow \mathbb{Q}) \Leftrightarrow (\neg\mathscr{P} \vee \mathbb{Q}) \qquad \text{(Cond)}$$
$$\neg(\mathscr{P} \rightarrow \mathbb{Q}) \Leftrightarrow (\mathscr{P} \wedge \neg\mathbb{Q})$$

$$(\mathscr{P} \leftrightarrow \mathbb{Q}) \Leftrightarrow ((\mathscr{P} \rightarrow \mathbb{Q}) \wedge (\mathbb{Q} \rightarrow \mathscr{P})) \qquad \text{(Bicond)}$$

$$\neg(\mathscr{P} \wedge \mathbb{Q}) \Leftrightarrow (\neg\mathscr{P} \vee \neg\mathbb{Q}) \qquad \text{(DeM)}$$
$$\neg(\mathscr{P} \vee \mathbb{Q}) \Leftrightarrow (\neg\mathscr{P} \wedge \neg\mathbb{Q})$$

$$(\mathscr{P} \vee \mathbb{Q}) \Leftrightarrow (\mathbb{Q} \vee \mathscr{P}) \qquad \text{(Comm)}$$
$$(\mathscr{P} \wedge \mathbb{Q}) \Leftrightarrow (\mathbb{Q} \wedge \mathscr{P})$$

$$(\mathscr{P} \wedge (\mathbb{Q} \vee \mathscr{R})) \Leftrightarrow ((\mathscr{P} \wedge \mathbb{Q}) \vee (\mathscr{P} \wedge \mathscr{R})) \qquad \text{(Dist)}$$
$$(\mathscr{P} \vee (\mathbb{Q} \wedge \mathscr{R})) \Leftrightarrow ((\mathscr{P} \vee \mathbb{Q}) \wedge (\mathscr{P} \vee \mathscr{R}))$$
$$(\mathscr{P} \vee (\mathbb{Q} \vee \mathscr{R})) \Leftrightarrow ((\mathscr{P} \vee \mathbb{Q}) \vee \mathscr{R}) \qquad \text{(Assoc)}$$
$$(\mathscr{P} \wedge (\mathbb{Q} \wedge \mathscr{R})) \Leftrightarrow ((\mathscr{P} \wedge \mathbb{Q}) \wedge \mathscr{R})$$

$$(\mathscr{P} \vee \mathscr{P}) \Leftrightarrow \mathscr{P} \qquad \text{(Id)}$$
$$(\mathscr{P} \wedge \mathscr{P}) \Leftrightarrow \mathscr{P}$$

$$(\mathscr{P} \wedge (\mathscr{P} \vee \mathbb{Q})) \Leftrightarrow \mathscr{P} \qquad \text{(Abs)}$$
$$(\mathscr{P} \vee (\mathscr{P} \wedge \mathbb{Q})) \Leftrightarrow \mathscr{P}$$

$$(\mathscr{P} \wedge (\mathbb{Q} \vee \neg\mathbb{Q})) \Leftrightarrow \mathscr{P} \qquad \text{(Simp)}$$
$$(\mathscr{P} \vee (\mathbb{Q} \wedge \neg\mathbb{Q})) \Leftrightarrow \mathscr{P}$$

$$(\mathscr{P} \vee (\mathbb{Q} \vee \neg\mathbb{Q})) \Leftrightarrow (\mathbb{Q} \vee \neg\mathbb{Q})$$
$$(\mathscr{P} \wedge (\mathbb{Q} \wedge \neg\mathbb{Q})) \Leftrightarrow (\mathbb{Q} \wedge \neg\mathbb{Q})$$

# *Glossary*

**antecedent** The sentence on the left side of a conditional.

**argument** A connected series of sentences, divided into premises and conclusion.

**atomic sentence** An expression used to represent a basic sentence; a sentence letter in TFL, or a predicate symbol followed by names in FOL.

**biconditional** The symbol ↔, used to represent words and phrases that function like the English phrase "if and only if"; or a sentence formed using this connective.

**bound variable** An occurrence of a variable in a formula which is in the scope of a quantifier followed by the same variable.

**complete truth table** A table that gives all the possible truth values for a sentence (of TFL) or sentences in TFL, with a line for every possible valuation of all sentence letters.

**completeness** A property held by logical systems if and only if ⊨ implies ⊢.

**conclusion** The last sentence in an argument.

**conclusion indicator** A word or phrase such as "therefore" used to indicate that what follows is the conclusion of an argument.

**conditional** The symbol →, used to represent words and phrases that function like the English phrase "if ... then ..."; a sentence formed by using this symbol.

**conjunct** A sentence joined to another by a conjunction.

**conjunction** The symbol ∧, used to represent words and phrases that function like the English word "and"; or a sentence formed using that symbol.

**conjunctive normal form (DNF)** A sentence which is a conjunction of disjunctions of atomic sentences or negated atomic sentences.

**connective** A logical operator in TFL used to combine sentence letters into larger sentences.

**consequent** The sentence on the right side of a conditional.

**consistency** Sentences are jointly consistent iff the contradiction ⊥ can*not* be proved from them.

**contingent sentence** A sentence that is neither a necessary truth nor a necessary falsehood; a sentence that in some case is true and in some other case, false.

**contradiction (of FOL)** A sentence of FOL that is false in every interpretation.

**contradiction (of TFL)** A sentence that has only Fs in the column under the main logical operator of its complete truth table; a sentence that is false on every valuation.


**disjunct** A sentence joined to another by a disjunction.

**disjunction** The connective ∨, used to represent words and phrases that function like the English word "or" in its inclusive sense; or a sentence formed by using this connective.

**disjunctive normal form (DNF)** A sentence which is a disjunction of conjunctions of atomic sentences or negated atomic sentences.

**domain** The collection of objects assumed for a symbolization in FOL, or that gives the range of the quantifiers in an interpretation.


**empty predicate** A predicate that applies to no object in the domain.

**equivalence (in FOL)** A property held by pairs of sentence of
FOLs if and only if the sentences have the same truth
value in every interpretation.

**equivalence (in TFL)** A property held by pairs of sentences if
and only if the complete truth table for those sentences
has identical columns under the two main logical operators, i.e., if the sentences have the same truth value on
every valuation.

**existential quantifier** The symbol $\exists$ of FOL used to symbolize
existence; $\exists x\, F(x)$ is true iff at least one member of the
domain is $F$.

**formula** An expression of FOL built according to the inductive
rules in §26.2.

**free variable** An occurrence of a variable in a formula which is
not a bound variable.

**functional completeness** Property of a collection of connectives
which holds iff every possible truth table is the truth table of a sentence involving only those connectives.

**inconsistency** Sentences are inconsistent iff the contradiction $\perp$
can be proved from them.

**interpretation** A specification of a domain together with the objects the names pick out and which objects the predicates
are true of.

**invalid** A property of arguments that holds when the conclusion
is not a consequence of the premises; the opposite of
valid.

**joint possibility** A property possessed by some sentences when
they are all true in a single case.

**main connective** The last connective that you add when you
assemble a sentence using the inductive definition.

**metalanguage** The language logicians use to talk about the object language. In this textbook, the metalanguage is En-

glish, supplemented by certain symbols like metavariables and technical terms like "valid".

**metavariables** A variable in the metalanguage that can represent any sentence in the object language.

**name** A symbol of FOL used to pick out an object of the domain.

**necessary equivalence** A property held by a pair of sentences that, in every case, are either both true or both false.

**necessary falsehood** A sentence that is false in every case.

**necessary truth** A sentence that is true in every case.

**negation** The symbol ¬, used to represent words and phrases that function like the English word "not".

**object language** A language that is constructed and studied by logicians. In this textbook, the object languages are TFL and FOL.

**predicate** A symbol of FOL used to symbolize a property or relation.

**premise** A sentence in an argument other than the conclusion.

**premise indicator** A word or phrase such as "because" used to indicate that what follows is the premise of an argument.

**provable equivalence** A property held by pairs of statements if and only if there is a derivation which takes you from each one to the other one.

**satisfiability (in FOL)** A property held by sentence of FOLs if and only if some interpretation makes all the sentences true.

**satisfiability (in TFL)** A property held by sentences if and only if the complete truth table for those sentences contains one line on which all the sentences are true, i.e., if some valuation makes all the sentences true.

**scope** The subformula of a sentence (of TFL) or a formula of FOL for which the main connective is the operator.

**sentence (of FOL)** A formula of FOL which has no free variables.

**sentence (of TFL)** A string of symbols in TFL that can be built up according to the inductive rules given on p. 51.

**sentence letter** An letter used to represent a basic sentence in TFL.

**sound** A property of arguments that holds if the argument is valid and has all true premises.

**soundness** A property held by logical systems if and only if ⊢ implies ⊨.

**substitution instance** The result of replacing every free occurrence of a variable in a formula with a name.

**symbolization key** A list that shows which English sentences are represented by which sentence letters in TFL.

**tautology** A sentence that has only Ts in the column under the main logical operator of its complete truth table; a sentence that is true on every valuation.

**term** Either a name or a variable.

**theorem** A sentence that can be proved without any premises.

**truth value** One of the two logical values sentences can have: True and False.

**truth-functional connective** An operator that builds larger sentences out of smaller ones and fixes the truth value of the resulting sentence based only on the truth value of the component sentences.

**universal quantifier** The symbol $\forall$ of FOL used to symbolize generality; $\forall x \, F(x)$ is true iff every member of the domain is $F$.

**valid** A property of arguments where there conclusion is a consequence of the premises.

**validity** A sentence of FOL that is true in every interpretation.

**validity of arguments (in FOL)** A property held by arguments; an argument is valid if and only if no interpretation makes all premises true and the conclusion false.

**validity of arguments (in TFL)** A property held by arguments if and only if the complete truth table for the argument contains no rows where the premises are all true and the conclusion false, i.e., if no valuation makes all premises true and the conclusion false.

**valuation** An assignment of truth values to particular sentence letters.

**variable** A symbol of FOL used following quantifiers and as placeholders in atomic formulas; lowercase letters between $s$ and $z$.

In the Introduction to his volume *Symbolic Logic*, Charles Lutwidge Dodgson advised: "When you come to any passage you don't understand, *read it again*: if you *still* don't understand it, *read it again*: if you fail, even after *three* readings, very likely your brain is getting a little tired. In that case, put the book away, and take to other occupations, and next day, when you come to it fresh, you will very likely find that it is *quite* easy."

The same might be said for this volume, although readers are forgiven if they take a break for snacks after *two* readings.

Made in United States
Troutdale, OR
12/20/2024

26969361R00239